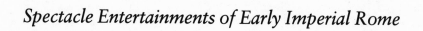

Spectacle Entertainments of Early Imperial Rome

RICHARD C. BEACHAM

Spectacle Entertainments
of Early Imperial Rome

Yale University Press
New Haven &
London

For Neil, for everything

Published with assistance from Amasa Stone Mather, 1907.

Set in Postscript Sabon type.
Printed in the United States of America.

Library of Congress Cataloging-in-Publication Data

Beacham, Richard C.
   Spectacle entertainments of early imperial Rome /
Richard C. Beacham.
      p.   cm.
   Includes bibliographical references and index.
   ISBN 0-300-07382-8 (alk. paper)
   1. Entertainment events — Political aspects — Rome — History.
2. Popular culture — Political aspects — Rome — History.
3. Processions — Political aspects — Rome — History.   4. Pageants — Political aspects — Rome — History.   5. Theater — Political aspects — Rome — History.   6. Power (Social sciences) — Rome.   7. Spectacular, The.   I. Title.
PA6074.B43   1999
394'.4'0937 — dc21   99-11449
                                                                 CIP

A catalogue record for this book is available from the British Library.

The paper in this book meets the guidelines for permanence and durability of the Committee on Production Guidelines for Book Longevity of the Council on Library Resources.

10   9   8   7   6   5   4   3   2   1

Contents

Acknowledgments

I would like to extend thanks for the assistance I received from colleagues and institutions in preparing this book. Foremost among these are the J. Paul Getty Museum and its curator of antiquities, Dr. Marion True, who arranged for me to work both at the museum and at the Getty Center for the History of Art and the Humanities during 1994 as a guest scholar. The staff at these institutions gave generously of their advice, encouragement, and expertise as I pursued my research and writing. I am grateful too to the University of Warwick for granting me a period of study leave and for assistance in preparing the illustrations. I received further support from the British Academy. I am indebted to Mr. Jerry Glover for his careful and imaginative preparation of a number of the drawings I have used, and to Larry and Barbara Fleischman for permission to use a photograph of an artifact from their collection. I thank colleagues in Theatron Ltd., for their help in researching and preparing designs of Pompey's theater. I acknowledge with gratitude the opportunity to present portions of my research as lectures to the Interdisciplinary Humanities Center at the University of California, Santa Barbara, the Department of Classics at U.C.L.A., the Art Institute of Chicago, and the Getty Museum. I am grateful to the editors of Yale University Press for their confidence, encouragement, and patience.

Introduction

"For you will live as it were in a theatre in which the spectators are the whole world." Dio Cassius placed these words in the mouth of Maecenas in a lengthy speech that the historian imagined this adviser making to Octavian in 29 B.C. In it he counseled the thirty-four-year-old master of the Roman Empire (who two years later would assume the title Augustus) on how he might "enjoy fully the reality of monarchy without the odium attaching to the name of 'King'" (Dio 52.34.2, 52.40.2). In researching this book, I found this passage most suggestive, because it epitomizes several of the themes and the attendant difficulties in my subject. It introduces the notion that the emperor himself was part of the show, both a provider and a participant in the spectacles that figured so prominently in the early principate. It also invites the reader to consider how, through the provision and shaping of such entertainments, the imperial ideology — both what was celebrated and what was left unsaid — might be formulated and communicated to Roman citizens and subjects. Maecenas's advice, however, appears in a historical account composed more than two centuries after the event it claims to represent; inevitably Dio's version is colored by his knowledge of how the imperial role was subsequently fashioned by Augustus, and then pervasively redefined and refined by his successors up to the time in which Dio himself was living. Dio provides important evidence — he is himself a witness of the state of play in his own day — but the facts and interpretations of earlier events contained in his history have to be handled with a degree of skepticism. Ideally, his account and those of Suetonius and Tacitus, the other major historians who wrote of the early imperial period long after it, must be examined in light of other forms of evidence.

But the situation is far from ideal; in a great many instances, apart from the support that the three historians may mutually provide to one another's account, there is little or no independent corroboration. The particular qualities and limitations of each of these historians have long been scrutinized and recounted. Without detailing them again, I want to remind the nonspecialist reader (as I shall do occasionally in the text as well) that, like others writing about this period (including these early historians themselves), I have had to make innumerable choices, formulating arguments and suppositions while making the best of limited and unsatisfactory evidence. I have also attempted to subject this evidence, in a manner not previously undertaken on so great a scale, to the particular insights, criteria, and preoccupations that a theater historian may bring to bear upon it. Such an attempt, although far from infallible or exhaustive in its treatment of the subject, does seem to me to have merit.

I provide a basic narrative that might be termed a "theatrical history" of Rome from the last decades of the Republic to the death of Nero. Apart from *Roman Life and Manners in the Early Empire,* a translation of Ludwig Friedländer's *Sittengeschichte Roms* (7th ed., 1906), there is no comprehensive account of the topic in English. There have been numerous articles and several provocative books such as Veyne, *Bread and Circuses,* Barton, *The Sorrows of the Ancient Romans,* and Bartsch, *Actors in the Audience,* that deal with particular aspects of the subject, as well as several important new studies of the perennially popular topic of gladiators. In addition, in 1996 a valuable collection of essays, *Roman Theatre and Society,* was published, which further refines our understanding of several highly important areas and points the way to work still to be undertaken.

Such specialized and detailed work on discrete topics indicates lively and timely interest in at least some portions of a broad area of investigation that has long been relatively neglected. This neglect may derive in part from a reluctance of many scholars either to acknowledge fully or at least to confront and assess what even a superficial survey of the period in question brings starkly into focus: that games, displays, and entertainments were of vital importance to the manner in which the Roman emperors and their subjects defined their roles and relationships, and crucial therefore to understanding the cultural and political life of the early imperial era. The reason for this scholarly reticence lies partly in the unsatisfactory state of much of the evi-

dence referred to above. I believe, however, that it also is due to a disinclination by many who (in an age of increased specialization) are finely trained in
such fields as classical philology, archaeology, art history, or history to take on
a topic that partakes of all of these, while simultaneously drawing upon, for
example, political science, aesthetics, sociology, architecture, religion, and
performance studies. In the absence of an extensive body of conventional
dramatic texts, even ancient theater specialists have tended to look elsewhere
in their studies.

Maecenas was said to have advised Octavian to "adorn this City with utter
disregard for expense and make it magnificent with festivals of every kind"
(52.30.1). Whether Dio is correct in suggesting that such advice was explicitly
given, there is no question that Octavian and his successors followed it. The
public entertainments in Rome were so pervasive, massive, and influential,
and therefore so instructive to our understanding of a great range of activities,
that to formulate an analytic account of them and their meanings demands a
dauntingly synoptic approach. Even to define the scope of such a study is
intimidating, because the spectacular and the theatrical became pervasively
embedded in every aspect of public life under the emperors. These qualities
were so much a part of the language, style, and gestures through which the
period defined and imagined itself at every level and in every manifestation,
that at times determining lines of demarcation seems arbitrary, and defending
them futile. Why, for example, do I define public funerals or banquets as
"spectacle entertainments" while denying that claim to myriad other examples
of ceremonial pomp or ritual display? If the topic were confined to "scenic"
occasions, it might certainly encompass triumphs, but what becomes of such
phenomena as the mock naval engagements (*naumachiae*) or the great animal
hunts (*venationes*) in the arena? Because I believe that these and many other
activities are linked by shared (but not exclusive) aesthetic values, which may
be usefully identified and viewed in their various permutations, I have applied
a relatively wide-angled lens in focusing on the topic, although I had to sacrifice a degree of detail in my treatment. To compensate for this, I have limited
my discussion almost exclusively to events in Rome itself, and to a period
terminated by the death of Nero. This approach may raise questions and provide a tentative agenda for those who wish to pursue the subject in greater
detail; certainly a large selection of topics and historical periods are still to be
explored.

While preparing this book I have also held firmly in mind a second quotation, in this instance from a prominent contemporary historian, Fergus Millar:
"Those who study and teach the history of the Ancient World suffer from a
great disadvantage, which we find difficult to admit even to ourselves: in a

perfectly literal sense we do not know what we are talking about. Of course we can dispose of a vast range of accumulated knowledge *about* what we are talking about. We can compile lists of office-holders in the Roman Empire, without our evidence revealing how government worked.... We can study the remains of temples, the iconography of gods and goddesses, the nature of myth, ritual and sacrifice; but how and in what way did all this provide an important or intelligible context for the peasant in the fields?" (1981, 63).

I cannot claim to "know" the reality that Roman spectacle had for its participants anymore than one can experience a great range of phenomena that characterized the everyday life of antiquity's inhabitants. Those confronting the past unavoidably suffer an estrangement from the immediate empathy and understanding that arises from a shared experience of a world like our own. At best, through analogy and imagination we may conjure up some secondhand sense of that experience. I have attempted here to provide a narrative framework, together with identification of primary sources and a range of topics inviting further examination, that will be useful to the general reader and to those with a scholarly interest in this extensive and provocative subject.

I

The Setup
Public Entertainments in the Late Republic

"We do not know what we are talking about." Historians examining the last decades of the Roman Republic are in one sense fortunate in such ignorance; direct experience of things that even a vivid imagination can scarcely evoke, such as war, at home and abroad, the collapse of civic order, famine, conspiracy, dictatorship, oppression, and the slaughter of innocents, which are all-too-familiar horrors in our own century, but remain comfortably remote for most of us. Historians contemplating the death throes of the Republic, however lively their imaginations, are still sheltered by one thing: they know the shape of things to come. They perceive, for example, that 44 B.C. marked the beginning of a process that unleashed forces that fundamentally altered the Roman world. The contemporary onlooker, of course, had no such perspective; one's personal assessment of events, depending on the degree to which one was involved or touched by them, might range from chaos to continuity but could achieve only a fragmentary awareness of their larger meaning and consequences.

What the historian lacks in comprehensive and immediate knowledge is partially compensated for by the ability to see things from a distance and to discern their lines of direction and patterns. To detect such development one has to take periodic readings, however incomplete, and compare them, in effect juxtaposing a series of snapshots to approximate a moving picture. At a time of changes as dramatic as those at the end of the first century, when Rome moved from republic to principate, the transitions revealed are particularly striking.

The focus of my survey is spectacle entertainments. As closely observed as the fragmentary evidence will allow, these can be seen during this period to have changed significantly. By employing as a sort of filter the particular insights and clarification that an analysis of the technique and function of theatrical art provides, we may produce a picture able to reveal to us more than we knew before.

The Occasions for Performance

By the middle of the first century B.C., Rome's inhabitants had ample opportunity to participate in a variety of public entertainments, many of which arose from venerable — if still evolving — traditions. Most of these were centered on the formal religious festivals and the public games *(ludi)* that marked them. The earliest such games were chariot races, but by the mid-fourth century, stage shows *(ludi scaenici)* had been introduced, and occasions for these (which were first given at the *ludi Romani*) and other entertainments at annual official games multiplied in the third and second centuries to include the *ludi Plebeii,* in honor of Jupiter (which were scenic by 200), the *ludi Apollinares* for Apollo (instituted in 212 and probably scenic from the start), the *ludi Megalenses,* dedicated to the Great Mother (begun in 204 and incorporating plays from 194), and the *ludi Florales,* honoring the goddess Flora (begun by 240 or earlier and scenic by 173). These amounted to about fifty days of performances per year. Further increases then took place in the first half of the first century B.C. with the *ludi Ceriales* (established by 201) enhanced by games; shows in honor of Sulla, the *ludi Victoriae Sullanae* (82); and in 46 B.C. Julius Caesar's *ludi Victoriae Caesaris* — honoring himself — to bring the number of days devoted to formal holidays to about seventy-five per year.

Three quarters of these included stage shows, with most of the other days reserved for contests in the Circus, but the actual length of a holiday was frequently increased through the practice of instauration, whereby if the ceremony attending the game was in any way interrupted, or if there was the smallest omission or mishap, the performance had to be repeated from the beginning, just like any other formal religious ritual. In addition to these formal annual games *(ludi sollemnes)* held by the civic authorities, there could be *ludi extraordinarii* given to mark particular events such as the celebration of a military victory; the dedication of a temple; an end to some natural disaster; *ludi funebres,* in honor of deceased notables, which at least as early as 174 could be scenic (Livy 41.28.11) and incorporated gladiatorial displays; and even occasional *ludi privati* sponsored by a donor anxious to impress the public. Privately provided spectacles at funerals or other occasions were also known as *munera,* literally, "gifts." From the end of the third century B.C. it had also become common for Roman commanders to dedicate games — *ludi votivi* — to appropriate deities, not on the authority of the Senate for the general welfare of the state but to mark their own success, thus deftly linking thanksgiving to the gods with the achievement of a particular individual.[1]

The provision of the various state games and their management was the responsibility of the elected magistrates with the *ludi Romani* and *Megalenses* given by the two curule aediles, the *ludi Plebeii* and *Ceriales* by the two plebeian aediles, the Floralia first by the plebeian aediles, but from 173 on by the consuls, and the *ludi Apollinares* by the urban praetor. In addition, other officials occasionally acted as patrons. In the beginning, the Senate had voted a fixed sum in advance for use by the appropriate magistrate for particular holidays, but after 200 B.C. the individual had considerable latitude, a condition that by the late Republic had led to a situation in which, to ensure splendor and win popularity, the magistrate supplemented state funds (the *lucar*) with his own wealth, confident of recouping it later from the enrichment secured by a successful political career. In addition to providing authority for the entertainments to take place, aediles were responsible for the purchase of plays and the contracts for production and staging. Although earlier the provision of shows probably had little direct effect on subsequent electoral success, such benefaction in the unsettled conditions of the later Republic had become an indispensable instrument for political advancement; indeed, any politician who had not served as an aedile (and thus provided games) compromised his chance of achieving higher office (Cicero *De Off.* 2.58–59). Thus, magistrates could manipulate the provision of official games so that increasingly they came to be seen not just as public religious ceremonies but also as gifts from the responsible official. "In the late Republic one could assume a connection between sponsorship of handsome spectacles as aedile and subsequent attainment of the highest offices" (Gruen 1992, 189).[2]

The same was probably true of ambitious individuals who had not yet held office but could significantly improve their future prospects by sponsoring private games. Although the Republic was strongly oligarchic in character, it did display significant democratic features as well, including the necessity of winning elections to attain office, and often victory depended on securing decisive support not just from the upper strata but from the general urban population of Rome. Particularly toward the end of the Republic, the role of popular political expression in determining fundamental questions of citizens' rights, the conduct of foreign and military affairs, and the exercise of leadership was crucial, leading to greatly increased competition between rival factions and individuals.[3] "No *nobilis* aspiring to reach the highest offices could ignore the possibility that he would need the votes of what to him must have been the lowest dregs of the city populace: not just in distributing bribes before the elections, but as an aedile, as an organizer of private *munera,* in his social life, and whenever he had occasion to display generosity or be charged with a lack of it" (Yakobson 1992, 47).

Votes therefore were a "marketable commodity" and, although widely lamented as regrettable, a degree of reasonably discreet bribery was considered inevitable.[4] As Cicero noted (*De Off.* 2.57) — even while deploring the practice — "I realize that in our country even in the good old times, it was an established custom to expect magnificent entertainments from the very best men in the year of their aedileship." Elsewhere he observed that although the people might dislike private *luxuria,* they greatly appreciated public *magnificentia,* and he went on to advise that "the Roman plebs should not be prevented from enjoying games, or gladiatorial contests, or banquets — all these our ancestors established — nor should candidates be restrained from showing that generosity which indicates liberality, rather than bribery" (*Mur.* 75–77). Consequently, by the middle of the first century B.C., a trend toward ever greater sumptuousness was well established. As I discuss later, such extravagance was expressed not only through the length and content of the various games but increasingly through their embellishment and the settings in which they took place.

Drama in Rome

By the last decades of the Republic, the composition for performance of new works of both comedy and tragedy had all but ceased. These genres, which had appeared in Rome by the middle of the third century B.C., had evidently lost their appeal to those writing for the stage.[5] Dramatic composition in these traditional genres appears to have devolved to scholars and dilettantes and away from professional playwrights. There were also a number of politicians in the late Republic who composed tragedies, suggesting a degree of cross-fertilization between oratory and theatrical rhetoric, which some Roman writers on the art of public speaking call attention to, and possibly reflecting as well the increasing importance of theater as an extension of political activity and expression.[6]

In Rome both comedy (*fabulae palliatae,* or plays in Greek dress) and tragedy (*fabulae crepidatae,* buskin-plays) had been based on Greek models. A third type of play, the *fabulae praetextae,* had evolved, which, by contrast, drew directly on Roman themes and subjects. The relevance of these latter works, and their propaganda value both to noble patrons with illustrious ancestors and to prominent men still living who had a congenial playwright at hand willing to celebrate their own greatness, encouraged the composition of *praetextae* (and probably their performance as well) into the first century A.D.[7]

There existed also a domestic variety of "situation comedy" with Italian subject matter: the *fabulae togatae* (plays in Roman dress). Because we know little of these except the names of several playwrights, a list of titles, and a few scraps of text, it is difficult to assess either the nature of the genre or the extent to which it was still viable in the late republican theater.

Despite the apparent lack of new plays, staged revivals of earlier works were, however, common in the late Republic. Cicero, for example, frequently records performances of tragedy and refers to a production of Plautus's *Pseudolus* in the first quarter of the first century B.C.[8] He also mentions a *togata,* the *Simulans* ("Pretender") by Afranius, performed at the *ludi Apollinares* in 57 (*Pro Sest.* 118), and there is a reference to a performance of Afranius's *Incendium* ("Fire!") in the time of Nero (Suet. *Nero* 11.2). Horace confirms that the works of other early Roman playwrights, including the tragedians Ennius, Pacuvius, Accius, and the comedians Naevius (who also composed some tragedies), Plautus, Caecilius, and Terence, continued to hold the stage in the late first century B.C. (fig. 1). These plays he claims "mighty Rome learns by heart, and these she views packed into her crowded theater" (*Epis.* 2.1.50– 61). From the evidence provided by the theatrical topics examined by the historian and critic Varro in the same period, it seems certain that the theater was also the subject of lively scholarly interest.[9]

Although the composition of tragedy evidently had lost its earlier vitality, becoming an academic and aesthetic exercise, it is hardly surprising that in a time of cultural and political upheaval, the restaging of time-tested works of serious drama reflecting traditional values still had popular appeal. "The province of Roman tragedy was firstly the celebration of contemporary aristocratic ideals through myth . . . next, the stimulation not of the intellect but of the emotions; thirdly, the cultivation of rhetoric; lastly, to a limited extent, the retailing of current philosophical-scientific views" (Gratwick 1982, 130). Such qualities, even though embedded in an archaic or bombastic language, no longer attractive to writers of a more sophisticated age, might still have found a ready response in a late republican audience. At the same time, there is evidence — particularly in the quickness of the spectators to interpolate

Fig. 1. Comic scene. Wall painting from the House of Casca Longus, Pompeii. Second quarter of first century A.D. (Fototeca Unione at the American Academy in Rome)

contemporary political references into the performance — that the traditional form may have lost something of its innate attraction and that, when tragedies were produced, some elements were distorted or "hyped" to give them greater popular appeal.

Horace's analysis of tragic writing in the *Ars Poetica,* although ostensibly aimed at advising would-be playwrights on their craft — "work with Greek models by day; and work with them by night!" (268–69) — may plausibly be considered as highlighting those characteristics of earlier tragedy that contemporary audiences found most attractive (fig. 2). He stresses, for example, that although some events are unsuitable for the stage, in general things should be

Fig. 2. Tragic actor and attendant. First century A.D. wall painting from Herculaneum, now in the Naples Archaeological Museum. (Fototeca Unione at the American Academy in Rome)

enacted, because "the mind is less affected by what it perceives through the ears, than by that presented to the faithful eyes, and what the spectator can see for himself" (180–82). Elsewhere he again endorses an apparent bias toward greater realism, "fictions which find favor should be close to reality; a play may not demand belief for whatever it chooses" (338–39). In analyzing the role of the chorus, Horace strengthens the impression gained from the few surviving fragments of Roman tragedy, which indicate that the chorus was dramatized in a more realistic fashion than was customary in earlier Greek practice, taking an active role in the dramatic action and not confined to providing mere commentary or poetic interludes. "Let the chorus take on the part and active role of an actor, and interject nothing between the acts which does not advance and fit appropriately with the plot" (193–95).

Horace also makes the point explicitly that (at least toward the end of the century) the taste for the "vain delights" of spectacle was well established, lamenting how readily the more cultured sections of the audience could be overwhelmed by the "stupid and ill-educated" rabble that greatly outnumbered them (*Epis.* 2.1.188, 183–84).

Serious drama may increasingly have found refuge in private performances given in the great houses of the nobility. With the growing interest in Hellenistic culture, a portion of the upper strata of Roman society began to offer patronage to Greek artists and intellectuals, including playwrights and actors.[10] Cicero characterized such sophisticates as "the smart and fashionable— people with the best chefs and confectioners . . . [who] go in for shows and what follows shows; the sort of things without which Epicurus says the Good can't be known" (*De Finibus* 2.23). Others of more traditional taste disdained such ostentatious indulgence — Marius referred with contempt to those who employed expensive actors for their banquets and, indeed, would not sit through public performances of Greek drama even when these were given in his own honor.[11]

Nevertheless, the occasional performance of Greek plays was a further example of the variety of late republican theatrical practice. It was a venerable tradition. Greek performers had visited and performed at Rome for ten-day periods twice in 186 B.C. and are recorded again in 167 (Livy 39.22.2, 39.22.10; Polybius 30.22.12). In 145 L. Mummius sponsored shows to commemorate his conquest of Greece; these included Greek theatrical fare, signifying "Roman expropriation of Hellenic artistry to serve national ends" (Gruen 1992, 196; cf. Tac. *Ann.* 14.21.2). Greek plays were evidently presented periodically thereafter, probably by visiting troupes from Magna Graecia, although Cicero suggests that they were perhaps more fashionable than popular (*Ad Fam.* 7.1.3). Presumably they presented a selection of the tragedies, comedies, and even satyr-plays characteristic of the later Hellenistic repertoire.[12]

By the late Republic, tragedy and comedy, certainly with regard to new composition, and possibly too if measured by their popularity in the public theaters, faced growing competition from the mime, which had coexisted with them since the third century. Both Latin tragedy and comedy in Rome, although long established, were essentially foreign imports whose subject matter, settings, and dress were Greek. This aspect may have appealed to a limited segment of the audience, but its hold on the broad mass was more tenuous. In particular, the attraction of comedies — certainly those by the prominent Roman comic author Plautus — was partly based on elements that directly sub-

verted and used as a source of comic fun those very qualities that were quintessentially "Greek."

Plautus had introduced into his rather mild-minded and urbane Greek models an element of anarchic buffoonery within complex and unlikely plots,
supported by language that was cruder, more ribald, and richer in complex
and sometimes fantastical imagery than anything found in his Greek New
Comedy models. He also used a great variety of complex lyrical meters together with music and dance. In all of these elements it is likely that Plautus
astutely drew upon the example of unscripted popular entertainment, enhancing the appeal of and in the process distancing his work from his ostensible
Greek sources.

Other writers of the *palliatae* were evidently less successful, including Terence, whose far more serious and respectful treatments of his original sources
may have elevated Roman drama as literature but, in the process, alienated
much of his audience with the very remoteness of their themes and milieu.
Those interested in the ideas and problems addressed by Greek comedy had by
the late Republic turned to other forms of literature more amenable to assimilation. Those attracted by the madcap absurdities of Plautine drama had
recourse to the mime.[13]

Mime, although well established and popular by the late Republic, is not
easy for modern scholars either to define or to confine to a particular genre. It
was formally introduced into the Roman holiday calendar in 173 at the *ludi
Florales* as an unscripted and virtually plotless entertainment that, unlike literary drama, was presented without masks and included female performers in
what were evidently uninhibited, versatile, and exuberant celebrations of fun
and frailty. From the first it was noted for its obscenity and license (including
female nudity) and, consequently, was perennially popular.[14] For those attempting to assess it, however, the diversity of the varieties of performance
covered by the term dictates some degree of caution. For the most part its
presenters concerned themselves with dramatic caricature, sensationalized enactments from everyday life (the bawdier the better, with adultery a favorite
theme), as well as more exotic subjects such as kidnappings, shipwrecks, and,
occasionally, plots drawn from mythology. But the mime could also embrace
every other form of broad entertainment, with acrobatics, song and dance,
jokes, and conjuring grafted onto the flimsiest of impromptu scenarios to
create a variety show. It is not surprising therefore that the word "mime" was
frequently used indiscriminately to designate "players" or "stage-folk."

The salient difference between mime and traditional comedy was the mime's
maskless enactment, but undoubtedly there was a rich stylistic interchange
between the genres and perhaps even some movement by performers from one

Fig. 3. Terracotta figure of a mime performer, now in the J. Paul Getty Museum, Malibu. (Gift of Barbara and Larry Fleischman)

type of "show business" to another (fig. 3). The mime had the advantage that it could be presented (typically by a cast of two or three) at any time or place, on its own, as an interlude or afterpiece with other drama, at private dinner parties, or in conjunction with any other form of public or private entertainment. By the middle of the first century B.C. its popularity elevated it to an object of literary endeavor as writers began to compose mimes in comic meters and occasionally to exploit its potential for topical allusion.

A comedic genre even more ancient than the mime was the Atellanae. Originally associated with the town of Atella in Campania, these native farces of the Oscan people were at first unscripted rural entertainments based on stock characters and situations. They relied heavily on slapstick and buffoonery, with performers wearing exaggerated masks. These entertainments were taken up by the Romans at an early date, leaving an indelible mark upon Latin scripted comedy, which did not, however, wholly displace them. There are frequent references to their continued performance in Rome well into the imperial period. Although the Oscan language in which the farces were originally performed was evidently incomprehensible to ordinary Romans, the Atellanae were translated or modified for a popular audience.[15] This difficulty would have been mitigated too by the nature of their material: short, crude, and boorish, highly physical and largely improvised. Eventually they were chiefly employed as afterpieces following the primary entertainment. As with mime, a literary version of the Atellanae appeared early in the first century B.C.

At the other end of the dramatic spectrum was poetry recitation (sometimes accompanied by music), which, while displaying a minimum of "performance values," enjoyed sufficient popularity to justify its public presentation in the late republican theater. Horace took some pride in *not* reciting his poetry except privately to friends, although noting that "there are many who recite their works in the middle of the Forum or in the baths: the confined space pleasantly echoes their voice" (*Sat.* 1.4.74–76). Elsewhere he specifically disdains "to recite my trifles in crowded theaters" (*Epis.* 1.19.41–42) but confirms that others do. The practice may have been borrowed from the Greeks (for whom it had long been the custom) and possibly first appeared in Rome in the first century; certainly in the imperial period it became firmly established.[16] It was not just his words, but his voice, demeanor, and gestures that demanded the skill of the poet and ensured the close attention and, if done well, the admiration of his audience. Such recitation must be viewed in light of the evidence that ancient audiences had developed extraordinary sensitivity to every nuance of language as performance — a capacity to hear and respond that we now find difficult to understand or even imagine, much less emulate. Cicero notes that the audience possessed a natural sense of poetic rhythm, so that the slightest failure by an actor to observe the metrical form of his speech, to give too much or too little stress to a syllable or to fail to move in the proper rhythm would be hissed and booed, and the same would occur if the chorus missed a note. "Although all actors labor to regulate the expression, voice, and the movements of the body, everyone knows how few there are or ever have been whom we could bear to watch" (*De Orat.* 1.5.18). Consequently, actors were careful to choose parts best suited to their particular talents, with some taking roles in which movement and gesture were emphasized, and others preferring those in which the quality of the voice and delivery was stressed (*De Off.* 1.114). The audience was so sensitive that it could determine which character was about to speak from the first note played by the *tibicen* (double-pipe).[17]

Alongside such refined entertainment, other diversions took place that are far more difficult for us to appreciate — such as the public slaughter of animals and humans for entertainment, which, after modest beginnings, was becoming a familiar spectacle, although it had not yet approached the horrific scale attained in the imperial period.

Animal Displays

The earliest display of animals in staged hunts (*venationes*) consisted of little more than public hunting of foxes, hares, and wild goats in the Circus Maximus as part of the *ludi Ceriales* and the Floralia; this probably merely formalized ancient folk customs with obscure religious or magical associations. At the festival in honor of Flora, a goddess of fertility, the choice of such animals seems particularly appropriate to the theme, which was also evoked when the spectators were showered with various seeds and legumes (Horace *Sat.* 2.3.182). From the third century to the late republican period, such games were still chiefly devoted to the display of these and other indigenous animals (boars, bulls, stags, bears), with the exhibition and hunting of beasts from abroad a rarity. Yet this in turn encouraged the more ambitious politicians, avid to impress the public by presenting something exceptional, to compete with one another and their predecessors, ensuring that a premium was placed on the ability to attain the most exotic animals available, in the largest possible numbers.

In 275 B.C. four elephants captured from Pyrrhus of Epirus by M. Curius Dentatus were displayed as the chief ornament of his triumph, marking the earliest record of such use and the beginning of a long tradition associating elephants with military success. In 251 L. Metellus displayed over one hundred Carthaginian elephants in the Circus, where they were involved in a mock battle with slaves armed with blunt weapons. It was then only a short step to incorporate the use of foreign animals into the games, and this was so well established by the beginning of the second century, that Plautus satirized it.[18] In 186 M. Fulvius Nobilior gave votive games following his victories in the Aetolian War.[19] Over ten days he provided a variety of entertainments, including Greek performers and athletics and, for the first time in Rome, staged a hunt displaying lions and leopards (Livy 39.5.7–10, 39.22.2). The trend thus established encouraged the spectators to associate military prowess and the geographic expansion of Roman influence with various animals from the distant realms subject to Roman might. Through the display of such exotic booty, power was rendered both graphic and entertaining (fig. 4).

This new trend concerned the Senate, which in 179 stipulated that expenditure for such entertainments should not exceed that spent by Nobilior for his triumph seven years earlier (Livy 40.44.8–12) and, at about the same time, banned the use of imported beasts in *venationes* (Pliny *N.H.* 8.17.64). But the appeal of the practice both to the people and to aspiring politicians was already sufficiently established to ensure that the decree was modified to permit African animals to be shown in the Circus Maximus (a display there in 169 included sixty-three African animals, together with forty bears and some elephants) and then somewhat later was allowed to lapse altogether (Livy 44.18.8).

The show must go on, and it did so with heightened extravagance. In 99 B.C. the memorably sumptuous games of the aedile C. Claudius Pulcher included elephant combat, and in the same period the aedile Q. Mucius Scaevola staged

Fig. 4. Cast of a relief showing
gladiators fighting animals in a
venatio. Terme Museum, Rome.
(C. M. Dixon)

the first lion fight (Pliny *N.H.* 8.19, 8.53). Sulla, celebrating his praetorship in
93, displayed one hundred lions that for the first time were allowed to run
freely in the Circus, where, as an added attraction, they were hunted by javelin
throwers donated by Sulla's friend, King Bocchus of Mauretania (Seneca *De
Brev. Vitae* 13.6; cf. Pliny *N.H.* 8.16).[20] In 61 B.C. the aedile L. Domitius
Ahenobarbus pitted one hundred Numidian bears against the same number of
hunters from Ethiopia (Pliny *N.H.* 8.36). Searching for ever-greater novelty,
M. Aemilius Scaurus in 58 used one hundred and fifty leopards and panthers
from Syria and at the same games — which proved legendary for their extravagance — displayed (in a purpose-built tank) a hippopotamus for the first time,
together with five crocodiles. Eventually the hunts' menagerie included such
rarities as giraffes, lynxes, rhinoceroses, and ostriches.[21] And still greater extravagance would follow to ornament the rises of Pompey and Caesar.

Gladiatorial Shows

In attempting to understand the nature of the occasions at which gladiators appeared, it is important to mark an important distinction between such
events *(munera)* and the other entertainments introduced thus far. During the
Republic, gladiators were not normally presented as part of the established
public games *(ludi)*, nor were they provided as an official and customary
responsibility of any of the elected Roman magistrates. The *ludi* can be seen as
offerings to the gods provided by public officials on behalf of the entire community; the *munera* were provided by citizens acting in a private capacity to

honor a recently deceased relative.[22] Nevertheless, because such citizens and the relatives they sought to commemorate were invariably prominent, and may well have held important office, the *munera* inevitably acquired a public dimension. Indeed, they offered to the family an ideal occasion to publicize the wealth, prestige, and accomplishments of the deceased and in the process, of course, to enhance the prestige (and thereby the future electoral ambitions) of his surviving relatives. This encouraged those offering such displays to present them at a moment propitious to their own advancement, which meant that frequently it proved convenient for them to take place some considerable time after the death they commemorated.

Thus, despite the important distinction of being offered by private citizens entirely out of their own resources and at a time of their choosing, they shared with the *ludi* certain characteristics. Just as the *ludi,* although honoring the gods, could nevertheless draw attention to the power, magnificence, achievement, and — particularly in the case of the votive games — the military prowess of those sponsoring them, so too the *munera* could celebrate and extol such virtues. Indeed, by their very nature, such combats, in addition to their great entertainment value, served as a collective celebration of courage and fighting skill, as well as a demonstration of the power these had to overcome death.

Their precise origin is unknown and their beginning was modest. Once thought to have been imported as an Etruscan practice — one Roman tradition believed they were introduced by the Etruscan kings — more recent speculation ascribes them to Campania. Some scholars, however, have argued for an Oscan-Samnite origin.[23] Livy claims (9.40.17) that in 308 Rome's Campanian allies had used the spoils of victory over the Samnites to arm gladiators who performed at private banquets. In 264 gladiators were employed for the first time in Rome in *ludi funebres* (which previously had been scenic) by Marcus and Decimus Brutus Pera at the funeral of their father, Junius, who had served as *Consul* in 292. Three pairs of gladiators fought in the Forum Boarium, which lay between the Palatine and the Tiber (Livy *Periocha* 16; Val. Max. 2.4.7). It is difficult to assess how quickly the new practice became established because later historians did not record the occasions systematically. Nevertheless, the few references there are do indicate a steady increase in both scale and frequency. In 216 the three sons of the former *Consul* Marcus Aemilius Lepidus marked his passing with combats in the Roman Forum between forty-four gladiators (Livy 23.30.15); in 200 Marcus Valerius Laevinus was honored by fifty; Publius Licinius was seen off in 183 with a show involving one hundred and twenty fighters, followed by gifts of food and a banquet in the Forum; at the games given in 174 by the younger Titus Flamininus honoring his deceased father, only seventy-four fought, but did so as part of a four-day commemoration, enhanced by an opulent public banquet, distribution of food, and the presentation of stage plays (Livy 42.28.11). A little over a century later, in 65 B.C., Caesar (commemorating his father who had died twenty years earlier) exhibited three hundred and twenty pairs of gladiators, and the numbers continued to grow—spectacularly—in the imperial era.[24]

Although little is known about the organization of these shows, throughout the period and until the end of the Republic they were enormously popular, partly because of their infrequency. Other entertainments could not compete in drawing power or excitement, as Terence had cause to complain when at the presentation of his play the *Hecyra,* given as part of the funeral games of Lucius Aemilius Paullus in 160, "the cry came that a gladiatorial display was on offer," causing such tumult that the show could not go on (*Hec.* 39–40). By the end of the century it became customary to commemorate notable gladiatorial shows permanently by depicting them in murals placed in public venues (Pliny *N.H.* 35.52). Such notoriety clearly made the shows particularly attractive as propaganda, not least because they could be given at the discretion of private citizens—so long as there was a conveniently deceased relative at hand—without official permission or regulation.

It was a capital offense in Rome to seek office by openly offering gifts, but shows given by prospective candidates, regardless of the potential for abuse, were not usually regarded as bribery.[25] Gladiatorial displays and the public banquets that frequently followed them were extremely expensive: Polybius, writing in the second century B.C. (31.28.5–6), placed the cost of a show of a grandeur befitting a leading aristocrat at around 720,000 sesterces.[26] Nevertheless, ambitious Romans evidently saw these events as good investments and opportunities to demonstrate family prestige, achievements, and wealth. Furthermore, by the late Republic, the public *expected* such munificent display, and those who failed to provide it suffered a loss of face, whose value was deemed beyond cost. In defending L. Murena, *Consul*-elect for 62 B.C., against electoral bribery, Cicero urged the prosecutor (*Mur.* 38–39) "not to despise so completely the splendor of the games and the magnificence of the spectacles that he gave. These helped him considerably. For why should I speak of the great delight the people and ignorant crowd take in games? It is not to be wondered at. . . . Elections are a question of numbers and a crowd. So if the splendor of the games pleased the people, it is no wonder that this helped Murena with them. But if we ourselves . . . are delighted by games and attracted to them, why should you be surprised at the ignorant crowd?"[27]

Measures were taken periodically to curb the expenditure, and Senate laws on *ambitus* (bribery) such as those passed in 181 and 159 may have attempted to deal with the problem as well, with little lasting effect. A law of 67 (the *Lex*

Calpurnia de ambitu) permanently disqualified from office those guilty of electoral corruption, and two years later both *Consuls*-elect (Autronius and Sulla) were prosecuted, convicted, and exiled for electoral bribery. During his consulship of 63, Cicero tried yet again to deal with the problem by means of the *Lex Tullia de ambitu*, which forbade anyone from "giving gladiatorial shows during the two years that he is a candidate for office actually or prospectively" (Cicero *Vat.* 37). In the same year, the Senate had decreed during Catiline's conspiracy that gladiators should be removed from Rome as a precautionary measure, no doubt influenced by the memory of Spartacus, whose rebellion of 73, spearheaded by fellow gladiators, had managed to defeat and resist numerous Roman armies for three years.[28]

The gradual increase in the frequency and scale of the shows led to the establishment of schools of gladiators in Rome and Campania that were run as commercial establishments to supply the demand; indeed, Cicero's friend Atticus had invested in one. The establishment of such institutions, and thereby the rise of men whose professional interest in promoting the activity complemented that of the actual sponsors, ensured that the shows received a great deal of publicity. Wall paintings and mosaics depicting gladiators are abundant, as are inscriptions and graffiti referring to particular games or to individual fighters who achieved enormous personal fame and following. Public interest and anticipation was further fueled by the practice of holding a solemn procession of gladiators decked out in all their pomp and tackle through the streets prior to the performance. Then the arms were formally presented to and examined by the presiding officials, after which a preliminary fight with blunt weapons was held as a "curtain-raiser."

A few voiced objections to the shows, although the objections were not on moral or humanitarian grounds but rather because of the wasteful extravagance of the displays and the lamentable trend toward using combatants other than slaves and criminals. Cicero observed, "A gladiatorial show is likely to seem cruel and brutal to some eyes, and I tend to believe that it is as currently practiced. But in the time when it was criminals who fought with swords in a struggle to the death . . . there could be no better instruction against pain and death" (*Tusc. Disp* 2.17.41). The role and scale of gladiatorial games had substantially evolved during the Republic, setting the scene for further change and expansion at the end of that period that would accelerate in the imperial era to establish the practice as one of the most notorious and noxious legacies of Rome. However difficult for the modern mind to comprehend, these displays are central to understanding the function of public entertainments within Roman culture.

Funerals, Triumphs, and Circus Processions

The rites attending the deaths of prominent citizens could be transformed into spectacular public shows not only through the gladiatorial entertainments that were associated with them, but also by the capacity of the
funeral itself for suggestive splendor. This potential was particularly significant in Roman society, in part because, apart from the funeral, the remains of
the dead, once honored and disposed of, played little role in the religious or
symbolic life of the community. Until Augustus built his great Mausoleum
(breaking a taboo and thereby making an unambivalent statement about his
preeminent position), even the greatest of Roman families were not allowed to
build spectacular tombs in the city through which graphically to assert political dominance. In the absence of such lasting memorials the burial rite itself
assumed enhanced importance.

Prior to a funeral, the corpse was initially prepared and set out in the atrium
of the deceased's house, dressed in clothes indicating the rank of office he had
held, including all the appropriate honorary insignia, such as wreaths acquired
in battle, and, in the case of generals who had triumphed, the revered triumphal garments and decorations *(insignia triumphalia)*. On the day of the
funeral ceremony, a procession was formed in front of the house (with lictors
to keep order), led by a band including up to ten *tibicen* players and a brass
section playing the *tuba, tuba longa,* and sometimes, the *cornu.* It was not
a muted performance, but, on the contrary, loudly and publicly proclaimed
the importance of the occasion; indeed, the din was proverbial (Horace *Sat.*
1.6.43). The couch and body were customarily carried by close family members and preceded by torch-bearers, even though the ceremony took place
during the day.

An official herald announced the funeral and formally invited the public to
attend. Along and behind the bier were more family members, while in front,
professional female mourners sang a repetitive dirge, the *nenia* (which in early
times, and possibly later as well, was led by a soloist, the *praefica*), of lamentation and praise for the deceased (Varro *De Vita P.R.* 3.110; Servius *Ad Aen.*
6.216). Accompanying these was a retinue of actors who might recite both
tragic and comic passages, and often one of them directly impersonated the
deceased with jests and mockeries (fig. 5). Next came other actors portraying
the dead man's ancestors, decked out in their historic clothes of office and
masks *(imagines)* fashioned to depict them individually. Even in this there was
an element of conspicuous display and competition, with ever more images
employed to depict the lines of descent of other related families. In 208 B.C.

Fig. 5. Artist's conception of a Roman funeral procession. (Drawing by J. Glover)

M. Claudius Marcellus's funeral had some six hundred masked men representing his ancestors; Sulla's procession in 78 was said to have used six thousand.[29] These masks may in some cases have been actual death-masks taken from the face of the deceased and were probably made of light material, perhaps thin clay or wax. According to Pliny (*N.H.* 35.6), in former times the faces of ancestors had been enshrined in the atria of houses, and these may have provided the ensemble employed in the funeral.[30]

The procession, which might be vast, ended at the Forum where the family, together with its ancestors represented by the mask-wearers, took seats before the *rostra,* while the larger public massed behind them. A speech was given before this congregation of the living and the "dead" praising and listing the achievements both of the deceased and of his ancestors, beginning with the most ancient whose images were in attendance (Polybius 6.53–54). Earlier the custom had been for such praise to be recited at private dinners, but from at least as early as the third century, the accomplishments of the deceased and his family were presented and celebrated in public and through oratory (Cicero *Tusc. Disp.* 4.2.3). This *laudatio* was probably interspersed with a chorus of lamentation by the professional mourners or the public (Kierdorf 1980, 104 ff.). In Roman society, the open, even ostentatious, expression of intense grief was customary, and one of the tasks of the orator was to provoke such a response from his audience. At the same time it was intended not just to lament the deceased and move the living but to provide a "great display of family status and a re-enactment of the society's values. By emphasizing the family's tradition and continuity, the loss would have been put in proportion and the status of the family re-asserted" (North 1983, 170). The tone and content of such orations is suggested by that given by Q. Caecilius Metellus on the death of his father, in 221 B.C., which Pliny recounts (*N.H.* 7.139–40): "He had to his credit ten of the greatest and best achievements which sages spend their lives trying to attain. That is, he wanted to be a warrior of the first rank; an outstanding public speaker; a most courageous general, one who won major military victories under his own auspices; to hold the highest offices; to have great wisdom; to be deemed the greatest senator; to acquire a great wealth honestly; to leave behind many children; and to be of great renown in the community."[31]

The entire ceremony — both the grandeur of the procession and the rhetorical hyperbole of the funeral oration — empowered such public funerals to become significant political events that the authorities even found expedient to prevent on occasion. After the failure of the sedition led by Gaius Gracchus in 121 B.C., his body and those of his companions were thrown into the Tiber, and the family was forbidden to go into mourning (Plutarch *G. Gracch.* 17.5). This was "intended to destroy the continuity of the culprits' family traditions . . . preventing their relatives from fulfilling their religious duties towards them and displaying their familial traditions in funeral processions" (Nippel 1995, 64). Eventually legislation was introduced to curb the cost and extravagance of funerals, including measures initiated by Sulla (Cicero *De Leg.* 2.60 ff.; Plutarch *Sulla* 35.3). But the futility of limiting such a highly effective political gesture was clearly demonstrated by Sulla's own funeral in 78 B.C., which surpassed all before it in the degree — if not the nature — of display it employed. In addition to the musicians, dancers, actors, and a vast retinue of ancestors, it exhibited some two hundred and ten carts carrying trophies, including two thousand golden crowns dedicated by foreign cities, his soldiers, and clients. The funeral couch was followed by magistrates, senators, priests, and priestesses, then members of the equestrian order, the general public, and Sulla's legionaries. In effect, it became an extraordinary postmortem triumphal procession.[32]

The formal ceremony of the actual Roman triumph was one of the most venerable and revered of all Roman customs. Because of its ritual and sacred elements, and the esteem in which it was held, its essential form appears to have changed relatively little throughout the republican period, while (possibly influenced by processions in the Hellenistic east), it became more spectacular. Its origins were evidently Etruscan and very ancient; indeed, as a sacred ritual it retained certain elements, the original meaning or function of which the Romans no longer fully understood. It is hardly surprising therefore that modern scholarship is deeply divided over its origin, form, and interpretation.[33]

Essentially the ceremony involved a processional rite honoring a victorious general, and bestowing sacred magic on the population and city that he had served. The terms for awarding a triumph were carefully laid down but inevitably subject to persuasion and manipulation.[34] The route was dictated as part of the ritual, and it passed from an assembly point near the temple of the Goddess Bellona (who personified frenzy in war) in the Campus Martius, through the Circus Flaminius and Circus Maximus, round the Palatine Hill, and along the Via Sacra through the Forum to end at the temple of Jupiter Optimus Maximus on the Capitoline Hill.

The general was clothed in ritual dress of purple and gold, consisting of a tunic embroidered with palm branches and a toga decorated with stars (fig. 6). In his right hand he carried a laurel branch, in his left an ivory scepter surmounted by an eagle, and he wore the *bulla,* a golden amulet of Etruscan origin. His costume and implements, the *ornatus triumphalis,* were identical to those of the statue of Jupiter on the Capitoline (Livy 10.7.10, 30.15.11–12). He rode on a high, two-wheeled chariot drawn by four horses, which were also adorned. The chariot was decorated with gold, ivory, and reliefs, as well as laurel branches, and was festooned with bells and whips, with a phallus fastened beneath it. The triumphator's face was painted red (imitating that of Jupiter's statue), as were those of the lictors in crimson tunics who preceded him. The general wore a garland, while another, a very large wreath of golden oak leaves — the *corona Etrusca* borrowed from the statue — was held over his head by a slave, who spoke the words, *"respice post te, hominem te esse memento"* ("look behind you, remember you are a man"). The triumphator was accompanied in the chariot by his small children, and his older children followed on horseback. In front of him were all the public magistrates and members of the Senate, as well as singers, musicians, and jesters. The procession progressed through the city streets and public spaces, which were decorated with flowers and banners, and the doors of the temples were opened, with incense and perfume spreading through the air. Displayed on large wagons within the convoy were the spoils and trophies of war, as well as banners, painted depictions of the battles and events of the campaign, models of the captured cities, and statues personifying the rivers and towns of the conquered territory. White oxen for the sacrifice to Jupiter were driven along, accompanied by various priests. Just ahead of the victor's chariot came the chained

Fig. 6. Artist's conception of a triumphal procession. (Drawing by J. Glover)

prisoners of war, the most prominent of whom — enemy kings, princes, and nobility — would also be sacrificed. In its wake followed the slaves who had been freed by virtue of the victory. Finally, at the end of the procession, the general's own soldiers marched, wearing laurel wreaths and chanting victory songs and derisive ditties about their commander. The throng of spectators applauded, threw flowers, and shouted *"Io triumpe!"*[35] while the entire retinue progressed to the temple where the general performed the sacrifices and returned the golden wreath to Capitoline Jupiter. Originally the triumph was performed on a single day, but, later, for particularly famous victories (and commanders) these were extended to two or even three days.

The antiquity of the triumph lent to it an immense authority, because to the Roman mind its age and continuity validated the ritual and enhanced the sacred magic it embodied. What we are inclined to dismiss or gloss over as mere ceremonial display and symbolism was seen as a vital rite suffused with numinous significance and efficacy. As Dionysius of Halicarnassus (writing at the beginning of the first century A.D.) observed of such religious ceremonies, the Romans (like the Greeks) "have preserved these for the greatest length of time and have never thought fit to make any innovation in them, being restrained from doing so by their fear of divine anger" (*Ant. Rom.* 7.70.3). He described, by way of example, the ceremony preceding the circus contests each September of the *ludi Romani* (the oldest of all the games), drawing upon the record of the "most ancient of all the Roman historians," Fabius Pictor (third century B.C.), but making clear in his account that much of what Fabius had described was still practiced in his own day.

The spectacle took the form of a procession, the *pompa circensis,* which was led by the responsible magistrates from the Capitol through the Forum and into the Circus Maximus, in effect following the path of a triumph in reverse.[36] The presiding official rode in a chariot, wore the same insignia as a triumphator, and was given the *ornatus Iovis* (wreath and scepter) in the temple of Jupiter (to whom the games were dedicated) prior to the procession. Heading the retinue on horseback were sons of the Roman nobility, followed on foot by other citizens' sons destined to serve in the infantry. Both groups were organized into military formation, and this part of the display served, according to Dionysius, to impress visiting foreigners with Rome's might. Next came those who would participate in the games: first the drivers in either double *(bigae)* or four-horse chariots *(quadrigae),* then the athletic contestants wearing only loincloths, which Dionysius notes was still the practice in his day. Groups of armed dancers followed the athletes and were accompanied by flautists and players of the lyre and a similar stringed instrument, the *barbiton.* The dancers wore purple tunics, elaborately plumed bronze helmets, and carried swords and short spears. Each group had one who led the others in a war dance consisting of a repeated rhythm of four short beats to the foot.

The armed dancers were followed by a dancing chorus of men dressed as satyrs or as *sileni,* the former costumed in goats' skins and high hairy manes, the latter in shaggy tunics garlanded with flowers. The dancers performed the lewd satyr dance, *sikinnis,* parodying the dance of the warriors in front of them. Dionysius notes at this point in his account that he has seen the same satyr choruses employed at Roman funerals, and that similar ribaldry and satire is directed at Roman commanders by their soldiers during a triumph. The *pompa circensis* continued with many more flute and lyre players following the satyrs, then bearers of censers burning perfume and frankincense, together with men displaying silver and gold vessels belonging to the state.

The final section of the procession (for which the other elements were essentially a prelude) consisted of embellished images of the gods, carried in chariots or on trays *(fercula)* borne on the shoulders of attendants. Boys pulled separate closed carriages *(tensae)* containing all the symbols, gifts, and other attributes *(exuviae)* associated with each god. Dionysius notes that images of all twelve Olympian gods were included, together with many others, both those that predated the Olympians and a host of demigods, muses, nymphs,

Fig. 7. Terracotta panel first century A.D. depicting a chariot race in the Circus. (C. M. Dixon)

seasons, and "countless others" (cf. Tert. *De Spect.* 7). These gods "attended" the games, with the most revered placed on chairs in a special viewing area, the *pulvinar*. First they were conducted on a circuit of the course to be welcomed by the crowd, with particular groups or individuals applauding their favorite deity: Mars by soldiers, Venus by lovers, and the like (Ovid *Amores* 3.2.43 ff.).

Subsequent Circus events consisted of a variety of activities tailored for the particular festival being celebrated. Probably all of the established games had at least one or two days set aside for entertainments, as too did the *ludi extraordinarii*. The most popular and frequent sport was chariot racing (involving four, three, or two horses), but there were variations in which riders finished the race on foot or leaped between two horses that were yoked together (fig. 7). These were followed by footraces, boxing, and wrestling, the winners of which were awarded a crown. During the republican era the Circus was also by far the most frequent location for *venationes*. It was less commonly used by gladiators and for theatrical entertainments, and, because of its size and sightlines, it was probably employed for more extravagant presentations. In 186 Greek athletes gave an exhibition there, and in 167, for the celebration of the triumph of L. Anicius Gallus over the Illyrians, a huge stage was erected for flute players, actors, and dancers (Polybius 30.22.1–12; cf. Athenaeus 14.613d–615e).[37]

The Circus eventually was also the customary venue for the *lusus Troiae,* the "Troy games," in which nobles' sons performed elaborate equestrian maneuvers. Two squadrons paraded in armor, then, after formal drills, fought a mock battle. This was one of the few "respectable" entertainments open to participation by free-born Romans during the later republican period. Like the "Troy games" the chariot races themselves had probably originally been imported to Rome from Etruria but subsequently appear to have been influenced by Greek practice, including the custom by which great men were allowed to compete and thereby bring honor to themselves and their families. For a while, wealthy members of the nobility, including senators, had both owned and sometimes raced their own horses in the Circus but, possibly because the state attempted "to restrict the fame of individuals, or [felt] that such fame should only be won by political and above all military exploits" (Rawson 1991b, 402), the practice was abandoned. After that the racers were of humble origin and frequently were slaves. Senators were forbidden to participate as contestants, and at some point they were also banned from contracting to provide racehorses for most of the games, with the exception of the *ludi Romani* and *Apollinares* (Polybius 6.17.1–3). Instead, the state paid breeders to supply the horses and contracted professional agents to provide the charioteers. Thereafter, leading citizens derived glory not as before by directly competing themselves but, as with the other *ludi,* by helping to sponsor, organize, and preside over the races.

Locating Performance: Place and Context

Although I have not attempted to survey the full panoply of occasions at which Romans of the late Republic could view spectacular entertainments or visually impressive ceremonies, I have outlined the most significant of these activities. But spectacle is three-dimensional and sequential, realized by taking place over a period of time, and its place, circumstance, and unfolding fundamentally shape what an audience both expects and experiences. The *place* is not simply the architecture or scenery that contains or displays the performance, it is also the range of associations of that location or material for the spectator, including historic activities that have occurred in the same place; the way it may have been specially fashioned or altered to take on unaccustomed symbolic meaning; and its location relative to other areas of urban space and their significance. It is important to bear in mind that most of the activities described here took place in or around the Forum, which not only provided in such features as its *rostra* and the theaterlike setting of the *gradus Aurelii* places ideal for public performance (Cicero *Clu.* 93; Steinby 1995, 332), but was also essentially "an open-air political stage." Here "everything happened out of doors, *sub conspectu populi Romani,* and nearly everything happened in this particular space—*contiones* [meetings], *comitia* [assemblies], triumphal processions, the procession . . . to the *ludi Romani* in the Circus Maximus, *quaestiones* [judicial hearings], theatrical performances, gladiatorial *munera,* funeral orations from the *rostra*" (Millar 1995, 240). The *context* of performance, moreover, is in part a function of the nature and frequency of the occasion (recurrent holiday, periodic religious ritual, special victory celebration) and the psychological effect of these upon the participants. It is conditioned too by the manipulation of language and imagery to inform, exhort, move, or amaze the audience, and of course by whom, and under whose patronage, the performance is given. Such elements are not incidental to the spectacle; in a real sense they *are* the event, which cannot be understood unless due regard be given them. Of course, imagining how they might have figured in the mind of an ancient Roman is impossible: the most I can hope to do— drawing upon what contemporary individuals might perceive if placed in some broadly comparable circumstance—is to sketch by inference what it may have been like for our Roman predecessors. In this area of experience, perception, and aesthetic response, we can "know," if at all, only through analogy.

Until the middle of the first century B.C., drama in Rome was performed on temporary stages built for many annual festive occasions and then dismantled. Such stages were therefore erected frequently during the republican era, and according to Vitruvius (5.5.7), writing after the construction in the mid-first century B.C. of the permanent theater of Pompey, they were still being built in his day in great numbers; indeed, they continued to be constructed during the imperial period. There were a large number of permanent theaters to the south in Magna Graecia and Sicily, and by the mid-second century B.C. there were many closer at hand in Campania and Samnium as well, which could have influenced the practice in Rome. Indeed (as detailed below), there was an abortive attempt made in 154 to construct a permanent theater in Rome itself near the Palatine Hill (Val. Max. 2.4.2). In the absence of a permanent structure, the frequent erection of temporary stages gave the Romans a continuous opportunity to mold these to reflect their own theatrical practice as it developed in its particular social and aesthetic context.

On the basis of the extant plays and dramatic fragments we can begin to construct a model of the early Roman stage by identifying the minimal elements necessary to stage republican drama. This was performed on a raised wooden stage, backed by the scene building, which was often referred to as the *scaena*.[38] The front of this building, facing the stage, had openings — two or three for comedy, and one for tragedy — that could be fitted with serviceable doors. Probably the doorways occasionally had a small raised porch, the *vestibulum*, attached to them. The area in front of the doors was thought of conventionally as an open street, and the doorways functioned as entrances to houses located along that street. In addition, comic plots frequently make use of a passageway *(angiportum)* behind the houses, an open area that afforded access to the rear of the houses (or to the gardens, often referred to as behind them). It was used as a theatrical convention to account for necessary movement of the characters when the plot would not permit such movement to take place on the street into which, also conventionally, the houses were thought to open: the stage.

This fundamental format in the earliest phase of Roman theatrical activity, dating back to the fourth century B.C., was probably realized in very basic platform stages, possibly similar to the type that were copiously illustrated on southern Italian vases of the period by the inhabitants of Magna Graecia. These vases show rudimentary stages backed by a simple facade, which sometimes had doors. The stages often have an overhanging roof and stairs to ground level. But in the course of time, as theater acquired a larger role in the city's cultural life and as the strong tide of Hellenization swept through Roman culture in the second century B.C., it is likely that alterations and embellishments of the earliest stages took place.

It is logical that some of the alterations in Roman theater architecture reflect an assimilation of Greek practice, in a process analogous to that of dramatic literature and many other aspects of Roman cultural evolution. The few pieces of evidence documenting the construction of temporary theaters during the republican period support this assumption. In 194 B.C. the censors instructed the curule aediles to set aside special seating at the games for the approximately three hundred members of the senatorial order (Livy 34.44.54; Val. Max. 2.4.3). This indicates a new element of stratification contrasting with the earlier impression (conveyed in particular by Plautine prologues) of socially unself-conscious spectators. "The symbolic character of the move stands forth. The theater would reassert the preeminence of the *nobiles*" (Gruen 1992, 204). The innovation in dramatic content and presentation observed in the plays of Terence some thirty years later (as well as the controversy they engendered, as recorded in his prologues) also suggests some change in audience composition, which began to exhibit tensions based on taste, education, and sophistication. The provision of special seats is an architectural feature frequently found in the remains of the Hellenistic theaters of southern

Italy, from which it may have been borrowed. In addition to prominent places reserved for the presiding officials, these senatorial seats were probably located in an orchestral area between the stage and the wooden tiers of the auditorium.[39] The provision of such an orchestra may represent a further architectural innovation that presumably was now occupied by privileged spectators (including the current magistrates and leading priests) but cleared when required by such special events as the visits by Greek performers referred to earlier.

To understand the context (which was often too the cause) of further development in the temporary stages, it is useful to examine some aspects of the occasions for performance more closely. The games were often preceded by a procession *(pompa)* from a temple to the theater, similar to that preceding the *ludi circenses,* and this was followed by customary sacrificial rites. Before the performances, a chair was carried into the theater and placed in either the orchestra or the main seating area *(cavea)* to honor the god or gods in whose name the games were being held. This ceremony, the *sellisternium,* used a special chair that was probably prepared in a ritual taking place prior to the games at an appropriate temple, where it was draped and emblems of the gods placed on its cushions. It was then carried in procession to the theater "from which the god . . . could watch the performance, through the medium of the symbol which represented him" (Hanson 1959, 85). An altar was probably located in the orchestra, and both it and the stage itself were sprinkled with incense or sweet-smelling saffron. In addition to such immediate religious elements, the temporary theaters were constructed near temples to enable their gods to observe the performances.[40]

Thus the leading political and religious figures of the Republic as well as the symbolic presence of its deities were continually in view during the entertainments. In addition, the erection of the theaters in the midst of civic monuments, shrines, and temples placed the spectators in a suggestive historic and religious context. In the late Republic there was a strong impulse toward the development of "cults of personified values" (Yavetz 1983, 46), such as *pietas, victoria, concordia,* and *clementia,* and the theater was an ideal venue for representing such concepts. Visually, emotionally, and psychologically, by means of the spectacle a close synthesis could be established between the state and public values. Thus the ordinary spectators' perception was modulated by and *through* the presence of a group of important mortal and divine guests as well as by the evocative setting of the entertainments.

Such theaters were erected periodically (in the Forum and the Circus) for the annual scenic games (fig. 8). Because the historians recording the period (principally Livy) pass over such recurrent constructions, it is likely that the

Fig. 8. Reconstruction of a temporary Roman stage, based on the evidence of wall paintings. J. Paul Getty Museum, Malibu. (R. C. Beacham)

structures they do mention were in some way special — possibly in that they were intended to be permanent — although few details are provided. For example, a stage and auditorium authorized near the temple of Apollo in 179 B.C. by the censors M. Aemilius Lepidus and M. Fulvius Nobilior, probably for the *ludi Apollinares,* is mentioned (Livy 40.51.3; cf. Hanson 1959, 18–24), but may never have actually been built. In 174 the censors Q. Fulvius Flaccus and A. Postumius Albinus arranged for a stage to be constructed for games given by the aediles and praetors (Livy 41.27.5), although its special significance is not indicated. What is likely is that by this period the Roman audience's taste for public extravagance was well established (although its members were frequently exhorted or constrained to private austerity), and the tendency continued undiminished despite documented Senate attempts to curb it.[41]

Just as the *ludi* and their entertainments may have offered temporary relaxation of the constant pressures of piety and propriety, so too the stage settings provided an opportunity to indulge vicariously in acceptable excess. From the beginning of the second century B.C. until the construction of the first permanent theater, the temporary stages and the performances taking place in them were increasingly lavish — sometimes astonishingly so. As Jory notes (1986a, 146), "Theatrical activity was intimately connected with three interlocking facets of Roman life; worship of the Gods, the honoring of the dead, and individual self-glorification or, put another way, with religious ceremonial, eulogy of the family and vote-winning. All three aspects tend to stimulate and encourage extravagant display and excessive expenditure." In addition to a variety of theatrical genres and the use of many costumed performers, attention was focused on the embellishment and scenic requisites of the temporary theater structures themselves. The impulse toward spectacle itself led to experiment and innovation, in the process making earlier versions of the stages obsolete — old-fashioned — and encouraging the borrowing of architectural and scenic refinements from the long-established Hellenistic theater. An example of this may be found in the show mentioned earlier that was produced at the triumph of L. Anicius Gallus in 167, when, according to Polybius (30.22.12), "a very large *skene*" and an orchestra for dancers were erected. This was at a time of growing interest in Hellenistic painting, encouraged by the presence of Demetrius of Alexandria, who painted townscapes, shrines, and the like. Similar paintings were already being used as scenery in the Hellenistic theater, and it is possible that the stage facade of 167 made use of painted effects.[42] The introduction of some such painting would have been an enhancement and a novelty, one likely to be welcomed both by ambitious and munificent patrons and by an audience seeking entertainment and diversion.

In 154 B.C. an attempt was made to build Rome's first permanent theater, which was to be prominently located near the Palatine Hill and would place the city on a par with communities in Campania and Samnium, as well as elsewhere in Latium, that acquired theaters at about this time.[43] By order of the censors C. Cassius Longinus and M. Valerius Messalla, the project went forward, building materials were collected, and the construction was evidently well underway (if not indeed completed) when, three years later, the former *Consul* and senior statesman P. Scipio Nasica, who had been against the project from the start, persuaded the Senate to order the demolition of the structure on the grounds that it was "useless and injurious to public morals." It was dismantled, the materials were auctioned off, and a ban was placed on the provision of seating at games held within the city limits (Livy *Epit.* 48; Val. Max. 2.4.2; Appian *B.C.* 1.28). "The event must have left a powerful impression. Dismantling a large stone theater on the brink of completion, one that would have accommodated a good portion of Rome's citizenry, could hardly go unnoticed" (Gruen 1992, 207). The city did not acquire a permanent theater for another century. The ban on seating, however, evidently was not enforced for long. In 145 B.C. Lucius Mummius erected seating for the plays (at which he employed Greek actors) given at his triumph that marked the sacking and destruction of Corinth (Tac. *Ann.* 14.20).

Nevertheless, the incident is a graphic example of the ambivalence toward theatrical shows, arising both from their potential for abuse by ambitious politicians and generals and by the threat that some felt the games and their increasing extravagance posed to moral values. Popular resentment was periodically aroused by criticism of the growth of private luxury and the decadent lifestyles of the wealthy. Strict traditionalists, epitomized by Marcus Porcius Cato, also regarded some intellectual and artistic innovations as dangerous and subversive and rallied public opinion against them (Polybius 31.25.5). During his censorship in 184, he had instituted a number of notoriously repressive measures intended to halt the growth of foreign-inspired luxury, and other measures were enacted from time to time that reflected some ambivalence, now tolerant, now repressive, toward fashionable new ideas and practices, mostly Greek-inspired ones. His censure, however, in light of the deep engagement with Hellenism that he and many other members of the Roman elite experienced and actively pursued, did not indicate mere xenophobic prejudice but rather "aimed to throw Roman values into deeper focus, to augment national pride, and to sharpen a sense of cultural identity" (Gruen 1992, 261). The theater was easily drawn into the midst of the controversy, involving as it did foreign elements, extravagance, new modes of art and, of course, political catering to the mob with the threat of manipulation and riot. Resisting the provision of a permanent facility expressed "the *severitas* of the State . . . the clearest example of public values" (Vell. Pater. 1.15.3). After periodic attempts to curb the cost of the games, in 115 B.C. the censors took direct measures against theatrical personnel, expelling at least some of them from the city, although the extent and length of the ban are uncertain (Cassiodorus *Chron.* 115 B.C.).

A public theater represented a site where a large and unpredictable mass of people could assemble at any time, without warning and therefore, potentially, with no means at hand to control them. Theaters were, after all, built for mass communication. In the Greek world, including the Hellenized parts of Italy, they had long been used for all sorts of public meetings, including political assemblies. In an atmosphere of social unrest and the ever-present threat of violent upheaval that characterized the second century, it could certainly be argued (particularly by those with little sympathy for the theater in the first place) that this was unacceptably dangerous. Clearly rhetorical objections of this sort were used to block a permanent theater but may not have fully disclosed the genuine motivation of those voicing them. In fact there is no evidence that prior to the last decades of the Republic the theater in Rome had ever been used to express popular discontent or subversive opinion, nor had any determined attempt been mounted to abolish the theater as an activity. On the contrary, members of the Roman elite offered substantial patronage to both the institution and its professionals. It was, however, important that the provisional quality of that support be maintained, together with reaffirmation of aristocratic privilege and control, if patrons were to be suitably appreciated for their generosity and indulgence of a popular pastime. "The ritual of erecting and then dismantling temporary structures gave annual notice that the ruling class held decisive authority in the artistic sphere. A permanent theater, whatever its advantages in cost and convenience, would represent a symbolic relaxation of that authority" (Gruen 1992, 209).

Despite the absence of a permanent facility (and as a manifestation of the cultural control that the aristocracy continued to exercise over theatrical activity), the impulse toward the display of scenic and architectural virtuosity on the temporary stages became more pronounced in the late republican period. In 99 B.C. Claudius Pulcher created an elaborate, multicolored *scaena* that attracted great admiration. It made such effective use of trompe l'oeil technique to imitate architectural details that, according to Pliny the Elder, "crows were deceived into flying to the painted image of roof tiles" (*N.H.* 35.23). The spectators subsequently enjoyed further refinements as patrons of the games produced new effects to dazzle them. At the shows given by Quintus Lutatius Catulus in 69 B.C. to celebrate a project (entrusted to him) to rebuild the temple of Jupiter on the Capitoline, he added an additional pleasure borrowed, according to the account, "in imitation of Campanian luxury" (Val. Max 2.4.6; cf. Pliny *N.H.* 19.23). This was the *vela,* or *velarium,* a system of awnings — the Greeks termed it *petasos,* a wide-brimmed hat — that could be stretched over the auditorium. Brightly colored and embroidered with designs, these pleased the eye and protected the spectators from the sun, and they must have created a singular atmosphere (gently rising and falling on the breeze) as the colored rays of light played through them onto the crowd and stage. Earlier, the Roman wooden theaters may frequently have been roofed, but as they grew in size, this was eventually no longer technically possible. "Partial covering by *vela* was a compromise which fulfilled both the requirements of the artistic and architectural concept of a closed theater building and the practical exigency of a sun shelter" (Graefe 1979, 1:221). The *vela* soon became a standard feature of Roman theater structures; as early as July 60 B.C., Catulus's awning (presumably made of coarse linen canvas) was superseded by a more impressive version fashioned from finer linen, or possibly cotton, for the *ludi Apollinares* given by the praetor Lentulus Spinther.[44]

At about the same time, legislation suggests that the theater audience was becoming further stratified and self-conscious. A law was passed in 67 B.C. under the tribune L. Roscius Otho stipulating that citizens of equestrian status had the right to occupy seats of honor in the theater: the first fourteen rows behind the senators, with two rows reserved for ex-tribunes. It was evidently not a popular measure with the general public. Four years later when Otho entered the theater (possibly at the *ludi Apollinares,* for which he would have been responsible if, as seems likely, he was Praetor in 63 B.C.), he was applauded by the knights but roundly hissed by those sitting behind them. Confrontation ensued — "the two parties turned on each other, shouting out insults; the whole theater was in a state of turmoil" (Plutarch *Cic.* 13) — and would have ended in violence had Cicero, who was *Consul,* not calmed the audience with a judicious speech.[45] In it he apparently argued that "the crowd's behavior politicized and hence violated the spirit of what was essentially a religious event. . . . This is consistent with the idea that the crowd would have felt the religious nature of the *ludi*" (Crawford 1993, 217–18).

As I discuss later, political expression in the theater greatly increased in this period. As Cicero comments elsewhere, however, the audience did indeed attend the theater not just to be entertained (or to express political opinion) but also "out of religious feeling" (*Har. Resp.* 2.22 ff.). Indeed, in his analysis of Roman society, the Greek historian Polybius suggested that religious belief, spectacle, and political stability were all closely linked together. "The quality in which the Roman Commonwealth is most distinctly superior is in my opinion their religious beliefs. . . . What in other peoples is an object of reproach — I mean superstition — is the very thing that maintains the cohesion of the Roman State. These matters are clothed in such pomp and introduced to such an extent into their public and private life that nothing could exceed it. . . . Their object is to use it as a check upon the common people. . . . Since every multitude is fickle, full of lawless desires and violent passion, it must be kept in check by invisible terrors and suchlike pageantry."[46] It is important therefore while assessing the place and sense of occasion and its impact upon the aesthetic event experienced by the audience to bear in mind the powerful catalyst provided by the religious fervor that was an essential element of all such entertainments.

Innovation quickened and the shows became more ostentatious when, according to Valerius Maximus (2.4.6), in the course of the decade following the new controls on seating, "C. Antonius decorated the stage entirely in silver, Petreius, in gold, and Q. Catulus with ivory. . . . P. Lentulus ornamented it with scenic devices of silver." Finally, in 58 B.C. three years prior to the dedication of Rome's first permanent theater, the aedile M. Aemilius Scaurus (whose father had been *Consul* in 115 when theater personnel were expelled from Rome) produced what was the last word in scenic excess in the temporary theaters. According to Pliny (*N.H.* 36.114–15), Scaurus "constructed during his aedileship, (and merely for a few days' temporary use), the grandest edifice ever wrought by man, even when meant to be permanent. I refer to his theater. The structure had three stories, supported by three hundred and sixty columns. . . . The lowest level was marble; the next glass — a luxury never heard of since — and the top was fashioned from gilded boards. The lowest columns . . . were thirty-eight feet high, and between them were placed three thousand bronze statues. . . . The rest of the equipment, including cloth of gold, painted panels, and various theatrical properties, was so lavish that when those remnants suitable for everyday use were taken to Scaurus' villa at Tusculum, and the villa then burnt by angry servants, the loss was calculated at thirty million sesterces."

Pliny considered that Scaurus's aedileship, crowned by the construction of his theater, "did more to undermine morals than any that I know of" (*N.H.* 36.113) and earlier (36.4–8) had specifically condemned the failure of the laws to forbid such sumptuousness as this theater — according to him a thirty-day wonder — displayed. "But it was for the delight of the public, of course, that the laws were being indulgent . . . for by what route do vices more commonly make inroads than the route of public interest?"[47] Even allowing for a degree of exaggeration in Pliny's assessment (written in the time of the emperor Vespasian, well over a century later), it indicates the extent to which the patrons' desire — and popular pressure — for ever-greater grandeur had come to characterize public entertainments in the late Republic.

The objection to extravagant architecture arose in part from an antipathy to what would now be termed "conspicuous consumption," an unseemly indulgence of frivolous tastes, which was perceived as a form of decadence both reflecting and encouraging moral laxity. It was also an expression of the rising intensity of competitive politics in the later Republic through which ambitious aristocrats sought to surpass one another in the grandeur of both their private homes and their public benefactions.[48] Such "private" display provoked suspicion and condemnation. At a somewhat more profound level of aesthetic criticism, objections were raised that the type of public embellishment of which the decor of the temporary theaters was an example reflected a morally dangerous departure from reality, likely to diminish the sobriety and delude the common sense of the spectator. Such objections had long been part of ancient critical theory, most cogently developed by Plato, but found resonance in the particular social and moral beliefs espoused by the conservative factions prominent in Rome. Vitruvius (7.5.3–5), writing only a half century or so after the construction of Scaurus's theater, condemned "paintings of monstrosities, rather than truthful representations of definite things" as decadent and criticized a temporary theater that echoed and complemented the account of Scaurus's stage, calling to mind the depictions of theatrical decor found in many wall paintings of the period.

> At Tralles, Apaturius of Alabanda skillfully designed the stage of the small theater . . . on which he depicted columns, statues, and centaurs holding up the architraves; rotundas with rounded domes; the angles of projecting pediments; and cornices formed of lions' heads to carry off rainwater from the roofs. Moreover, the story above this had rotundas, porticoes, half pediments, and all the types of painted embellishment displayed on a roof. When the appearance of this stage, by virtue of its high relief, pleased its viewers, Licymnius the mathematician came forward and said . . . let us take care lest this painted stage make of us Alabandines or Abderites [peoples renowned for, respectively, extravagance and stupidity]. For which of you could have buildings, or columns or elaborate pediments above the tiles of your roof? . . . If we approve of such pictures which can have no basis in reality, we shall, like those other communities, be deemed idiots, because of such faults.

Vitruvius pointed out (7.5.4) that such artistic deceits delighted the spectators, whose "understanding is darkened by decadent critical principles, so that it is not capable of giving its approval authoritatively and on the principle of propriety only to that which really can exist." But the essence of theater is make-believe, and its experience would naturally be enhanced by taking place in buildings whose architecture and decoration were infused with fantasy. Vitruvius also noted that the popularity of the type of art he condemned arose from its extravagant use of color and bold display, and by the "expenditure of the patron." Thus the experience and approval of the spectator was conditioned, apart from the actual subject matter and staging of dramatic fare, by what Cicero termed the conspicuous public *magnificentia* provided by the games' sponsors and by the splendor of the stage architecture and its decoration.

Rome was a highly stratified and therefore immensely self-conscious society characterized by complex systems for defining, signifying, and acknowledging status. In the last decades of the Republic "these appear to have grown ever more subtle and elaborate . . . walking, sitting, reclining, facial expressions and gestures, and above all speech — its tone and tenor, rhythm and accent — were subject to regulation according to a set of increasingly refined stylistic models" (Barton 1993, 115). Moreover, one's status and personal power were in part a function of *dignitas,* an elusive but pervasive concept whose practical substance (apart from a code of elaborate etiquette) consisted of the expectation that an individual's honor and authority enabled him to protect and reward his clients, friends, and dependents, from whom in turn he demanded deference, tangible forms of respect for his status, and the assurance that his sense of "face" would not be slighted, or if it were, that any affront would attract swift and forceful retribution. So strong was this association between the visible expression of power and its effective reality that often at times of potential or actual violence the mere display of the emblems of status and authority was enough to awe the unruly and restore peace. For example, although republican Rome remarkably had no municipal police force (nor permanent garrison of soldiers) responsible for maintaining law and order, the magistrates "could generally secure obedience to their authority without re-sorting to coercive measures. The lictors [bearing their *fasces*] well illustrate the point: if it came to conflict, they could do little to enforce a magistrate's will, but they were a potent symbol of his authority" (Rich 1991, 194; cf. Livy 1.8.2; Nippel 1995, 12–16).

Part of this concept, particularly in the late Republic and early imperial period, demanded the externalization of one's status not just through the formal insignia of public office but through a variety of appropriately impres-sive displays. As Tacitus commented (*Ann.* 3.55), at least until the age of Nero "the more handsome a man's fortune, house, and establishment, the more imposing his reputation and his following." In addition to such "private" manifestations of *dignitas,* and however much Vitruvius or other critics might deplore its more fanciful or frivolous forms, elaborate spectacle freely pro-vided to the public was an immediate and effective gesture for expressing and validating individual power, and in turn the perception and evaluation of such power was a vital factor in how the audience experienced the event.

The Politics of Performance

The power and prestige of Rome's aristocratic class derived from family descent as well as personal achievement, and the renown of the former and the actuality of the latter were crucially dependent upon attaining office. As Yak-obson points out (1992, 50–51), "the Roman nobles . . . perhaps more than any other social élite in history, were dependent on popular elections for the very definition of their relative status in society. . . . The ultimate test and measure of *dignitas* for a republican *nobilis* was his ability to reach higher office." Such individuals suffered from a version of acute "performance anx-iety" that could be relieved only by winning elections. To achieve this, am-bitious politicians went to great lengths to display their status and enormous expense to distribute generosity when it was politically expedient. Although on one level this could be seen (and occasionally was punished) as mere elec-toral bribery, on another it could also be construed as an important expression of benefaction and esteem for the Roman people. The theater and related entertainments offered a convenient medium through which the dominant elite could simultaneously assert its public-spirited largess and its control of culture and the arts. The populace too possessed a *dignitas,* worthy of homage, that might be defended by law if abused.[49] According to Cicero (*Leg. Agr.* 2.71), such a quality counted among the major benefits enjoyed by the Roman people; he exhorted them to "keep possession of your liberty, your votes, your dignity, your city, your Forum, your games, your festivals, and all your other enjoyments."

Elaborately embellished public entertainments therefore simultaneously validated personal power while contributing to the public's sense of being paid the honor and enjoying the splendor that was its due. Thus the bestowal and reception of such gifts established a socially significant transaction between both parties, as patron and client. The theater was the most obvious occasion for such an exchange, but the sense of significant spectacle permeated other public entertainments as well, because of their lavish decoration and by virtue of the urban landscape in which they took place.

Gladiatorial combats *(munera)* were not presented as part of the annual public *ludi* during the Republic and therefore would not normally have been presented in the temporary theaters constructed for those occasions. The earliest gladiatorial combats (264 B.C.) were staged in the Forum Boarium, site of Rome's cattle market (Val. Max. 2.4.7). This was located southwest of the Forum near the Tiber and was an important hub where several major streets converged and direct access was afforded to Rome's two earliest bridges, the Pons Sublicius and Pons Aemilius. In addition, it was the site of several important cults, notably the earliest dedicated to Hercules, whose altar, statue, and various temples and dedications were located in it (see Palmer 1990; Steinby 1995, 221–23, 295–97). One part of it contained the market, and nearby was the Emporium, the major site of warehouses and wholesale commerce in Rome. It was also adjacent to one end of the Circus Maximus. The earliest combats took place, presumably in an open square, at the center of this complex of commercial and religious buildings.

In such a context, it is likely that the immediate occasion of the gladiatorial display transformed urban space from its normal function and associations into something extraordinary — just as an act of street theater or other out-of-the-ordinary events can temporarily "theatricalize" a public space today. At the same time, the perception of the events themselves might also be "colored," and the spectator's perception conditioned, by the suggestive power of the surrounding architecture and monuments. For example, the Forum Boarium contained a bronze statue dedicated to the Roman general Titus Flamininus, and this would have been an appropriate and evocative site for the extensive funeral games given in his honor by his sons in 174 B.C. (Plutarch *Flam.* 1.1; Livy 41.28.11; cf. Palmer 1990, 237–38). To speculate further, the gladiatorial displays may have been in part rituals that celebrated the redemptive qualities of manly combat as well as the ability to confront, and for some contestants to overcome, death. Hercules, according to the myths associated with his cult, was a supreme warrior-hero as well as a mortal who had experienced and survived the terrors of the Underworld. Gladiatorial combats staged upon or adjacent to ground hallowed to Hercules could be seen as taking place in a most appropriate physical as well as imaginative space.

Throughout the republican period, however, the most frequent venue for gladiatorial shows at Rome was the central Forum (Vitruvius 5.1.1–2), where from very early times shops on one side and the temple of Concord on the other delineated a rectangular arena. When the first combats took place, spectators simply stood about or sought the best available vantage point, perhaps with a sense, as Auguet suggests (1972, 19), that they "were taking part in a ceremony rather than attending an entertainment. . . . The lack of distance conferred a violent and strongly emotional character on the bloodshed."

As Jory points out (1986b, 538), "Once the Forum became accepted as the appropriate venue for the paying of honors to the dead, it was natural that both gladiatorial shows and *ludi funebres* should take place there, and as seating accommodation was provided for the *ludi scaenici* in the temporary theaters so provision was made for the spectators in the Roman Forum." Thus, although *munera* were not included in the annual games, those presenting *ludi funebres* might borrow from the games the practice of erecting seats for their spectators in a temporary theater for the theatrical shows and the gladiatorial combats that were staged in honor of the deceased. From the late fourth century, galleries *(maeniana)* had been provided in the Forum (Fest. 120.L); next, permanent balconies suitable for viewing were built, and later additional temporary seating was constructed with places rented to spectators. These were called *spectacula,* the term used for arena structures throughout the republican period (cf. Welch 1994, 61, 78). In 122 B.C. Gaius Gracchus attempted to remove these seats (first by persuasion, but ultimately by force) to allow "the common people an opportunity of seeing the entertainment" (Plutarch *G. Gracch.* 33.5–6). Later, Cicero (*Pro Sest.* 124–26) mentions seats *(spectacula)* at displays held to honor Metellius Pius, who died in 63 B.C. In the mid-first century B.C., passageways were built beneath the Forum, probably by Caesar — who later also provided silk awnings for a gladiatorial show he gave there (Pliny *N.H.* 19.23; Dio 53.22) — that allowed the gladiators to emerge suddenly in a dramatic manner. The Forum probably continued to be used for *munera* until it was repaved following fires in 14 and 9 B.C.[50]

Gladiators were presented as part of the funerary rites of important public figures, and, as noted earlier, the formal orations following the funeral procession also took place in the Forum. Like all rituals, funerals provide pattern and predictability, order and continuity, which connect past, present, and future — as well as the living and the dead — a continuum arising from tradition and experience, which transcend history and time. The associated orations and ceremonies can enable the deceased person in effect to become "a commentary upon his life, his history, and his community, mirroring his social world to itself and to himself at the same time" (MacAloon 1984, 150).

The Forum was ideal for presenting such a ritual. By the middle of the second century B.C., it formed an increasingly integrated complex of temples, public monuments, and spaces reserved for particular political activities.[51] It also was lined with statues of prominent individuals or monuments recalling their achievements. Not only might statues be erected on the *rostra* to honor the deceased, but in exceptional cases areas could be permanently reserved — also on the *rostra* — for their descendants to view "the games and the gladiators" (Cicero *Phil.* 9.7; cf. Welch 1994, 76–77; Steinby 1995, 332). A number of buildings in the Forum (as well as the trophies and shrines associated with them) had been constructed, repaired, or enhanced through the benefaction of one or another of Rome's leading families, and by the end of the Republic this represented an important expression of political competition between rival *gentes*. Therefore, a range of associations immanent in this formal public space displaying a microcosm of Roman history and culture over the centuries inevitably informed the perception of a funeral. Indeed, as Cicero pointed out (*De Orat.* 2.266–67), speeches given there could use the Forum's landmarks as highly effective "visual aids,"[52] while elsewhere (*De Amic.* 97) he characterized a public meeting as a stage performance. Certainly the buildings provided an extraordinarily splendid backdrop. In the late republican period, an audience facing the *rostra* from the open central area of the Forum had on their right the imposing Basilica Aemilia.[53] Extending their gaze to the left, they saw successively the Curia Hostilia behind the rostra, the lofty temple of Concord, and finally the temple of Saturn. Behind them stood the temple of Castor and Pollux.

In such an architectural setting, the funeral of a member of a prominent family acquired greatly enhanced significance, both as homage to an individual and as powerful propaganda drawing the public's attention to the past accomplishments and future promise of the family staging the ceremony. "A funeral speech which recalled the glories of ancestors and triumphs of the distant past could also be playing its part in securing political success for the survivors" (North 1983, 170). Consequently, the orations were often preserved and even published. The funeral was itself a deeply significant rite of transition, through which the family member formally became an ancestor, joining the congregation of his predecessors who, as described earlier, were present in the form of carefully masked and costumed participants. The deceased did not cease to exist but rather remained part of a larger integrated collective of the living, the dead, and those yet to be born. Such a ceremony not only helped to establish and sustain powerful bonds between members of the deceased family but also, in the case of major public figures, encouraged a broader social cohesion embracing much of the Roman community. In exceptional circumstances the funeral was officially "public," financed by the state; even when it was not (which was usually the case), it might be attended by virtually the whole population of Rome and neighboring towns, as Diodorus noted (21.25) in the example of the funeral of Aemilius Paullus in 160 B.C. As described by Polybius (6.53), a funeral provided a highly theatrical and effective pageant.

> Whenever any famous man dies, at the funeral he is carried with all the funerary trappings to the *rostra* in the Forum, sometimes sitting erect and conspicuous or more rarely reclining. Then with all the people standing around, an adult son . . . or some other relative mounts the *rostra* and speaks of the virtues and achievements of the dead man. Thus the people are reminded of what had been done and made to see it with their own eyes — not only those who took part in these achievements but also those who had not, and are moved to such sympathy that the loss seems to be not confined to the mourners, but a public one affecting the whole people. . . . When [the masked impersonators] reach the *rostra,* they all sit in a row on ivory chairs. There could not be a more inspiring sight. . . . For who would not be moved by the sight of the images of men renowned for their excellence, all together as if alive and breathing? What spectacle could be more glorious than this? Besides, the speaker . . . when he has finished telling of [the deceased], recounts the successes and achievements of the others present, starting from the most ancient. Thus by the constant renewal of the good report of brave men, the celebrity of those who performed noble deeds is rendered immortal, while the fame of those who did good service to their country becomes known to the people and a heritage to future generations.

The "performance" of a triumph, like a funeral, could draw on both the emotion of the occasion and its architectural setting to create a highly impressive event and an expressive mise-en-scène. Instead of taking place at a single venue, the triumph was a moving spectacle that displayed its procession of dazzling trophies, captured enemies, and victorious soldiers to vast numbers of the population thronging its route as it traversed the heart of Rome. It progressed through a symbolic landscape of public monuments, temples, and shrines, which lent significance to the ceremony through their presence and, in turn, were thrown open, decorated, and embellished with spoils of past wars to mark the importance of the event. Pliny notes, for example (*N.H.* 34.33), that the statue of Hercules Triumphalis in the Forum Boarium was dressed in triumphal clothing for such occasions. In fact, it is likely that temples were deliberately constructed on sites located along the course of the triumphal procession. As in the Forum, the erection of such temples was frequently financed by leading Roman families, whose members' electoral prospects would be significantly enhanced by military success. Of the thirty temples dedicated in the period between the First and Third Punic Wars, eighteen were erected on this route, and others close by it. As Patterson (1992, 196) points out, these "had a double function: to remind those participating in triumphal processions of the achievements of their ancestors, and to remind voters of the achievements either of candidates for election themselves or of their families."[54]

The triumph itself was in essence a particularly magnificent parade, whose impact as a spectacle performance arose from a number of aesthetic elements common to this genre of public procession. The primary expressive element of a parade is, of course, the ranks of marchers, who in a manner similar to that of massed choruses of dancers are simultaneously the "performers" as well as a highly effective living scenic device, whose controlled and coordinated movement and sounds can stimulate a powerful emotional response in the spectators, particularly when its movement is underscored by a strong rhythmic pulse. The effect is strengthened when the performers themselves — heroes and soldiers — evoke such feelings as solidarity, thanksgiving, and pride in the onlookers. The event is also defined and the emotional response to it informed by a motivating purpose: in the case of the triumph, to celebrate an entire panoply of entities — the gods, the state, the conquering general, his soldiers, the captured plunder, and the victory. As the cavalcade of military ranks and orders passed by, displaying centuries-old standards recalling past struggles, there must also surely have arisen from such pomp and grandeur an emotional reaction to the power and majesty of Rome itself. The event could also, of course, condition such feelings to contribute to the underlying political agenda or goal of an individual or faction.

By progressively sequencing the participants and objects as they were observed by the spectators, the triumph modulated and ordered the aesthetic impact and response of the audience so that moments of high intensity, such as the appearance of the victorious general or visual depictions of "high points" from the campaign, were balanced by lighter sequences in which booty was displayed or jesters performed ribald dances. An emotional response could be encouraged by juxtaposing, for example, captured and condemned enemy chieftains and the newly rescued Roman victims of their oppression, just as a selected sequence of images in television ads can strongly affect modern viewers.

As a performance, the triumph approached a "total" work of art, supporting the emotional content of the occasion by using such expressive elements as rhythmic movement, music, song, mimicry, elaborate costumes, dazzling booty, scenic displays in the form of carts (floats) carrying *tableaux vivants,* banners, incense, and, not the least of these, the participating presence of the crowd itself reacting to these elements and its own cohesion and psychology to intensify the event. Plutarch's account (*Aemil.* 32 ff.) of the triumph of Aemilius Paullus in 167 B.C. — who had himself noted that a skillful military commander could also arrange and administer an impressive public festival (Polybius 30.14; Livy 45.32.11) — illustrates some of these qualities.

> The people occupied the parts of the City which offered a view of the procession and watched it wearing white clothes. All the temples were open and filled with garlands and incense, while many attendants and lictors held back the disorderly crowds which were rushing about. . . . The first day was hardly sufficient for displaying the captured statues, paintings and colossal figures which were carried in two hundred and fifty carts. On the second day the finest and richest of the Macedonian arms were paraded in many wagons, glittering with freshly polished bronze and steel. . . . As they were carried along, they clashed against each other, with a harsh and terrifying sound. . . . Then followed three thousand men carrying silver coins in seven hundred and fifty vessels . . . each borne by four men, while others carried mixing bowls of silver, drinking horns, bowls and cups. On the third day at dawn trumpeters led the way, sounding a battle-cry, not a marching or processional tune. After them one hundred and twenty oxen with gilded horns, bedecked with fillets and garlands, were led to sacrifice by young men. . . . Boys carried gold and silver libation vessels. Next came bearers of gold coins . . . divided into seventy-seven vessels. After them came the bearers of . . . the gold plate of Perseus' table. These were followed by the chariot of Perseus [King of Macedon], with his armor on which lay his diadem. Then came the King's children, led along as slaves, and with them a throng of weeping and supplicating foster-parents, teachers and tutors. . . . Behind walked Perseus himself . . . followed by a company of sorrowing friends. . . . Next came those who carried four hundred golden wreaths, which the cities had sent with their embassies to Aemilius as prizes for his victory. Next, mounted in a magnificently adorned chariot came Aemilius himself . . . wearing a purple robe interwoven with gold and holding in his right hand a branch of laurel. The whole army also carried sprays of laurel, following the chariot . . . and singing.[55]

The *pompa* described earlier that preceded the games in the Circus was also essentially a parade and shared many of the elements found in the triumph. But its form differed in that the procession concluded in the Circus Maximus itself, where it was observed by the huge crowd assembled there for the contests. The triumph marked the climax and culmination of a lengthy process — the outbreak of hostilities, the subsequent military campaign, and the eventual victory — which concluded in celebration. The circus procession, by contrast, functioned as a sort of prelude: a rite anticipating the exciting contests immediately to follow rather than one of closure for a process already completed. Psychologically, therefore, the mood would have been different because the *pompa,* celebrating a military victory, engendered emotions quite unlike those aroused by athletic contests or animal displays.

Although the space of the Circus itself probably was not fully integrated architecturally until the comprehensive works begun by Caesar had been completed by Augustus, by the middle of the first century B.C. it had already acquired a number of monuments and structures, including ornamentation along the central barrier *(euripus)* and the turning posts. Moreover, from ancient times the site was considered sacred to the sun and moon, possibly incorporating shrines to these within or adjacent to it. Whatever its architectural format in the late republican period, the Circus Maximus accommodated an enormous number of spectators — probably around 150,000 — and the size, self-awareness, and participation of this crowd was crucial in determining the aesthetic quality of the occasion. In addition, the audience included the entire panoply of the gods, the appearance of whose images and sacred attributes had marked the climax of the procession and who, after being paraded in a circuit before the applauding spectators, were positioned in their place of honor to preside over the games (Ovid *Amores* 3.2.43–58.).

This sequence of events, and the fact that it immediately preceded a range of competitive contests that were both enormously popular and highly partisan, inevitably lent the scene a sense of high drama and compelling spectacle. The nervous excitement of the crowd — encouraged by the grandeur of the parade, the religious fervor it inspired, and the keenly anticipated events about to begin — became an essential part of the occasion. As Ovid points out (*Ars Amat.* 1.140; *Amores* 3.2.19–24), despite the assignment of individual seats, the audience had to sit closely packed together in narrow rows, and therefore there would have been a physical sense of unity, collective energy, and response. In the Circus, moreover, men and women were allowed to sit together, and the social orders intermingled, a condition that apparently also applied to gladiatorial shows but not to the theater, where the organization of the audience was subject to formal guidelines.[56] This blurring of social barriers in

turn would have further encouraged festive relaxation and a sense of the spe-
cialness of the occasion in the vast Circus crowd. Indeed, its size and diversity
may have conveyed the illusion to those assembled — as they looked upon the
unparalleled spectacle of *themselves* — that the crowd constituted (or at least
represented) the entire Roman people. Such a situation, although volatile, had
the potential to direct and bestow a great deal of popular goodwill and gratitude upon those politicians, patrons, and presiding officials associated with
the event. It was also ideal for organized and spontaneous political expression.

Mid-First-Century Rome: The State of Play

The public events outlined here — theater, gladiatorial and animal shows,
funerals, triumphs, and the circus — which constituted the major Roman spectacles in the later republican era, had by then existed for centuries, during
which they had all undergone extensive modification, whether in their inherent
form or, crucially, in the uses to which they were put and the manner in which
the public perceived and responded to them. Increasingly the officeholding
Roman nobles displayed their *dignitas* at such occasions and, while attracting
attention to their personal grandeur, won popular favor by dispensing largess
in the form of ever more lavish entertainments. This situation, however, also
had severely negative consequences for these officeholders, because it "imposed the cost directly on themselves and continuously increased that cost
through competition, which forced them to demean themselves before their
inferiors, incur enormous debts, and sometimes risk a criminal prosecution
and severe penalties" (Yakobson 1992, 50).

Although such traditionalists as Cicero deplored this developing tendency
and the "profligates who squander their money on public banquets, doles of
meat among the people, gladiatorial shows, and wild-beast fights" (*De Off.*
2.55), nevertheless, as the established republican institutions began to break
down, and competition for office became more ruthless, politicians both clung
to this system and relentlessly intensified and exploited it. The importance of
public benefactions distributed en masse in the form of such shows seems to
have increased in part because the traditional system of client-patron relations
(which had long controlled large sections of the electorate) was in crisis, and
this led to widespread electoral corruption. To curb the games, however,
risked arousing popular resentment and the loss of crucial votes to anyone
advocating such measures.[57]

The increased importance of the games as elements of political competition
and advancement in turn changed their nature. Not only had the character
of the occasion at which games were given become more politicized, thus

affecting how they were perceived and judged by the audience, but the intensified competitive element tended to express itself most directly both in the frequency and in the increased scale and sumptuousness of the presentations. The emphasis progressively was placed on more marvelous display and what today might be termed "production values": lavish decor, extravagant props, large numbers of performers (animal and human), lengthy duration, marvelous architecture, a varied program, and plenty of noise and movement. In short, patrons endeavored, and were evaluated by the electorate on their capacity, to put on a show. This phenomenon can be seen as part of a broad evolution in Roman society toward what may be termed the "theatricalization" of culture, which became more pronounced at the end of the Republic and intensified in the imperial era. Whether in architecture, sculpture, painting, the literary arts, political rhetoric, or other manifestations, it is possible to discern an increased emphasis on image over essence, style over substance, fantasy over reality, and emotional gesture over reasoned analysis or discourse. All of these are abundantly evident in the characters and events that constitute the last act of the republican era.

2

Playing for Power
The Age of the Dynasts

An observer seeking to discern the facts of Roman history may be likened to a spectator attempting to make sense of the characters and actions on what is, at the best of times, a darkened stage and, at the worst, a stage with the curtain drawn. He or she can sometimes make out some shadowy movement or hear an occasional intelligible phrase but, for the most part, must rely on imagination to interpret the dimly lit scene. The last two decades before the death of Caesar are a stark exception to this: thanks to the extensive public and private writings of Cicero, we have more detailed information about Roman political life during this period than for any other aspect or era of antiquity. His observations and insights cast a veritable spotlight upon, if not always the entire scene, at least the principal actors and their movements. Of course, the illumination he offers can distort, obscure, or emphasize elements, while adding emotion and color to what we observe and how we perceive it; nevertheless, the impact and expressiveness of the mise-en-scène benefit enormously from it.

Polybius (6.9.6–9), writing long before Cicero, gives a prescient analysis of how political structures collapse, providing a useful "program note" outlining the drama that unfolds at the hands of ambitious politicians in the last years of the Republic:

Setting out to seek power, and unable to gain their objectives by their own resources and through their own qualities, they dissipate their property, using every means to bribe and corrupt the masses. Then again, when they have rendered the many receptive and greedy for largess through their insane appetite for prestige, the essential character of democracy is destroyed, and it evolves into a state of violence and government by force. The populace, once it is accustomed to feed off the property of others, and expects to live off the property of its neighbors, and when it finds a champion who is ambitious and daring, but is excluded by poverty from political rewards, brings the rule of force to completion, and gathering together, carries out murders, exiles and redistributions of land — until, having come to live in the manner of beasts, it finds once again a master and monarch.

Every aspect of this analysis is richly illustrated by the events that led to the collapse of the Republic and the establishment of one-man rule.

Political and Social Changes

As a result of the Social War of 91 to 89 B.C. and, following the civil war, the emergence of Sulla as dictator from 81 to 79, profound changes occurred in the Roman constitution itself and, consequently, in the nature of political life and the exercise of power. Reforms took place that, although alleviating a number of structural problems, also laid the basis for future discord. The extension of citizenship and voting rights to a much larger population had encouraged proletarian masses from throughout Italy, with little property except their vote, to swarm to Rome to take part in the popular assembly, causing the population to grow rapidly and electoral bribery to explode. To keep them satisfied and gain their support, entertainments, amenities, and other forms of largess were distributed on an increasingly lavish scale, which in turn made urban existence relatively attractive and encouraged further migration. As Sallust pointed out (*Cat.* 37.7) "Young men who had maintained a wretched existence by manual labor in the country, had come, tempted by public and private doles to prefer idleness in the City to their hateful toil."

During the strife at the beginning of the century and the subsequent rule of Sulla, a great many politicians had been killed, while others had their property confiscated or were barred from holding office. The generation following was in many cases extremely anxious to restore both their family fortune and their own status and *dignitas* by attaining public office. Sulla's constitutional changes had created a situation with more political opportunities for young men — the number of quaestors, a junior office, had been doubled to twenty — although their chances for further advancement were thwarted because the number of higher offices had not been similarly increased. Thus there was great competition between peer-group members as "each age group, equal in years and notionally equal in prestige, progressed together through a series of elections in which they competed with each other for public favor and political power" (Beard and Crawford 1985, 53). Rather like a struggle for academic tenure, or appointment as a partner in a law firm, the situation, far from fostering cooperation or consensus, encouraged high anxiety, intrigue, and ruthless pursuit of individual self-interest.

At the same time that it became more difficult to win office, the potential rewards increased dramatically. Men not only saw the prospect of restoring family status and formally returning themselves through elections to the senatorial class, they also contemplated a range of dazzling "prizes."

Extraordinary wealth could be amassed quickly through, inter alia, entrepreneurial activities, confiscations, war profits, or appointment to provincial office — each offering opportunity for entirely legitimate enrichment. The expanding empire also provided increased scope to gain prestige through military achievement and — the ultimate accolade — being awarded a triumph. Those fortunate enough to be elected consul thereby ennobled their family forever. The risks, however, were also great. To rise to high office was potentially to become an object of resentment and even violence at a time when, as Cicero claimed, the title of *Consul* had come to confer more envy than prestige (*Pro Sulla* 29.81). Apart from the personal danger they faced in an increasingly turbulent political situation, politicians had to invest a great deal of money both in getting elected, and, while pursuing their careers, displaying their *dignitas* through sufficient splendor. If they were unable to meet or somehow secure their debts they faced the danger of having their goods sold by court order and, as a probable consequence, incurring *infamia,* the "formal banning of a man from Senate, magistracies and the law-courts — in other words political death" (Frederiksen 1966, 128). This made them vulnerable and prone to compromise their principles.

At the same time, the old patronage system could no longer be relied upon to "deliver" the vote. The traditional bonds between clients and patrons, which had lent some degree of stability and control, could not encompass the expanded and volatile urban electorate (numbering perhaps 200,000 male citizens out of a total city population approaching one million) generated from the massive recent migration into Rome.[1] This increasingly heterogeneous population, and in particular the lower element that Tacitus referred to later (*Hist.* 1.2) as the *plebs sordida* (whose living standard was probably not much above subsistence level), could be manipulated by demagoguery and bribes. Such manipulation, however, required a great deal of effort and expenditure, as well as ingenious and aggressive electoral campaigns. This encouraged a high degree of "rugged individualism" in ambitious politicians, who had to struggle to put together and maintain an unstable constituency of friends, allies, and "ingratiated" portions of the broad electorate to secure victory. Some sense of the demands made upon even the most honest and scrupulous of politicians can be gained from the vivid "Handbook" on electioneering prepared for Cicero, probably by his brother Quintus *(Comment. Petit.)*. In addition to placing emphasis on such obvious requirements as oratorical eloquence and intellectual agility (2–3) and putting as many people as possible in one's debt, the "Handbook" advised the politician to show off the number, variety, and quality of his friends (4–6) who should attend him at home and on his public walks, and who ought to crowd about him whenever he appeared in the Forum. But above all, throughout the campaign it was crucial to stage what Quintus termed *pompae plena* — a "good show" — which should be "brilliant, resplendent and popular, with the utmost display and *dignitas*" (52). All the while, the candidate should encourage gossip about the crimes, lusts, and briberies of his rivals.

Of course, as noted in the previous chapter, by the first century B.C., the pressure of competition ensured that the provision of public entertainments played a major role in determining the outcome of elections. Near the end of his life, Cicero himself detailed the role of such public benefactions in securing office, noting that "if entertainment is demanded by the people, men of right judgment must at least consent to furnish it, even if they do not like the idea. . . . The whole system of public bounties in such extravagant amount is intrinsically wrong, although sometimes necessary; even then they must be limited by our means, and subject to moderation" (*De Off.* 2.17.58 ff.).

Moderation, however, had little appeal to Romans anxious to achieve public office, whose "preoccupation with personal achievement and competition for the greatest glory . . . stands out as the most conspicuous characteristic of the Roman ruling class [and] can be traced right through the history of the middle and late republic and into the early Empire" (Wiseman 1985, 4). Whether in the form of an abiding sense of an Homeric heroic ethos or a more visceral hunger for personal glory and wealth, the pursuit of excess was a dominant trait in Roman psychology.[2]

Unfortunately, officeseekers viewed honor and glory as limited commodities and believed that sharing them with others diminished oneself, because (in the phrase of the late republican mime Publilius Syrus) "profit cannot be made without loss to another" (337). Consequently, the striving for these distinctions and the *dignitas* arising from them was relentless, drawing upon the desire to surpass anything achieved by either one's predecessors or immediate rivals. As Horace observed, "The envious man grows thin on the plenty of another" (*Epis.* 1.2.57–59), and for aspiring Roman politicians, in a period in which "the boundaries of competition and rules of the game [were] unclear, *invidia* [envy] toward the winners increased" (Barton 1993, 151). In addition to the cruder forms of direct bribery or the persuasive appeal of benefactions, there were of course other talents that advanced one's career and assisted in the accumulation of authority and the power that accompanied it. According to Cicero (*Pro Mur.* 30), "There are two skills which can raise men to the highest level of *dignitas:* one is that of a general, the second that of a good orator."

Pompey the Great, Triumphator

Pompey was not an outstanding orator, but his skills as a general were extraordinary, and his career demonstrated that, when expedient, the prestige they lent could now be used to circumvent the constitutional and customary procedures for attaining office. Victories in the civil war in Italy, and subsequently in Sicily and Africa, first allowed him to pressure Sulla into granting him a triumph, probably in 80 B.C. when he was twenty-six.[3] This was particularly remarkable in that he had held no public office at all (much less the consulship or praetorship required for triumphators) and had initially been granted no formal authority to raise an army. He was now and henceforth hailed as *Magnus* as a mark not only of his supremacy as a general but also for the distinction of being the first and only member of the equestrian order ever to celebrate a triumph. The event was marred only when (possibly trying to evoke the aura of Alexander) he attempted to enter the city on a chariot drawn by elephants instead of horses, which was unable to pass through the triumphal portal (Plutarch *Pomp.* 14.6; Pliny *N.H.* 8.4). A decade later in 71, after further victories in Spain, he triumphed a second time when, with his army provocatively positioned outside Rome, he extorted from a reluctant Senate permission to stand for *Consul,* despite remaining innocent of any previous office and being well under the minimum eligible age of forty-two. Ambition would suffer no delay, and certainly not one imposed by mere technicalities of constitutional law, in the pursuit either of military glory or of consequent political preeminence.[4]

Employing a keen understanding of theater to display his unique status, Pompey appeared in the Forum at the ceremony that took place every five years in which the censors questioned young knights (to whose order Pompey still belonged) about their military service. There, with his full consular regalia and train of lictors, he led his horse through the astonished crowd, answering the censors, to the delight of the assembled throng who — shouting and applauding — accompanied him to his home. With a keen sense of show business, he subsequently appeared in public infrequently, and only when surrounded by supporters. As Plutarch records (*Pomp.* 23.3), "He sought to surround his presence with majesty and pomp, believing that he should keep his dignity free from contact and familiarity with the masses."

During the next decade, having been given unprecedented powers, made supreme commander of the sea, and granted the right to raise a huge fleet and army, Pompey attained further stunning victories, first destroying the pirates who had systematically terrorized the Mediterranean cities and disrupted vital commerce, and then vanquishing Mithridates, king of Pontus, who for more than forty years had been an affront to Roman power in the East. These were complemented by further victories in Syria and Judaea and extensive administrative organization of the far-flung conquered lands. On his return west he "proceeded with increasing pomp and magnificence" (Plutarch *Pomp.* 42.4), and along the route at Mytilene on Lesbos had an opportunity to admire the theater there, which inspired in him plans for securing further future glory. Arriving in Italy in December 62 B.C. he disbanded his army despite widespread fear that he intended to install himself as Rome's monarch, and by such "generous" action secured yet more popularity. As he approached the city, he was met by various processions of citizens, and finally by the Senate itself "lost in wonder at his exploits" (Appian *Mith.* 116.). Over the next nine months he choreographed the most magnificent triumph ever seen at Rome, determined to provide a spectacle so dazzling that it would totally eclipse both the memory of his predecessors and the prestige of his rivals, setting him in the public imagination on the level of Alexander the Great.

It was staged on September 28, 61 B.C., the day before his forty-fifth birthday. As Plutarch observed, "Others before him had celebrated three triumphs, but what most enhanced his glory and had never been achieved by any Roman before, was that he celebrated his third triumph over the third continent. His first was over Africa, his second, Europe, and now he triumphed over Asia, thus it seemed, encompassing all the World in his three triumphs" (*Pomp.* 45.5).

The spectacle lasted two days and, despite its splendor, left out enough to have "dignified and adorned yet another triumph" (Plutarch *Pomp.* 45.1). In it marched hundreds of captives representing the fourteen nations and nine hundred cities that Pompey had defeated, together with the families and generals of the conquered kings. A vast amount of plunder — innumerable wagonloads of it — was carried in a glittering stream, above which towered a twelve-foot statue of Mithridates made of solid gold. In its wake came Pompey himself drawn by four horses in a great bejewelled chariot.

The triumph was arranged as a consummate piece of propaganda, meticulously stage-managed to record indelibly in the imagination of its Roman audience an image of Pompey's power and majesty. Through him, Roman power had been projected further east than ever before, and the triumph evidently also sought to emphasize the scope of the new conquests and the exotic and dramatic qualities of the people and places that had figured in them. Placards were carried ahead of the procession inscribed with the names of all the defeated nations: Pontus, Armenia, Cappadocia, Paphlagonia, Media, Colchis, Iberia, Albania, Syria, Cilicia, Mesopotamia, Phoenicia, Judaea, and Arabia. Other inscriptions recorded the vast sums of money that Pompey's victories had contributed to the public treasury. The ranks of captives — all splendid in their native costumes — included, in addition to the pirate chieftains, defeated generals; the king of the Jews, Aristobulus; innumerable relatives of the conquered kings Mithridates and Tigranes of Armenia and those of lesser potentates, together with a vast number of trophies and such suggestive props as Mithridates' throne and scepter, the couch of Darius, and the bronze prows of some of the eight hundred captured ships (Pliny *N.H.* 33.151, 37.12–14). One trophy, the *Oikoumene,* was particularly evocative of Pompey's power: it represented the entire world in the shape of a globe or some form of personification (Dio 37.21.2). The most compelling displays of all were the dramatic mobile *tableaux vivants,* which, like elaborate parade floats, depicted some of the campaign highlights in a manner calculated to convey a strongly theatrical effect as they slowly rolled past the upturned heads of the spectators. According to Appian (*Mith.* 118), these included "images of Tigranes and of Mithridates, representing them as fighting, as vanquished, and as fleeing. Even the besieging of Mithridates and his silent flight by night were represented. Finally it was shown how he died, and the daughters who chose to perish with him were pictured also, and there were figures of the sons and daughters who had died before him, as well as images of the barbarian gods decked out in the fashion of their countries."[5]

Prelude to a Permanent Theater

It was the grandest spectacle ever seen in Rome, but Pompey, elevated to godlike status by the ceremony, must soon have recalled that evocation of his mortality relentlessly repeated by the slave who accompanied him in his triumphal chariot. For as Cassius Dio noted (37.50.6), Pompey quickly realized that "he did not have any real power, but merely the name and envy resulting from his former authority." Cicero said the same thing, noting in January 60 B.C. (*Ad Att.* 1.18.6) that "Pompey wraps that triumphal cloak around him in silence," unable to assist in a deteriorating political situation. The Senate had awaited the return of so formidable a warlord with anxiety, but once Pompey's army had been safely disbanded, and influenced by the resentment of those whose accomplishments and ambitions Pompey had eclipsed, it reasserted its authority. Pompey had reentered political life with two major requests: that the various *acta* encompassing the political organization and settlement he had made in the East be ratified and that his veterans be rewarded with land grants. The Senate obstinately frustrated these requests, alienating Pompey and eventually causing him to form a political alliance with Crassus and Caesar, in 60 B.C. Following Caesar's election to the consulate the following year, Pompey's demands were satisfied as Caesar forced through the necessary measures — with scant regard for established legal procedures — in the process causing violence and virulent resentment. Pompey himself suffered a drastic loss of popularity, as Cicero, who was on generally friendly terms with him but opposed to the conditions of the land settlement, documents. Whereas earlier in June 61, prior to Pompey's triumph, he had noted that because "the wretched starveling mob thinks I am a prime favorite with the great man Pompey . . . at the games and gladiatorial shows I have been the object of extraordinary demonstrations, without any hissing or catcalls" (*Ad Att.* 1.16), the situation had so deteriorated by July 59 that he reported "disgust is beginning to conquer fear" (2.18) and that "to my great sorrow, by dear friend Pompey has shattered his own reputation" (2.19). Cicero further noted an ominous change in public behavior, with "feeling best observed in the theater and spectacles": "For at the gladiatorial show both the patron [probably Pompey's associate Aulus Gabinius] and his guests were overwhelmed with hisses. And at the *ludi Apollinares,* the actor Diphilus made an impertinent attack on Pompey, 'by our misfortunes thou art "Great," ' which was encored repeatedly. 'A time will come when thou wilt regret your strength,' he declaimed amidst the cheers of the entire audience. . . . 'If neither law or custom can restrain . . .' was received with a tremendous clamor and shout. . . . The general public now speaks with a single voice, but founded not on resolution, but hate."

When Curio the Younger, who at the time opposed Caesar and Pompey, entered the theater, he was roundly applauded by those sitting in the section reserved for the *equites,* and Cicero recorded that in consequence there was some talk of punishing the knights by repealing the seating privileges granted their order under Roscius's law and of punishing the people by suspending the grain laws. The effect of such a rapid reversal of fortune upon Pompey who, as Cicero characterized it, "had fallen from the stars," was devastating. "Unused to such contempt, and having always been surrounded by an aura of praise and glory, he is now disfigured in stature and broken in spirit, and doesn't know what to do" (*Ad. Att.* 2.21).

Like others before him, as he contemplated the transience of his triumphal glory, Pompey realized that the most effective way to preserve it was to embody it permanently in public monuments. Indeed, in Cicero's view (*De Off.* 2.17.60), it was to the long-term advantage of every politician to favor building over the provision of lavish entertainments; "the expenditure of money is better justified when it is made for . . . those works which are of service to the community. There is, of course, more immediate satisfaction in what is doled out, nevertheless, public improvements win us greater gratitude with posterity." Twenty years before, Sulla had undertaken the most ambitious building program ever seen in the Republic, monumentalizing the Forum and conceiving in the Tabularium (subsequently completed by Quintus Lutatius Catulus) a great elevated theatrical backdrop for what took place below. Even before Pompey returned from the East, Caesar as praetor in 62 had attempted to provide him with a suitable opportunity for prestigious construction by transferring to him the responsibility for rebuilding the great temple of Capitoline Jupiter, which had earlier been entrusted to Catulus, who apparently had not yet entirely fulfilled the commission (Suet. *Div. Iul.* 15). This move "to enable Pompey to gain the glory for its completion and inscribe his own name" (Dio 37.44) was blocked in the Senate. In contemplating other possibilities during the dispiriting period following his triumph in 61, Pompey conceived the idea of building what would be Rome's first permanent theater. An account of the background helps to explain why.

During his absence of almost six years from the city, events had occurred that would have directly influenced Pompey's decision and, eventually, its consequences. The first significant appearance of Caesar on the political stage, as aedile in 65 B.C., was marked by extraordinarily lavish provision of the games for which he was responsible—the *ludi Romani* and *Megalenses*—which, possibly with the financial assistance of Crassus, Caesar had given with memorable scale and style. Even before their enactment, he had staged a prelude that stirred admiration by displaying the splendid decorations and objects to be employed in them "not only in the Comitium and the Forum with its adjacent temples, but in the Capitol as well, building temporary colonnades" (Suet. *Div. Iul.* 10.1). In the same year, he gave gladiatorial games commemorating his father, at which all the decor and appointments of the arena were of silver (Pliny *N.H.* 33.53) and were planned on so grand a scale that the number of scheduled combatants had to be curtailed because "the huge band assembled from everywhere so terrified his opponents that measures were taken to restrict the number of gladiators that anyone could keep at Rome" (*Div. Iul.* 10.2).

Following this success, and when, according to Plutarch (*Caes.* 6.1), "the ambitious efforts of his aedileship were at their height," Caesar used the goodwill and prestige achieved through the games to pursue a political agenda. The first of these was to overshadow totally the contribution of his fellow aedile Marcus Bibulus, who thereafter remained a bitter and at times troublesome opponent, particularly when, in 59, the two shared the consulate. In fact, in Plutarch's estimation (*Caes.* 5.9) such "lavish provision for theatrical performances, processions, and public banquets, quite washed away all memory of the ambitious efforts of his predecessors in the office. . . . People were so pleased that everyone sought to heap new offices and honors upon him." Three years prior to his aedileship, during the funeral procession of his aunt Julia, the widow of Marius, Caesar had boldly arranged to display images of his uncle. He then used his delivery of the oration as an opportunity for self-advertisement, taking as his theme "the origins and traditions of the two sides of Julia's family, one descended from kings, the other from gods" (North 1983, 170). These were bold gestures. Ever since the conflict between Marius and Sulla, which laid the basis for the civil war, Marius, who once had been revered as the savior of the country, had been a veritable "nonperson"; indeed his corpse had been exhumed and scattered on Sulla's orders and the trophies commemorating his famous victories removed from public display (Cicero *De Leg.* 2.56; Suet. *Div. Iul.* 11). Nevertheless, his memory, despite formal disgrace, was still cherished by a large portion of the population and, in particular, by the urban plebs, who consequently admired Caesar and were grateful for this calculated gesture.

Drawing upon his enhanced popularity as aedile, Caesar repeated the gesture on a grander scale in the hope of winning further support. He again secretly prepared images of Marius, together with trophies from his many great military victories, and had them installed by night on the Capitol. Their discovery at dawn was a veritable theatrical "coup" as word of the brilliant display spread, and a huge crowd of Marian partisans, moved to tears by the sight, gathered to applaud Caesar's act. Although denounced by some in the Senate for his impudence, Caesar carried the majority and scored an impressive display of authority and *dignitas* that strengthened his popular following.

The propaganda of Caesar's games and the public relations value of permanently displaying the trophies of military conquest must have been evident to Pompey, as only a few years later he considered the course of his own political career: the dedication and provision of a permanent theater would, of course, provide Pompey with the opportunity to secure both effects at a single stroke.

Other events that had occurred in Rome during his campaigns in the East offered Pompey further encouragement. In 64, in response to growing political violence, the Senate had banned the Collegia Compitalicia. These had been essentially religious, trade, and neighborhood associations—some of great antiquity—based in the various city districts *(vici)* that, by virtue of their organization as small local units, were vulnerable to domination and manipulation by opportunistic politicians, who could use them to intimidate rivals and generally foment electoral mischief. From about 70 B.C. onward, they were increasingly politicized and used to organize claques and cause disturbances in election campaigns. Traditionally, the Collegia had also been responsible for planning and celebrating the annual games of the *Compitalia* festival. This took place early in January, shortly after the *Saturnalia,* and it was a popular festival in which slaves, freedmen, and humble citizens enjoyed a relaxation of their duties. The heads of the city districts were even allowed to don the *toga praetexta,* a formal garment ordinarily reserved for the top magistrates, for the occasion (Livy 34.7.2). The associated games, which as neither state-sponsored *ludi* nor private benefactions had an ambiguous status, were aimed solely at the urban plebs, arose out of the mood of holiday abandon, and evidently offered—or could be manipulated to provide—a release for subversive sentiment. "These games implied a symbolic abolition of the status boundary between free and slave" (Nippel 1995, 72). The ban on the Collegia was extended to suppress the festival as well (Cicero *In Piso.* 8).

The ban remained a contentious issue, arousing the indignation of the lower orders. In December 61, just a few months after Pompey's triumph, a tribune attempted to revive the festival but was thwarted by the consul designate, Metellus Celer. On January 1, 58, shortly after entering office as tribune, P. Clodius Pulcher, ignoring the prohibition still in effect, summarily revived the Compitalia, in the process upstaging the consuls who by tradition formally took office with suitable ceremony on the same day. He then passed four major contentious laws (including one formally reinstating the Collegia) in an assembly held only three days after the festival.[6] Apart from such immediate results, as a champion of the lower sections of the city population—particularly recently manumitted freedmen and slaves—and an accomplished demagogue, Clodius had a strong long-term political motivation because the network of the Collegia could be used to assist in the recruitment of the gangs of violent supporters that he employed systematically to advance his populist political agenda. He superbly organized these partisan thugs into well-disciplined groups of ten, recruiting both slaves and freedmen. "No power except for the army or well-trained units of gladiators was a match for them [as they] terrorized the whole City" (Yavetz 1983, 91; cf. Cicero *Pro Sest.* 34, 55, 78, 85).[7] Clodius—a patrician by birth—had formally sought, and after some delay been allowed to become, a plebeian through adoption. This was primarily to qualify as a candidate for the tribuneship (a powerful and effective political platform from which to champion the interests of the lower orders), and his self-interested desire to reestablish the Collegia was obviously an important motivation.[8]

It seems likely, however, that the earlier suppression of this popular festival had other repercussions apart from its impact on Clodius's career. The date of the ban roughly coincides with the earliest reports of a new phenomenon: the persistent expression of political sentiments in the theater by sections of the audience. The disappearance of the Compitalia, including the "rough and ready" theatrical activity—satiric farces and lampoons of current political issues—that is thought to have figured in them, simultaneously embittered a large section of the population and cut off a benign outlet for the release of generalized social resentment and unrest. In effect, the ban may have inadvertently channeled the expression of these sentiments into the ready alternative venue provided by the formal entertainments taking place in the theater at the annual and extraordinary festivals.[9]

As noted in Chapter 1, Roscius's law reserving special seating for members of the equestrian order had been enacted in 67, but it was not until later, probably in 63—shortly after the suppression of the Compitalia—that resentment of it erupted into violent disorder in the theater (Plutarch *Cic.* 13.2–4; Pliny *N.H.* 7.117). The earliest reference found in Cicero's letters to theatrical unrest or the expression of political sentiments at the games is that quoted above for June 61, but from then on he frequently mentions such occasions. For example, in July 54, writing to his brother Quintus, he even predicts that the year will be quiet on the basis of the "demonstrations in the theater" (*Ad Quint. Frat.* 2.15.2). This suggests that once the theater audience had become "politicized" and acquired a taste for expressing itself on current issues, it continued to do so despite the eventual reinstatement of the Collegia. "The combination of autonomous organization and spontaneous articulation of the masses' material and cultural interests with cynical manipulation of their wishes in the power struggle between Senate and certain politicians constituted an often explosive mixture" (Nippel 1995, 82). Thereafter such expression was not, however, voiced only by members of the lower orders: the theater became a sounding board for diverse elements in the population, depending upon their representation in the audience at any particular occasion.

Cicero records that in 59, Gabinius, a candidate for the consulship, was hissed together with his supporters at gladiatorial shows he had himself organized; an indication that even such "private" occasions could not be entirely controlled by those sponsoring them (*Ad Att.* 2.19.3, 2.24.3). Much depended upon which interest groups marshalled its partisans to voice their concerns from the midst of the audience.

In addition to demonstrations arising from the spectators themselves, the theater also became a place at which elements of the population would assemble outside to dramatize their political stance there before the influential audience comprised of the Senate, magistrates, and other members of the upper strata. "Besides . . . staging high-handed imitations and usurpations of official sanctions, Clodius resorted to rituals of popular justice against Cicero in 57 and Pompey in 56 as responsible for the famine of the time" (Nippel 1995, 76). Thus, for example, in 57, Clodius led a crowd protesting grain shortages, first in July at the *ludi Apollinares,* forcibly ejecting the spectators (Asconius 48C), and again in September at the *ludi Romani* (Cicero *Ad Att.* 4.1.6–7; *De Dom.* 6–7, 10–16; Dio 39.9.2–3). On the latter occasion, the crowd, after rushing the theater, threatened the Senate itself, which was meeting at the temple of Concord. Cicero and Pompey were accused of being responsible for the food shortage. Clodius's attack backfired, however, when the Senate, as a consequence of its disrupted deliberations (and at Cicero's suggestion), formally entrusted control of the grain supply *(cura annonae)* to Pompey; a highly prestigious responsibility for which Pompey was long remembered. The following year, in March 56, in a speech at the trial of the former tribune Publius Sestius, Cicero provided his own invaluable analysis of the recent political role of the spectacles, while supplying some detailed and striking examples of the audience demonstrations.[10]

In 58, under threat from Clodius, and in imminent peril of prosecution under legislation about to be brought in at his enemy's instigation, Cicero fled the country, after which Clodius declared him an exile and employed his hooligans to destroy or vandalize much of Cicero's property. Earlier (prior to his departure), citizens had graphically demonstrated their support for Cicero by donning mourning. Now — and again for its value as an act of political theater — the razing of Cicero's house on the Palatine "took place in full view of well-nigh the whole City" because such destruction had traditionally been employed against public enemies (Cicero *De Dom.* 100; Dio 38.17.6; Vell. Pater. 2.14.3). Later, however, at gladiatorial shows given in the Forum the following year, "the type of spectacle attended by crowds from all classes, and which are particularly enjoyed by the masses," one of Cicero's defenders, Sestius, then tribune, deliberately attended to test and demonstrate the degree of public support Cicero enjoyed. "At once from all the spectators . . . was heard such applause that it was said the entire Roman people had never demonstrated greater or more obvious unanimity for any cause." By contrast, Clodius's brother, Appius Claudius, who was praetor, attempted to slink in unseen to avoid popular condemnation; when the crowd spotted him, the hisses were so strong that they "alarmed the gladiators and frightened the horses!"

Even more graphic scenes took place in the temporary theater. During a production of the *Brutus* of Accius, a line referring to the sixth-century king Servius Tullius — "Tullius, who secured the people's freedom" — was deemed by the crowd to be a reference to Cicero (whose middle name was Tullius) and "encored a thousand times." Early in 57 Clodius used armed gangs (including gladiators belonging to his brother) to prevent a vote for Cicero's recall at an assembly of the plebs (*Pro Sest.* 75–78, 85). Later, in May 57 when the Senate passed resolutions favorable to Cicero during the period of the *ludi Florales,* the theater audience once more took the opportunity to demonstrate its feelings. When the news of the Senate's actions came, the famous actor Aesopus, who was performing in Accius's *Eurysaces,* repeatedly "pointed" whatever passages could be fashioned to apply to Cicero, even interpolating appropriate lines from another play (the *Andromacha* of Ennius) and as he did so was wildly encored by the audience. Cicero later asserted that "he pleaded my cause before the Roman people with far weightier words than I could have done myself" and described "how [Aesopus] wept as he spoke of the burning and destruction of my house. . . . His acting was such that after describing his former happiness, when he turned to utter the line 'all these things I have seen in flames' it drew tears even from my enemies and rivals!"

The audience was so inflamed by this that a little later, when the senators entered the theater, they were roundly applauded, and as the consul P. Lentulus Spinther (who gave the games) arrived, he received a standing ovation from a crowd "weeping with joy." When Clodius entered, he had first to endure the "clamor of cries, threats, and curses" that rained down upon him, and then sat totally dispirited during a performance of the comedy *Simulans,* "The Pretender," by Afranius, every possible passage of which was construed by the entire audience to compound his humiliation. At one point the entire cast "leaning forward threateningly, and staring right at the foul creature, chanted in unison the line 'This Titus is the sequel, the end of your vicious life!'" Shortly thereafter the Senate passed a resolution finally enabling Cicero's recall, with Clodius alone casting a dissenting vote.

In reflecting on this episode, Cicero noted that there were "three venues where the opinion and feeling of the Roman people could be most directly expressed about public affairs: at meetings *(contiones),* at assemblies *(comitia),* and at a gathering for plays and gladiatorial shows." The opinion expressed at meetings was not entirely reliable, because the meetings could be packed with those bribed to attend, and assemblies did not always represent all segments sufficiently. Cicero concluded that the best expression of opinion was to be found at the shows, which displayed the broadest representation of the general population, including a good number of inhabitants from the surrounding countryside who came to attend them. Cicero's analysis, however, was probably colored by self-interest. As Vanderbroeck argues (1987, 79–80),

> The composition of the public was subject to manipulation. The shows were free, but not freely accessible. Providing tickets for clients or the members of a tribe was a proven means to gain popularity. . . . The spectators in the theater differed from the participants in the popular assembly and they were not representative of the Roman citizenry. We should not forget that the games were not merely a popular entertainment of the lower strata, but that they were popular with the entire population. The members of the élite enjoyed the spectacles as much as the plebs. The possession of separate seats gave senators and *equites* the possibility to act as a claque. The composition of the public was determined . . . partly by the organizer and other important persons who could furnish tickets to city-dwellers and country folk.

Only a few weeks after the delivery of Cicero's speech at the trial of Sestius, the theater was the site of another politically charged demonstration, for which once again he provides a graphic, suggestive, and highly informative account. The occasion was the week-long celebration of the *ludi Megalenses* (April 4–10), six days of which consisted of theatrical entertainments in honor of the Great Mother, taking place by tradition close to the site of her temple on the Palatine Hill. They were the responsibility of the two curule aediles, the senior one of whom presided over them. In 56 B.C. that magistrate was P. Clodius himself, who, notwithstanding his recent humbling in the Senate, had retained sufficient popularity among the general public since his tribunate two years earlier to secure election, which conveniently enabled him to avoid prosecution for the mob violence carried out at his orders against Cicero and others the previous year.

The *Megalesia* was the first major festival of the year, an important opportunity for the responsible aedile to impress the public. Thus Clodius, who, as described above, had earlier been the object of various humiliations in the theater, now had an attractive opportunity to stage-manage some theatrical mischief of his own, and it is this that Cicero describes in his oration *De Haruspicum Responso* (21–26) presented some six weeks later. This speech ostensibly sought to find the cause for some recently occurring omens suspected to be of supernatural origin. Even allowing for a degree of exaggeration and possibly some rhetorical sleight-of-hand, Cicero's account provides both a unique glimpse into the nature of theatrical ritual in the late Republic and an intriguing account of the scene staged by Clodius and his supporters on this occasion.

Following the opening ceremonies and the *pompa theatralis,* led by dancers and flautists into the theater, where the turreted crown representing the Great Mother was placed on a throne of honor in the orchestra — something altogether untoward occurred. According to Cicero, the temporary theater was invaded "by a great mob of slaves, mustered from every district of the City, and incited by this pious aedile, which at his signal were let loose to burst onto the stage from every passage and entrance." In the ensuing uproar, with "the Senate and Roman people trapped and helplessly fettered . . . exposed to a mob of mocking slaves," the consul Lentulus Marcellinus stood up. Although not presiding, he was the most distinguished public official in the audience and at his closely observed gesture other senators and knights rose and left the theater. Cicero suggests, perhaps with a degree of hyperbole, that had Lentulus not attended, and by "[his] name, [his] authority, [his] utterance, [his] presence" restored a degree of order, "we should not have been permitted to survive and raise our present protest."

Although it is impossible to assess the actual degree of physical danger to members of the audience, there can be no doubt that, at the least, Clodius, "in turning the *Megalesia* into a sort of *Saturnalia,* was committing an especially outrageous crime against Roman propriety" (Lenaghan 1969, 124). This would have been intensified by the nature of the Megalesia itself, because the cult of the Great Mother was strongly supported by members of aristocratic and patrician families, who also by venerable tradition entertained their friends lavishly during this holiday (Aul. Gell. 2.24.2, 18.2.1). Clodius's band of supporters may not have been (as Cicero asserts) entirely composed of slaves, who were probably formally excluded from attending this festival. His retinue, however, drawn from the lower orders, was likely to have included in addition to many freedmen at least a good number of slaves who, wearing no distinctive clothing, could certainly have taken part in the invasion of the theater and the occupation of places reserved for citizens. Cicero chose to emphasize this aspect: "slaves gave these games, slaves watched them — in his aedileship the whole *Megalesia* was a slaves' festival."[11]

Cicero asserted that the violent disruption with slaves actually stalking the stage and hijacking the ritual amounted to gross sacrilege, and that this was the cause of the recent manifestations of divine anger that his speech ad-

dressed. In passing, he briefly detailed the type of flaws that normally subjected the games to *instauratio* — the obligation to repeat them. These were
1) an interruption of the ceremony itself, 2) some error in performing the
ritual, or 3) an offensive crime or act of violence. This, together with the sense
his entire account conveys of the high seriousness with which the games were
viewed, both as religious and political events, further emphasizes their importance in Roman culture and in turn the attention paid to them by such men of
affairs as Cicero — and Pompey.

It may be significant that the disruption of the Megalesia by Clodius's followers took place only two months after the Senate, in February 56, had in
effect called for reinstating the earlier ban imposed upon the Collegia in 64 but
then rescinded by Clodius as tribune in January 58. It decreed that "political
clubs and organizations should be broken up and a law dealing with them
should be proposed" (Cicero *Ad Quint. Frat.* 2.3.5).[12] This action may well
have further agitated Clodius's gangs (at which it was aimed) and certainly
reflected an increasingly chaotic and dangerous political situation. Clodius had
manipulated the Collegia and "created countless new ones formed from the
slave-scum of the City" (Cicero *In Piso.* 4.8). Pompey himself was subjected to
vicious personal attacks and barracking in the Senate and at times could not
even leave his house for fear of being ambushed in the street. He confided to
Cicero that he believed there was a plot against his life (*Ad Quint. Frat.* 2.3.4).

Pompey suffered a further affront in April when Cicero — in a major politi-
cal miscalculation — sought to reopen the emotive question of the legality of
the land settlement forced through by Caesar during his consulship in 59. Both
Crassus and Pompey saw in this a dangerous threat to their alliance with
Caesar. Pompey immediately undertook to pacify Clodius (fresh from his
Megalesia antics), gaining his support in blocking discussion of the land acts,
and later in the month attended a fateful meeting with Caesar and Crassus at
Lucca, together with some two hundred senators. There the triumvirate was
renewed and strengthened to secure for its members political domination of an
exhausted and emasculated Republic. For Pompey, humiliated, constricted,
and seeing Caesar's rising military reputation in Gaul eclipsing his own, recourse to the triumvirate was one way of reasserting his prestige and securing
popular support. But there was another as well.

The Theater of Pompey

As detailed above, the role of theater in Roman political life became
more important during Pompey's absence abroad on military campaigns and
subsequently in the period following his great triumph of 61. Both its dangers

and its opportunities were formidable. Traditionally, the provision of a permanent theater at Rome had been vehemently opposed on moral, political, and security grounds. The nobility had resisted a permanent site perhaps primarily because its existence would compromise their ability to manipulate patronage to their advantage. "Retention of the old system entailed annual decisions to purchase plays, mount productions, and construct makeshift stages and accoutrements that reaffirmed senatorial control of popular entertainment" (Gruen 1992, 222). Now, in the increasingly volatile conditions of the late Republic, earlier rhetorical objections to the supposed danger posed by a permanent structure to public order acquired greater legitimacy and force. As Cicero pointed out in 59 B.C., such venues in Greece had frequently been the site of destructive events "when in the theater, untried men, quite inexperienced and ignorant, brought on harmful wars, put subversive men in charge of public affairs, and expelled men of merit from the city" (*Pro. Flac.* 16).[13] Recent events in Rome offered plenty of examples of unruly proceedings in the temporary sites. But now as the republican government and its institutions were wracked by factional struggles, what had earlier been feared by many as perilous might be seen as desirable by one who knew how to benefit from it.

As Pompey contemplated his maligned *dignitas* and loss of prestige, the provision of a permanent theater was distinctly attractive. By tradition, returning triumphators had used some of their war booty to build religious shrines as a lasting memorial to their achievements. Pompey himself had dedicated a temple to Hercules in 70 and erected one to Minerva in 61, probably on the Campus Martius, together with the dedication of a large sum of money to the goddess (Palmer 1990, 236; Diod. Sic. 40.4; Pliny *N.H.* 7.97). But, as we have seen, by the mid-first century the surest way to secure the greatest (though transient) popularity was through the provision of games. In providing a permanent theater, Pompey could assert his political preeminence in a most graphic manner by in effect co-opting for himself a prominent form of display and patronage and an important means through which to assert aristocratic control of cultural activity, which, by venerable tradition and collective will, the political elite had reserved for themselves. A theater could raise Pompey's prestige by in effect providing a continuous "triumph." The actual stagings, as Cicero's account cited below of the style of the two inaugural tragedies suggests, could be used to remind an audience of Pompey's own spectacular triumph, and the building itself could permanently display such evocative trophies as the fourteen allegorical statues representing the nations conquered on his eastern campaign (Pliny *N.H.* 36.41), statues which may eventually have adorned the piers of the theater's exterior arcade. But beyond that it "would associate his name permanently with pleasure and detract from the glory of whoever happened to put on a show there. For the beauty of a theater was that it could bear his own name" (Greenhalgh 1980, 175–76). Pompey would effectively "corner the market" in memorable monuments.

The establishment of a theater, particularly one of the size and sumptuousness that Pompey had in mind, could (as events demonstrated) accommodate a great variety of entertainment. It might even provide an outlet for the type of "rough" theater that was probably not represented among the limited activities customarily allowed to take place in the temporary constructions provided by individual politicians and dedicated to a particular festival, entertainments whose banishment from the popular street festivals had caused such embitterment and reaction. Although perhaps easing such resentment by providing a new civic venue for such popular expressions to take place, a permanent facility offered a place of display and celebration that, unlike those in the streets, could be "stage-managed" and more easily controlled in any volatile situation.

Pompey, moreover, had the means to realize his audacious plans. In addition to some fourteen houses and estates and a considerable inheritance from his parents and freedmen, he had accumulated a vast war booty, much of which had been invested lucratively in the East.[14] Apart from the glory from such conspicuous and extravagant munificence (which might raise him in contemporaries' eyes to the status of a Hellenistic monarch), the provision of a theater may also have appealed to Pompey on an intellectual level. He was well trained in Greek and Latin literature, and he had a circle of artists and intellectuals as friends. Foremost among these was Terentius Varro, the greatest of all Roman scholars, who had written extensively about theatrical art.[15] Pompey had fashioned himself as a successor to Alexander and the master of the Hellenistic East. For generations, prominent Roman statesmen and commanders had freely "demonstrated not only enthusiasm for Greek culture, but confiscation of it" (Gruen 1992, 248). What grander gesture or more extravagant demonstration of Pompey's status and ability to exploit Hellenic culture for the greater glory of the Roman people (and himself) could there be than to adorn the city with the most striking and venerable icon of all, a magnificent and permanent theater?

In September 55, exactly six years after his triumph and some eighteen months after the fateful conference at Lucca that had enabled Crassus and Pompey to share the consulship of that year, Pompey held games dedicating the theater, which may have been substantially complete by then, although the temple associated with it was apparently not finished for another three years and was consecrated during Pompey's third consulship in 52 (Aul. Gell. 10.1.7; cf. Vell. Pater. 2.48.2).

The games were keenly anticipated, as Cicero reveals in a speech in which, as an aside, he dared a political opponent to show himself at them: "We are close upon the celebration of the most elaborate and magnificent games in the memory of man, which have no equivalent in the past, and which it is difficult to imagine can ever be seen on such a scale in the future" (*In Piso.* 65). The shows were, of course, meant to be commensurate with Pompey's achievements in Rome and abroad. In addition to a variety of dramatic performances, there were athletic contests, music, gladiators, and hunting of wild beasts in the Circus. The last was not performed merely to delight the public by displaying exotic creatures. The menagerie had a message; it represented the distant lands that Pompey had subdued. With greater numbers of traditional animals than had ever before been seen at Rome—six hundred lions (three hundred and fifteen with manes), four hundred and ten leopards and panthers, and eighteen elephants—Pompey displayed such novelties as baboons, a lynx (possibly a gift from Caesar in Gaul), and, for the first time on any stage, an Indian rhinoceros.[16]

Although Pompey's popularity and acclaim undoubtedly soared with the mass of spectators whose favor and taste were his chief concern, Cicero's more fastidious (but private) opinion, as expressed to his friend Marcus Marius, must have been shared by a portion of the audience. "As for the Greek and Oscan plays, I don't suppose you were sad to miss them . . . and, as for the athletes—I can't conceive you regret forgoing them—you who scorned the gladiators. . . . All that's left is the hunts; twice a day over five days. Magnificent to be sure; who can deny it? But what pleasure can a man of culture derive from seeing some poor mortal torn to pieces by a mighty beast, or some fine animal impaled on a spear? And even if such things were worth seeing, you've seen it all before. I certainly saw nothing new" (*Ad Fam.* 7.1). Cicero adds that "the last day was for the elephants, which greatly impressed the crowd and rabble, but gave them no pleasure. In fact there was a degree of compassion, and a kind of feeling that this huge beast has a fellowship with the human race." His account is echoed by others, including Dio, who records that the elephants at first refused to fight in the battle staged in the Circus, protesting as they "walked about with their trunks raised toward heaven" (39.38.3), and Seneca describes how one of them put up an extraordinary fight, attacking its javelin-throwing opponents and tossing their shields in the air (*De Brev. Vit.* 13.6). Some of the beasts attempted to break through the iron fence separating them from the spectators, who were so moved by their pitiful trumpeting that they burst into tears and cursed Pompey (Pliny *N.H.* 8.21).

This undoubtedly militated against the aim of the festivities, which was of course to glorify Pompey and ingratiate the masses. The case highlights an important aspect of the potential and limitations of the games as public rela-tions exercises. Comparing Caesar and Pompey, Yavetz comments (1983, 55), "It is apparent that concern for the physical well-being of the masses was only one factor. All Roman rulers bribed the people with bread and circuses, and yet the one was popular and the other hated. Seneca provided the answer: the giving is not the decisive factor but the manner of its giving. The people were more easily swayed by how a ruler did than by what he did, and respected the one who at least took the trouble to appear popular" (cf. Seneca *De Benef.*).

Pompey, in attempting to secure popularity entirely by awing the spectators, while remaining aloof from any expression of "the common touch," had only limited success. Cicero recorded how in the *Clytaemestra* of Accius, a parade of six hundred mules carried the plunder of Agamemnon as he returned from Troy and, amidst hundreds of performers, some three thousand bowls were used in the *Equus Troianus* (of Naevius?) to display booty upon the stage. Evidently the themes and staging were fashioned to flatter Pompey's own triumphal militarism through mythological associations. Cicero indicates that although the approach did not entirely please the spectators, it did impress them, which may suggest the extent to which cross-fertilization between the art of the theater and that of the public spectacle conditioned audience reac-tion as it viewed the variety show assembled for the dedication.

But there was more to see and experience: the great theater itself hailed as Rome's most magnificent building, along with its complex of public amenities, gardens, and displays of art. According to Pliny (*N. H.* 36.115), Pompey's theater could seat forty thousand spectators, a figure that has long been doubted, but that more recent work has shown may not be too greatly exag-gerated, for what is believed to have been the largest Roman theater ever built (figs. 9 and 10).[17] The diameter of the auditorium was almost five hundred feet, while the stage itself was nearly three hundred feet in width, equivalent to the length of an American football field. Behind it the great facade of the *scaenae frons,* which may initially have been constructed of wood, probably rose to the full height of the upper tiers of the auditorium opposite: three stories (fig. 11). The outer semicircular wall was composed of three tiers of columns carved from red granite, possibly with the fourteen statues of Pom-pey's conquered nations placed around the perimeter (*circa Pompeium,* Pliny *N.H.* 36.41). Although nothing of the external structure of Pompey's theater remains visible above ground, it was probably similar to that surviving from the theater of Marcellus, erected forty-four years later. If so, then the engaged columns of the ground level were Tuscan, the second level Ionic, and the third Corinthian. This impressive facade was adorned with stone and stucco and embellished with numerous statues of stone and bronze (cf. Pliny *N.H.* 7.34).

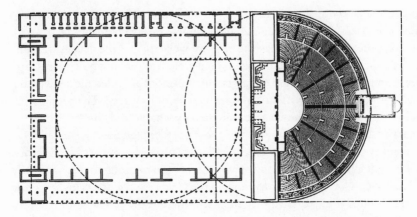

Fig. 9. Diagrammatic design of the theater of Pompey complex. (Created by Theatron Ltd.)

Hinting at the sumptuous architecture and spectacle within, it formed a series of forty-four huge vaulted arches at street level, from which a system of passages and staircases efficiently conducted spectators to their seats above, using tickets organized according to entrance, section, level, etc. This helped to ensure public order by eliminating competition for seats or confusion and congestion in locating them.

The most striking element in Pompey's edifice (although probably not completed or formally incribed until 52) was the provision of a temple to Venus Victrix crowning the top and rear of the auditorium and placed directly opposite the stage and *scaenae frons* (fig. 12). It was the largest of several shrines along the upper rim of the *cavea* in honor of *Honos, Virtus, Felicitas,* and *Victoria* (Pliny *N.H.* 8.20; cf. Suet. *Claud.* 21.1), "a small pantheon of the political rallying cries of the Sullan period" (Richardson 1992, 411). Apparently this temple was constructed so that the monumental ramp of steps leading to it formed the central bank of seats in the auditorium. It was said that when Pompey's political rivals objected to a permanent theater, he claimed that he was building a temple beneath which steps would be provided for watching the games (cf. Tertullian *De Spect.* 10). Allowing for the sophistry that was the privilege of a powerful man, the circumstances do indicate the continuing integration of theatrical performance and religious rites and the custom of close physical proximity between theater buildings and religious shrines. Indeed, according to Vitruvius, temples should be so arranged that "the images of the gods may seem to rise up and gaze upon those who make vows and sacrifices" of the sort customarily performed in the theater, and their

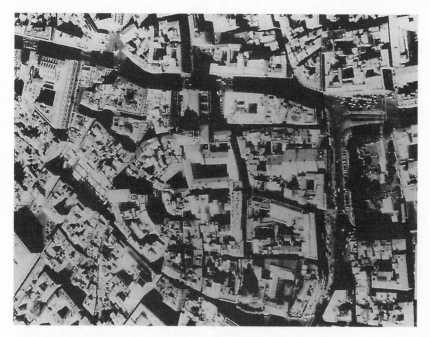

Fig. 10. Aerial photograph showing the site of Pompey's theater. (Fototeca Unione at the American Academy in Rome)

altars should always be placed lower than the statues in the temples so "those sacrificing may look upwards toward the divinity" (4.5.1, 4.9).[18] By sanctifying his theater with a temple dedicated to the goddess to whom he credited his military victories, Pompey both avoided any quibble about whether the provision of such a building was an appropriate benefaction from a triumphator and ensured the survival of a "private" monument glorifying an individual in a manner never before practiced in Rome.

Curving outward from either side of the temple was a covered and colonnaded gallery that extended around the top of the auditorium to connect with the two large lateral wings of the scene building, the *versurae,* which formed the recess for the (possibly temporary and wooden) scenic facade and framed the stage (fig. 13). At regular intervals around the external perimeter of this colonnade were attached the vertical masts from which projecting horizontal booms suspended a huge, bright-colored linen awning, the *vela,* that shaded the auditorium. According to Valerius Maximus (2.4.6), writing three quarters of a century later, the structure even was provided with a form of air-conditioning; "Pompey was the first to have water flowing down the aisles [of

Fig. 11. Artist's conception of the interior of Pompey's theater. Giuseppe Gatteschi. (Fototeca Unione at the American Academy in Rome)

the theater] to cool the summer heat." The permanent provision of such luxuries, which included as well the use of a fine saffron-scented spray *(sparsio)*, was undoubtedly intended to please and flatter the Roman audience.[19]

In addition to the theater itself, Pompey's architectural complex—which was designed as a single integrated unit—included an assembly room, or *curia;* a new meeting place for the Senate that was dominated by a statue of Pompey, provided, according to Plutarch *(Brut.* 14), by the Roman people to demonstrate its gratitude. Its prominent position was an unsubtle reminder of Pompey's own political eminence before a Senate that had too often displayed scant regard for it (cf. Steinby 1993, 334–35). Pompey also provided himself with a new residence conveniently a short distance away. Because, like the theater itself, its location in the Campus Martius was outside the formal boundaries of the city *(pomerium)*, proconsuls and other officials holding military authority (including Pompey himself) could attend while retaining their imperium, their formal right of command.[20] Pompey's theatrical sense had earlier been displayed in the design of his first house, the vestibule of which he prominently decorated with ships' prows captured from the Cilician pirates (Suet. *Gramm.* 15.1; Cicero *Phil.* 2.68; S. H. A. *Gord.* 3).[21] Now, adjacent to his theater, he constructed an even finer house, fashioned so that in

Fig. 12. Computer design of the theater of Pompey and the temple of Venus Victrix. (Created by Theatron Ltd.)

relation to that massive edifice it appeared, according to Plutarch, "like a boat being towed behind a great ship" (*Pomp.* 40.5, 40.9).

The house and *curia* were located within a spacious park extending several hundred feet behind the theater, the Porticus Pompeii, which quickly became one of the most popular places in Rome to stroll (Cicero *De Fat.* 8; Catullus 55.6; Ovid *Ars Amat.* 1.67; Martial 11.1.11). Within were rows of trees, shaded streams, and numerous fountains. It formed a rectangle, framed on each side by the columnar facade of different buildings (fig. 14). The side extending along the back wall of the theater itself probably had three great ceremonial doors (corresponding to those opening into the interior of the theater from the *scaena*), the middle one of which was aligned along the central axis of the park and was balanced by the *curia* at the other end, which in turn was flanked by two secondary structures to echo the tripartite arrangement of doors opposite. Along the north side was the Hecatostylon, "the portico of the hundred pillars." This great colonnade was festooned with heavy golden curtains from Pergamum and displayed a collection of statues and paintings, some hundreds of years old, works of outstanding merit and elegance (Pliny *N.H.* 35.59). One of these represented Pompey's role model, Alexander the Great, painted by Nicias the Younger in the fourth century B.C. Adjacent to the colonnade was a grove of plane trees, and possibly along the

Fig. 13. Computer design of the theater of Pompey complex. (Created by Theatron Ltd.)

south side opposite were possibly markets and shops. The large central court in between was composed of a double grove of trees *(nemus)* either running alongside an arcade or with rows of statues spaced between the trees (Martial 2.14.10; Propertius 2.32.11–12). This park was used on the days of performance as a place for the audience to promenade between the entertainments without leaving the theater complex or causing disruption in the streets, and at other times it provided a splendid recreational site for the Roman citizenry where they could escape from the summer heat or was used for amorous assignation.[22] As Vitruvius noted (5.9), this space could also be used to provide space for preparing the stage sets and machinery.

Pompey's complex was an amenity with a message. To walk through the central court of the park, with trees and possibly monuments placed along its sides at regular intervals to emphasize the perspective, "was processional in character, perhaps intended to recall Pompey's own triumphal procession" (Gleason 1990, 10). Moreover, the layout of the buildings, and in particular the placing of the theater and the *curia* at opposite ends of the site's central axis, tended to raise the status of the former (crowned by its temple) to that of a formal political space when faced from the front porch of the *curia* that was also itself a sacred precinct (Aul. Gell. 14.7.7). The entrance to the latter was dominated by a huge painting of a warrior by the fifth-century painter Polygnotus, which may have reminded visitors of the famed military prowess of its

Fig. 14. Artist's conception of the Porticus Pompeii. Giuseppe Gatteschi. (Fototeca Unione at the American Academy in Rome)

builder (Pliny *N.H.* 35.59). The political and religious nature of the building dominating each pole of the axis was therefore visually emphasized by being mirrored. Moreover, because the complex was located in the Campus Martius, which — in addition to its venerable military connection — had long been a place where voters were impressed by monumental architecture (and from time to time bribed with largess), in effect it extended and refined associations that this area already had. But, beyond that, the site comprised Rome's first "leisure complex," providing an alternative focus for public life to that traditionally centered on the Forum. In that sense it anticipated imperial practice, when such entertainments virtually displaced the republican electoral procedures and venues — as well as their by-then obsolete political function.

After its construction and for many decades to come, architecturally speaking, Pompey's theater was "the only show in town." Temporary stages continued to be built well into the imperial period, and other politicians still sought to exceed one another in the lavishness and ingenuity of their games, but nothing would surpass Pompey's great edifice for over a century, when the Colosseum was built. It did not, however, put an end to the corruption and violence that had come to be associated with electoral competition, nor to overt political expression at the games. Moreover, we know of one further curious example of architectural virtuosity that suggests that the splendor of Pompey's permanent theater engendered something approaching a desperation for novelty in those seeking to construct temporary theaters in its shadow. In the period 53 to 52 B.C., when Pompey's theater was new, C. Scribonius Curio built a theater in connection with the funeral games honoring his father. In fact, he built two large wooden theaters adjacent to one another, each revolving on a pivot. In mornings they were positioned back to back for the performance of plays, and in afternoons they were wheeled about to form a single amphitheater for gladiatorial displays.

Clearly, although *munera* were presented not as part of the annual state *ludi,* but only in the context of particular *ludi funebres,* "the Romans saw no anomaly in presenting gladiatorial shows at the same venue as other forms of entertainment which we more usually associate with 'the theater'" (Jory 1986b, 539). According to Pliny (*N.H.* 36.117–20), who deemed the affair a mad folly, after a while spectators even remained seated while the structures revolved. The image is in one sense emblematic of the conditions in Rome at the time: a population transfixed with its pleasures and diversions, while the state swung perilously toward revolution. Prior to Curio's *ludi,* his friend Cicero had vainly attempted to dissuade him, asserting that "no one admires the capacity to give *munera,* for it's only a display of wealth, not native ability, nor is there anyone who is not already bored to death with them" (*Ad. Fam.* 2.3).[23] Afterward it was claimed that Curio was so impoverished as a result of his theater and games that when, a little later, Caesar offered to assist him financially with some of his Gallic gold, he found in Curio (tribune in 50) a willing and extremely useful political ally (Suet. *Caes.* 29.1; Appian *B.C.* 2.102; Dio 40.60–62).

The electoral campaign of 53 was notorious for its corruption and violence, as the three consular candidates competed "not only by lavish and open bribery but also by gangs of armed supporters" (Asconius 30C). One of these candidates was Titus Annius Milo, who for several years had opposed Clodius's street gangs (augmented by gladiators) with bands of his own to whose service Cicero attributed the salvation of the country (*De Off.* 2.17.58 ff.; cf. *Ad Att.* 4.3.2–5; *Ad Quint. Frat.* 2.5.3; Dio 39.8.1). Milo's consular campaign, however, resorted to games and bribery on such a massive scale that Cicero feared for his future. "He is preparing to give the most magnificent games, at a cost, I assure you, that has never been exceeded by anyone" (*Ad Quint. Frat.* 3.8). A little later Cicero reiterated his concern, writing his brother that "anything more corrupt than the men and the times of today cannot be conceived," although noting that he hoped Milo's campaign would be successful "unless all is lost by absolute violence; but it is his private estate that I am afraid for 'and now is he beyond endurance mad' [quoting *Iliad* 8.355] since the games he is going to give will cost a million sesterces" (*Ad Quint. Frat.* 3.9).

As it happened, the elections had to be delayed because of the intensity of disruption, although "Milo desired they be conducted at once, placing his faith both in the support of the 'best' men because of his opposition to Clodius, and of the people because of his generous largess and great expenditure upon stage plays and gladiatorial displays" (Asconius 31C; cf. Lintott 1974, 64–68). In January 52, with the postponed consular election still pending, Milo killed Clodius in a brawl on the Appian Way and was subsequently charged and convicted (despite Cicero's frustrated attempt to help) first of murder and subsequently of electoral bribery (Lintott 1974, 73–75). Meanwhile, in enraged reaction to the murder of their champion, the *plebs urbana* staged their own spectacular "state funeral" for Clodius by conveying his body into the Senate House where they burned both the corpse and the structure and then "with deliberate purpose, held the funeral banquet in the Forum itself with the building still smoldering" (Dio 40.49.2–3). The Senate summoned Pompey and assembled under guard outside his theater (presumably in the *curia* attached to it), where it resolved to gather up the ashes of Clodius and to rebuild the Senate House (Dio 40.50.1–2). Pompey was appointed sole *Consul* as an emergency measure. It was his third consulate, and during it he formally inscribed his name upon the temple of Venus at his theater (Aul. Gell. 10.1.7).

As political instability deepened into virtually continuous crisis, politicians, desperate to secure power within a collapsing system, still looked to the games and associated diversions to validate their prestige and dignity. Again, Cicero's correspondence dramatizes this. In 51 he was sent as proconsul to Cilicia in southern Asia Minor. Throughout his sojourn there he was pestered by his protégé M. Caelius Rufus, anxious back in Rome to acquire panthers for the games he must give when elected aedile.

June 51: "I beg you to interest yourself in the matter of the panthers."
June 51: "If I am elected, I shall probably be so with a colleague wealthier than myself."
August 51: "About the panthers . . . you should send for some men from Cibyra and see that the animals are shipped to me."
September 51: "In almost all of my letters I have mentioned the panthers. That Patiscus has sent Curio ten panthers and you have failed to send ever so many more will reflect no credit upon you. . . . Curio has made me a present of that ten, and another ten from Africa. . . . My anxiety on this point is all the greater now, since I expect to have to provide everything myself apart from my colleague. For love's sake please do this . . . "

October 51: "If Curio had not made me a present of the beasts sent to him
from Africa for his games, my games might have been altogether dis-
pensed with; as it is since I must give them, I do ask that you take the
trouble—I have been forever asking you this favor—to let me have
something in the way of beasts."

February 50: "It will be a disgrace to you if I have to go without any Asian
panthers."

In April 50, Cicero replied, "About those panthers, the business is being
carefully attended to by those who hunt them; but it is surprising how few
there are, and they tell me that these few bitterly complain that in my province
no snares are set for any living creatures except themselves; they have decided,
it is said, to emigrate from here to Caria. . . . All the animals caught will be at
your service, though I cannot say how many. Your aedileship, I assure you, is
of intense interest to me."

On a far more somber note, a few months later in August 50, with the
constitutional crisis between Pompey and Caesar at its most threatening, Caelius wrote, "I see the imminence of violent discord which only the sword and
force will settle. . . . If it could only be done without personal risk to yourself, a
drama *(spectaculum)* of infinite entertainment is about to be staged for you by
Fortune." Within only a few years, the unfolding of this drama would cost all
of them, Pompey, Caelius, Caesar, and Cicero, their lives.

Enter Caesar

"Would that Pompey had died two years before the outbreak of the Civil
Wars, after he had completed his theater and the other public works with
which he surrounded it!" (Vell. Pater. 2.48.2). In fact Pompey, in conceiving
his theater as he did, had dramatically intensified a tendency already evident in
republican political life that, ironically, Caesar was quick to extend still further. By the late 50s he had acquired reputation and stature that placed him on
a level close to Pompey. But he had not yet been granted outward expressions
commensurate with what he felt his achievements demanded. And as Cicero
observed ominously, "for his *dignitas* he is prepared to do anything" (*Ad Att.*
7.11.1). Despite formidable military successes, Caesar had never triumphed.
Earlier, after his victories in Spain, his claim had been frustrated by the Senate's refusal to let him stand for the consulate of 59 unless he reentered the city,
which disqualified him for the triumph he had been granted. Caesar viewed
the complicated political intrigues of 51–50 that eventually caused the Senate
to demand that he lay down his Gallic command and to recall him to Rome

with the loss of his imperium as a far worse affront, particularly because Pompey by contrast would continue to command an army. As Gruen argues (1974, 75), "Caesar's *dignitas* was an obsession. Aristocrats from more influential houses could take their station for granted; Caesar insisted upon his. . . . He was generous, gentle, compassionate, a friend in need, a solace for the unfortunate, an expansive and open personality . . . but Caesar would hurl Rome into war in order to provide a stage for his own talents."[24]

Pompey, in fact, had unwittingly helped to construct that stage. His career had been embellished with splendid honors and exceptional privileges, such as the right to wear full triumphal garb and a golden crown when attending the Circus or a magistrate's dress *(toga praetexta)* and crown or laurel wreath in the theater, although according to Velleius Paterculus, "he refrained from using this honor more than once, and indeed, that was itself too often" (2.40.4; cf. Dio 37.21.4; Cicero *Ad Att.* 1.18.6). He had celebrated the longest and most sumptuous triumph ever seen to mark his extension of Rome's mastery over the world. In constructing and dedicating his theater as a monument bearing his name, he had ensured in a quite unprecedented fashion that the Roman people—not as individuals but massed together collectively—would be constantly reminded of his achievements and unsurpassed glory. After a period during which, as we have seen, the significance of the spectacles as political events had steadily increased together with their scale, Pompey's innovation was the ultimate political gesture by which he skillfully used the theater to focus attention and admiration upon himself *personally,* in effect becoming part—if not indeed the focal point—of the spectacle. This was a development of far-reaching significance, for it established a precedent by which first the dynasts, and in their wake, the emperors, functioned as a crucial element in the mise-en-scène.

Caesar saw a challenge in Pompey's exploitation of the theater. Early in his career, as described above, he had been adept at using public entertainments to enhance his prestige, particularly with the urban plebs. In the 50s he made extensive use of the gold acquired in Gaul to finance further public spectacles and an ambitious building program at Rome, including plans for a new forum (to include a *curia*) that would bear his name.[25] The outbreak of civil war in 49 following his entry into Italy across the Rubicon soon involved him in foreign campaigns against Pompey and his allies, whom he defeated at Pharsalus in August 48 (or June according to the new Julian calendar which Caesar was to introduce in 46). Acting on a vow made before the battle to build in his new forum a temple to Venus Victrix, he later chose instead to dedicate it to Venus Genetrix (the ancestress of his family, the Gens Iulia), thus personally and publicly associating himself with her (Steinby 1995, 306–7). In clear imitation of Pompey's configuration of his temple, theater, *porticus,* and *curia* complex, Caesar too provided a *porticus* to link the temple to his new *curia*, which displayed impressive works of art, including depictions of Ajax and Medea by a renowned contemporary painter, Timomachus of Byzantium, a golden statue of Cleopatra, and, in the square in front of the temple, a portrait statue of his favorite horse (Appian *B.C.* 2.68, 2.102; Pliny *N.H.* 35.26, 8.155; Dio 51.22.3; Suet. *Div. Iul.* 61).

Following further successes in the civil war, and wishing to mark these with a grandeur surpassing even that for which Pompey was renowned, Caesar raised the spectacles to an entirely new level of significance. Conditions favored his endeavors. After the devastation of the wars, the inhabitants of Rome must have greatly welcomed such diversions. During the three years of conflict there had been a considerable reduction in population; indeed Appian suggests (probably with exaggeration) that the citizenry of Rome itself had been depleted by one half (*B.C.* 2.102), and Pliny places the total number killed in the wars at one million one hundred and ninety two thousand — the reason, he claims, that Caesar failed to mention the casualty figures in his writings (*N.H.* 7.91–92).[26] This, together with deprivation, disruption of social values, and the collapse of normal life must have made for a highly "receptive" audience, one that could easily be manipulated by a skillful and determined demagogue.

After his decisive victory over the remnants of Pompey's forces in Africa at Thapsus early in 46, Caesar was awarded distinctions different in kind and degree than any Pompey had attained. A chariot was erected as a votive offering in his honor on the Capitol, facing the statue of Jupiter, and close by, a bronze statue of Caesar with a globe at his feet, inscribed "demigod" (Dio 43.21.2). Earlier, Caesar had issued coins showing his Gallic trophies and a personification of Roma with her foot on the globe. Now, perhaps with the memory of Pompey's claim to have conquered the world (projected by the image of the globe carried in his triumph), Caesar appropriated the symbolism for himself, confirming the opinion expressed by Cicero that he "wished to see himself as master of the World" (*De Off.* 3.83). The votive chariot too was highly suggestive, because its use at Rome was strictly limited to athletes at the races, triumphators during their triumph, presiding magistrates at the Circus and representations of gods. On the pediment of Jupiter's Capitoline temple, adjacent to Caesar's shrine, the god himself was depicted in a chariot (Pliny *N.H.* 28.16, 35.157). But, beyond that, the inscription at the base of Caesar's statue explicitly suggested for the first time that he was himself divine.

The chariot was set up in anticipation of Caesar's great triumph in 46, and its timing and nature inevitably colored the public perception of that event and its meaning. So too did the fact that the bestowal of triumphal honors on Caesar had been so long delayed. First in 59, and then again a decade later upon his return from Gaul during the crisis of 49, his unavoidable entry into the city had made it legally impossible (Appian *B.C.* 2.163; Plutarch *Caes.* 35.6 ff.). Then, after the victory over Pompey's Roman forces at Pharsalus, he had eschewed a triumph, deeming it unseemly in the circumstances. Now, at last (able to ignore or demand dispensation from the requirement not to have entered the city since his victory), in August 46 he triumphed.

He did so in a chariot drawn by four white horses (instead of the customary dark ones), which because of their association with Jupiter (as well as Aeneas and Romulus) further enhanced the symbolism of the occasion. The celebrations took place on four nonconsecutive days (thus surpassing Pompey's in duration) and also broke all precedent by consisting of four separate triumphs: Gallic, Alexandrian, Pontic, and African, each of which was distinguished by emblems and decor fashioned from, respectively, citrus wood, tortoise shell, acanthus, and ivory . These triumphs exceeded in length and excelled in grandeur anything preceding them. The money resulting from the sale of spoils was recorded as more than six hundred million sesterces (Vell. Pater. 2.48.2). According to Appian, restraint was shown in not carrying the actual names of the Romans that Caesar defeated, while, however, graphically "representing their misfortunes by various images and pictures, except for Pompey, since he was still greatly mourned by all" (*B.C.* 2.101–2). Dio (43.19) notes that most of these displays pleased the public, although they were offended by the sight of the numerous lictors captured from defeated fellow Roman citizens. Following the processions, Caesar held a great public banquet at which some twenty thousand dining couches were set up (Plutarch *Caes.* 55.4). Then, "garlanded with all kinds of flowers," he was escorted by the populace to the site of his forum (where work had been under way for several years) and subsequently accompanied home in a torchlight convoy enlivened with music and a train of forty elephants.

Immediately following the triumphs, Caesar held games to mark the consecration (29 September) of his temple to Venus Genetrix (fig. 15). The *ludi Veneris Genetricis* took place in the Circus and, like the triumph, surpassed all that had gone before them in splendor and expense (Dio 43.22.2–23). At the same time, other entertainments honoring Caesar's deceased daughter Julia were held in the Forum where a temporary wooden amphitheater was erected, in which both gladiatorial and animal combats were staged; the first time this combination (which subsequently became the norm) was presented. Julia had been dead since 54, but Caesar, evidently wishing to enhance the occasion with such popular votive commemorations (normally confined to private *ludi*

Fig. 15. Terracotta panel depicting combat between men and animals in the Circus, of the type stages at Caesar's games. The figure on the left is armed as a gladiator; that on the right has a long spear *(venabulum)* to keep the animal at a distance. The oval "eggs" were used to mark off the laps (usually seven) of the chariot races. (C. M. Dixon)

funebres), broke with custom by presenting them in conjunction with the *ludi* arising from his triumph and the dedication of the temple and in the process subtly merged this public religious festival with a private display honoring his own family. Apart from its innovatory character, honoring Julia with *munera* under these circumstances is curious (at least to a modern sensibility) because she had been married to Pompey, who had been defeated and killed in the very conflict for which Caesar was now celebrating victory.

In addition to the gladiatorial displays in the Forum, Caesar also staged large-scale combats in the Circus Maximus, including both cavalry and infantry units, and even a battle waged with elephants. He also presented the *lusus Troiae*: equestrian displays by noble youths that, according to tradition, had first been introduced by Rome's founder, Aeneas, and had been revived only once before, by Sulla. Caesar's use of them now was a further example of self-serving myth-making, because it allowed him to dramatize the prominent role in the original games of his ancestor, Aeneas's son Ascanius-Iulus, and in the process also emphasize Rome's — and Caesar's — Trojan origins (cf. Vergil *Aen.* 5.545 ff.). Dio asserts that, apart from the Troy games, "in all of the contests the captives and those condemned to death took part," although noting that exceptionally some knights also fought in single combat, a novelty that must have excited popular interest. He goes on, however, to suggest that the scale of the bloodshed (considered to be in bad taste in the light of the recent sufferings of the population) and the games' enormous expense drew some criticism, and he notes as an example of their extravagance the provision of vast awnings to shade the spectators from the sun. Although such luxurious comfort — some accounts claimed these *vela* were fashioned from silk — was condoned by the mass of spectators, envious soldiers rioted, objecting that the money ought better to have been spent on them (Dio 43.24; cf. Coleman 1996b, 9; for the awnings, cf. Pliny *N.H.* 19.23).

To accommodate the activities in the Circus, Caesar made substantial changes in its architecture and arrangement. He removed the turning posts in order to set up in their place opposing "camps" for the combatants and presumably removed other structures that interfered with the spectacle (Pliny *N.H.* 36.102; Suet. *Div. Iul.* 39.2). Other changes were permanent, giving the Circus its "canonical shape . . . with its two long sides meeting in a semicircular end" (Humphrey 1986, 73), although the rebuilding was completed only under Augustus. Caesar created a large canal *(euripus)* some ten feet wide in front of the seating tiers to protect the spectators from the animals that fought in the games. With the magnificent example of Pompey's theater to inspire both envy and emulation, Caesar may have seen in this project the opportunity to create a similarly effective and stunning "festive" space in which large numbers of spectators could be convened and influenced. Indeed, the Circus (which may now have been enlarged to contain perhaps as many as two hundred thousand spectators) dwarfed even Pompey's great edifice. It was approximately 2,150 feet long and 410 feet wide, with the arena itself (between the opposite banks of spectators) about three hundred feet in width.

In addition to events in the Forum and the Circus, Caesar staged novel combats in an entirely new venue, which was created for the occasion in the Campus Martius (Dio 43.23.4; Appian *B.C.* 2.102). According to Suetonius, "After a lake had been excavated biremes, triremes, and quadriremes of the Tyrian and Egyptian fleets, manned by a large number of combatants, clashed in a naval battle" *(Div. Iul.* 39.4). This was Rome's first *naumachia,* a new form of entertainment combining spectacle and combat that would figure prominently under the emperors. The emphasis — constantly given visible expression — on fighting and military prowess in all these activities was clearly intended to work to Caesar's advantage. The panoply of diversions staged by

Caesar following his triumphs combined spectacular shows with personal propaganda, by reminding the audience at every occasion of his role as Rome's mightiest warrior. Military success, thus "packaged," appealed to patriotic and imperialist impulses in the public, while providing a potent form of entertainment and winning admiration and gratitude for Caesar's achievements as both soldier and showman.

He also planned, according to Suetonius (*Div. Iul.* 44), to follow Pompey's example by creating a theater of his own of enormous size situated in the heart of the city between the Palatine and Capitoline Hills. A little later he began to clear a portion of the area for its construction, which required the demolition of numerous shrines and buildings including the temple of Pietas, for which he was criticized (Dio 43.49.3). He did not live to complete the project, which was eventually carried out (on a smaller scale) by Augustus, to become the theater of Marcellus.

The extent to which all of these activities contributed to what would later be termed "a cult of personality" with the leader as "impresario" is highlighted in an anecdote recording an event that took place at this time in the theater during performances there. Two prominent writers of mimes, Decimus Laberius and Publilius Syrus, were present. Syrus was a former slave, whose writings were highly regarded (and later widely circulated in the imperial period), who also acted in his own mimes. After touring the provinces, he challenged other performers to compete with him in Rome (Pliny *N.H.* 35.199; Macrobius *Sat.* 2.7.7). Laberius, by contrast, was a Roman knight whose literary works were admired for their pungency and ready wit. In one of them, "The Descent into the Underworld," a number of people come forward who have witnessed strange portents and wonders. One reports seeing a husband with two wives, whereupon Laberius has a second character exclaim that this is even more remarkable than the recent dream of a soothsayer about six aediles. Caesar had in fact recently nominated six aediles instead of the usual four (adding two *aediles ceriales* with particular responsibility for the grain supply) and was rumored to favor polygamy. As Mommsen observes, "one sees from this that Laberius understood how to exercise the fool's privilege and Caesar how to permit the fool's freedom."[27]

Caesar may, however, have seen an opportunity for revenge at the games of 46. He challenged Laberius, then aged sixty, to perform in a competitive improvisational presentation (with Syrus) of one of his own mimes. Laberius (as he noted wryly) could hardly "deny anything to a being to whom the gods have granted everything." Nevertheless, "I left my household gods today a Roman knight; I shall return a mime. In very truth, today I have lived a day too long." By appearing publicly on the stage — the first recorded case of a member of the equestrian order doing so—he sacrificed both his dignity and possibly his formal status as a knight. He redeemed the former, however, by acting the role of a slave who rushed on stage crying, "thus O Romans do we lose our liberties!" and later pointed out that "many must he fear whom many fear." The latter was secured for him by Caesar himself with a gold ring (the formal mark of a knight) and half a million sesterces; one hundred thousand more than the sum needed to maintain his equestrian rank (Macrobius *Sat.* 2.7.1–9). Suetonius noted that this enabled Laberius "to walk directly from the stage through the orchestra . . . to a seat in the fourteen rows" reserved for his order (*Div. Iul.* 39).

His fellow knights, however, begrudged allowing him to resume his place, perhaps because technically Caesar's payment meant Laberius had performed for profit, and they smarted in resentment of Caesar's casual irreverence in alternatively removing and bestowing equestrian status. Cicero (in an exchange that conveys the flavor of the occasion) called out in a barbed reference to Caesar having recently packed the Senate with his supporters, "I would offer you a seat, were I not so short of space myself!" Laberius scored a hit with his riposte to Cicero, who had been frequently criticized for his political vacillation, "It's not surprising you lack for space, since you generally perch upon two at the same time!" (Seneca the Elder *Contr.* 7.3.9). Caesar awarded the prize to Syrus, and even "got in on the act" by improvising a line of verse, "thereby following in the footsteps of Laberius and Syrus [and emphasizing] the playfulness of the whole contest" (Lebek 1996, 46). Syrus, in turn, accepted it with a line of verse in which he gracefully noted that Laberius was a writer and spectator, not a professional performer.[28]

The games were a supreme piece of political and personal propaganda, and to give them lasting value, Caesar decreed that they should become annual, creating and endowing a special college for their maintenance (Pliny *N.H.* 2.93). Henceforth they would be called the *ludi Victoriae Caesaris* and would take place every July. This was extremely significant because "*Victoria Caesaris* . . . was created to be a personal goddess of Caesar" (Weinstock 1971, 91), and her festival was now to be added to the traditional calendar of yearly *ludi,* thus in effect establishing an annual religious holiday in honor of Caesar.

Taken together, the conduct of the triumphs and games in 46 and the subsequent establishment of a new annual festival honoring Caesar suggests that far from resting content with surpassing the *dignitas* of Pompey, he aspired to the ultimate glory: divine status. Subsequent events strengthen this inference.[29] In the meantime, other, unprecedented mortal honors were bestowed upon him. Following his victory over the last remnants of the Pompeian forces (led by his sons) at Munda in Spain, the Senate in the spring of 45 granted

Caesar and his male descendants the unprecedented honor of using the title *imperator* before — and therefore as part of — their name (Suet. *Div. Iul.* 76.1; Dio 43.44.2). In becoming a permanent *imperator* (a term traditionally obtained only when, following a victory, the general was thus hailed by his soldiers), Caesar also became a perpetual victor and therefore was entitled to display this status by wearing a laurel wreath and enjoying certain other related honors all the time. As victor he was granted the right *permanently* to wear the triumphal garb; a privilege that earlier had been restricted to a triumphator on the day of his triumph and exceptionally, in the case of Pompey, extended to his attendance at the Circus games as well.[30]

The Senate further decreed that an ivory statue of Caesar should be carried in the *pompa circensis,* in the company of those of the gods and goddess traditionally displayed in that procession (Dio 43.45.3). Cicero confirms that in July 45 when the new *ludi Victoria Caesaris* were first celebrated — although Caesar had not yet returned to Rome from his campaign in Spain — his statue was carried alongside that of the goddess Victoria. He noted with satisfaction that the usual custom of applauding the gods as they appeared in the procession was not followed in the case of Caesar; "the people were splendid not even to applaud Victoria on account of her bad neighbor!" (*Ad Att.* 13.44.1). The following October, Caesar was given another triumph (his fifth, with the emblems now made of polished silver), although no attempt was made to match the splendor of those held the year before. It was marked by an event that strengthens Cicero's hint that Caesar's new honors and powers were engendering some resentment. As his chariot passed the location reserved for the tribunes of the people, one of them, Aquila, pointedly remained seated, which caused Caesar to rebuke him with the taunt, "Come, then Aquila, take back the Republic from me you mighty tribune" (Suet. *Div. Iul.* 78.2). The exchange at such a public and formal occasion was highly charged, and it elevated Aquila's passive protest to a significant political act. As Yavetz notes (1983, 194), "possibly he belonged to Pompey's camp and could not forgive Caesar for flouting tradition by celebrating a victory that had been gained in a civil war."

Further honors (including explicitly divine ones, all of which were given visible expression) were granted by the Senate early in 44. Caesar was declared *Dictator* for life. He was given a golden throne in the theater (corresponding to that placed there by custom for the god in whose honor the *ludi* were being held) on which his symbol would be placed, and a golden crown decorated with jewels like that carried over the head of a triumphator (Dio 44.6.3). This throne, imbued with powerful symbolic value, was reserved for the theater and never in fact displayed during Caesar's life, although it figured in events shortly after his death, and under Augustus was frequently exhibited.

The theater was habitually conceived of as a place with profoundly sacred significance, and this was most graphically expressed through the use of the god's throne and emblems to represent visibly the divine presence. For Caesar to be granted this attribute in such a quintessentially public venue conveyed an immensely charged and expressive image. In a similarly significant act, the Senate—in addition to the previous right to display his ivory statue at the *pompa*—now also gave Caesar a carriage to carry his attributes *(exuviae)* in the Circus procession, corresponding to those of the other gods (Dio 44.6.3; Suet. *Div. Iul.* 76.1).

According to Weinstock (1971, 284 ff.), this last honor was particularly potent. Caesar's symbols were to be conveyed in a *tensa,* an ivory and silver carriage drawn by four horses, which carried the attributes of the Capitoline deities (Jupiter, Juno, and Minerva) to their particular place of honor, the *pulvinar,* at the Circus. Following Caesar's assassination, Cicero specifically emphasized these extraordinary honors: "What greater honor had he obtained than to have a *pulvinar,* a statue, a [templelike] pediment to his house, a priest?" In the same passage Cicero noted the addition of a fifth day specifically honoring Caesar to the four days dedicated to Jupiter at the *ludi Romani.* There could be no more compelling assertion of Caesar's divine status, which according to Dio was then underscored by the erection of his statue in the temple of Quirinus, inscribed "To the Invincible God" (43.45.3).

Apparently not all of these tributes were put into practice during Caesar's lifetime; possibly they represented elements of a program of progressive deification to be introduced gradually and in part while Caesar was absent on a projected campaign in Parthia. But it is important to recognize the manner in which religious ideology and political propaganda (in this case virtually indistinguishable) were promulgated using the spectacles in the Circus and theater as an effective means for delivering them. Traditionally these spectacles had been an occasion for enhancing the *dignitas* and prestige of the magistrate or benefactor associated with them; now an individual was in effect himself becoming part of the spectacle — an expressive element — used to convey through his presence, costume, props, and numinous "aura" a forceful message to the spectators. The spectacle provided the context for his own highly meaningful performance. As we have observed, during the last decades of the Republic, the games had increasingly been characterized by audience demonstrations and by performances that were fashioned (or could be interpreted) to make direct political statements. At the same time, the manner of their provision — their architecture, length, frequency, and extravagance — had increasingly enabled their sponsors to employ them as effective elements of a political program or campaign: what Quintus Cicero had referred to as "putting on a good show." Now under Caesar, these elements, the political content of the actual performance, and the occasion and circumstances of its enactment had in essence fused: the patron had become a performer. Caesar embraced his role with alarming enthusiasm, indeed, according to Cicero, "He wasted all the power of his intellect . . . in pandering to popular humors" (*Phil.* 5.18).

This synthesis of method and message could clearly be an effective means of winning support — indeed adulation — from the urban plebs, which again, as an eyewitness, Cicero asserts; "having for many years sought to reign, Caesar by great labor and perils, had succeeded: by shows, buildings, benefactions, and banquets Caesar charmed the ignorant multitude" (*Phil.* 2.45). If over-played, however, it could also alienate, as indicated in a speech given at the time by Cicero in which he suggested there were rumors (which he thereby subtly helped spread, even while discounting them) that Caesar's behavior had so angered a portion of the public that they failed to applaud at his public appearances. Cicero (no doubt with intended irony) suggested that the specta-tors must have been so thrilled at the very sight of Caesar that they were struck dumb and unable to applaud, and that in any case such a vulgarity commonly extended to ordinary mortals was beneath Caesar (*Pro Reg. Deio.* 33–34). Nevertheless, Cicero's suggestion (even if exaggerated) that the mere presence of Caesar might exercise a powerful effect upon the spectator, strengthens the theory that he sought to become a performer — and prop! — in a spectacle of his own devising.

Whatever the truth of popular feeling (which in retrospect was evidently fatally misjudged by many at the time), Caesar's actions played poorly to those who had traditionally exercised power and validated their *dignitas* in the elective positions for which they so ruthlessly competed. Caesar's increasing monopoly on the offices and institutions of political life — he had the right to nominate all the magistrates below the consulship — frustrated the competi-tive impulse and vaunting ambition that for centuries had motivated members of the upper order as they progressed through the *cursus honorum*. Moreover, when in 44 he became *Dictator perpetuo,* it seemed to deny in a most dan-gerous manner the republican principle of regular elections of its magistrates, as a new office "totally different from those common under the Republic had sprung into being before their very eyes. There were no limitations, such as annual tenure *(potestas ad tempus)* or collegiality *(par potestas)* — the office was lifelong and unshackled by the obligations of accountability" (Yavetz 1983, 205). Indeed, Caesar was rumored earlier to have displayed an unnerv-ing and dangerous attitude when he defined the Republic as "nothing, a title without form or content" (Suet. *Div. Iul.* 77). These developments and Cae-sar's apparent insensitivity or indifference to both the affront they caused to politicians' self-interest and the deep alarm they aroused in those who did not share his belief that the stable operation of the republican government required the direct and permanent supervision of one man were perceived by many senators as an extremely perilous threat to their *libertas.*

These feelings could only have been intensified by the extraordinary acts of political theater that were staged early in 44. What exactly took place at the first of these, in conjunction with the celebration of the *Feriae Latinae,* is not entirely clear, although the evidence is suggestive. The venerable festival took place at the temple of Jupiter Latiaris on the Alban Mount some thirteen miles southeast of Rome and commemorated the old Latin League and the kings of Alba, from which, significantly, Caesar claimed descent. A sacrifice was made in which the members of the League reaffirmed their loyalty to the god and to their kinship with the other Latin peoples. Once Rome gained control of the League, officiating at the festival was one of the most important tasks of the consuls, who were accompanied by the other senior magistrates. Eventually regular *ludi* lasting a couple of days and including a chariot race in Rome itself were instituted as part of the ceremony.

In the festival the successor to the Alban king, later termed *Dictator,* whose office had evolved into one of the public priesthoods of Rome, took part. In the previous year, 45, Caesar began to wear the red boots that by tradition were symbols of the Alban kings. As Weinstock notes, "he could not have done it without the authorization of the Senate, and the Senate in turn could only have done it by appointing him *Dictator* of Alba" (1971 324).[31] But why would Caesar, who was now both *Dictator* and *Consul* of Rome itself, take an interest in securing this antiquarian and virtually meaningless title? The answer may lie in the fact that this role allowed him to costume himself as a king: to assume by legitimate if curious means a dress whose significance lay in its symbolic value.

At the same time as this festival took place, two other closely related events occurred. Caesar's statues on the *rostra* were decorated with a diadems, the symbol of kingship, possibly as a plot by Caesar's opponents to discredit him by spreading the rumor of his desire to become king (Dio 44.9.2; cf. Appian *B.C.* 2.108). In addition, on returning from the Alban Mount where he had celebrated the Feriae Latinae and reentering Rome in a solemn procession (an *ovatio*), Caesar was acclaimed by sections of the spectators as king (Dio 44.9–10; Suet. *Div. Iul.* 79.1).

An *ovatio* normally was granted to a general only after a victory in war for which the technical requisites allowing a triumph had not been fulfilled. The ceremony took place (as did the Feriae Latinae) on the Alban Mount, with homage paid to Jupiter Latiaris rather than the Capitoline deity honored in a triumph. The awarding of such a ceremony by the Senate to Caesar was entirely unprecedented and apparently inexplicable. But, viewed as a piece of theater, its meaning and motivation become clearer. Caesar (like any general celebrating an *ovatio*) would have processed on horseback through the streets of Rome (which otherwise, as *Dictator,* he was forbidden by ancient law to do), still wearing the kingly garb donned earlier for his role in the Feriae Latinae. He would have been accompanied by a bodyguard, a large number of lictors, and the magistrates and senators who had to attend the *ovatio,* as well as by his fellow *Consul* Mark Antony. The population would have been in a festive frame of mind because of the ovatio and the fact that the days just after the rite of the Feriae Latinae were holidays. Indeed, Suetonius says that the mood was "extravagant and unprecedented" (*Div. Iul.* 79.1).

The overall effect would have been markedly similar to that of a royal entry *(adventus)* by a king, an established regal ritual of investiture in the Hellenistic world, in which an acclamation by the public and the decoration of statues with kingly props was customary. The connection was made explicit when some in the crowd shouted *"Rex!"* It is possible that this was staged as a "dress rehearsal" to test public opinion on Caesar becoming king. In the event, two tribunes intervened, punishing those responsible for the demonstration, but were in turn dismissed from office and insulted by Caesar, who claimed the tribunes were conspiring to spread false rumors about his wish to be king (Appian *B.C.* 2.16.108; Plutarch *Caes.* 61.9 ff.; Val. Max. 5.7.2). In doing so, he must have further alienated the other tribunes (already offended by the incident with Aquila), a breach undoubtedly welcomed by Caesar's enemies in the Senate. For Caesar's regard among the ordinary Roman populace who traditionally looked to the tribunes as their special protectors, it was a public relations disaster, because it raised the suspicion of kingly ambition. "The rejection of monarchy was an essential part of Roman political culture. . . . It was assumed that anyone was entitled to kill a would-be tyrant" (Nippel 1995, 61). A man who had earlier crossed the Rubicon claiming to protect the rights of the tribunes, and in doing so had brought on an immensely destructive civil war, "a man who claimed a crown while infringing the tribunes' *sacrosanctitas* was also capable of aiming at royal status" (Yavetz 1983, 200).

A second, even more graphic event took place only two weeks later, on February 15, at the festival of the *Lupercalia,* and this time the evidence that it was deliberately stage-managed by Mark Antony is compelling. The ritual was an elaborate and ancient one — essentially a "beating of the bounds" — in which young men dressed only in goatskins ran along a designated route to effect a magical purification of the community and promote fertility. In the previous year the two existing collegia traditionally responsible for conducting the festival had been augmented with a third, specifically in honor of

Caesar. Seated on the *rostra* on a gilded chair that had recently been provided for his use (Dio 44.6.1), he now watched the festival, wearing the triumphal garb and crown that, exceptionally, he was allowed to wear on any public occasion. According to Appian, Antony, who was the leader of the new collegium, the Iulii, "sprang upon the *rostra* and put a diadem on Caesar's head. At this sight some few clapped their hands, but the greater number groaned, and Caesar threw off the diadem. Antony again put it on him and again Caesar threw it off. When they were thus contending the people remained silent, in suspense to see how it would end. When they saw that Caesar prevailed they shouted for joy and at the same time applauded him because he did not accept it" (*B.C.* 2.16.110).

Cicero (an outraged eyewitness) notes that Antony "came naked, naked and anointed, into the Forum." He adds the additional details (together with Suetonius) that Antony harangued the spectators, then pleaded on his knees, and that Caesar ordered the diadem (the accepted symbol of kingship) to be placed in the temple of Capitoline Jupiter — Rome's only king — stipulating that it be officially recorded that by order of the people Antony had offered the kingship to him (Cicero *Phil.* 2.34, 3.5, 13.8; Suet. *Div. Iul.* 79.2; cf. Dio 45.30–34).

According to Dio (44.11.2), Antony explicitly referred to Caesar as "King," and this, with the other evidence, supports the conclusion that "the assumption of deliberate staging best explains why Caesar wore his new purple cloak and golden crown and sat on his golden throne when he received the offer of the diadem" (Weinstock 1971, 338). Here in the midst of a venerable popular ceremony, at a moment of high civic and religious importance, before a greatly excited and attentive audience, after a lengthy process during which Caesar had been awarded ever greater and more extravagant honors, the props, costumes, and actions of a coronation were brought together. It is possible therefore that what took place both at the Lupercalia and only a little earlier at the ovatio were in effect abortive performances in which Caesar and Antony twice seriously misjudged the mood of their audience and had to resort to improvisation to save the situation. In the light of the able stagecraft and deft sense of theater consistently displayed by Caesar on other occasions, however, an alternative interpretation is possible.

It may be that both performances closely followed their intended scenario. Caesar may well have *wished* publicly to be seen to renounce the title of king (and officially to record his renunciation) because, as Rawson has persuasively argued, "he did not need the name of King, for he had the essence: he was the Roman descendant of kings, who was also consul, *imperator,* above all *triumphator,* and reuniting the powers split and delimited in time at the beginning of the Republic, *dictator perpetuo.* . . . Why should he have done so? It would have brought him, with considerable odium, neither more absolute power nor more spectacular ceremony" (1991a, 170 ff.; 188).

As he had stated after the attempt to acclaim him King during his ovatio, "I am not King, but Caesar" (Appian *B.C.* 2.108). Indeed, according to Suetonius, the reason he gave for rebuking the tribunes was that by punishing the offenders so swiftly they "had robbed him of the glory of refusing it himself" (*Div. Iul.* 79.1). This "unscripted" intervention, as noted above, badly compromised the intended outcome of the scenario: popular acclaim. Thus the act of renunciation at the Lupercalia, at a point when divine honors had already been granted (which by contrast, he had made no effort to spurn), far from diminishing Caesar's prestige and authority may well have been intended to enhance them, while winning for him increased popularity with the Roman people for whom the title (if not, apparently the essence) of kingship still remained, as it had always been, repugnant.[32]

If this interpretation is correct, then either the stagecraft on these occasions was too subtle for Caesar's watchful enemies in the Senate, who were spurred on by what they deemed the genuine threat of Caesar's kingly ambitions or, more likely, the message Caesar intended had been all too effectively conveyed: that he was already a king (and far more) in everything but name and could safely ignore senators' traditional privileges, career aspirations, and *libertas*.

At the Base of Pompey's Statue

The evidence suggests that Caesar was a consummate theatrical impresario who skillfully drew upon and extended all the means that had evolved under the Republic for employing spectacle as an invaluable political tool. Constrained to play before a diverse and temperamental audience, however, Caesar seriously misjudged the reaction of one highly influential section of spectators. For these, Caesar's critics, he had fatally overplayed his part. They too, however, in retrospect disastrously miscalculated the popular support their own actions would enjoy. "The conspirators did not have a positive political plan; they simply believed that Caesar's standing in public opinion had reached an all-time low, that his murder would not cause a ripple of excitement, and that the Senate could easily manage the aftermath" (Yavetz 1983, 191). On the Ides of March, these enemies struck. After considering such alternative venues to stage their tyrannicide as the Via Sacra in the Forum, the Campus Martius when Caesar presided over elections, or even in the theater as he entered it, they chose Pompey's *curia,* part of the great theater complex where the Senate was meeting on that day. Much of the urban working population was conveniently away from the city's center, celebrating the festival of

Anna Perenna with picnics, singing, and general merrymaking at her grave on Rome's northern outskirts (Scullard 1981, 90). At the same time, within the theater itself, attention would be distracted by a gladiatorial show. Caesar died in the *curia* at the feet of the statue of his rival, Pompey.[33]

Following the assassination, by way of seeking to appease Caesar's followers and in the vain hope of avoiding further strife, the Senate agreed to provide a public funeral. This meant that it would be presented not by Caesar's family, but at public expense by the government magistrates. It was a highly unusual gesture, last seen in Rome when Sulla's memorable funeral took place thirty-five years earlier. Cicero recalled ruefully some six weeks later how Atticus and others (evidently gauging the true state of public opinion more accurately than the conspirators) had "exclaimed that all was lost if Caesar had a public funeral. How right that was!" (*Ad Att.* 14.14). The funeral took place on March 20 and was in the event a masterful piece of theater as Appian's (probably reliable) account vividly conveys (2.143–48): "When Caesar's body was brought into the Forum a countless multitude ran together with arms to guard it, and with acclamations and magnificent pageantry placed it on the *rostra*."[34] The venue had a particular significance and poignance (Dio 44.49.3), because Caesar himself had very recently erected this *rostra* (displaced from its original site when he dismantled the old *curia*) and only a few weeks earlier had presided from it over the memorable events at the Lupercalia. It displayed two recently dedicated statues of him — those that had briefly been adorned with diadems (Dio 43.49.1, 44.4.5, 44.11.2–3, 44.49.3; cf. Richardson 1992, 336–37).

Now a great mass of people streamed into the Campus Martius from all over the city and then into the Forum where the traditional gladiatorial displays honoring the deceased took place. Caesar's body, placed beneath a wax image, was carried on an ivory couch hung with gold and purple cloth and then placed on the *rostra* within a golden shrine that had been fashioned to resemble Caesar's temple of Venus Genetrix. This model was a highly effective "scenic element" because it suggested emblematically the magnificent temple that Caesar had provided (as well as his other building projects) and the divine ancestry and renowned military achievements that the temple itself evoked. Moreover, a similar shrine (known as a *baldachin*) had long been used in Greece and the East to display images of gods and kings or, as in the case of Alexander the Great, employed as a funeral conveyance (Diod. 18.26). These sacred and regal associations would have further enhanced its expressive power in the highly emotional context of Caesar's funeral.

Mark Antony gave the extraordinary funeral oration, an action for which Cicero later expressed profound contempt. "You most wickedly presided at the tyrant's funeral, if that's what it was. Yours was that beautiful pane-gyric, yours the pity, yours the exhortation; you, you I say, who kindled those torches" (*Phil.* 2.36). It was a masterful performance, and highly effective as political theater. Antony first reviewed Caesar's achievements and then read the various official decrees by which the Senate had honored him, "with a severe and gloomy countenance . . . dwelling especially on those decrees which declared Caesar to be superhuman, sacred, inviolable, and which named him the father . . . of his country." As he recited each honor he turned toward Caesar's corpse and added an appropriate comment "full of grief and indigna-tion," to indicate how utterly Caesar had been betrayed by those who earlier had thus revered and praised him. He emphasized the remarkable clemency that Caesar had shown to his enemies and had recited the oaths by which all had sworn to protect him. "Here lifting up his voice and extending his hand toward the Capitol behind him, he exclaimed 'Jupiter, guardian of this city, and ye other gods, I stand ready to avenge him as I have sworn.'" Earlier, at the urging of Cicero and others (Dio 44.23–34; Appian *B.C.* 2.132–35), the Senate had agreed there must be a general amnesty and no recriminations, and at this point the senators present became agitated, causing Antony to modify his demand and express the hope that more bloodshed could be avoided. But of course, fatal damage to any notion of reconciliation had been done. He finished with a call for hymns and lamentations.

What followed was quite unprecedented — gaining potency from its viola-tion of conventions — and staged as a veritable theater piece; indeed, its overtly theatrical quality is specifically underscored in Appian's account. "Having spoken thus, he gathered up his garments like one inspired, girded himself so that he had the free use of his hands, took his position in front of the bier as in a play, bending down to it and rising again, and first hymned him as a celestial deity, raising his hand to heaven in order to testify to Caesar's divine birth." Antony then rapidly incanted all of Caesar's war and military achievements, and his great benefactions to Rome. Speaking "in a kind of divine frenzy, he then lowered his voice from its high pitch to a sorrowful tone, and mourned and wept as for a friend who had suffered unjustly. . . . Carried away by an easy transition to extreme passion, he uncovered the body of Caesar, lifted his robe on the point of a spear and shook it aloft, pierced with dagger-thrusts and red with his blood. Whereupon the people, like a chorus in a play, mourned with him in the most sorrowful manner and from sorrow became filled again with anger."

In a surge of empathy and brought to a high pitch of emotion by Antony's histrionics, the crowd formed two choruses and began to chant the *nenia,* a funeral dirge (cf. North, 1983, 170). Someone evidently impersonated Caesar, naming his murderers and quoting a line from the tragedy of *Armorum Iudicium* by Pacuvius, "Have I saved them that they might murder me?" with similar sentiments from a Latin version of Sophocles' *Electra* (Suetonius *Div. Iul.* 84.2). "The people could endure it no longer. . . . Somebody raised above the bier an image of Caesar himself made of wax. . . . The image was turned round and round by a mechanical device, showing the twenty-three wounds in all parts of the body and on the face, that had been dealt to him so brutally. The people could no longer bear the pitiful sight."

Gathering all the combustible material at hand, they cremated Caesar there in the Forum, in effect restaging the climax of the dramatic funeral of Clodius of 52 B.C., including an attempt once more to burn down the Senate House (Plutarch *Brut.* 20.5). "Then the musicians and actors tore off their robes . . . rent them to pieces and threw them into the flames, and the veterans their arms which they had worn to the funeral; women offered up their jewelry and the robes of their children" (Suet. *Div. Iul.* 84.4). The crowd then surged in a violent frenzy out of the Forum and raced through the streets in search of Caesar's murderers.

The State Craft and Stagecraft of Augustus

May it be my privilege to establish the Republic in a firm and secure position, and reap from that act the fruit that I desire; but only if I may be called the author of the best possible government, and bear with me the hope when I die that the foundations which I have laid for the Republic will remain unshaken.
— *Suetonius Aug.* 28.2

Calling in his friends and asking whether it seemed to them that he had played the mime of life well, he added "since well I've played my part, all clap your hands and from the stage dismiss me with applause."
— *Suetonius Aug.* 99.1

Caesar's will, read in the Forum on March 19, 44 B.C., named Octavian, his eighteen-year-old nephew, as heir. Over the next few years, as Octavian moved to consolidate that legacy, his behavior was widely condemned as ruthless, unprincipled, and tyrannical — he even condoned the murder of Cicero, who earlier had been an invaluable supporter and been viewed as a father figure by Octavian — and yet, long before the end of his life he was universally admired (and widely worshipped) as a benevolent patron of the best in Roman culture, the father and savior of the country. This remarkable transformation was achieved, as Augustus himself implied on his deathbed, in part through his sense of the dramatic and his formidable skill in producing potent acts of theater.

The first demonstration of these qualities came only a few weeks after Caesar's assassination as Octavian undertook to sway public opinion — much of which in the volatile atmosphere favored the "liberators" — to his support. On April 8, Cicero (*Ad Att.* 14.2) noted that he had the day before received a letter from Atticus reporting on "the theater and Publilius [Syrus, the mime], good signs of the unanimous feeling of the people." By this, Cicero meant that those present in the audience were at least inclined to be sympathetic to the conspirators, and they demonstrated this through their response to some topical references by Syrus during the Megalesia. The following day he wrote again to Atticus (*Ad Att.* 14.3), specifically asking him to "give me full details as to who were cheered by the people at the mimes, and the epigrams of the actors." At about the same time, the consul Dolabella bloodily suppressed a demonstration by the pro-Caesar faction, for which he was subsequently applauded in the theater (Cicero *Phil.* 1.2, 1.12).

Mark Antony was soon exercising almost monarchical power in Rome, following the departure for their own safety of most of those directly involved in the conspiracy against Caesar, including Marcus Brutus and Cassius, who left Rome on April 13 (Yavetz 1983, 191). Octavian returned to Italy from Macedonia early in April, assumed the name Gaius Julius Caesar Octavianus, and won the vital support of Caesar's veterans. Later (about mid-May), when in Rome, he lobbied for passage of the *Lex Curiata,* which would make his adoption as Caesar's son legal, but in the meantime Antony refused his demands for payment of the legacies and money left him in the will. Antony received Octavian coldly and briefly in the gardens attached to Pompey's house (which Antony had been given by Caesar following his rival's death), then arrogantly dismissed him. In approaching Antony, Octavian shrewdly cited his wish to honor the benefactions (including *ludi*) that Caesar had promised to all of Rome's citizens.

The *ludi Apollinares* ran from July 6 until July 13. Gaius, Antony's brother, the second praetor, presided over the games in the absence of Marcus Brutus, who as urban praetor was responsible for them. Prior to his taking charge, "lavish expense was incurred in the preparations for the games, in the hope that the people, gratified by the spectacle, would recall Brutus and Cassius" (Appian *B.C.* 3.24). However, in place of a performance of the *Brutus* (which might have reminded the audience that Marcus Brutus was himself a liberator in the tradition of his legendary namesake, the sixth-century regicide) another play, the *Tereus* of Accius, was substituted, probably at the behest of Gaius, who hoped thereby to curtail sympathy for Brutus by, in effect, highjacking the spectacle. Nevertheless, according to Cicero, at references to tyranny there was a tremendous public demonstration in favor of Caesar's assassins from every section of the audience (*Phil.* 1.15). "Did the applause bestowed at the *ludi Apollinares* — or rather — the testimony and judgment of the Roman people appear to you insignificant? . . . Was it not Brutus, though not present himself at the games he sponsored, the one whom the Roman people in that most elaborate spectacle paid the tribute of their zeal, and soothed their regret for the absence of their liberator with continued applause and shouts?"

In a letter to Atticus written shortly after the event, Cicero reported that Brutus "seemed delighted at the *Tereus* incident. . . . For my part the better the news is the more it annoys and pains me, that the Roman people use their hands not for defending the constitution but for clapping" (*Ad Att.* 16.2).[1] Appian (*B.C.* 3.24) suggests, however, that following the initial demonstrations, opposition crowds loyal to (or bribed by) Octavian surged in and halted the demands that Brutus and Cassius be recalled. In any case, only a few days later Octavian had a chance to give his own games, the third annual *ludi Victoriae Caesaris,* to which he added complementary gladiatorial displays (as Caesar had done in 46, commemorating Julia) and which he dedicated to the memory of Caesar.[2]

Octavian gave these *ludi Victoriae Caesaris* (which followed close upon those of the *Apollinares* and took place from July 20 to July 30) as a personal benefaction. Although Caesar had provided an endowment and established a collegium (of which Octavian was a member) to administer them, in the unsettled circumstances the collegium was unwilling to exercise its responsibility because to do so would have been in effect a political act. Antony, moreover, was using every available means to delay giving Octavian the money left him by Caesar. Frustrated by Antony, but determined that the shows must go on, Octavian sold some of his own property and borrowed to raise the required sums, acts for which he gained a great deal of popularity (Appian *B.C.* 3.23). In fact, Octavian's generosity (and Antony's high-handed behavior) made a greater impression upon the Roman populace than had Brutus's competing celebration of the Apollinares, the last day of which — July 13, Caesar's birthday — Octavian had probably "upstaged" by distributing on that occasion (from his own funds) the legacies left to the public by Caesar.

Somewhat earlier, possibly at the *ludi Ceriales* in mid April, Octavian had attempted to put into effect the Senate decree stipulating that a throne with a golden crown representing Caesar should be carried to the theater and placed among those of the gods. Antony, as consul, blocked this attempt (at the

suggestion of the responsible aedile Critonius). Octavian tried again at Caesar's own games and was once more frustrated by Antony, possibly, as Cicero
suggests, through intervention by the tribunes and some expression of disapproval from the knights in the first fourteen rows (Appian *B.C.* 3.28; Cicero
Ad Att. 15.3). It may have been that Antony, who earlier had been instrumen-
tal in the process of Caesar's incremental deification, now hesitated, because
as the heir to a "god," Octavian — despite his youth and inexperience — would
have been a formidable rival. In any case, Antony, thereby, had set himself
firmly against Caesar's elevation to divine status, incurring a great deal of
unpopularity.[3]

Octavian, by contrast, scored a tremendous propaganda victory over Antony with the benefit of a veritable stage manager's dream: an extraordinary
act of celestial pyrotechnics. As Octavian himself recorded it: "During the very
time of my games a comet was seen for seven days in the northern region of the
sky. It . . . was very bright and conspicuous in all lands. This comet, the people
thought, indicated that Caesar's soul had been received among the immortal
gods." As his subsequent career demonstrates, Octavian was not one to miss an
opportunity, heaven-sent or otherwise, and he continues: "For this reason this
symbol was placed above the head of the statue of Caesar which I consecrated
in the Forum soon afterwards" (Pliny *N.H.* 2.93–94). At about the same time,
a prominent soothsayer, Vulcanius, conveniently interpreted the comet as heralding a new golden age under a new god and promptly died without providing
further details (Servius *In Verg. Buc.* 9.46–47; cf. Suet. *Div. Iul.* 88; Dio
45.7.1). Although Octavian initially encouraged the interpretation that the
prophecy referred to Caesar, privately (according to Pliny) he associated it with
his own destiny, which he wished linked to his adoptive father. Because the
common people of Rome (whose support was crucial to Octavian's ambitions)
had displayed a strong desire to institute some form of worship of Caesar, it
was greatly in his interest to encourage this impulse.[4] Cicero records that on
November 10 Octavian, in a remarkable speech, explicitly proclaimed by oath
to a popular assembly: " 'May it be granted to me to attain the honors of my
father,' and at the same time stretched out his hand towards Caesar's statue"
with histrionic effect (*Ad. Att.* 16.15.3). Although Cicero's somewhat con-
descending reaction — that Octavian's reach in effect exceeded his grasp — was
doubtlessly shared by others, he was clearly intent on developing skills commensurate with such lofty ambition (cf. Galinsky 1996, 43).

On January 7, 43 B.C., at Cicero's urging, the Senate formally granted
Octavian imperium and propelled him along the *cursus honorum* by excusing
him all offices up to and including the praetorship, a position he could not

normally have attained until his mid thirties. The following August, Octavian coerced the Senate into appointing him consul, a month before his twentieth birthday.[5] In November he formed the triumvirate with Antony and Lepidus, which under the *Lex Titia* was authorized to exercise virtually absolute power for a term of five years.

On January 1, 42 B.C., Caesar was officially declared a *divus*. As pointed out by Price (1980, 36), this was "an intermediate category . . . between man and god" (*homo* and *deus*), and thus Octavian became *Divi Filius*, "son of one divine." Senators and magistrates swore scrupulously to honor all of Caesar's official acts, while in the Forum a temple to the "Deified Julius" was planned. Eventually, bowing to the inevitable, Antony at his own request was inaugurated as the *flamen*, or special priest, assigned to the new cult of Divus Iulius, which, having been established as one of the four *flamines maiores* of the Roman state, enjoyed an honor otherwise restricted to Jupiter, Mars, and Quirinus. Octavian had thus successively secured the support of Caesar's veterans, the Roman citizenry, and the Senate, while maneuvering his rival first into forming a political alliance and then into endorsing the divine status of Caesar, which thereby enormously enhanced Octavian's own prestige and authority.

Octavian, however, soon faced grave popular opposition as he aggressively consolidated his rapid rise to power, as well as the threat from a second formidable rival who had also assumed the desirable role of "son of a god." Following the death of Pompey (who earlier had been celebrated on coins as a prince of peace and conqueror of the world), his two sons undertook to promote him posthumously into quasi-divine status. One of them, Gnaeus, was killed in April 45 after Caesar's victory over the remaining Pompeian forces at Munda in Spain; the second, Sextus (assuming the name "Pius" to emphasize his filial devotion), remained at large, positioned to attract and command formidable forces. To appease him, Antony had even suggested in 44 that he be invited to return from Spain, compensated for his father's confiscated property, and made commander of the fleet (Appian *B.C.* 3.4).

Instead, Sextus established a naval power base in Sicily, from which to raid and blockade Italy, and provided a refuge for prominent fugitives from the bloodbath of the triumvirs' proscriptions in Rome and for the remnants of the conspirators' forces following their defeat at Philippi. In 44–43 he began to issue coins depicting his father in the guise of Neptune, held triumphal spectacles, staged mock naval battles, and "assumed a certain additional glory and pride by representing himself to be the adopted son of Neptune, since his father had once ruled the whole sea." He even affected a sea-blue costume and sacrificed to his father by lowering horses into the sea. When his opponent's fleet was destroyed by a storm, he attributed it to divine intervention (Dio 45.48.5, 48.19.1–2; App. *B.C.* 5.100; Pliny *N.H.* 9.55). Thus, as a sort of epilogue, a curious replay of the long-running conflict between Caesar and Pompey was now reenacted at the hands of heirs, each claiming to be the adopted offspring of a god.

. Sextus Pompey's deliberate use of role playing to embellish a name that, because of his father, the populace readily associated with benefaction, in particular, the provision of grain, evidently gained him some popular following among the lower orders in Rome. These had earlier been greatly distressed by the struggle between Octavian and Antony and now suffered a devastating famine as Sextus, having achieved complete mastery of the sea, periodically disrupted the grain supply (App. *B.C.* 5.18). This, together with Sextus's propaganda, caused public esteem for Antony and Octavian to decline sharply. Dio relates (48.31) that although only a little earlier the two men (following their reconciliation under the Pact of Brundisium, in 40) had been granted triumphal dress and special honors, now their attendance at public spectacles became the occasion for popular demonstrations urging them to make peace with Sextus. During the *pompa circensis* in 40 B.C., at the customary appearance of the statue of the sea god, the crowd avidly demonstrated its support for Pompey. When at subsequent ceremonies that statue was pulled from the show and not allowed to appear, the populace reacted violently, pulling down images of Antony and Octavian. Later the urban population used riots and, in effect, a "strike" during which they closed their businesses and workshops to force an accommodation with Sextus under the treaty of Misenum in 39 (App. *B.C.* 5.18; Dio 48.37.2; Vell. Pater. 2.77).

In the meantime, Octavian countered with his own propaganda, seeking to enhance his prestige by holding magnificent entertainments and festivals at his own and the public's expense while denigrating Sextus as little more than a "commander of pirates." Vergil's *Fourth Eclogue,* heralding the start of a golden age (and possibly inspired by the hope that the marriage of Octavian's sister, Octavia, to Antony in 40 marked the end to the dangerous rivalry between them), may have been one expression of a transitory sense of public optimism. But any improvement in Octavian's status or the state of public opinion proved brief as Sextus's activities again raised anxiety and resentment. At one point both Antony and Octavian were stoned by an angry crowd in the Forum, and only through armed force and great loss of life was order restored. In 37 (after Antony and Octavian had extended their triumviral powers for another five years), hostilities with Sextus were renewed; after inflicting several severe defeats upon the triumvirs' forces, he was eventually vanquished and subsequently executed in 35. The extent of Sextus's popularity may be seen in the fact that, according to Velleius Paterculus, years later (in 31) the consul Marcus Titius, the man responsible for his execution, "when celebrating games in Pompey's theater, was driven amid the curses of the people from the spectacle which he himself was giving" (2.79.6). Nevertheless, the removal of Sextus and the downfall of the triumvir Lepidus in the same year, while Antony remained continuously engaged in his eastern domain, left Octavian master of the western Roman Empire.

Duel of the Titans:
Octavian "Apollo" Caesar vs. Mark "Dionysus" Antony

Following the struggle with Sextus and the public antipathy it aroused against him, Octavian throughout his long public career took great pains to present himself as a ruler whose basis of power and ability to protect the populace from civic strife was not simply an expression of brutal military force or consequence of political tyranny. He embarked on a campaign to achieve lasting popularity. After the victory over Sextus, he declined various honors offered him, abolished debts owed by private citizens to the state from the period before the civil war, and greatly reduced taxes (Dio 49.15.3). He also rewarded his soldiers and officers and bestowed on Agrippa (victor over Pompey at the decisive naval battle of Naulochus) a golden crown uniquely adorned with tiny ships' prows, which he was permitted to wear whenever generals donned triumphal garb (Dio 49.14.3–4). But if the struggle with Sextus Pompey was something of a postlude to that between Caesar and Pompey, it was also a curtain-raiser to the epic one between Octavian and Antony. Once again, role playing and a complementary skill at stage management figured significantly in the struggle.

Octavian, of course, could claim association with the now-deified Caesar, and through him with such suggestive antecedents as Aeneas and, ultimately, the goddess Venus. Antony countered with a less impressive claim to descent from Hercules, with whose appearance he liked to be compared; indeed, he cultivated such comparison by imitating the demigod in his attire (Plut. *Ant.* 4). But, following the battle of Philippi and his first sojourn in Asia, he began to fashion himself as Dionysus, and a little later issued coins in the East depicting his image with a Dionysian crown of ivy. Making a triumphal progress through the Hellenistic cities of the East, he was hailed as divine, while as Plutarch (quoting *Oedipus Rex*) asserts, all Asia was filled "with offering of incense, paeans, and the sound of deep groaning." Moreover, "as Antony entered Ephesus, women dressed as maenads, men and youths as satyrs and pans all led the way before him, and the city was filled with ivy and thyrsus wands, with the music of the flute, pipes and lyre. All welcomed him as Dionysus, bringer of joy, gentle and kind" (*Ant.* 24).

In 39, following his marriage to Octavia, the couple went to Athens, and there Antony continued a highly theatrical lifestyle, donning Greek attire, giving elaborate festivals, and holding revels in the theater of Dionysus, where he constructed a setting designed to resemble a Bacchic cave in which to hold his banquets. The indulgent Athenians set up inscriptions hailing him as the "New Dionysus." After 37, when he had abandoned Octavia and settled permanently in the East, he increasingly embraced this role, which in its embodiment as the Egyptian god Osiris complemented and added mythical luster to his alliance with Cleopatra. She was accordingly represented as Venus, or Isis, come "to revel with Dionysus for the good of Asia," and accompanied him with a retinue of pages and handmaidens costumed as cupids, Nereids, and Graces (*Ant.* 26). In fact, it is likely that the public presentation of their relationship was deliberately stage-managed to enhance the prestige and aura of each. Cleopatra could extend her power over the new dominions presented to her by Antony, while in forming an alliance with the mistress of Julius Caesar (who had borne him a son, Caesarion, as a potential rival to Octavian), Antony could lay claim to a share of Caesar's heritage. After their first liaison, in 40, Cleopatra gave birth to twins, whose names, Alexander Helios and Cleopatra Selene, with their evocation of the sun and moon, may have been chosen to suggest that they were divinely destined to rule the world.

Antony had long been accused of debauchery and self-indulgence — indeed, Cicero had earlier savaged him repeatedly for drunkenness, consorting scandalously with mimes, and following a generally depraved life (e.g., *Phil.* 2.2 ff., 2.24 ff., 2.28 ff.). In particular, he never tired of taunting him for his behavior at the Lupercalia when he had run into the Forum "naked, anointed, and drunk" (*Phil.* 3.5; cf. Dio 45.30.5). Now his conduct made him vulnerable to an intensive campaign of propaganda asserting that he was guilty not just of thoroughly un-Roman indulgence in oriental decadence at Cleopatra's sumptuous court but also, in his administration of the East, of behaving like some contemptible oriental god-king. Although his Parthian campaign of 36 was unsuccessful, denying him a great victory to burnish the splendor of the "unconquered Dionysus," in 34 a minor victory over the Armenians provided the excuse for a grand display when he returned in triumph to Alexandria. It imitated the traditional form of the triumph at Rome with the usual panoply of soldiers, booty, and royal captives. Antony followed in the customary chariot but then grossly violated sacred precedent by presenting all the spoils of Roman arms not to Capitoline Jupiter, to whom they were due, but to Cleopatra, seated on a golden throne. The ceremony was marred when the royal captives refused to worship this new divinity — the "New Isis," as she styled herself (Dio 49.40.3–4).

Further outrage followed. As "a theatrical piece of insolence and contempt for his country" (Plut. *Ant.* 54), Antony appeared at a magnificent pageant with Cleopatra (costumed as Isis), both seated on golden thrones set on a raised silver dais. He then conferred a vast dominion and exalted titles upon their children. Little Alexander, decked out in Persian garb and tiara, was proclaimed "King of Kings" and given Media, Armenia, and Parthia (which had not yet been conquered); Antony's other son, the infant Ptolemy, appearing in the costume and diadem of a Macedonian king, was awarded Syria, Phoenicia, and Cilicia and granted the same title.

When Octavian reported these things to the Senate, they aroused immense indignation. A sharp rebuke and warning were sent to Antony, who responded by preparing for war with Rome. His forces and those of Cleopatra assembled at Samos, where, as Plutarch records, with the gathering of "all munitions necessary for war, it was also proclaimed that all stage-players should appear, so that, while virtually the entire world was filled with groans and lamentations, this one island resounded for days with the sound of the lyre and pipe, full theaters, and the sounds of choruses. . . . Then Antony gave the island of Priene to his actors to inhabit and set sail for Athens where fresh sports and play-acting employed him" (*Ant.* 57). Nevertheless, the speed and extent of Antony's war preparations evidently alarmed Octavian, who quietly began both to further secure his position with the public and to organize resources for the decisive conflict now looming.

While Antony had been playing the god-king in the East, Octavian had displayed an effective talent for manipulating public opinion through propaganda, benefaction, and carefully crafted imagery. In doing so he learned from the mistakes of Caesar and sought to create a telling contrast between his own behavior and that of Sextus Pompey and Antony. He did this by taking pains to appear to adhere to traditional Roman practices wherever possible, subtly shaping these to enhance his own authority and secure his political program. Although he accepted such honors as the setting up of his statues and annual celebration of the anniversaries of his victories, he carefully avoided taking explicitly divine or regal honors, and in 36 he declared his intention to restore the Republic as soon as Antony returned from his Parthian expedition.

Although he enjoyed the title of *Divi Filius,* he dropped the provocative honorary name of Romulus used earlier and eschewed the use of coinage or other imagery either presenting him as a god or displaying overtly divine attributes. He pursued important domestic reforms, and by championing the peace and prosperity of Italy he presented himself as its patriotic defender from the strife that had characterized the age of the dynasts and from the new threat of oriental despotism embodied by Antony. He further consolidated his position by marrying Livia Drusilla in 39, a move that won him vital social and political prestige within the same aristocratic and senatorial circles that Caesar had so alienated. These groups were further ingratiated by an agreement at this time allowing the republicans, who had earlier taken refuge with Sextus, to return to Italy.

Octavian's effort to highlight the clearest possible contrast between his own espousal of traditional Roman values and Antony's indulgence in oriental decadence did not prevent him from using mythological imagery to publicize himself and communicate the developing ideology of his principate to the Roman audience. As Zanker has persuasively demonstrated, "In the struggle between Mark Antony and Octavian we can observe how mythological figures and imagery gradually shaped the protagonists' own view of themselves and began to affect their behavior. . . . The uncertainties of the present and the capriciousness of politics in Rome . . . provided irrational longing for a savior, and predictions of a new and blessed age. . . . The only language available in which to express such ideas was that of Greek myth" (1988, 44). From the beginning, Octavian had been the subject of various portents suggesting that divinity had shaped his destiny as the harbinger of a new age and as a ruler who would save his people. Gradually these coalesced in the course of his career into a mythological framework, centering upon Octavian's special relationship to Apollo. The Julian family had provided the earliest temple to Apollo in Rome in 431 (Livy 4.29.7). It had been dedicated on July 13, the day later reserved (from 208) as the principal day for the *ludi Apollinares,* which, centuries later, Caesar (whose birthday was also July 13) had used to enhance his glory. After Philippi (where the god's name had been given as the watchword by the forces of his adversaries), Octavian increasingly employed Apollonian imagery to convey his own cause and specifically ascribed to the god's intervention — together with that of his twin, Diana — the critical victory over Sextus Pompey at Naulochus off the northeast tip of Sicily in 36 (Appian *B.C.* 5.484). Although the principal hero of that battle had been Agrippa, a shrine to Diana close to the camp of Sextus's land forces and the assertion that Octavian had vowed before the battle to build a temple of Apollo on the Palatine allowed him to highlight and validate his own mission (Vell. Pater. 2.81.3). This was confirmed shortly thereafter when a thunderbolt conveniently struck the Palatine, seemingly designating the site (adjacent to Octavian's own house) where the temple should be built. The Palatine was the most hallowed location in Rome, marking the spot where Romulus and Remus had been nourished by the she-wolf. The thunderbolt allowed the future site to be declared public land, thereby making it legal to build a temple upon it. It was begun that year (connected by a ramp to the house of Octavian) and was completed and dedicated in 28 (Dio 49.15.5, 53.1.3; cf. Galinsky 1996, 213–20).

Shortly after the Peace of Brundisium in 40, Octavian was said to have appeared costumed as Apollo at a banquet representing the twelve Olympian deities. According to Suetonius, this display caused a scandal, particularly because it took place while the Romans were still suffering from the famine arising from the conflict with Sextus, and prompted the people to proclaim that "Caesar is indeed Apollo, but 'Apollo the torturer'" (*Aug.* 70). Antony publicized the occasion later to counter the criticisms that Octavian directed at his own unseemly amateur theatrics. This incident aside, however, Octavian consciously strove to avoid excessive personal display or provocative claims of divine status. Instead, he underscored his role as one who could command respect and allegiance from all sectors of a society that for decades had been so grievously divided by individual warlords that the Republic was ultimately rendered ungovernable. The carefully nurtured notion that Octavian enjoyed the particular favor of Apollo was an important element in how the public was encouraged to regard him. In contrast to the sensual self-indulgence and licentious Dionysianism so thoroughly embodied by Antony's antics under the alleged spell of Cleopatra, Apollo stood for discipline, morality, and moderation: traditional Roman virtues now urgently demanded for the vital mission of creating a new order, worthy of Rome's past.

In essence, these rival performances by Antony and Octavian, which in the end caused the Roman audience to favor the latter (perhaps because he was the more persuasive actor), cast an obscuring veil of "make-believe" over what in reality was a civil war between rivals for political preeminence. What Octavian succeeded in portraying as a great moral crusade to defend the integrity of Roman values and institutions from eastern barbarism and decadence could be construed in a less flattering light to be little more than a continuation of the recurrent baleful struggle for individual supremacy — indeed for virtually monarchical power — that had characterized the malignant political life of the Republic for the past century. "Each of them desired to be master not only of the city of Rome, but of the entire world" (Nepos *Vit. Att.* 20.5).

The aedileship of Octavian's friend and ally Marcus Agrippa in 33 (during Octavian's second consulship) on the eve of the final conflict with Antony amply demonstrates Octavian's use of the time-tested methods of political persuasion to enhance his *dignitas* and authority and, in particular, to reinforce support among the urban masses. Although Octavian sought to amplify a reputation for soldierly prowess by securing the eastern frontier through the Pannonian expedition, Agrippa, who had been primarily responsible for the regime's most important military victories (and had already served as consul in 37), assumed the relatively junior office of aedile that, moreover, had been left vacant for several years. This unprecedented move might have been seen as an extraordinary diminution of status, but in fact Agrippa (and Octavian) deliberately used the post (which traditionally had been an important means by which aspiring politicians won advancement) to demonstrate that—in the absence of any genuine political life—the ruler was concerned about the welfare and happiness of the common people as well as about upholding the customs and values of the Republic. Thus, not for the last time, a traditional office and institution was subtly reinterpreted and employed to support the new order, without too grossly offending the established forms of the old one it displaced.

Agrippa used his office and "without taking anything from the public treasury repaired all the public buildings and all the streets" (Dio 49.43.1), even cleaning the sewers and, crucially, securing the city's water supply. Thus, in telling contrast to Antony's frivolous self-indulgence in the flesh-pots of the East, at home Octavian was carrying out public works of vital importance— and lasting influence. Agrippa, however, was far from disdaining the more glamorous pursuits traditionally associated with his office. He gave extraordinarily lavish and prolonged games, complementing them with extensive gifts of money, oil, and salt. Free year-long admission was provided to the public baths for both men and women, as was free access to barbers, while at the theater he literally "rained upon the heads of the people tokens that were good for money in one case, in another clothes, or yet again for something else, while displaying vast quantities of goods for all and letting the people scramble for them" (Dio 49.43.2–4). He also gained favor with the masses who attended the races in the Circus Maximus by installing symbols of Neptune in the form of silver dolphins (perhaps reminding the spectators of Octavian's famous victory over the "Son of Neptune") to record the number of completed laps. Lest the effect of the message conveyed by such generosity be undermined by rival propaganda or prophecy, Agrippa secured a monopoly on such things by expelling all of the astrologers and magicians from Rome (Dio 49.43.5).

While thus strengthening broad popular support, Octavian also distributed consulates and triumphs to useful members of the upper orders, who in turn were encouraged to record their achievement (and gratitude) by embellishing Rome.[6] Recognizing the unique value of buildings for public entertainment, Octavian allowed Statilius Taurus (following his victories in Africa and subsequent triumph in 34) to begin construction of Rome's first permanent amphitheater, to be used for gladiatorial displays and hunts (Dio 51.23.1). In 32 Octavian restored Pompey's theater at considerable personal expense (*R.G.*

20). Close to it he is said to have constructed a portico with images of different nations, possibly incorporating the fourteen such statues placed by Pompey adjacent to the theater (Servius *Ad Aen.* 8.721; cf. Pliny *N.H.* 36.41; Suet. *Nero* 46). Modestly refraining from adding his name to the dedicatory inscription of the theater itself (or effacing that of Pompey), Octavian took advantage of the refurbishment to move the statue of Pompey from the curia (subsequently sealed up), where Caesar had died, to a place adjacent to the theater where its thought-provoking presence was prominent (Suet. *Aug.* 31.5; cf. Dio 47.19.1). In this he was following the precedent of Caesar himself, who in 44 B.C. had permitted a statue of Pompey (which had been smashed by a mob) to be reerected on his newly repositioned Rostra Caesaris (Dio 42.18.2, 43.49.1; Suet. *Div. Iul.* 75.4). Cicero had observed that "in setting up Pompey's statue, Caesar firmly fixed his own" (Plutarch *Caes.* 57.4); a similar interpretation could be applied to Octavian's act.

As Octavian recorded later, in 32 B.C. "all Italy of its own accord swore an oath of allegiance to me and chose me as its leader in the war which I won at Actium" (*R.G.* 25). As well as securing the home front for the struggle with Antony and fostering a sense of national purpose, the oath (extended later to other regions of the empire) had the practical effect of creating a direct relationship of mutual loyalty and responsibility between Octavian and every Roman citizen. The population thereby became his personal clients: "He fed them with doles, amused them with games and claimed to be their protector against oppression" (Syme 1939, 322). He thus skillfully exploited (while seeking to reverse) the deep sense of despair that had afflicted the population through decades of seemingly interminable atrocities, strife, and civil war, a mood summed up by Horace a few years earlier: "Already a second generation is being ground to pieces by civil war, and Rome through her own strength is tottering. . . . This City we ourselves shall destroy, an impious generation of an accursed race; and the ground shall again be held by beasts of prey" (*Epode* 16.1–2, 9–10). Yet in the same poem, Horace had concluded with the prophetic hope that "a happy escape may be granted the righteous" (66).

The war against the forces of Antony and Cleopatra was carefully presented to Romans not as a continuation of civil strife but rather as the decisive event marking their liberation from crimes of the past and from alien impediments to lasting peace and the triumph of Roman values: "a war to end wars." It was therefore declared not against Antony but against his villainous foreign and female accomplice, Cleopatra, who had seduced him into befouling Roman virtues and imperium. Octavian portrayed Antony as a man who had taken leave of his senses; the true object of the war was Cleopatra and her eunuchs, servants, and chamberlains (Dio 50.5.1–4, 6.1). In effect "written out" of the script by Octavian, Antony stubbornly refused to relinquish his part, celebrating the outbreak of hostilities with sumptuous costumed feasts and going into battle in the guise of Dionysus still leading the sacred band — *thiasos* — of his followers. Like Pirandello's *Enrico IV,* trapped within the role he had assumed and no longer able to separate his own personality from his dramatic persona, he played his part to the end. Cleopatra too refused to play the role that Octavian wished to assign her, choosing to take her life rather than be paraded as the chief ornament of his triumph.

The triumph duly took place without her upon Octavian's return in August 29, when, celebrating in the course of three days a triple triumph over the Dalmatians and Pannonians, Cleopatra at Actium, and the Alexandrians, "an effigy of the dead Cleopatra upon a couch was carried by, so that in a way she, too . . . was a part of the spectacle and a trophy in the procession" (Dio 51.21.8). As a further act of suggestive staging, Octavian broke with precedent to arrange for the public magistrates, who traditionally came out to meet the victorious general and then preceded him into the city to process *behind* him instead, thereby graphically demonstrating his position as leading citizen *(Princeps)* of the state. Such symbolism was complemented by a more concrete expression of his position; he made lavish gifts to his soldiers and gave some four hundred sesterces apiece to citizens (and later to their children as well), which, with a magnanimous cancellation of the extensive debts owed to him, helped the Romans "to forget all their unpleasant experiences and to view his triumph with pleasure, quite as if the vanquished had all been foreigners."

The Pageantry of Peace

The victory was soon claimed to have been divinely ordained, a response to Horace's prayer in an ode (composed at this time): "What god can the people call on to shore up our toppling Empire? . . . Whom will Jupiter appoint to expiate our crimes?" (*Odes* 1.2.25, 29), which the poet had himself helpfully answered by concluding, "Here may thou have glorious triumphs, the name of father and of *Princeps* . . . while thou art our leader, O Caesar" (49–52). In attempting to understand the causes of the awful destruction that had been endured for so long, it was widely felt that "the outraged gods have visited unnumbered woes on sorrowing Hesperia" (*Odes* 3.6.7–8), and that to secure lasting peace, it was first necessary to atone for the sins of the past, particularly the neglect of religious rites and honors. "You will pay for the sins of your ancestors, Romans, until you repair the crumbling temples of the gods, and the images begrimed with smoke" (*Odes* 3.6.1–4). Seeking to exploit this feeling of collective guilt, Octavian embarked on a great mission of "moral

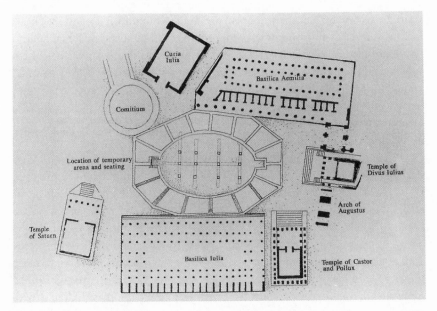

Fig. 16. Diagram showing the central area of the Roman Forum at the time of Augustus, with a space representing the placement of a temporary arena for the performance of *munera*. (Drawing by J. Glover)

rearmament" and religious revival, quickly giving it visible expression. The existing priesthoods were replenished and the archaic guild of the Arval Brethren (concerned with sacrifices and prayers for the fertility and prosperity of the land) was revived. After Actium he held a solemn ceremony (such as had not been seen for centuries) to close the doors of the temple of Janus and thereby mark the beginning of an age of peace, followed by a vast project to restore the shrines of the gods (Livy 1.19.2, 4.20.7). "I rebuilt in my sixth consulship [28 B.C.] on the authority of the Senate eighty-two temples and overlooked none that needed repair" (*R.G.* 20.4). He also honored the families of those who had earlier dedicated temples by making them responsible for their continued maintenance and repair (Dio 53.2.4).

In addition to such comprehensive refurbishment and restoration, new temples were constructed, with prominence given to that of Divus Iulius, which Octavian had begun to build around 36 in the Forum on the site of Caesar's cremation (fig. 16). It was now formally dedicated in August 29, immediately after his triumph, and thereby recalled Caesar's dedication of the temple of Venus Genetrix at the time of his triumph seventeen years earlier. Octavian decorated it with spoils from the war and constructed in front of it a new speaker's platform (Rostra Iulia) garnished with the prows of the Egyptian ships captured at Actium. To make the connection with Octavian even more explicit, the Senate ordered the erection of a triumphal arch (probably immediately adjacent to Caesar's temple) commemorating the victory.[7] The inauguration of the temple was accompanied by suitably sumptuous games. According to Dio (51.22.4–9), these consisted of a great variety of entertainments, including as special attractions the *lusus Troiae* performed by noble youths, and horse races among competing members of the equestrian order. Combats were staged between bands of exotic fighters from Dacia and Germany, and both domestic and foreign animals (including a rhinoceros and a hippopotamus) were slaughtered in gratifyingly large numbers. In the same year the new, permanent amphitheater of Statilius Taurus located in the Campus Martius and begun several years earlier was completed and dedicated with gladiatorial combats (Dio 51.23.1; Suet. *Aug.* 29.5).

Even greater pomp was lavished on the dedication of the temple of Apollo on the Palatine in 28. First vowed in 36, it had subsequently gained particular significance after the story was put about of the god's appearance at the Battle of Actium — close to the shrine of Actian Apollo — to assure, through his miraculous intervention, Octavian's victory. Long before that victory, Vergil's *Fourth Eclogue* (40 B.C.), in heralding a new age of peace and happiness, had announced, "Your Apollo now reigns" (10). Octavian, prudently benefitting from Caesar's example by not seeking to be worshipped as a god during his lifetime, nevertheless clearly perceived that the evocation of benevolent divine force could strengthen the basis for his power and lend luster to his authority. In the mood of thanksgiving and relief that prevailed after his triumph, he was widely viewed as virtually divine. "There was nothing that men could ask of gods, nothing that gods could offer to men, nothing that prayer could conceive of, nothing that ultimate bliss could achieve, which was not vouchsafed to the State, to the People, to the World after his return to Rome" (Vell. Pater. 2.89).

Apollo, functioning as a surrogate for his favored mortal, soon figured prominently in the ideology and imagery of the new regime.[8] By linking the temple to Octavian's house via a ramp from its forecourt, "the bond between the god and his protégé could not have been more explicitly conveyed" (Zanker 1988, 51). Octavian underscored the association by holding a festival during the same period (paid for from his private resources) commemorating the victory at Actium that had been secured by Apollo's intervention. This festival and its games were thereafter repeated every four years, organized by consuls and priestly collegia in turn. Octavian himself later recorded that they were held to honor vows made for his welfare (and were to take place only during his lifetime), which they duly did in 28, 24, 20, 16, etc. (Dio 51.19.2, 53.1.4; Aug. *R.G.* 9.1). They were celebrated throughout the empire, where, in contrast to Rome, they continued after his death (Suet. *Aug.* 59).

This established a pattern that continued during Octavian's long reign. "As a showman, none could compete with Augustus in material resources, skill of organization and sense of the dramatic. . . . Each and every festival was an occasion for sharpening the loyalty of the people and inculcating a suitable lesson" (Syme 1939, 468–69). In addition to the numerous traditional public *ludi* held annually (including now the *ludi Victoriae Caesaris*) and those commemorating his Actium victory every fourth year *(Actia)*, each year Octavian celebrated the date when he first was granted imperium (January 7, 43 B.C.) and each September 3 commemorated his victory at Naulochus in Sicily over Sextus Pompey (Dio 49.15.1; Appian *B.C.* 5.130). In 27 B.C., another festival was instituted to mark each date that his imperium had been renewed for periods of ten or five years. Dio notes that this practice was followed by subsequent emperors up until his own day (53.16.2–3). Eventually there was yet another periodic festival, the Augustalia (October 12), marking Augustus's safe return from Syria in 19 B.C., which became the annual *ludi Augustales* after his death in A.D. 14 (Dio 54.10.3, 54.34.1–2, 56.46.4; Aug. *R.G.* 11; Tac. *Ann.* 1.15). After the dedication of his temple in 2 B.C., annual games *(ludi Martiales)* were held on May 12 honoring Mars Ultor. Finally, games were given from time to time to enhance the public celebration — *ludi Natalicii* — marking Augustus's birthday (September 23), which were first decreed in 30 B.C.; these too became annual in 8 B.C.[9]

On January 13, 27 B.C., at the beginning of his seventh consulship, Octavian formally returned control of the state to the Senate and thereby claimed to have surrendered all his extraordinary powers and fulfilled his promise to restore the Republic. "Since that time, while I have exceeded all others in respect and influence *(auctoritas)*, I have possessed no more power than any of those who were my colleagues in any office" (*R.G.* 34). In recognition of his prestige and authority, three days after the "restoration" the title Augustus was conferred upon him. Apart from being a synonym for "sacred" and "divine," this title conveyed a suggestion of *auctoritas*, and its association with *augurium* invited an affinity with Romulus, whose augury had figured in the founding of Rome but whose title of king Octavian was loathe to take.[10] Otherwise he accepted few honors, desiring, he said, only to be first citizen: *Princeps*. He made no formal changes in the institutions of the Republic or his own official role. None of the old offices were abolished. He was scrupulous in respecting the function and prerogatives of the Senate.

Yet Rome (if not yet technically an hereditary monarchy) was now an autocracy in everything but name. Although most people realized this, to say so would have been bad taste. All, more or less willingly, acquiesced in an elaborate charade to mask the displacement of a city-state constitution that over the past century had been unable to encompass Rome's situation as a world power, and unworkable, had proven intolerably dangerous and destructive. Sallust observed of that period, "All who took part in government used slogans that had a good ring to them, some in order to defend the rights of the people, others to enhance the *auctoritas* of the Senate. All pretended to care for the public good, but in reality strove to increase their own power" (*Cat.* 38.3). Now, "by pretending to be something he was not in reality, Augustus succeeded in reconciling the new reality of the monarchy with the old one of the Republic" (Meier 1990, 68). Syme (1939, 516) termed this the "necessary and salutary fraud" of the principate, but it was perhaps not so much blatant deceit that was demanded as a degree of "make-believe." Such theater required a "willing suspension of disbelief" on the part of all concerned. How was this collective condition achieved?

In strictly tangible terms, Augustus's power rested on his enormous personal wealth as the richest man in the Roman Empire and on his control of the armed forces. Apart from the state treasury, he drew upon a personal fortune inherited from Caesar, vastly swollen by proceeds from confiscations during the triumvirate, and upon income from the provinces under his control.[11] This was later augmented by further substantial inheritances, which, according to Suetonius, Augustus claimed he spent entirely for the public; these amounted to 1.4 billion sesterces between 6 B.C. and A.D. 13, the year before his death (*Aug.* 101.3). Apart from its many other uses, this fortune enabled Augustus to follow the exhortation that, according to Dio, his friend and adviser Maecenas gave to "adorn this capital with utter disregard for expense and make it magnificent with festivals of every kind" (Dio 52.30). Except for its scale, there was nothing intrinsically new in Augustus's provision of buildings, gifts, and celebrations — Roman politicians had long flaunted such munificence — but Augustus extended the practice to provide land allotments and secure the corn supply at his own cost. "His private finances were entwined with those of the state; so began a long process with important consequences during the imperial period" (Shatzman 1975, 371). The same was true of his control of the army, which, following Philippi, had numbered some sixty legions, or more than a quarter of a million soldiers. From these he created a professional force, most of whom were under his personal command and whose loyalty he cultivated, while curbing the power of any overambitious general to subject the state to the sort of blackmail and threat of civil war mounted by Sulla in 88 and 82, Pompey in 71, Pompey and Caesar in 60, Caesar in 49 — and by Octavian himself in 43.

The ultimate foundation of Augustus's power, however, rested not upon such vital material support but on the intangible, yet indispensable, compliance and approval of the Roman people: in effect, the "consent of the governed." Unlike previous aspirants to one-man rule, who had or could be perceived as having championed one faction against another, Augustus attracted the endorsement of all classes of society, precluding significant opposition. In the case of the upper stratum from which any serious rivalry was likely to arise, he was careful to avoid humiliating those he now commanded. He respected their rights and traditional privileges while curbing opportunities for abuse. The accumulation in himself of so much power had the virtue of preventing it from being exercised (as in the past) by politicians competing with one another. The same had been true under Caesar, of course, with the crucial difference that Augustus, unlike his predecessor, did not ignore or treat with contempt those whose power his presence curtailed. In place of the destructive fighting for office that earlier had operated, he made political careers a function of his favor for "good behavior." He had the right to make binding nominations of candidates for office. He even gave financial assistance to some responsible senators to encourage them to take on the office of aedile, which in the late Republic had so often proven a volatile means for gaining access to higher office (Dio 53.2.2).

In 22 B.C. Augustus prudently transferred responsibility for those state festivals, traditionally managed by the aediles, to the praetors, at the same time "commanding that an appropriation be given from the treasury, and forbidding any of them to spend more than another from his own resources, or for a gladiatorial combat to be given except by Senate decree, or with more than one hundred and twenty men" (Dio 54.2.4). This curtailed two major sources of public contention and discord — the provision of official *ludi* and of private *munera* — while ensuring that the splendor of allowable entertainments offered by others did not outshine his own.[12] At the same time, he checked another (less orthodox) opportunity for competitive display by extending a ban against public performance, which had already applied (since 38 B.C.) to senators and their sons, and to their grandsons as well should these belong to the equestrian order, to whom a similar ban was henceforth applied. The measures against knights were eventually relaxed, if not lifted entirely, more than thirty years later, in A.D. 11 (Dio 56.25.7–8).

Although the number of senators was reduced, their individual prestige was enhanced. Augustus took care to cultivate and flatter them but hardly ever threatened them. By ingenious sleight of hand, he even plausibly styled himself as the defender of the old system to which his protection was indispensable, while undertaking its reform. The old oligarchy had benefitted only those belonging to it, often at great cost to others, and worst, in the case of Caesar, it had led to virtual monarchy, although still incapable of solving many of the urgent problems confronting the state. What mattered to most senators was now not its restoration but a leader who could ensure peace, prosperity, and a degree of fairness and hope in the pursuit of their ambitions. "In — probably difficult — disputes with the Senate, new agreements and compromises were reached. In such repeated give-and-take, however, Augustus always took a little more than he gave" (Meier 1990, 67).

The equestrian class also greatly benefitted from Augustus's reforms. Its members, who under the republican oligarchy had tended to remain at the margins of much public life, now could look forward to upward mobility as they were drawn into the imperial administration and provincial government, in turn ensuring a responsiveness and efficiency never attained in the late Republic. With the spread of Roman authority, quickening urbanization, and the wealth and culture generated by prosperity and security, such men now became enthusiastic supporters of the ethos and ideals of the emerging principate.

Augustus's greatest achievement, which provided the strongest bulwark of his system, was the creation of a strong and cohesive constituency among the urban masses. These had suffered severely during the protracted death throes of the Republic when, as Plutarch noted (*Caes.* 28), "There were many who dared to say publicly that only monarchy could cure the diseases of the State, and that this remedy ought to be welcomed when offered by the gentlest of physicians." Whereas the upper orders were to give their support through the so-called restoration of the Republic, "the *plebs urbana* had to be approached in ways which demonstrated . . . concern for both their material and their cultural demands" (Nippel 1995, 85). The people now looked to Augustus above all to restore and maintain the order and prosperity that dire experience had taught them to value more dearly than any abstract notion of *libertas*. In analyzing Augustus's reign long after it had ended, Dio concluded (undoubtedly with prudent regard to the realities of his own age) that "by combining monarchy with democracy he preserved their freedom while establishing order and security, so that they were free both from the license of a democracy and the insolence of tyranny, living simultaneously in a liberty of moderation and a monarchy without terror; they were royal subjects, but not slaves, democratic citizens without strife" (56.43.4). Augustus strove convincingly to fill the role of one assiduously working for the welfare of the people, while at the same time creating a sense of mission and patriotism — above all a belief in their destiny as Romans — that could be mobilized to support his regime and its program. He still faced, however, the dilemma that while the broad mass of people wanted someone to champion their interests, "from time immemorial the upper classes shrank from the worship of a personality in any shape or form, and every dictatorial regime was abhorrent to them" (Yavetz 1969, 92).

Augustus ingeniously addressed the problem in June 23, when, resigning the consulship that he had held since 27, he accepted a power traditionally adhering to a particular office, that of tribune of the people (from which office members of the patrician class were barred), without taking the office itself. He held this power for thirty-seven years, until the end of his life, briefly assuming the consulship again only twice (in 5 and 2 B.C.). This unprecedented bestowal of continuous *tribunicia potestas* gave him the power — despite his standing as a private citizen without office — to protect the interests of the plebs, proposing legislation on their behalf and vetoing any deemed inimical.[13]

It was a curious innovation and became the keystone of the principate by giving the emperor effective control of the state. In the late Republic (as the example of Clodius's tenure in the office had demonstrated), the tribuneship could be dangerously disruptive, although through its espousal of the concerns of the lower orders, it could also, if used judiciously, help to prevent such disorder. In assuming its prerogatives, Augustus mollified the upper orders by exercising a power sanctioned by republican practice without offending the constitution by continuously holding the actual office, while, on the other hand, the lower masses, less concerned by constitutional niceties, saw in his action a declaration that Augustus would work on their behalf. And yet, even in offering them such security, Augustus also gained for himself a further measure of autonomy, while calming the elites' anxiety that *their* interests might be threatened in the future by populist politicians. "No protest from the plebeians was now possible through traditional channels. Instead of relying on their tribunes, the populace was now compelled to use more informal methods of protest: choruses in the theater, at the Circus, and like places" (Galsterer 1990, 14). The support that Augustus had attained in the urban population was demonstrated the following year, 22 B.C., in the wake of a series of natural disasters that the people were convinced had arisen because Augustus was no longer Consul. Instead of looking to the traditional magistrates for assistance, they stormed the Senate demanding that Augustus be made *Dictator* and *Censor* for life (Dio 54.1.1–3; Suet. *Aug.* 52). He refused, instead prudently assuming formal responsibility for the grain supply.

In light of the novel relationship with the people that Augustus had fostered, it is hardly surprising that thereafter "he surpassed all his predecessors in the number, variety and splendor of his games" (Suet. *Aug.* 43). Such occasions gave the people direct contact with their patron and protector. During the late Republic, the theaters increasingly became venues for overt political expression by the audience; in the case of Caesar they had been employed to communicate the power and glory of the leader as he literally became part of the show. But Augustus did not exploit such occasions primarily to enjoy popular adulation or promulgate a cult of personality; indeed, he actively discouraged such use. "On one occasion when he was watching a comedy, one of the players spoke the line 'O just and generous Master [*Dominus*],' whereupon the whole audience rose to their feet and applauded, as if the phrase referred to Augustus. An angry look and a peremptory gesture soon quelled this gross flattery, and the next day he issued an edict of stern reprimand" (Suet. *Aug.* 53). Instead he fashioned the occasions for the games subtly to convey an ideological message and thereby strengthen the political basis for the principate. The games had a long tradition as important religious events, but (perhaps because of their growing politicization) during the late Republic their religious character appears to have eroded somewhat. As part of his thorough revival of religious practice — responding to and fostering a genuine increase in popular piety — Augustus sought to link worship and devout feeling to his own program of comprehensive renewal and reform. As so often observed in the official poetry of Vergil or Horace, to honor the gods was to revere Roman power and destiny and, in turn, the emperor. At moments of high pageantry in the theater, reverence was focused on Augustus and through him on the state and its gods.

In what were essentially state spectacles, Augustus and the imperial family functioned not simply as revered leaders (their popularity waxing and waning according to changing circumstances) but also as dynamic emblems that attracted and inspired deep patriotic and religious sentiment. Augustus did not find it necessary to follow Caesar by assuming divine attributes and styling himself as a living god. Instead, acting more circumspectly (and shrewdly), he encouraged the worship of his divine spirit through the cult of the Numen Augusti, which provided an outlet for Romans to express their religious feeling in a beneficial fashion without "proclaiming his full divinity, but [leaving] the possibility that he was indeed divine wide open for posterity to decide" (Ogilvie 1969, 122). Outside of Italy, the new imperial cult was often closely modeled on preexisting rites honoring other gods. Early in Augustus's reign, for example, sacred games established at Mytilene on his behalf patterned on the practices of the cult of Zeus, with annual sacrifices at a temple of Augustus. For good measure, "the Mytileneans promised that if any more distinguished honors were later discovered their zeal and piety would not fail to carry out anything which further deified *(theopoiein)* Augustus" (Price 1980, 35). As

Horace observed in his *Epistle to Augustus,* written about 13 B.C., "Upon you, while still among us, we bestow timely honors, set up altars to swear by your *numen,* and confess that none such as you has arisen or shall arise" (*Epis.* 2.1.15–17).[14]

Popular Revival: Staging "The Golden Age"

In this same letter (which was largely devoted to recounting the history of the Roman theater), Horace alludes to the great *ludi Saeculares* of 17 B.C., the occasion at which more than any other during Augustus's reign the religious and patriotic themes of the principate were given visible expression, using all the powers that poetry and pageantry could provide (*Epis.* 2.1.131 ff.). Long before Augustus, by custom celebrations were held every century to mark the sequence of the *saecula,* which spanned the period from Rome's founding. The first such *ludi* had been held in 249 and were repeated in 146 (Censor. 17.8, 17.11; Livy 49). Although due to occur again in 49 or 46 (during the civil war), they were postponed, possibly in anticipation of a victorious conclusion to Caesar's projected Parthian campaign and then indefinitely following his assassination. The concept of a *saeculum* was linked with the notion of divine intervention in the form of a heaven-sent hero who would bring great victories and lasting peace, marking the beginning of a new age. Following Caesar's death and the attendant portents, such belief became more firmly established.[15] In his *Fourth Eclogue* (40 B.C.), Vergil announced the arrival of a new golden age when the gods would return to the land of Saturn, Italy, the last place they had lived. Later (circa 23 B.C.), when plans for the Augustan celebration of the *ludi* may already have been in hand, in book six of the *Aeneid,* Vergil has Romulus himself identify and praise the promised hero who will usher in the new age: "This, this is the man so often promised to you, Augustus Caesar the offspring of a god, who again shall found the golden age in Latium, throughout the land once ruled by Saturn" (791–94).

The ludi Saeculares began on May 31, 17 B.C., and consisted of several days of formal and sacred ceremonies intermingled with and followed by a week of entertainments, all carefully coordinated as an act of myth-making designed to provide a visually impressive and emotionally engaging manifestation of the achievements of the Augustan regime and its role in ushering in a new epoch of peace, prosperity, and happiness. In addition to the positive developments since Augustus restored the Republic ten years earlier, its immediate impetus was the accord reached with Rome's ancestral enemies, the Parthians. This had allowed Augustus to claim honorable victory in finally securing Rome and her empire from external danger, while extensive moral legislation and religious reforms passed the previous year were intended to protect society from the inner danger of decadence and discord. The events of the *ludi* were stage-managed by the Quindecimviri Sacris Faciundis (one of Rome's four major political priesthoods), whose college of priests was associated with Apollo and responsible for consulting the Sibylline books. The priests consulted these prophetic books, now housed in the new temple of Apollo on the Palatine, and revealed that the oracle had ordered the celebration of the *ludi* at this time. Augustus and Agrippa had been elected to the college as its masters and presided over its management of the ceremonies (*R.G.* 22).

The festival was clearly intended to be a piece of consummate propaganda, which would both make an unforgettable impression upon those experiencing it and, in time, would become one of the enduring myths of the principate. In the absence of the type of firsthand accounts through which a participant (such as Cicero) conveyed events in which he figured, it is difficult to imagine what was undoubtedly a potent act of theater. The discovery in 1890 of an inscription recording the events of the celebration, however, together with further fragments that came to light more recently, allow us to reconstruct some aspects of the performance.[16] It was contrived to fulfill the directions contained in the oracle itself, the text of which was recorded in the fifth century A.D. by Zosimus (2.6).

Long before the celebration, heralds announced "a festival of a type which has never before been seen, nor shall again" (cf. Suet. *Claud.* 21.2). Coins issued at the time that depict these heralds reveal that they wore archaic dress including a distinctive helmet adorned with two towering feathers.[17] This element evokes the helmet that Vergil had described Romulus wearing in the passage just prior to his own heralding of the coming golden age of Augustus, quoted above. "See thou how the twin plumes stand upon his crest? . . . Lo under his auspices, my son, that glorious Rome shall measure her empire by earth, her courage by heaven" (*Aen.* 6.778–80). To emphasize the connection, the reverse side of the coin showed the head of Augustus himself with the symbol of Caesar's comet, which had appeared in 44 B.C. and, remarkably, was expected again in the summer of 17. Thus the audience was conditioned to anticipate a highly unusual festival and was made receptive to its symbolic message.

To enhance expectation, in the days immediately prior to the *ludi* the members of the College of the Quindecimviri provided materials for purification—sulfur, tar, and torches—which the people were to use in private rites of expiation, thereby marking the beginning of their own direct participation in the festival. In fulfillment of the oracle's command, "let everyone bring from his own home a gift from his own store . . . to offer as expiation," the day before the festival priests collected these, in a manner suggestive of a long-vanished harvest festival from Rome's rural past. On the evening of May 31, the first of the nightly sacrifices in the Campus Martius were held. A decade earlier Agrippa had completed and dedicated the Saepta Iulia, a large rectangular enclosure east of the Pantheon, surrounded by a lofty portico and adorned with numerous pictures and reliefs, and the Senate had convened there on May 23 formally to pass decrees relating to the imminent *ludi*. It may be that some of the subsequent activities were also held in this suitably spacious and public venue for the ceremonies.

At the sacrifice Augustus presented nine sheep and nine goats to the Moirae (fates), which were "wholly burnt in accordance with the Greek rite." In a lengthy prayer he called upon these to protect and increase the power of the Roman people, to bless their empire and armies with victory and good fortune, and to "be gracious and favorable to the Roman people, to the College of the Quindecimviri, to me, my family, and my household." The meaning of the occasion was thus powerfully conveyed both by the content of the prayer and by the visible form of its enactment, as Augustus officiated to invoke divine support for himself and his household *(mihi domo familiae)*, now inseparable from the larger welfare of the Roman people and the empire. Augustus had recently adopted Gaius (the son of his daughter, Julia, and Agrippa) and evidently hoped that he would continue the dynasty, the legitimization of which was a principal element in the formulation of the new official mythology. "It is apparently here for the first time that we have his house mentioned . . . indicative of the new position which the *Aeneid* had given to the past of the house of Augustus, and the new hope of the future, which Augustus himself had reason to feel because of the heir that he now had" (Taylor 1975, 178). Indeed, with Agrippa (Augustus's son-in-law) also officiating at the ceremonies, the spectators must have been impressed by the extent to which Rome's destiny was now closely bound to its "first family."

Following this first ceremony, some form of torchlight entertainment was presented during the night, on a stage "with no auditorium or seats for spectators," while "one hundred and ten wives of free citizens chosen by the *Quindecimviri*" held a *sellisternium,* a procession and ritual banquet where symbols or images of gods were carried in chairs and then placed to preside over and watch the ceremonies and entertainment (Hanson 1959, 82–85). Two chairs were reserved for Juno and Diana. Thus the theatrical entertainment was presented as a direct extension of the earlier ritual, sharing its religious context. Possibly to preserve the moral tone, young people were allowed to attend these nighttime performances only if accompanied by an adult relative (Suet. *Aug.* 31). The following morning, June 1, the oracular instruction to "let white spotless bulls be led to Zeus's altar by day, not night for to heavenly gods sacrifice is made by day" was duly followed as Augustus and Agrippa each sacrificed full-grown bulls at the temple of Jupiter on the Capitol. The record of their prayer indicates that after invoking Jupiter, the ceremony followed the same formula as that used the previous night. Following that, "performances in Latin were presented in the wooden theater that had been erected in the field beside the Tiber," and then by additional entertainments and a repetition of the sellisternium. A proclamation was also issued, calling for general rejoicing, and afterward Augustus sacrificed a selection of prescribed cakes to Eilithyia, the Greek goddess of childbirth.

The same pattern was followed on June 2, though this time cows were sacrificed to Juno Regina and a prayer offered on behalf of the one hundred and ten Roman matrons "praying on bended knee," asking for the same blessings invoked earlier by Augustus. This underscored the festival's emphasis on fertility, which complemented the recent moral legislation of Augustus, itself part of the careful ideological preparation for the *ludi*. This included a number of measures designed to encourage marriage and propagation. Unmarried men could, for example, be denied seats at the theater and other festivals—which had led to opposition and demonstrations in 18 B.C.—but an exception was made for these *ludi,* perhaps in the hope that bachelors would be inspired by it to go forth and multiply.[18] Games and nocturnal ceremonies again followed, and this time "Augustus sacrificed beside the Tiber a pregnant sow to Mother Earth [*Tellus*]," goddess of fertility. This was the same offering that Aeneas had made beside the Tiber, marking his arrival in the promised land of Italy (*Aen.* 3.390 ff., 8.81–84), and must therefore have been profoundly suggestive, perceived by the spectators as a symbolic refounding and reaffirmation of Roman destiny.

On June 3 the high point of the festival was reached, when Augustus and Agrippa offered sacrifice on the Palatine to Augustus's patron deities, Apollo and Diana, which was followed by a solemn ceremony in fulfillment of the oracle's instruction that "hymns be sung in Latin in the gods' temples; let youths and maidens sing, each in separate choirs." The inscription records that (presumably first) on the Palatine, and then "in the same fashion on the Capitol," twenty-seven boys and the same number of maidens were chosen to sing a hymn composed by Horace. Indeed, this chorus, written in an intricate sapphic meter, was conducted by Horace himself, who recalled his role a few years later in *Epistle* 2.1. (132–33): "Where together with chaste youths would the unwedded maid learn the suppliant hymn if the Muse had not given them a poet?" This hymn, the *Carmen Saeculare,* whose full text survives, might almost have been dictated by Augustus himself. Its imagery, themes, and the evocation of particular gods and goddesses closely followed that of the festival, in many cases explicitly detailing the meaning of what had been presented, while, as a performance, the very presence and participation of the chorus of young people implicitly incorporated and expressed the concepts of fertility, social and religious renewal, and hope for the future, which the ceremonies of the past several days had sought to impress upon all taking part. "Already Faith and Peace and Honor and ancient Modesty, and neglected Virtue are venturing to return, and blessed Plenty with her cornucopia appears" (*Carm. Saec.* 57–60). As Horace himself summed it up, "The chorus asks for aid and feels the presence of divine spirits, begs for showers from heaven, pleasing it by the prayer they have been taught, turns away disease, drives out fearful dangers, gains peace and a season fertile with fruits. Song wins grace from the gods above, song from those below" (*Epis.* 2.1.134–38).

The final instruction of the oracle was "day and night without interruption, let the people be festive sitting in richly adorned seats, and let merriment and laughter mingle with solemnity." Accordingly, the festival concluded with further dramatic performances, and then, "an auditorium and a stage were erected, the turning posts set up, and four-horse chariot races began," which continued for another day. Then came the following proclamation: "We present seven days of performances in Latin in addition to the prescribed festival, in the wooden theater by the Tiber beginning on June 5; Greek musical shows in Pompey's theater at 9 A.M.; Greek stage plays in the theater in the Circus Flaminius at 10 A.M. . . . On June 12 we shall present a hunt . . . and circus performances."

The ludi Saeculares were the most detailed and carefully crafted example of a synthesis of Augustan propaganda and pageantry known to us, but the elements they comprised figured in many other festivals that punctuated and emphasized the continuing message of the principate. As an example of the "higher art" of spectacle, with all its diverse elements coordinated into a richly expressive mise-en-scène, they may well have been unique; nevertheless, on innumerable other occasions the same messages and images were reiterated as the developing political and ideological concepts informing the regime's policies and programs were fashioned and communicated through the artistic media. This "aestheticization of politics" ultimately came to condition and then to determine how the Roman people perceived, and imagined their rulers and government.

The aesthetic of the principate — apart from the intellectual or emotional appeal of the ideas and ideals it espoused — also drew heavily upon the innate and unreflective sensual satisfaction provided by the grandeur, opulence, and scale of its various public manifestations. Horace again provides direct evidence that the "vain delights" of such spectacles were well established, while lamenting the fickleness of fashion and how readily the more cultured sections of the audience, whom he identifies as the equestrian order (in the front rows of the auditorium), could be overwhelmed by the "stupid and ill-educated" — the urban plebs — that greatly outnumbered them. "All pleasure even for the knights has now passed from the ear to the empty delights of the restless eye. For four hours and more . . . cavalry and infantry sweep past; soon kings are dragged in with bound hands. . . . Hurtling along come chariots, carts, wagons and ships, with spoils of ivory and Corinthian bronze carried in triumph. . . . What voices have ever been heard above the din to which our theaters resound? . . . Amidst such clamor and works of art and foreign luxury, the play is seen, when, buried beneath this, the actor steps onto the stage to the crash of applause. 'Has he said anything?' 'Not a word.' 'Why then the uproar?' 'It's his woolen robe, dyed in violent violet in the Tarentine fashion!' " (*Epis.* 2.1.189–207).[19] Similar sentiment was expressed in the same period by the historian Livy (7.2.13), who condemned the lavishness of theatrical art, "the insanity of which is now almost beyond the means of wealthy kingdoms." But the very sumptuousness of the performances and their venues was itself an important element in the aesthetic experience and meaning of the occasion. In common with the other Augustan spectacles, "their purpose, above all . . . was to distract from the reality, to lull the onlooker. In an aesthetically attractive and architecturally impressive setting, the question of the political organization of power becomes secondary as long as this power does not encroach upon the realm of private life" (Edler 1990, 84–85).

Theatrum Populusque Romanus

Augustus was mindful of the usefulness of the theater as an element in the legitimization and stability of his regime, and to complement Pompey's monument and the continuing provision of temporary theaters such as that used at the ludi Saeculares, he acquired two more splendid edifices: the theater of Balbus in 13 B.C. and, two years later, that of Marcellus. Lucius Cornelius Balbus (who had himself composed a tragedy based on contemporary Roman history and staged it while quaestor at Gades in Spain in 43)[20] had been allowed a triumph in March 19 B.C., a unique distinction for one not born a Roman citizen and an exceptional honor in that thereafter traditional military triumphs were not granted to those outside the imperial family. Indeed, even the donning of triumphal dress was soon reserved for the emperor, although magistrates were still permitted this attire while presiding over official games. Balbus was subsequently permitted to construct and lend his name to what would be the last building erected in Rome by anyone other than the emperor or Senate (often on his behalf) until the city ceased to be an imperial capital (Veyne 1990, 469). Constructed in the Campus Martius, it probably accommodated about eight thousand spectators, and its decoration (particularly four columns of onyx that presumably embellished the *scaenae frons*) was regarded as sensational (Pliny *N.H.* 36.60).

It was dedicated by Balbus (while Augustus was absent in Gaul) with lavish games, which were overshadowed first by the flooding of the Tiber at the time (making the theater accessible only by boat) and then by the announcement of Augustus's imminent return to Rome. Evidently careful not to upstage Balbus, he slipped into the city, refused various honors voted by the Senate (tactfully proposed by Balbus) that he regarded as unseemly, but demonstrated yet again his mastery of the "common touch" the next day by welcoming the people into his relatively modest home on the Palatine, while also "placing baths and barbers at the service of the people free of charge for the day" (Dio 54.25.4). A little later he underscored his munificent modesty: at the games vowed for his return, when the entire theater audience stood to cheer his adopted sons, Gaius and Lucius, Augustus sternly rebuked the crowd for such inappropriate display (Dio 54.27.1; Suet. *Aug.* 56).

Meanwhile, his own — far more impressive — theater of Marcellus was at last nearing completion; at the time of the ludi Saeculares it was already sufficiently advanced for some of the entertainments to be staged there (*ILS* 5050). It had originally been one of Caesar's most grandiose building projects but was evidently delayed by the civil war. Its actual construction may not have begun until the death of Marcellus, to whom Augustus then dedicated it as a memorial, probably in 11 B.C. Not to be overshadowed by Balbus, Augustus recycled for use in the Marcellus theater's *scaenae frons* the famous thirty-four-foot high marble columns that Scaurus had used some forty-five years earlier in his extravagant temporary stage and which later had graced the atrium of his house (Pliny *N.H.* 36.4–8; Ascon. *In Cic. Scaur.* 45). The auditorium probably held around thirteen thousand spectators, considerably more than that of Balbus's theater (fig. 17).

Marcus Claudius Marcellus, Augustus's nephew by the first marriage of his sister, Octavia, died in 23 B.C. at age nineteen, at the beginning of a career for which Augustus had nurtured great hope. He was the first husband of Augustus's daughter, Julia (who subsequently married Agrippa) and, because he was considered the probable heir to his uncle, his advancement along the *cursus honorum* had been accelerated. In the final year of his life, the magnificent games he gave as aedile — the last such to be given, because from 22 on they were entrusted to praetors — were enhanced when Augustus provided

Fig. 17. The eastern side of the theater of Marcellus as it appears today. (Fototeca Unione at the American Academy in Rome)

awnings to shelter the Forum throughout the summer (Dio 53.31.2; Pliny *N.H.* 19.24; Vell. Pater. 2.93). Following his untimely death, Marcellus was interred in the great Mausoleum that Augustus was constructing for the imperial family. Marcellus's widow, Octavia, dedicated a superb library to him (Ovid *Tr.* 3.1.69–70; Plutarch *Marc.* 30.6), and Augustus ordered that as a memorial a golden statue of him, with a golden wreath and curule chair, be carried in the ludi Romani and displayed in the theater among the responsible magistrates (Dio 53.30.6). The rare use of such chairs of honor in the theater had first been granted to certain (living) officials at the time of Sulla and had been used most recently by Antony and Octavian in 40, and subsequently only by the latter (Weinstock 1957, 146–52).

Marcellus's greatest memorial was of course the massive theater that now bore his name. Little is known about the interior layout of the stage and its facade, although new excavations and analysis began in 1997. Apparently there was another large structure behind the stage, facing and approximately the same size as the auditorium, and this raises the possibility that both the stage and a basic *scaenae frons,* consisting essentially of three doorways with minimal decorative detail on the facade, could be removed to create a large, open oval area suitable for gladiatorial combats and animal displays (Richardson 1992, 383). If so, it lends weight to the possibility noted earlier that the theater of Pompey may also have first employed a temporary and removable *scaenae frons.* According to this hypothesis, the theater of Marcellus was dual-purpose — like the earlier temporary structure of Curio — suitable for the staging of dramatic performances and, as an amphitheater (complementing that constructed by Statilius Taurus a decade earlier), other entertainments as well. If so, it could have catered to the fickle taste that Horace claims could unnerve "even a courageous poet" when those in the audience "greater in number, but poorer in honor and virtue . . . call in the middle of the recitations [*carmina*], for a bear or boxers; the sort of things that thrill the 'little people' [*plebecula*]" (*Epis.* 2.1.182–86). Although Horace characterizes this section of the audience as "stupid and ill-educated," even they would know better than to demand such things if they *never* took place in the same venue as the *carmina!*

The theater of Marcellus (like that of Pompey) incorporated a system of corridors and stairs to lead spectators to their seats with a minimum of confusion, and the seating itself is believed to have been divided horizontally by concentric passageways *(praecinctiones)* into "three principal zones, with an extra zone of broader steps for the senators along the orchestra and a colonnade containing seating for the less privileged at the top" (Richardson 1992, 383). Rising vertically from the orchestral level were eight *cunei:* wedge-shaped segments separated on either side by staircases. The architectural format thereby helped embody the extensive regulations detailing the disposition of the various sections of the audience laid down by Augustus's *Lex Iulia Theatralis,* which had been enacted probably six or seven years earlier.[21] In this legislation he carefully controlled the allocation of seats, and even the *appearance* of the audience, which suggests that it too was part of a meticulously managed mise-en-scène, giving force to Horace's assertion that whatever the object of the crowd's attention, a critical observer would "gaze more intently on the audience itself than on the performance, since it provides by far the better spectacle" (*Epis.* 2.1.197–98). According to Suetonius, Augustus "issued special regulations to end the wholly confused and lax way of watching shows and introduced order. . . . The senatorial decree provided that at every public performance, wherever held, the front section must be reserved for senators. . . . Other rules included the separation of soldiers from civilians; the assignment of special seats to married plebeian men, to young freeborn boys, and close by to their tutors . . . and a ban on those wearing dark clothes except in the upper rows; Augustus confined women to the back rows, even at gladiatorial shows, although previously men and women had sat together" (*Aug.* 44).

That no distinction is made between theatrical events and gladiatorial shows — the law was subsequently applied to both theaters and amphitheaters — provides further circumstantial evidence that the *munera* were no longer confined to the Forum or Circus but now, in addition to Statilius's amphitheater, might also take place in the new permanent theaters, thereby justifying (for the first time) a rule separating the sexes. The increased regulation of gladiatorial combats (indicated too by the restrictions placed on their expenditure, frequency, and number of combatants in 22 B.C.) suggests that Augustus was concerned not just about crowd control and decorum but also about tighter constraint over such traditional expressions of private aristocratic patronage. The seating regulations came during a period when he was putting into effect a number of new laws governing marriage and morality, which he claimed revived earlier admirable practices from former times and introduced new ones that subsequent generations could emulate (*R.G.* 8.5). In the case of theater, he was establishing new practices that appear to have been followed (with occasional lapses, subsequently corrected) for centuries.[22]

The poorest seats, at the very top of the auditorium *(summa cavea),* were probably allocated to slaves, together with freedmen and the poor who were not wearing the white togas required for entry into the middle section *(media cavea)* of the audience. This assumes that slaves were allowed to have seats (or even be present) in the theater at all, which (with the possible exception of some particular festivals) is likely.[23] When Horace and later writers refer to the less-educated and ill-behaved section of the audience, they usually have this group in mind. Women too were relegated to this section, a fact that is frequently alluded to in literature — for example, Propertius's Cynthia warns him to "take care that you strain not your neck, gazing at the upper section of the theater" (4.8.77). It is not clear whether any further distinctions based on status applied to the seating of women, except for the Vestal Virgins, who were given a prominent place of honor in the lowest section at one side of the orchestra. After Augustus's death, his wife, Livia, was allowed to sit with them as a singular privilege (Tac. *Ann.* 4.16).

The stipulation that boys should not be far removed from their *paedagogi* echoes the requirement noted earlier that they be accompanied at the nocturnal events of the ludi Saeculares; Augustus seems to have been particularly concerned for their education and morals, as well as anxious to curb rowdiness — in light of Horace's lament: "What voices have ever been able to be heard above the din with which our theaters resound?" (*Epis.* 2.1.200–201). Poorer boys lacking a tutor (and presumably the stipulated *toga praetexta*) were probably relegated into the upper galleries. The rest of the freeborn boys were located somewhere in the middle of the *cavea* (possibly with one or more cunei reserved for them), with most of the other sections in the same area occupied by Roman citizens of the *plebs urbana*. It is not clear whether any distinction was made between the *plebs frumentaria,* the quarter of a million citizens formally enrolled to receive free grain, and the rest, nor whether there were divisions representing the thirty-five tribes. Although Suetonius mentions a section for married men (*Aug.* 44.2; cf. Martial 5.41.8), thus implying that unmarried men sat separately, bachelors initially may not have been admitted at all. As mentioned earlier, they had been allowed at the Secular games only by special temporary lifting of the ban then in effect and — as the inscription makes quite clear — "because of religious duty and since no one will ever see such a spectacle again." In 12 B.C., just prior to the dedication of the theater of Marcellus, bachelors again received special dispensation to take part in the celebrations of Augustus's birthday (Dio 54.30.5). Certainly the ban upon them was later abolished (although special seats continued to be reserved for those married),[24] but it is likely to have been among the regulations detailed in the *Lex Iulia Theatralis.* How it could be enforced is unclear — indeed the special indulgence for the ludi Saeculares was granted in part to discourage attempts at deception.

The section reserved for soldiers probably made some distinction between those currently in service and veterans. In front of them sat civil servants and functionaries, including the officials and attendants comprising the *familia Caesaris* — the imperial household — whose presence and importance Augustus would wish to be given visible emphasis just as they had been stressed in the formal prayers at the ludi Saeculares. An area may have been reserved too for members of the various *collegia,* the most important of which — "long-standing and formed for legitimate purposes" (Suet. *Aug.* 32.1) — had after earlier bans been licensed by either Caesar or Augustus himself.

The lowest section of the *cavea* contained the fourteen rows established for members of the equestrian order by the *Lex Roscia* in 67 B.C. This category was likely restricted to some smaller number than all those who met the property requirement of the equestrian census — 400,000 sesterces — because this would have resulted in a group much greater than the approximately 1,600 seats provided by fourteen rows. Possibly seating was limited to those *equites* enrolled on the jury lists, the *decuriae,* which would have yielded a far smaller number (Rawson 1991c, 531–33; Henderson 1963, 61). Probably because of concern for social cohesion, Augustus gave a special dispensation to men who, impoverished in the civil wars, no longer met the property qualification, granting them seats if their fathers had qualified (Suet. *Aug.* 40.1). He also awarded access to a number of minor magistrates as well as to those who had served as regimental commanders, the *tribuni militum.* In any case, the number qualified for and seeking seats often resulted in overcrowding the fourteen rows. Quintilian records that Augustus once reprimanded a knight for drinking in his seat rather than doing so outside the theater, as Augustus himself did, to which the knight replied that the *Princeps* need not fear losing his seat (*Inst.* 6.3.63).[25] Horace describes the whole theater audience as *stipata,* "packed" (*Epis.* 2.1.60). In A.D. 5, the provision of separate seating for knights was extended to the circus (Dio 55.22.4).

The lowest section of the theater of Marcellus contained some twenty rows, which suggests that in addition to the area reserved for the equestrian order, distinguished foreign visitors, envoys, and some of the more important government officials who were not formally members of the equestrian order may have been placed here. Seats were allocated here too for the assistants and ceremonial attendants *(apparitores)* on magistrates (Rawson 1991c, 99–100; Edmondson 1996, 92, 106). Included here also were holders of the *corona civica,* a crown of oak leaves awarded to those who had saved the life of a fellow citizen — men so highly regarded that when they entered the theater, all present gave them a standing ovation (Pliny *N.H.* 16.13; Livy 10.47).

Senators sat, as they had done by right since 194 B.C., in the foremost seats, which by the late Republic probably placed them in the orchestral area, immediately in front of the stage, except when activities there — athletic contests or animal fights — precluded their presence. In the theater of Marcellus, several broad, shallow steps in the orchestral area were probably used for senatorial seating, which Augustus may have distinguished from equestrian seating by the provision of *subsellia* — movable, backless benches accommodating several people. The foremost serving magistrates and priests probably qualified for *prohedria,* thrones of honor with canopies (a custom of Greek origin), and there may also have been a special bench, the *bathron,* reserved for the tribunes. Finally, the most highly honored persons sat on a *sella curulis,* or the curule chair, a folding stool whose curved legs were placed crosswise.

This chair was the customary privilege of those magistrates holding imperium, but its use in the theater was more restricted. Augustus normally had the right to take his seat on a *sella curulis* as in effect the third colleague of the two current consuls (Dio 54.10.5). In his case, however, the right to its use was extended to the theater. It may also have been allowed to the *Flamen Dialis,* the chief priest of Jupiter (Weinstock 1957, 151), as well as to the magistrate presiding at the particular *ludi* and exceptionally to others to whom it was granted as a mark of distinction.[26] As noted above, such a chair was also placed in the theater as a memorial to Marcellus. Augustus inaugurated the theater with dedicatory games of appropriate splendor, marred only when his *sella curulis* collapsed while he was presiding at the opening ceremonies, causing him to be thrown to the ground (Suet. *Aug.* 43.5). In the Circus, the *lusus Troiae* (in which his adopted grandson, Gaius, aged about ten, took part) was performed, and—possibly in the new theater itself—a *venatio* with six hundred imported African animals was staged.

The theater of Marcellus and its seating arrangements were fashioned to resemble a microcosm of society and to convey this hierarchy in visual terms. In effect it was color-coded: "In the front, the senators with the wide purple stripes on their tunics [*latus clavus*], the curule magistrates wearing the *toga praetexta* with its purple stripe [and] the knights with the narrower purple stripes on their tunics [*angustus clavus*]. Behind them the plain white toga and tunic of the ordinary citizens and at the very back, the poor wearing dark tunics of cheap wool" (Parker forthcoming).

It became the prototype of the buildings widely constructed during the subsequent centuries of the imperial period. Social and political conditions encouraged their provision. The most important factor was the establishment of the principate itself, both as the basis for the administration and governing of Rome and its provinces and as the head of a new, more clearly defined social hierarchy that could be celebrated and in a concrete sense demonstrated in the very layout and seating of these theaters. The practice of providing boxes, *tribunalia,* over the vaulted passages that afforded access at either side into the orchestra gave prominence to the presiding magistrate (acting on behalf of the emperor) and to other honored guests (including the Vestal Virgins) and ensured that throughout the far-flung empire, when entertainments were provided a symbol of the imperial authority responsible for such munificence was always visible. The new system of imperial government (facilitated by predominantly peaceful conditions) assisted the integration of the provinces and their population into the Roman state and Roman society and, crucially, led to their cultural development and urbanization. In the empire there were close to a thousand cities, and although many of these had relatively small populations of under fifteen thousand inhabitants, by the end of the first century A.D., frequently even the smallest towns had acquired a collection of monumental public buildings, including a theater (fig. 18).[27] With the spread of Roman authority that quickened urbanization and the wealth and culture generated by prosperity and security, provincial citizens now became enthusiastic supporters of the ethos and ideals of Roman government and customs. Within the new conditions governing status and position, one effective way for a provincial

Fig. 18. The theater and amphitheater at Arles, France, typical of those widely built through-out the Roman Empire in the time of Augustus. (Fototeca Unione at the American Academy in Rome)

to distinguish himself and attract favor was through public patronage. Thus the theaters operated as both an engine and an object of propaganda.

The conditions favoring the provision of theaters also encouraged opulence and grandeur in entertainments. The place and occasion symbolized Roman prestige and imperial glory and were an important expression of the official ideology that justified, gave meaning to, and secured public support for the operation of the principate. Inside Rome's imperial theaters the audience was often presented with dazzling spectacles calculated to impress and to cast glory upon the rulers and patrons (or their representatives), whose presence frequently added to the excitement and splendor of the occasions and ceremonies. Augustus attended his own games and often presided at those given by other officials. He took great care to be *seen* to share the crowd's enjoyment — Caesar had been criticized for being observed attending to his correspondence during the shows — and made his excuses when forced to arrive late (Suet. *Aug.* 45.1). His keen awareness of the significance of his own role in the mise-en-scène is evident in a letter recorded by Suetonius in which Augustus worried that his great-nephew, young Claudius, would make a fool of himself in public. "I am against his watching the games in the Circus from the imperial box [*pulvinar*], where the eyes of the whole audience would be on him" (*Claud.* 4.3). The emperor was himself the star of the shows. They began with ritual homage to him — different sections of the crowd, assisted by the divisions imposed by the *Lex Iulia Theatralis,* chanted rhythmic acclamations that were gradually codified and accompanied by music — and all that followed was expected to be worthy of his magnificence.[28]

The crowd was also encouraged in a literal sense to *enjoy itself,* because its size, the sense conveyed through the subdivisions (each indicating its presence by its distinctive dress) that the whole of society was taking part, and its collective reactions and clamor must have been intoxicating. In addition to this aspect and the impressive architecture and embellishments, the audience must have felt flattered and impressed too by the enormous expense and technical refinements lavished upon the occasion. In addition to music for the ear and scenic devices to enthrall the eye, a scented saffron spray cooled the air, while high above, the great system of awnings, manipulated by teams of *velarii,* drew the senses into further fantasy. "The red, blue, and yellow *vela* suspended like inverted arches over the buildings, dipping them into their multi-colored shade, softly moving in every breeze, must have presented a striking sight" (Graefe 1979, 1:221). The tall masts from which these were suspended, which overtopped and ringed the structures, gave them the appearance of a crown from afar. In fact, the three theaters and other places of entertainment located in the Campus Martius were themselves an effective and compelling spectacle. As the contemporaneous remarks of Strabo record (5.236 ff.), "Pompey, Caesar, Augustus, his sons and friends, and wife and sister have outdone all others in their zeal for building and in the expense incurred." Indeed, the whole area "presents to the eye the appearance of a stage-painting, offering a spectacle one can hardly draw away from. . . . Colonnades in great numbers, sacred precincts, three theaters, an amphitheater, and very costly temples, in close succession to one another, giving the impression that they are trying to suggest that the rest of the City is a mere accessory."

The propagandistic aspects of the entertainments in the theater were also exploited on a smaller but highly effective scale throughout the diverse sections of the city. In 7 B.C. Augustus reorganized Rome into regions and local neighborhoods *(vici),* each of which was administered by a locally elected magistrate (Suet. *Aug.* 30; Dio 55.8.6–7). On certain days magistrates were allowed to display a degree of prestige and pomp in their dress and retinue. They were in charge of administering the ancient cult and sacred sites of the *Lares Compitales,* which incorporated a new element of worship and sacrifice to Augustus's own household, *Lares,* and his *Genius,* the attendant spirit of his family. As part of his widespread attempts to revive venerable religious practices, by about 12 B.C. Augustus began to restore these modest local shrines, which were widely sited at the numerous crossroads in Rome, adding to them *Lares Augusti* and a new image to represent his *Genius* (Ovid *Fast.* 5.143–46). As noted in Chapter 2, the earlier cult had long had a festival, the Compitalia, associated with it in which slaves, craftspeople, and others of relatively humble social status staged impromptu plays and games in the city streets but which in the late Republic had been suppressed with the responsible collegia because of the manner in which they were exploited politically (Suet. *Div. Iul.* 42.3). First under Caesar, and then Augustus, the oldest and least controversial of such collegia were permitted to form and function once again (Yavetz 1983, 85–96). Augustus now revived the festival as well, because he saw in it a means for encouraging a sense of communal spirit and local identity within the vastness of Rome. Moreover, because of its new association with himself, it could engender popular loyalty and affection, serving as a further binding element of the new regime. The cult soon found similar expressions in other Italian cities and provinces (Taylor 1931, 185–85, 217–18; Vanderbroeck 1987, 114; Galinsky 1996, 322–31). An impulse to secure a degree of cohesion within the ethnically diverse city population may account for the note by Suetonius that at Augustus's instruction, "sometimes plays were shown in all the various City districts, and on several stages, the actors speaking the appropriate local dialect" (*Aug.* 41). In addition, Propertius indicates that the Compitalia continued to be associated with singing, dancing, and the performances of the mimes (2.22.3–6).

The Mise-en-Scène of the City

The manner in which Augustus linked himself to the theatricalization of urban life and landscape through the provision of sumptuous and monumental buildings for mass entertainment as well as through more humble shrines and performances throughout the city was evident also in a variety of other architecture and the activities associated with it. Augustus is famously noted for claiming that he "found Rome built of bricks, and left her clothed in marble," but his reconceptualization of the city went far beyond mere beautification or monumentalization: it became an essential and highly theatrical expression of the ideology of the principate. Rome was to become *urbs pro maiestate imperii ornata,* "a City adorned for the splendor of the Empire" (Suet. *Aug.* 28.3). Vitruvius, in dedicating his great treatise on architecture to Augustus, noted precisely the same thing: "Not only has the State been enriched with provinces by your means, but the majesty of the Empire has similarly been expressed through the eminent dignity of its public buildings" (1.*praef.*2). Even the provision in 20 B.C. of a milestone in the Forum, the *milliarium aureum,* suggests both the center of the world and, by extension, the "New World Order" (Dio 54.8.4; Pliny *N.H.* 3.66). As noted above, after 29 B.C. Augustus had decided not to hold any further triumphs for himself, in part because his prestige was such that a triumph could not elevate it further (Florus 2.34). Instead, he perceived that a far more effective display of glory and power could be embodied in permanent form through public monuments, which, moreover, could communicate a detailed assertion of the new ideals and beliefs of the evolving principate.

The monopoly he exercised over building projects ensured that such architecture "spoke" with a single voice. For example, when he allowed Gaius Sosius — who had converted to Octavian's cause following the defeat of Antony — to renovate the temple of Apollo Medicus (near the future site of the theater of Marcellus), its interior was adorned with reliefs related not to Sosius's Judaean triumph of 34 B.C. but rather to the Pannonian and Dalmatian campaigns and their commemoration on the first day of Augustus's own triumph in 29, held shortly before Sosius's rebuilding (Hölscher 1985, 89; Galinsky 1996, 346, 383). The temple, moreover, was adjacent to that of Bellona, from which triumphal processions traditionally began — triumphs that henceforth would be granted only to members of the imperial family.

Thus Augustus simultaneously honored Sosius, while permanently linking his own name with victory, and Apollo. Sosius dedicated his lavish restoration on September 23, Augustus's birthday. "His loyalty did not go unrewarded: at the Secular Games this one-time follower of Mark Antony could be seen among the procession of priests, the *Quindecimviri Sacris Faciundis*" (Zanker 1988, 69). In a similar fashion to such opportunistic utilization of available architecture, Augustus co-opted the image of Victory (which in the late Republic was widely used as a triumphal symbol) to serve both as a universal icon for Rome and as a cult closely linked to himself, placing a statue of her — standing upon a globe and holding a wreath and palm branch — in the newly completed *Curia Iulia* soon after 29, the same year in which he dedicated the temple of Divus Iulius. "By establishing the cult of Victory in the Curia Iulia he transformed the senate house into a virtual dynastic shrine" (Galinsky 1996, 315). The image of Victory was soon widely reproduced as propaganda (Dio 51.22.1).

Following Augustus's victorious return from Spain and Gaul in 13 B.C., the Senate decreed that an altar marking the Pax Augusta be erected at the eastern edge of the Campus Martius (Dio 54.25.3–6; cf. *R.G.* 12.2). This "Altar of Peace," the most representative work of Augustan art, was dedicated on January 30, 9 B.C. Much of it has survived and been reassembled to give an excellent impression of the original monument, if not always a clear indication of the meaning of the scenes depicted in its exquisitely composed friezes. In particular, scholars have posited a variety of events constituting the ceremonial occasion illustrated along the north and south sides of the structure. These have included inter alia a representation of the dedication of the altar itself or the elevation of Augustus to the post of Pontifex Maximus in 12 B.C.

One particularly plausible suggestion is that the scene represented is a formal *supplicatio* honoring Augustus, which (according to this interpretation) was held immediately after his return from the western provinces in 13 B.C. (Billows 1993). Not only does this theory account for most of the evidence contained within the frieze itself, but it also has strong circumstantial support. *Supplicationes* were periods of public rejoicing and thanksgiving decreed by the Senate following events of national significance; these, in part through their relative informality, appear to have allowed ordinary individuals a more personal and emotional expression of worship than that afforded by other official rituals. Such expressions included a public procession during which the participants would kneel and venerate statues or emblems of the gods placed on platforms *(pulvinaria)* at their temples (Livy 22.10.8, 3.7.7, 40.37.3). "Senators, magistrates, priests and the general populace, including women and children, would dress in the best apparel, with crowns of laurel on their heads and laurel twigs in their hands, and go in procession around the various

Fig. 19. A relief panel from the *Ara Pacis* showing the procession of the imperial family. (Fototeca Unione at the American Academy in Rome)

temples thanking the gods by sacrifices of incense and wine" (Billows 1993, 88). In Augustus's own final record of his achievements (the *Res Gestae*), immediately after noting that "although the Senate decreed further triumphs for me, I declined them all," he records that "for successes on land and sea . . . the Senate decreed *supplicationes* on 55 occasions" (*R.G.* 4; cf. Dio 54.10.3). The friezes of the Ara Pacis would then be historical and realistic in the sense that they depicted an actual event that had taken place at the time the altar was decreed (fig. 19). At the same time, because it is doubtful that all of those depicted in the imperial entourage were actually present in Rome at the moment of Augustus's return, the friezes may also be "depicting an idealized version of history. . . . Everyone who should be present at such a symbolic occasion is shown as present: we see history as it ought to have been" (Billows 1993, 91).

Such an interpretation raises the scenes on the northern and southern sides of the altar to the level of a historical (yet ever-present) pageant, and this sense is greatly reinforced by the nature of the events of Roman myth and the legendary past depicted on the adjacent friezes along its eastern and western faces. These include Aeneas sacrificing a pregnant sow to his family gods after landing in Latium, the discovery of Romulus and Remus with the she-wolf, an iconic figure of Roma, and one of Tellus, goddess of fertility and the earth. All of these images convey levels of allusive meaning rich in religious and political significance and provide in permanent form an evocation of themes and emotions paralleling those memorably marked a few years earlier at the *ludi Saeculares*. Just as ritual seeks to represent sacred events through a form of hieratic reenactment, and pageantry redeems great moments of the past by releasing them from time through theatrical replication, so too the friezes of Augustus's altar place secular events into the eternal world of myth and interpret them to show that "actions from Rome's legendary history . . . reached their fulfillment with the contemporary Principate of Augustus" (Holliday 1990, 549; cf. Elsner 1991, 52, 55; Galinsky 1996, 106–7).

Other examples of this aspect of Augustan architecture have been widely discussed, particularly in terms of Augustus's own Forum (adjacent to that of Caesar) and its temple of Mars Ultor, dedicated probably in May of 2 B.C.[29] The completion of this complex, considered by Pliny to be one of the most beautiful edifices in the world (*N.H.* 36.101–2), was celebrated with magnificent games (repeated annually thereafter on May 12), including the *lusus Troiae* and slaughter of 260 lions in the circus, gladiatorial combats in the Saepta, and a great naumachia, staged in a huge basin constructed beside the Tiber (Suet. *Aug.* 43.1; Dio 55.10.7–8; Ovid *Ars Amat.* 1.171–72). This naumachia employed some thirty ships and three thousand men in what Ovid described as "a mock naval battle in which Caesar displayed Persian and Greek ships": the Battle of Salamis of 480 B.C. The reenactment has been interpreted both as "a piece of pageantry advertising Rome as the champion of Hellas against the Orient," the heir and defender of Hellenistic traditions (Syme 1984, 922), and as a retrospective allusion to Actium with the victory there of the civilized West over the barbaric East (Zanker 1988, 148; cf. Coleman 1993, 67 ff.).

Such pageantry, "for which the vast world was in the City" (*Ars. Amat.* 1.174), was intended "to fill the hearts and eyes of the Roman people with unforgettable images" (Vell. Pater. 2.100.2), and a similar desire was incorporated into Augustus's new Forum itself. The temple of Mars had Augustus's name emblazoned on its architrave, while enshrined within were statues of Mars Ultor, Venus, and the deified Caesar. The new Forum was used as a focal point for such important rituals as the assumption by boys of the *toga virilis,* the meeting of the Senate for declarations of war, sacrifices marking the inception and completion of military campaigns, the formal bestowal of triumphal honors, the display of war booty, and an annual ceremony by the steps of the temple honoring the cavalry commanders (Suet. *Aug.* 29; Dio 55.10.2–5). At its center stood a statue of Augustus clothed in triumphal garb and driving a four-horse chariot, which had inscribed on its base *Pater Patriae,* a title voted earlier that same year. The sides of the Forum were a veritable "Hall of Fame," with niches on the south side displaying statues of Romulus and other great heroes from Rome's past, and featuring on the north Aeneas and all the principal members of Augustus's Julian ancestry. In all, about one hundred men were thus honored, so that — as Augustus himself proclaimed — citizens would require him, while he lived, and future *Principes* to match their standard (Suet. *Aug.* 31.5). Elsewhere on the site was a variety of important artistic works and trophies, including the sword of Julius Caesar and famous standards that Crassus and Antony had lost to the Parthians and that Augustus recovered in 20 B.C.

Augustus had been offered the revered title *Pater Patriae* in what has been termed "a genuine Augustan masterpiece of political calculation and staging" (Alföldi 1953, 117): as he entered the theater of Pompey he was met by a huge crowd of ordinary citizens whose offer of the title was then formally bestowed on him in the Senate. Augustus accepted it "with tears in his eyes" (Suet. *Aug.* 58). The choice of site reflected the extent to which "theater and circus were the arenas in which *princeps* and *plebs* met . . . where the People could legitimize the *princeps'* extraordinary position" (Nippel 1995, 87). The beliefs and emotion of that occasion were permanently evoked through the new Forum and its imagery, which as a form of continuing spectacle, "provided a space where rituals might take place involving Senate, *Equites* and People, in a setting defined by Augustus' own achievements" (Patterson 1991, 209).

Similar qualities characterized what has recently been termed "the Julian topography of the center of Rome" (Millar 1993, 9), which so impressed Strabo at the time: "If on passing to the old Forum, you saw one forum after another . . . and basilicas, and temples, and saw also the Capitol and the works of art there and those of the Palatine and Livia's promenade, you would easily become oblivious to everything else. Such is Rome" (5.236). Even Augustus's own house on the Palatine Hill functioned as an expressive dramatic emblem. In 36 he had acquired what had been the house of the noted late-republican orator Hortensius Hortalus, which was described by Suetonius as impressively modest (*Aug.* 72). As noted earlier, however, immediately adjacent to it (virtually as an extension) Augustus constructed his new temple of Apollo, together with a portico and library, that was "universally admired as the most sumptuous and magnificent of all early Augustan buildings" (Richardson 1992, 14). In addition to exhibiting an important art collection and sculpture gallery, it was the repository of the sacred Sibylline books that Augustus had moved from the temple of Jupiter in 12 B.C., placing them in two gilded bookcases at the base of the cult statue of Apollo in the cella of the temple. Nearby were the venerable temples of the Magna Mater (linked with Aeneas and Troy) and of Victoria (embellished following the victory at Actium), and beneath the complex was the site of the Lupercal, the cave in which Romulus and Remus were suckled by the she-wolf. A hut believed to have been that of Romulus, whose name Octavian had once considered taking, "proclaimed the same message in a more subtle way" (Patterson 1991, 205; cf. Suet. *Aug.* 7; Dio 53.16).

Thus the overall visual and emotional impact of the Palatine area was very intense, especially if, as is likely, the main route of access to it during Augustus's reign was altered to lead directly from the Forum, past houses traditionally occupied by the ruling aristocracy, to the now appropriately preeminent house of Augustus (Wiseman 1987, 403–6). To further convey a message through this setting, the Senate (shortly after the dedication of the temple of Apollo and at the same session when it named him Augustus) had ordered that the house be distinguished by displaying a laurel tree on each of the two doorposts and an oak crown (the *corona civica*) permanently placed above the door, "to symbolize that he was always victor over his enemies and the saviour of the citizens" (Dio 53.16.4; cf. *R.G.* 34.2). In the later years of his reign, the Senate frequently met at the neighboring temple of Apollo, symbolically suggesting their subordination to the *Princeps*' authority (see Thompson 1981). Augustus's Palatine setting ultimately was so evocative of a more-than-mortal power that in the end Ovid even used it as a metaphor for the place where Jupiter himself summoned the Olympian gods, characterizing the scene as "the place which, were I allowed to speak boldly, I would not hesitate to call the Palatine of high heaven" (*Met.* 1.175–76).

The Augustan Repertoire

Amid the rhetorical eloquence of such architecture, the most persuasive and direct statement of imperial grandeur and power emanated from the theaters themselves and the spectacles they contained. The evidence for the extent and variety of Augustus's showmanship is overwhelming; what is far less clear, however, is the nature of the subject matter presented in the three theaters at his disposal, accommodating altogether perhaps as many as fifty thousand spectators. Horace says that the works of earlier Roman playwrights, including Ennius, Naevius, Pacuvius, Accius, Afranius, Plautus, Caecilius, and Terence, continued to be performed in his time. Their works, he claims, "mighty Rome memorizes, and these she views packed into her crowded theater" (*Epis.* 2.1.60–61). Yet elsewhere, as noted above, he complains that the audience is so noisy and boisterous the actors can barely be heard, and it is obsessed with spectacle. This suggests that—apart from the revival of tried and true staples from the repertoire—serious drama did not flourish in performance. Horace laments the tendency of even the more attentive element of the public to resist good new writing in preference to old favorites. "I am impatient that any work is censured, not because it is thought coarse or inelegant, but simply because it is not old." He condemns the reluctance to admit that much earlier Roman work is second-rate (*Epis.* 2.1.76–78 ff.).

As far as comedy is concerned, Horace thinks that the audience is too indulgent toward such earlier writers as Caecilius and Plautus and often too ready also to accept shoddy artistry in contemporary poets (*A.P.* 54, 264 ff.; *Epis.* 2.1.168–76). Elsewhere he asserts that one "Fundanius, alone of living poets can charm us with comic chatter" (*Sat.* 1.10.40–42). For the rest, he delights in ridiculing such practicing poetasters and buffoons as Tigellius Hermogenes, one-time friend of Caesar, who was evidently a contemporary actor and singer of some renown and had founded a school for mime artists. Horace evokes him as an example of vulgar popularity and bids him with contempt to "go whine amongst the easy chairs of your female acolytes" (*Sat.* 1.10.90–91). He suggests that would-be playwrights should study and imitate the great writers of Greek Old Comedy; "writers whom the fop Hermogenes has never read" (*Sat.* 1.10.17–18). Elsewhere he announces—possibly referring to a different Tigellius—"the flute girls' guilds, the drug quacks, beggars, actresses, buffoons, and all that breed are in grief and mourning over the death of the singer Tigellius. He was, forsooth, so kind" (*Sat.* 1.2.1–4; cf. Leppin 1992, 248–49).

Horace wanted an "art of poetry" that would engender a new repertoire and texts of excellence modeled on the masterworks of the Greek playwrights while encouraging contemporary authors to innovate in their artistic expression of Roman values and genius through arduous attention to detail. But he expressed a low opinion of the taste of the Roman audience and disdained himself to be judged either by the "contempt of a scornful spectator" or by his approval, because "the man whom Glory carries to the stage in her windy car . . . is left deflated by the apathetic spectator, but exulted by his fans" (*Epis.* 2.1.215, 177–81). While therefore bidding "farewell to show business" [*valeat res ludicra*] himself, he points out that "I do not begrudge praise when others handle well what I decline to try myself" and expresses admiration for "that poet able to walk a tightrope, who with airy nothings wrings my heart, inflames, soothes, fills it with vain alarms like a magician, and sets me down now at Thebes, now at Athens" (*Epis.* 2.1.209–13).

A poet for whom he had the highest admiration (and whose approval he valued) was Asinius Pollio (born 76 B.C.), who, after a political career culminating in the consulship in 40 B.C. and a triumph in 39, had retired while still young to pursue learning and the arts, including the composition of trag-edies.[30] Horace praised the mastery of rhythmic subtlety displayed in his dra-matic works "singing of kings' exploits" (*Sat.* 1.10.43). Vergil too, whom Pollio had befriended, had the highest regard for his qualities as a tragic play-wright, considering his verses "alone worthy of Sophocles" (*Ecl.* 8.9.10). Pol-lio abandoned drama, however, to write a history of the civil wars, a task that Horace characterized as "full of dangerous hazard, walking, as it were over fires hidden beneath treacherous ashes," although Pollio prudently stopped with Philippi, avoiding the more topical — and controversial — events leading to Octavian's rule.[31] Horace expressed (in vain) the hope that Pollio would soon "renew [his] high calling" and that his "stern tragic muse will be only briefly absent from the theater" (*Odes* 2.1.6–10).

Pollio did organize public recitations, but only before a limited and invited audience (Seneca the Elder *Contr. 4. praef.*). Like Horace, who was unwilling to subject his work to public criticism by letting it "return again and again to be looked at on the stage" (*Sat.* 1.10.39) or to "recite [his] trifles in crowded theaters" (*Epis.* 1.19.41), Pollio did not present his work in actual theaters, and still less could he be found among those "who recite their works in the middle of the Forum or in the baths" (*Sat.* 1.4.74–75). During the period in question the only permanent theater available was that of Pompey, but pre-sumably a more intimate venue was used for recitations, a precursor of the roofed Odea, soon built widely throughout the Roman Empire. The public recitation of poetry and works of rhetoric was traditional in the Hellenistic world and, according to Suetonius, by the mid-second century B.C. was estab-lished practice at Rome (*Gram.* 2.4). Cicero referred in 62 B.C. to his Greek client Archias having presented his work (possibly by private invitation) be-fore Aemilius Scaurus, and had himself heard Archias's recitation encored and applauded (*Arch.* 6, 18). In 45 Atticus had arranged a public reading — termed an *acroasis* — of the Greek scholar Tyrannios's Homeric criticism (*Ad Att.* 12.6.2). Cicero also noted that it was customary for poets to give readings of preliminary drafts of their works to the *vulgus* before completing the final version (*De Off.* 1.147).

Seneca the Elder provides a glimpse of such public readings in the early principate through his description of a recitation by Porcius Latro, a promi-nent orator, on the hypothetical question "Should a man adopt the grandson born to him through his disinherited son's liaison with a prostitute?" which he declaimed before an audience including Augustus, Maecenas, and the em-peror's adopted son, Agrippa. Agrippa, although not nobly born himself, was the father of Lucius and Gaius, Augustus's grandchildren and putative heirs. At one point in his presentation, Latro referred to the notion of a "fellow grafted onto the nobility from the dregs of society by adoption." Maecenas whistled, ostensibly to indicate that Augustus was in a hurry and that Latro should finish his declamation, but the suspicion was that he had done so maliciously to ensure that Augustus attended to the innocently delivered but potentially offensive allusion. "Latro could not even apologize for his error" without calling attention to it (*Contr.* 2.4.12–13). The episode illustrates the volatility of power relationships at public performances and the manner in which the political potential of these in part depended not just on the intention of the performer or even the audience reaction, but to an important degree on the interpretation the emperor chose to give it. "As the most conspicuous member of the audience, an emperor could remain unoffended in the face of speech that appeared allusive, in this way defusing the potential insult by denying its existence" (Bartsch 1994, 84). Reality itself became enthralled to a theatrical aesthetic and its dynamics.

In addition to Pollio and Latro, others in the circle of Augustan poets and orators also gave some type of public performance; Horace refers to the great patron Maecenas himself being applauded in the theater, even detailing that on one occasion "*thrice* the thronging people broke into happy applause in the theater" on his behalf (*Odes.* 1.20.3, 2.17.25–26). Tacitus records that once, upon hearing a quotation from Vergil, the theater audience spontaneously rose en masse to pay homage to the poet in their midst, "just as they would have done to the emperor himself" (*Dial.* 13). Indeed, according to Macrobius, Vergil's account of Dido and Aeneas was adapted for the stage (5.17.4), and Servius asserts that the same was true of his *Sixth Eclogue* (*In Ecl.* 6.11).

Two other major Augustan poets are known to have written tragedies that were highly praised, although apparently not repeated. Lucius Varius Rufus was commissioned to write an original tragedy, *Thyestes,* which was presented in 29 B.C. at the great triumphal games celebrating the victory at Actium. For this Augustus awarded him the enormous sum of a million sesterces, probably in public as a gesture of conspicuous munificence, which would certainly have justified Horace's characterization of Rufus (along with Vergil) as a poet whom Augustus loved and on whom he had bestowed gifts "to the giver's great renown" (*Epis.* 2.1.246–47).[32] The work survived to be read by Tacitus, who greatly admired it, and by Quintilian, who deemed it the equal of any Greek tragedy. Both had similar praise for the *Medea* of Ovid, which was probably written about a decade later (Tac. *Dial.* 12; Quint. *Inst.* 3.8.45, 10.1.98). But, like Rufus, who, following the success of *Thyestes,* devoted himself to the composition of epic poetry and the editing of the *Aeneid,* which Augustus had entrusted to him after Vergil's death, Ovid's muse (as he put it), having briefly allowed him to don the tragic buskins and scepter, did not thereafter let him seek applause in the theater (*Amores* 2.18.13–16, 3.1.67–70; *Tr.* 5.7.27–28). He notes, however, that some of his work (though not intended for the theater) had been staged, and this may have included his elegies or the monologues of the love-struck heroines in the *Heroides* (*Tr.* 2.519–20).

Ovid points out that Augustus, despite the high moral tone he sought to encourage, had a fondness for the low and bawdy farce of the mimes and condoned the considerable expense of producing them incurred by the praetors sponsoring the official *ludi* — "the stage is profitable for the poet, and the praetor purchases such immoralities at no small price" — as well as by the *Princeps* himself for his own benefactions. Not only the Senate and the Roman people — men, maidens, wives, and children — attended such "obscene mimes, which always contain crimes of forbidden love," but, moreover, "these you [Augustus] have yourself often viewed and displayed to others (so gracious is your glory everywhere) and with your own eyes, by which the whole world benefits, serenely watched staged adulteries" (*Tr.* 2.497 ff., cf. 2.513–14). Augustus also appreciated Greek drama. He particularly relished the works of Old Comedy and had them staged (Suet. *Aug.* 89); he awarded prizes at Greek play competitions (*Aug.* 45) and himself composed a tragedy, *Ajax*, which may have been influenced by Sophocles (*Aug.* 85). He undoubtedly encouraged his poets (in Horace's words) to "work with Greek models by day; and work with them by night!" (*A.P.* 268–69). Rome had for some time been caught up in a quickening tide of Hellenistic influence, leading to a profound and permanent transformation of its culture. The emphasis placed on the construction of new permanent theaters in Rome and throughout the empire reflected the importance that the Hellenistic world had long placed upon the theater, thus marking a cultural coming of age for Roman society. But it was only one manifestation of a much broader process under Augustus through which the principate was engaged by means of its festivals, rituals, and pervasive and reiterated iconography in propagating its own mythology, indeed even its own cosmology.

"The imagery of the new imperial myth, like the revived Roman religion, depended for its effectiveness to a large degree on ritual. . . . By the end of Augustus's reign a single integrated system of imagery had evolved which took in victory celebrations, the ruler cult, presentation and glorification of the Emperor, and honorific monuments. . . . Through the regular repetition of prescribed rituals and festivals and the unchanging visual formulas, the mythology of the Empire took on a reality of its own, removed from the ups and downs of the historical process" (Zanker 1988, 237). To lend authority, legitimacy, and stability to the ideological foundations of the new political order, the principate sought wherever possible to ground these in established belief and tradition, thereby encouraging the use (and frequently the revival or adaptation) of earlier rites, imagery, and forms of artistic expression.

The revival of classical forms, or even the use of strongly archaic elements, in art, architecture, literature, and language, through its emphasis on simplicity, harmony, clarity, and precision, conveyed not just an aesthetic quality but an ethical one as well. A form of aesthetic puritanism paralleling that promulgated in the social sphere by Augustus's moral legislation was widely evident in public works and in particular encouraged the study and emulation of Greek, especially Athenian, art forms from past centuries.[33] This process had the most profound impact on every sphere of artistic activity, and its influence continued to be felt long into the imperial period.

The theater, as an ancient and quintessentially Greek art form, provided a major focal point for these impulses. Its increasing function within Roman society as a medium of political display and a venue for the celebration of popular enthusiasms, however, meant that those controlling it (and therefore, ultimately, Augustus himself) could not risk losing their audience through any miscalculated exercise in aesthetic fashion. As the evidence of Horace suggests, traditional tragedy — except when hyped with such production values as outlandish costumes and gaudy scenic extravagance — struggled to hold a popular audience (fig. 20). In an age when even traditional comedy appears to have been increasingly displaced by the anarchic pleasures of the mime, tragedy with its sometimes obscure language and turgid dramaturgy risked being hooted off the stage or watched in pious boredom. The practice of composing in archaic styles and genres, which was employed by some writers at this time and brought praise from their peers and patrons, was not likely to be successful under the conditions prevailing in the theater. Tragedy was old-fashioned in a manner that an appeal to the purity and piety of antique practice could not redeem for Roman spectators out to have a good time. Increasingly, the audience, which crowded into the new theaters and carefully dispersed to their designated sections, was swollen by veterans, rural immigrants, and the urban underclass, who had little ability to appreciate the critical niceties of an arcane theatrical art of poetry as promulgated (but not practiced) by Horace. After all, "what taste could you expect of an unlettered throng just freed from toil, rustics mixed up with city folk, vulgar with the serious-minded?" (*A.P.* 212–13). Such an audience was liable to be alienated by tragedy.

It was not what Augustus wanted. If the occasion was to contribute to the greater glory of the regime, the audience so assiduously organized as a microcosm of the Roman people must not be divided into sophisticates and *vulgus* by the elitist fare offered the house: they must all — or at the least the masses who

Fig. 20. A carved ivory figure of a
Roman actor wearing traditional
tragic costume and mask. Thought to
date from the late second century A.D.,
it depicts a female character dressed in
a full-length tunic *(chiton)* and
apparently wearing the conventional
high clogs *(cothurni)*. Petit Palais
Museum, Paris. (C. M. Dixon)

chose to attend — *enjoy* themselves. Tragedy was evidently too antiquated —
its practice and conventions too drained of vitality — to hold again the popular
stages in its traditional format, although, as noted, recitations or minimalist
stagings may well have taken place in other venues before a cultivated minority audience.[34] Instead, a new type of theatrical entertainment, pantomime,
arose, which drew on the same mythological sources as tragedy (and may have

appealed to similar emotions) but embodied these in an altogether different and more accessible mode of performance. Just as classical forms and motifs were widely used by Augustan artists and architects synthetically, and "Roman poets in the period invented ways of using Greek mythology that had no parallel among the Greek poets since the fifth century" (Williams 1978, 111), so too in the theater old wine found its way into new skins. Pantomime had its roots in the venerable tradition of mimetic dance from which the earliest dramatic forms of tragedy and comedy had probably evolved and which continued to hold a central place in Greek education, religion, and modes of artistic expression. It presented characterization, emotion, and narrative through the movements and gestures of the body of an individual performer who neither sang nor spoke. Thus it drew on, shaped, and interpreted well-loved and suggestive myths that the audience could appreciate on a purely sensual level and respond to without having to follow a complicated verbal text.

Its first appearance in Italy took place (according to later tradition) in 22 B.C., although a more likely date would be the previous year at the games celebrated by Marcellus during his aedileship (Athenaeus *Deipno.* 1.20D; cf. Jory 1981, 148). It was said to have been fashioned by Pylades from Cilicia and Bathyllus from Alexandria, each of whom was a superb dancer as well as, apparently, a theoretician of considerable force and sensitivity (Leppin 1992, 217–19, 284–85). Although it was traditionally asserted that the elements of their art developed and were perfected in the East, more recent analysis has suggested an Italian origin, possibly arising from the venerable and versatile mimes (Jory 1996, 26–27). In any case, Pylades and Bathyllus evidently established it in Rome by virtue of their particular skills and personalities and through the assistance of fortunate contacts. Both achieved enormous personal renown and success, which enabled them to found schools that preserved their name and art long after their deaths.

Bathyllus was the freedman and darling of Maecenas, close companion of Augustus and patron of legendary wealth (Tac. *Ann.* 1.54; Hor. *Epod.* 14). He is credited with developing the comic pantomime, which was fairly simple in composition, though often lascivious and droll, and evolved as witty travesties of the more salacious Greek myths or burlesques of well-known ancient tragedies. Such contemporary works as Ovid's *Metamorphoses* and *Ars Amatoria* could also be adapted for pantomimic performance (Ovid *Tr.* 5.7.25–30). Bathyllus was remembered for playing such roles as Echo and Pan or an Eros and satyr, presenting these dramatis personae simultaneously. Horace may have had his protean skill in mind when he formulated his descriptive analogy of one "who wears the look of being at play and yet is on the rack, like a dancer who plays now a satyr and now a clownish cyclops" (*Epis.* 2.2.125).[35]

The comic pantomime was much in vogue during Bathyllus's lifetime but later faded away, displaced perhaps by the mime, whose broad and easily understood humor was able to hold the attention of a heterogeneous theater audience. But the much more extravagant tragic pantomime, first practiced by Pylades, a freedman of Augustus, endured for centuries. It was evidently fashioned from sensational moments from Greek mythology, and from the great tragedies in particular; the scenes were linked as lyrical solos, and all were performed by a single artist who was usually male.[36] Lucian, writing his critical account of the subject in the second century A.D., gives a long list of its subjects, including a vast range of Greek mythology along with a few subjects drawn from Roman, Egyptian, and Syrian myth. The themes are similar to those of tragedy, but the presentation is more varied and imaginative. He concludes, "To sum it up, [the pantomime] will not be ignorant of anything that is told by Homer and Hesiod and the best poets, and above all by tragedy" (*De Salt.* 37–71). This individual silent performer was backed by musicians playing such instruments as the tibia, cymbals, drums, cithara, and *scabellum* (a clapper operated by the foot) and accompanied by either a single actor or a chorus that sang the part and provided the narrative continuity, during which the pantomime impersonated all the characters, male and female, in a series of interlinked solo scenes consecutively arranged. Quintilian notes that there could be two *pantomimi* "contending with alternate gestures" and says that Augustus called one of them *saltator* (dancer) and the other *interpellator* (interrupter) (*Inst.* 6.3.65). The task of the performers was to give an impression of the whole ensemble and the relationship of one character to another while preserving the sense of the plot and creating graceful and expressive movements and gestures.

This formidable challenge demanded enormous skill and imagination on the part of the principal artist, who underwent extensive training to be able to depict both the actions as well as, simultaneously, the emotional state of several characters. He was aided in this daunting task by appropriate masks and often elaborate costumes — which he changed in the course of performance and used to help express his character (cf. Jory 1996, 11–12) — and by the conventional nature of the most prominent of the many roles he was expected to learn, the movements of which (a sort of gestic vocabulary) were set by firm tradition from which the actor strayed at his peril. The most important element was the complex and subtle movement of the hands and arms, which one observer, Athenaeus, likened to the creation of pictures as though using the letters of the alphabet (*Deipno.* 20CD). Even so, it is baffling to contemplate how such recorded subjects as Pythagorean philosophy or the dialogues of Plato could be intelligibly rendered in performance (Plut. *Mor.* 711C).

Lucian's account suggests why the versatility of the performer attracted such admiration from the audience: "In general, the dancer undertakes to present and enact characters and emotions, introducing now a lover and now an angry person, one man afflicted with madness, another with grief, and all this within fixed bounds. . . . Within the selfsame day at one moment we are shown Athamas in a frenzy, and at another Ino in terror; presently the same person is Atreus, and after a little, Thyestes; then Aegisthus, or Aerope; yet they all are but a single man. . . . The dancer should be perfect in every point, so as to be wholly rhythmical, graceful, symmetrical, consistent, unexceptionable, impeccable, not wanting in any way, blended of the highest qualities, keen in his ideas, profound in his culture, and above all, human in his sentiments." He notes the disgrace of a performer who, while dancing Chronos in the act of devouring his children, inadvertently slipped into the role of Thyestes committing the same act. Evidently the audience was familiar not only with the different myths but also (rather like contemporary devotees of the ballet) with the precise way in which they were to be danced. Lucian further records how one pantomime in presenting the madness of Ajax became so overwrought in the role that he snatched the tibia from one of the musicians and gave such a blow to the dancer portraying Odysseus that only his helmet saved him. His account provides an intriguing glimpse of the Roman audience: "The auditorium, however, all went mad with Ajax, leaping and shouting and flinging up their garments; for the riff-raff, the absolutely unenlightened, took no thought for propriety and could not perceive what was good or what was bad . . . while the politer sort understood, to be sure, and were ashamed of what was going on, but instead of censuring the thing by silence, they applauded to cover the absurdity of the dancing." When the actor returned to his senses later he was mortified by his unseemly indulgence and refused thereafter to repeat the role. "What irked him most was that his antagonist and rival, when cast for Ajax in the same role, enacted his madness so discreetly and sanely as to win praise, since he kept within the bounds of the dance and did not debauch the histrionic art."

This suggestion that the audience was composed of spectators of diverse taste and refinement agrees with the evidence discussed earlier. One segment (probably a minority) was keenly sensitive to the subtleties and nuance of the performance, was responsive to the more profound ideas and emotions informing the story, and, most significantly perhaps, could follow the libretto (often in Greek) that was sung while the dancer rendered his detailed interpretation. Nevertheless, the nature of the performance ensured that there was plenty for less sophisticated spectators to enjoy as well, and this undoubtedly helped to secure it official support and patronage. It was of course open to abuse and could lapse into bad taste. It was often lascivious and sensual. Juvenal notes the effect of this on susceptible members of the audience: "When the soft Bathyllus[37] dances the role of the gesticulating Leda, Tuccia cannot constrain herself; your Apulian maiden raises a sudden and longing cry of ecstasy, as though embraced by a man; the rustic Thymele is rapt: now is the time that she learns her lessons" (*Sat.* 6.6.6). Ovid warned of the same effects in the Augustan theater, advising the lovelorn not to "indulge in theaters until love has quite deserted your empty heart; zithers, flutes and lyres weaken the resolve, and voices and arms swaying in rhythm. Fictive lovers are constantly danced: the actor by his craft teaches you what to avoid and what pleases you" (*Rem. Amor.* 751–56).

It was probably the potential for sensationalism together with the extraordinary notoriety of some "stars" that accounted for the pantomime's enormous popularity with the masses. The less restrained element in the audience was at times highly volatile and quick to voice its criticism or approval and, if sufficiently charged, to riot. Indeed, five centuries later, the historian Zosimus judged the introduction of pantomime to have been one of the most damaging legacies of Augustus's rule (cf. Jory 1984 and Slater 1994). On one occasion when Pylades was performing the role of the "Mad Hercules," members of the audience began to mock and taunt him for not (in their opinion) observing a dancer's proper movements and rhythms; he appeared uncertain, or possibly inebriated. In a fury, Pylades threw off his mask and upbraided the audience in finest prima donna fashion. "Fools! I *am* dancing the role of a madman!" (Macrob. *Sat.* 2.7.12–16). On another occasion, his depiction of the god Dionysus was said to have "filled the entire City with that deity's unrestrained fury" (*Anth. Pal.* 290). Evidently high-strung himself, once "when a spectator began to hiss, he pointed him out to the entire audience with an obscene gesture of his middle finger" (Suet. *Aug.* 45).

Augustus exiled Pylades from Italy for this offense in 18 B.C. but soon called him back, possibly as one of a number of measures taken to appease popular opposition to the moral legislation of the same year.[38] In general, however, Augustus supported and enjoyed the new art form and considered his patronage of the people's pastime a democratic gesture (Tac. *Ann.* 1.54). Nevertheless, only a few years after its introduction he felt constrained to curb the "pantomania" rampant in the Roman audience. Rivalries between Bathyllus and Pylades (or Pylades' former student, Hylas) led to outbreaks of violence among their supporters. Augustus rebuked Pylades but was in turn admonished by him: "You are ungrateful, Master. Let the people kill their time with us!" (Dio 54.17.4). This suggests that "Augustus should be grateful that the people were concentrating on pantomimes rather than on more important matters, a story which if true suggests that the performer was both politically aware and on close terms with the Emperor" (Jory 1984, 58). Nevertheless, on one occasion Augustus ordered that Hylas be publicly whipped and was meticulous in curbing actors' licentious behavior (*Aug.* 45.4).

Together with other stage performers, the pantomimes (the great majority of whom were foreigners, many of them slaves or freedmen) were subject to severe restrictions. They were denied Roman citizenship, their descendants were banned through the fourth generation from marrying into the senatorial class, and if caught in adultery could be killed with impunity. Augustus was determined that however useful the theater, neither its partisans nor practitioners should be allowed to undermine public decorum or morality. Nevertheless, he indicated his favor and fairness by amending the law that had allowed public officials to beat performers on the merest whim: henceforth they could do so only for offenses committed during the games or other public performances (Suet. *Aug.* 45). From time to time, as a popular gesture, a performer who had won the crowd's support might be freed, and a successful pantomime could earn substantial sums of money. By the end of his life, Pylades was sufficiently wealthy to give private games at his own expense in 2 B.C. and sufficiently respectable to present both equestrians and women on stage without incurring Augustus's censure (Dio 55.10.11).

The advent and popularity of the new art of pantomime in Rome were probably in large part due to the encouragement and opportunities provided it by a regime that saw in its practice a useful medium both for mass entertainment and for embodying and popularizing the classical mythology and traditional beliefs so central to the ideology of the principate. As Augustus's own account of his career in the *Res Gestae* makes clear, the festivals and spectacle entertainments (of which pantomime became a major element) were — in addition to an expression of his *dignitas* and *auctoritas* — a major and defining element in the evolving relationship between the *Princeps* and his people.

> The Senate decreed that vows for my health should be offered by the consuls and priests every five years. In accordance with these vows, games have frequently been held in my honor during my lifetime, sometimes by the four principal colleges of priests, sometimes by the consuls. [9]
>
> In honor of my homecoming [19 B.C.] the Senate . . . ordered the pontiffs and Vestal Virgins to perform a yearly sacrifice on the anniversary of my return . . . and called the day *Augustalia.* [11]
>
> I built . . . a ceremonial box at the Circus Maximus. [19]
>
> I restored the theater of Pompey at great expense, without any inscription of my name. [20]
>
> I built the theater next to the temple of Apollo . . . to be named after my son-in-law Marcus Marcellus. [21]

Three times I held a gladiatorial spectacle in my own name and five times in the name of my sons or grandsons; in which spectacles some ten thousand men took part in combat. Twice in my own name and a third time in the name of my grandson, I provided a public display of athletes summoned from all parts. I held games four times in my own name and twenty-three times on behalf of other magistrates. . . . I held the Secular games. . . . In my 13th Consulship [2 B.C.] I was the first to hold the Games of Mars, which since then the consuls have held each year by decree of the Senate. . . . I have provided public spectacles of the hunting of wild beasts twenty-six times in my own name or that of my sons and grandsons, in the Circus or the Forum or the amphitheaters, in which some three thousand five hundred beasts have been slaughtered. [22][39]

I provided the public spectacle of a naval battle . . . having excavated an area eighteen hundred feet long by twelve hundred feet wide, where thirty beaked ships and many other smaller vessels joined in battle. In these fleets some three thousand men apart from oarsmen, took part in combats. [23]

Imitations of Immortality

It is interesting to observe that the *Res Gestae,* which Augustus commanded be inscribed on bronze tablets and placed upon his Mausoleum after his death, is in some ways a curiously ambivalent document. Only after his program had been successfully established could his own achievements be celebrated. But if political reforms were to be permanent, they had to be linked to a republican tradition, even while effectively establishing a one-man rule. They would only be successful once "a monarch succeeded in insinuating himself into the role of the foremost defender of the Republic" (Meier 1990, 70). Thus, while enumerating his achievements and many of the honors and offices bestowed upon him, throughout the document Augustus also underscores the restraint he had exercised in refusing many other distinctions: *dignitas* is balanced by decorum, for example, "Although the Senate decreed further triumphs for me, I declined them all. [4] . . . The Dictatorship offered to me both . . . by the people and the Senate [in 22 B.C.] I refused to accept. . . . The Consulship which was offered to me at that time on an annual basis for life, I refused to accept" (5).

Such political ambiguity permeated the Augustan principate, with attitudes ranging from sublime intimations of an idealized golden age of social harmony and universal happiness by some sincere enthusiasts, through tactful equivocation by others, to the squalid hypocrisy of still others who paid lip-service to nobler motives but in reality were content to base the state's institutions (and their own advancement) on brute force, mitigated by little more than wishful thinking and "make-believe."[40] A further level of ambiguity characterized the

presentation and perception of what might be termed the "divinity question."
As noted earlier, Augustus had long been recognized as *Divi Filius,* and the
worship of his *Genius* was already practiced, first privately and later as an
official state god. But in reality it was a "worship of himself, and though it was
veiled in much the same way that Augustus's political power was veiled, it was
effective in securing loyalty to his rule" (Taylor 1931, 245). The sense of his
own immanent (and imminent) divinity was pervasive.[41] Vergil, for example,
in his *Georgics* had not only celebrated early in Octavian's reign his coming
deification (1.22 ff.) but also suggested that it might occur before his departure from earth (40–42). Horace later had done the same: "Augustus shall be
deemed a god on earth for adding to our empire the Britons and dread Parthians" (*Odes* 3.5.1–4). Around 22 B.C. Propertius had referred to him simply
as Deus Caesar (3.4.1).

Augustus had declined during his lifetime formally to be worshiped as a
god, in a temple, content instead to act as one who had been chosen for his
mission by the gods and was their agent and representative on earth. He recognized that it was prudent and expedient for his program to present himself in
reality as a Roman citizen, yet at the same time his special relationship with
heaven encouraged richly ambiguous rhetorical and allegorical expression. It
was Ovid who perhaps best captured in artistic form in his *Metamorphoses* —
which may be interpreted as a metaphor for the world of the principate — the
sense of a *theatrum mundi* where everything was constantly undergoing pervasive transformation and nothing was ever quite what it seemed. In describing through his poetry "a world in which individual human agents are helpless
before the willful and apparently boundless power of the Olympians," he may
be suggesting in reality that "the political order as currently constituted is
dysfunctional; that the State may be dying — or already be dead" without
anyone noticing (Nugent 1990, 256).

Despite such potentially subversive expression (which may in fact have led
to his final disgrace and exile),[42] Ovid played the role assigned him as a poet of
the principate, pointing out that the ultimate and most stunning transformation, that of Augustus into a god, was yet to take place but surely would. As he
plaintively reminded Augustus from exile, in the *Metamorphoses* his account
of mythic transformations had culminated in the apotheosis of Julius Caesar
and the coming deification of Augustus: "We sang too, though the final touch
was missing from our undertaking, of bodies transformed into new appearances" (*Tr.* 2.555–56), although earlier, in the revision of the *Ars Amatoria* (in
about 1 B.C.),[43] he had boldly linked "Father Mars and Father Caesar . . . for of
the two of you, one is a god, and one will be" (202–3).

In addition to extensive political and artistic propaganda, not least that celebrated in the new theaters and festivals, the Roman spectators had had before them for decades the monumental "stage set" of Augustus's great Mausoleum. Traditionally in Rome the remains of the dead (once the funeral had taken place) did not figure in the religious or ceremonial life of the state and were confined outside the city, denying the great families an opportunity visually to assert their preeminence through the provision of spectacular tombs dominating the cityscape. By contrast, in the Hellenistic world, protocol had long dictated that the founder of a city had the privilege of being buried and commemorated near its center. In building his great memorial edifice, Augustus "was not only overcoming an ancient taboo, he was also making a clear political statement about his new position, and that which his successors would inherit" (North 1983, 169). He had begun its construction around 32 B.C. when he was only thirty years old, and his greatest achievements, including the crucial defeat of Antony, had not yet taken place. Indeed, it served graphically to remind everyone that, in contrast to Antony, who intended to be buried in Alexandria, Octavian and his family would be interred in Rome. It was prominently located in open ground in the Campus Martius, with a great public park attached to it (Suet. *Aug.* 100.4; Strabo 5.236). Its triumphal scale (almost 300 feet in diameter and 120 feet high) and isolation ensured that it physically dominated the landscape, while its suggestion of an archaic hero's grave of the distant past and its placement in the symbolic setting of the Campus must have had a strongly provocative impact on the imagination as well.[44] Even its name directly evoked that wonder of the world, the massive and magnificent tomb of Mausolus constructed over three centuries earlier at Halicarnassus.

Augustus's structure, moreover, had already provided the venue for the great and solemn state spectacles marking the funerals of his anticipated heirs: Marcellus, in 23 B.C., Lucius, in A.D. 2; Gaius, in A.D. 4; and that of Livia's son by her first marriage, Drusus the Elder (father of Germanicus and Claudius), in 9 B.C. On that occasion Augustus had himself accompanied the body of his stepson all the way from Ticinum (Pavia) to Rome. There a magnificent funeral took place, the bier (probably on the Rostra Caesaris) in the Forum surrounded by statues of Julio-Claudian ancestors, the eulogy offered by Drusus's elder brother Tiberius. A second oration was delivered in the Circus Flaminius by Augustus himself before the body was borne by a great concourse of knights to the Campus Martius, where it was cremated and the ashes interred in the Mausoleum (Dio 55.2.1–3.; Tac. *Ann.* 3.5). As a veritable temple-in-waiting for the Gens Iulia, crowned by a colossal statue of Augustus, the Mausoleum was a striking emblem of emergent imperial mythology and the focus of the regime's most potent pageantry (fig. 21).

Fig. 21. The Mausoleum of Augustus as it appears today after the excavations and restoration carried out 1936–1938. (Fototeca Unione at the American Academy in Rome)

Following their untimely deaths, Gaius and Lucius, Augustus's grandsons, were honored by Senate decree with a formal state cult, which included special offerings by magistrates on the anniversaries of their deaths, and they may have been further venerated by the designation of sections in the theater named in their honor.[45] Throughout the empire, arches, altars, and buildings were erected in their names, and in Rome a monumental portico was erected next to the temple of Divus Iulius — in effect for a triumph they never celebrated — and the Basilica Iulia was rededicated to them in A.D. 12. Their cult was suggestive of the type of hero worship long practiced in Greek cities but was also thoroughly integrated into the new Julian mythology that was increasingly concerned with the evolving cult of Augustus himself. In A.D. 2 Dio records that "a sacred contest was decreed in Naples . . . because its inhabitants . . . tried in a manner to imitate the customs of the Greeks" (Dio 55.10.9; Strabo 5.246). This festival, the *Sebasta,* modeled on the Olympic games, was to take place every four years, and it made use of a temple to Augustus, which evidently was similar to those already devoted to his worship in the Hellenistic East but which had previously been absent in Italy (Dio 51.20). In the Greek world, the imperial cult, with its assertion of the emperor's divinity, drew on symbols from traditional Hellenistic religious practice that thereby "helped to construct (in a social sense) the emperor and Roman power for the Greeks of Asia" in terms familiar to them (Ostrow 1990, 378; cf. Galinsky 1996, 322–26). Theater ceremonial undoubtedly figured significantly in such a process. During the last years of Augustus's reign, following the precedent of Naples, temples including special priests (ostensibly dedicated to the worship of his *Genius*) began to be established in Italy, and in Rome itself his cult continued to be recognized at his house on the Palatine, on the Capitol, and at the temple of Mars Ultor (Taylor 1931, 214 ff.).

At the games in A.D. 13 marking Augustus's birthday (September 23), during the Circus races "a madman seated himself in the chair dedicated to Julius Caesar, and taking his crown, put it on. This incident disturbed everybody, since it seemed to have some bearing on Augustus, as indeed, proved true" (Dio 56.29.1–2). The following August, the *Princeps* attended the musical and gymnastic events marking the fourth celebration of the Sebasta given in his honor at Naples (Suet. *Aug.* 98). Two weeks later, on August 19 (the anniversary of his first consulate fifty-seven years earlier), he died at age seventy-six in Nola, south of Rome.

After gazing at his image in a mirror, Augustus inquired as he died if he had played the mime of life well and deserved to be applauded as he left the stage. But a final vital postlude remained to be performed, for which he left detailed staging instructions. Through the ritual pageantry of the funeral his divinity, which had been the object of elaborate allegorical imagery, must now with the ultimate suspension of any lingering disbelief become "real." First, at a meeting of the Senate his will was read, making Tiberius his heir and distributing large sums of money to the citizenry. In four additional documents deposited the previous year with the Vestal Virgins, he provided detailed orders for his funeral; an extensive document for public display (the *Res Gestae*) listing his honors, his benefactions, his expeditions and conquests, and a statement about his position in the Roman state; an account of military and financial resources; and injunctions and advice for Tiberius and the Roman people.

The state funeral followed. At the head of the procession was the statue of Augustus's patron goddess, Victory, which he had placed on a pillar behind the seats of the consuls in the Curia Iulia at its dedication in 29 B.C., following his Actium triumph (Suet. *Aug.* 100; Dio 51.22.1). Augustus's body was borne from his home on the Palatine in a coffin placed on an ivory and gold couch, on the top of which rested a wax image dressed in triumphal garb. A second image of gold was brought from the Senate, and a third was carried in a triumphal chariot. These preceded the *imagines* of the Julian family, which were followed by one of Romulus, who headed up those of other deceased notable Romans (including Pompey). The wax images were accompanied by figures appropriately costumed to personify all the nations Augustus had added to the empire. The inclusion of nonrelations in a solemn procession traditionally limited to ancestors was a deliberate dramaturgical choice, which by breaking with convention imbued the event with a symbolic expressiveness conveying its timeless and universal significance. Earlier Augustus had done a similar thing in permanent form when "next to the immortal gods he honored the memory of those leaders who had raised the Roman Empire from small beginnings to greatness. Accordingly . . . when erecting statues of men in triumphal dress in the two porticoes of his forum, he declared he had done so in order that citizens might measure both himself and succeeding *principes* by the standard set by such men" (Suet. *Aug.* 31.5). Thus, even in his funeral procession, Augustus conveyed a political and religious message, visually locating himself and his family in the unfolding cavalcade of Roman history so that the centrality of their role would be communicated through the instructive spectacle of the procession that wound down into the ceremonial heart of Rome in the Forum. Because of his divinity, Julius Caesar was not impersonated among the ancestral images. His presence was felt, however, when, following a short eulogy by the younger Drusus at the Rostra Caesaris (which Caesar had established and which had probably been completed by Augustus), the main encomium was delivered by Livia's son Tiberius from the Rostra Iulia in front of Caesar's temple of Divus Iulius.

It was a highly evocative spot, the site where Caesar had been cremated and the earliest altar had been erected to his divinity; the interior of the temple now housed his colossal statue, while its pediment displayed a star representing the comet that marked his apotheosis. The platform of the *rostra* itself (some ten feet high) was decorated with the prows of ships taken at Actium, and immediately flanking it to the south stood the great triumphal arch voted by the Senate to honor Augustus in 19 B.C. on the occasion of the return of the standards from Parthia (Dio 51.19.2). Tiberius, clearly conscious of how the associations of the place would powerfully color his eulogy and amplify its emotional impact, had "issued an edict warning the public against the same excessive enthusiasm that they had displayed at the funeral of Julius Caesar," emphasizing that there was no question of the carefully scripted scenario being upstaged by an improvised cremation such as took place during the tumultuous performance of March 44 B.C. (Tac. *Ann.* 8). Following a lengthy laudatory account and interpretation of Augustus's legacy, the procession resumed and progressed through the Campus Martius, while choirs of children — sons and daughters from the great noble families — sang dirges. Augustus's body was carried by the consuls and other magistrates (with senators, knights, and much of Rome's population in their train) past the panoramic backdrop of the many shining monuments newly built or refurbished during his reign. At the pyre it was encircled successively by the priests, knights, cavalrymen, and infantry, all of whom threw upon it their various medals, decorations, and insignia. The centurions kindled it. "So it was consumed, and an eagle released from it flew aloft, appearing to bear his spirit to heaven" (Dio 56.42.3). The priestly colleges later gathered the ashes and interred them in the Mausoleum.

A senator and former praetor, Numerius Atticus, swore under oath (and on cue) that he had seen Augustus's spirit soaring up to Heaven through the flames, just as tradition recorded had occurred at the death of Romulus. Thus persuaded by the combined pressures of propaganda, pageantry, and direct evidence, on September 17 the Senate formally established the state cult of Divus Augustus, subsequently ordering annual games in his honor (the *ludi Augustales,* October 5–12) and the provision of a temple, with Germanicus appointed the first priest and Livia the first priestess. She bestowed a million sesterces upon Numerius in recognition of his perspicacious piety (Dio 56.46).

The first celebration of the new games was entrusted not, as was now customary for state *ludi,* to the praetors but to the tribunes. The Senate had decreed that the consuls should henceforth be in charge of the games established earlier to mark Augustus's birthday (September 23), and by placing these which followed only two weeks later in the hands of the tribunes, the Senate may have wished to symbolize "the twin pillars of Augustus's rule, *imperium* equal to the consuls and *tribunicia potestas*" (Jory 1984, 60). The tribunes thereupon petitioned to give the games at their personal expense and (perhaps in consideration of this) asked to be allowed to wear the triumphal gold-embroidered purple gown and use the chariot customarily granted magistrates presiding at games in the Circus. The Senate refused their offer, mindful perhaps of the troubles which such private expenditure by ambitious officials had caused in the past before Augustus curbed the practice. They were, however, granted the triumphal dress, though not the chariot (Tac. *Ann.* 1.15). Dio suggests that these and other decisions thought to have been made "nominally by the Senate . . . were actually made by Tiberius and Livia" (Dio 56.46.5). The attitude of Tiberius, who did not share his predecessor's enthusiasm for games, is thus probably reflected in the limited public grant allocated for the new games. This was so small that one of the most popular pantomime stars refused to appear for the allotted fee. Riots ensued, and to avoid further unseemly disruption of these, the first games honoring the deified Augustus, the tribunes summoned the Senate and persuaded it to increase its meager allowance (Dio 56.47.2). Nevertheless the atmosphere was soured and further disturbances occurred during the performances. It was an inauspicious beginning for the post-Augustan age. And there could be no more immediate or graphic demonstration of what Rome had lost when its great emperor-impresario retired to Olympus.

Playing for Keeps

The Politics of Pageantry in the Early Principate

Tiberius described himself as "holding a wolf by its ears" (Suet. *Tib.* 25) when, as Augustus's fifty-six-year-old heir, he was faced with exercising supreme power through a role and institutions that had been specifically molded for his stepfather and that thereby reflected a personality fundamentally different from his own. Indeed, his respect for Augustus's achievement and talents was so great that he almost certainly felt inhibited both by a sense of his own inadequacy in assuming his new role and by a concern not to diminish the luster of his revered predecessor. After the death of his natural father—Livia's first husband, Tiberius Claudius Nero—for whom he had delivered the funeral eulogy in 32 B.C. when he was nine, Tiberius had been raised in Octavian's household and duly participated in imperial pomp, riding one of the horses drawing Octavian's chariot at his Actium triumph, taking a leading role in the *lusus Troiae,* and sponsoring gladiatorial games for his father and grandfather in the Forum and Statilius Taurus's new amphitheater, respectively. Suetonius notes that there were theatrical performances as well but that, tellingly, Tiberius did not attend them (*Tib.* 7).

Later, however, as far as the demands of an impressive military career would allow, he attempted to avoid the glare of public life, first withdrawing to Rhodes, where he studied philosophy (6 B.C.–A.D. 2) and after returning to Rome, "merely attending his personal affairs and exercising no public functions" (Suet. *Tib.* 15). But his adoption by Augustus in June of A.D. 4 (following the deaths of Gaius and Lucius) and the formal bestowal of both the *tribunicia potestas* and proconsular imperium marked him as future *Princeps* and demanded public prominence. In A.D. 12, after military successes in his Illyricum campaign, Tiberius had celebrated a (postponed) triumph at which Augustus presided and (as custom urged) gave a great public banquet, distributed gifts of money, and also employed the spoils of victory lavishly to restore the temple of Concord and completely rebuild that of Castor and Pollux (*Tib.* 22; Dio 55.8.2, 55.27.4). Nevertheless, Tiberius appears to have been genuinely reluctant to assume the burdens of the principate, and his ambivalence was reinforced by his temperament and the lack of any precedent or formal procedure for determining the succession.

Augustus had deliberately created through his reform of the constitution a veritable hall of mirrors in which the boundaries and lineaments of imperial offices and powers were difficult to discern but which, consummate actor and impresario that he was, he had mastered with great skill and success. His gift for public relations overcame a problem noted by Oscar Wilde: "To be natural . . . is such a very difficult pose to keep up" (*An Ideal Husband,* act 1). By contrast, Tiberius (as Tacitus observed), although he valued dissimulation, was a poor actor, and lacked Augustus's unfailing sense of theatricality. "Even when he did not aim at concealment, he was — by habit or nature — always hesitant, always cryptic" (Tac. *Ann.* 1.11). When by contrast he was "determined to conceal his real feelings, his words became more and more ambiguous and obscure" (Tac. *Ann.* 1.11). "In fact, the true dissimulation stemmed not from the man, but from the system which he had inherited, the product of the great illusionist Augustus; it was only underlined by his successor's maladroitness" (Stockton 1988, 142). During the extended deliberations on the issue of succession, he found himself at once in difficulty with an essentially suppliant but still fretful and occasionally sullen Senate that became so exasperated at his diffidence and equivocation over assuming Augustus's title that one senator, tiring of the "impudent farce," finally cried out, "Let him take it or leave it!" In fact Tiberius was only tentatively engaging in a "comedy of refusing power" ostensibly offered by the Senate, which thereafter was conventionally enacted by both senators and emperors — each aware of the essential absurdity of the situation — at the beginning of each new regime (cf. Veyne 1990, 410). Despite repeated pressure (and as a mark of his undoubtedly genuine veneration of Augustus), he refused to assume various trappings of power or such overblown titles as "Father of his Country," although in the end he did accept the confirmation of his imperium "until I come to the time when it may seem proper to you to give an old man some rest" (Suet. *Tib.* 24). Indeed, he often attempted to maintain and enhance the constitutional role and responsibility of a Senate that did not trust him and to demonstrate respect for a public that, "unconvinced of his sincerity," felt little affection for him (Tac. *Ann.* 1.72). From the first, Tiberius's rule was marked by social and political tension.[1]

Tiberius does not appear to have been naturally ruthless, and still less a tyrant. Early in his reign he defended a knight charged with "admitting a mime actor who was a male prostitute to the cult honoring Augustus" by piously pointing out that "Augustus had not been voted divine honors in order to ensnare Roman citizens," and adding that the same actor "had often taken part in the games which Livia had dedicated to Augustus' memory" (Tac. *Ann.* 1.73). But, despite such tolerance, "even when acting fairly his essential austerity made a bad impression" (Tac. *Ann.* 1.75), and his lack of the "common touch" was graphically signaled during the same period by his absence from the sensational gladiatorial contests given jointly by his natural son, Drusus, and Germanicus, the son of Tiberius's deceased brother, Drusus, whom he had adopted in A.D. 4.[2] "Various reasons were given [for his antipathy toward such entertainments]. His dislike of crowds, or morose nature, or reluctance to be compared to Augustus, who had cheerfully attended" (Tac. *Ann.* 1.76). Tiberius by contrast not only stayed away but condemned the single combat of knights that had graced his sons' games and forbade such unseemly fun in the future (Dio 57.14.3). He displayed a similarly unfestive nature when, shortly after assuming power, he could be persuaded only with difficulty "to let his birthday [November 16], which fell on the day of the Plebeian games in the Circus, be honored by the addition of a single two-horse chariot" (Suet. *Tib.* 26).

The Emperor Who Was Not Amused

This apparent disdain for popular pastimes, coupled with an aloof personality, was a serious "public relations" error that caused suspicion and resentment, the expression of which did little to lend Tiberius confidence in the administration of what he viewed as vexatious burdens of office or to ease a melancholic disposition. Thus the great public entertainments that Augustus had so successfully employed as engines of personal popularity and celebrations of imperial ideology became for Tiberius an irksome responsibility at best and at worst a subversive threat in what Tacitus termed *theatralis licentia* (Tac. *Ann.* 1.77, 13.24). The lower classes in Rome not only desired that their *Princeps* provide for their physical needs and security but that he confront them face-to-face and seem genuinely to enjoy the popular entertainments that it was his duty to provide. To them, Tiberius's attitude seemed insulting, and his grudging and miserly provision of games humiliating.

In A.D. 15 trouble again broke out in the theater, when troops (who were probably regularly stationed there after the disturbances of the previous year) were forced to intervene to curb rioting and insults to the magistrates.[3] This resulted in the death and injury of spectators and soldiers. A centurion died, and a tribune of the Praetorian Guard was seriously wounded. This incident had to be handled judiciously, because under the new conditions of the principate, "whether their behavior was spontaneous . . . or organized, the spectators present at the public games were undoubtedly regarded as expressing the will of the Roman People" (Nippel 1995, 90). When the matter was debated in the Senate, it was proposed that praetors be given the power to whip pantomimes; the proposal was vetoed by the tribune of the people, however, on the grounds that Augustus had previously exempted the performers from such summary punishment and to change the practice would be an act of desecration. Augustus's wish must be respected. Tiberius was resented for allowing a sham debate as "the senators amused themselves with a show of liberty," although in fact whatever the outcome, "Tiberius would not presume to alter" the Augustan precedent (Tac. *Ann.* 1.77). Instead other measures were taken, including placing strict limits on pantomimes' pay, allowing performances only inside the theater, which could be adequately policed, and prohibiting performers from receiving senators in their homes or being accompanied in public by members of the equestrian order. Spectators who misbehaved were subject to banishment by order of the praetors.

The nature of the pantomime performances, with their emphasis on the interpretive skill, imagination, and physical virtuosity of an individual artist, naturally encouraged intense rivalry and partisanship. Moreover, as the commentator Lucian noted, the mythological selections enacted tended to depict characters in states of intense emotion, the performer "introducing now a lover and now an angry person, one man afflicted with madness, another with grief" (*De Salt.* 67). As Jory notes (1984, 63–64), "This concern with the portrayal of individuals in a state of emotional crisis . . . seems to have produced a reaction among the audience which was intensified by the fact that the performer was a soloist." The absence of an ensemble of characters through whom the spectators' attention and empathy could be diffused, together with the competitive nature of the performances (and consequently the development of factions fanatically devoted to one artist or another), introduced a volatile element into the theatrical performances in Rome that had not been present earlier and that, under the new political conditions dictating that the theater represent a veritable microcosm of society, inevitably demanded official intervention and control. In contrast, the chariot races and the violent contests in the arena provoked virtually no disorder, encouraging contemporary Romans to praise the morally edifying qualities of the *munera* while condemning theatrical performances as seditious and licentious.

The determined attempt to curb the increasing public passion for pantomimes, though prudent, was undoubtedly unpopular. Although Velleius Paterculus recorded with approval that "rioting in the theater has been suppressed" (2.126.2), the measures ultimately proved ineffective, in part because the performers enjoyed a degree of protection from Drusus, Tiberius's son. As Consul at the time, he refrained from taking strong action — indicating perhaps a greater deference to public opinion than that shown by his father (Dio 57.14.10). But for a while at least, Tiberius himself feigned an interest he did not feel in the festivals, attending them out of a sense of duty and "to ensure the orderliness of the crowd and to seem to be sharing their holiday. But in fact, he never felt the slightest enthusiasm for anything of the kind" (Dio 57.11.5–6).

To some extent Tiberius's disdain for the theater reflected his shyness and a marked antipathy to flattery. Like Augustus before him, he indignantly refused to be called *Dominus* (Tac. *Ann.* 2.87) but also resisted what he viewed as the unseemly pomp and spectacle that his predecessor had so astutely employed to impress the populace and encourage patriotism. His dislike, however, had other causes as well. Under Augustus, as an extension of the pageantry of state and to give the public a more active role and sense of involvement, it had become customary for individuals or groups within the audience to present requests to the *Princeps* at the venues for public entertainment. As Josephus noted, "The Romans are wonderfully serious about being spectators. They collect eagerly in the Circus and, forming a mob, make demands of the emperors for what they want; and those who decree that their requests should not be opposed never go without gratitude" (*Ant. Iud.* 19.24). This gave the crowd the vital sense, which it demanded and cherished, of enjoying the respect of the ruler, who also benefited from the exchange. "Provided that it did not get out of hand, even a hostile demonstration could ease a difficult situation. A grievance aired, even if fruitlessly, is a grievance halved" (Cameron 1976, 173).

Tiberius, however, appears to have resented the arrangement, either out of arrogance or, more charitably, because he genuinely felt that such demagoguery demeaned both him and the Roman people. According to Suetonius, one of the reasons he stayed away from the theater was to avoid having to receive and acquiesce to such requests, "particularly after the crowd forced him, on one of his rare visits to the theater, to buy the freedom of a slave-comedian named Actius" (*Tib.* 47). Dio adds that he resisted the demand until the performer's master had consented and been reimbursed (Dio 57.11.6). On another occasion spectators successfully pressured Tiberius to return to public display the famous *Apoxyomenos,* a statue of a naked athlete by Lysippus that Tiberius had removed from its place in front of the baths of Agrippa, allegedly to his bedroom (Pliny *N.H.* 34.62). In A.D. 19 he was forced to fix prices after a public protest over the high cost of corn (Tac. *Ann.* 2.87). The problem recurred more dangerously in A.D. 32 (when Tiberius was no longer in Rome), causing near insurrection in the city while "for several days sweeping demands were shouted in the theater with a presumption rarely displayed to emperors" (Tac. *Ann.* 6.13). Tiberius sternly reprimanded the officials for not taking the measures necessary to curb such popular demonstrations but when they subsequently did, kept silent, thereby vainly hoping to avoid public opprobrium.

A startling example of the manner in which public opinion might be expressed at the games occurred in A.D. 20 during the trial of Aemilia Lepida, great-granddaughter of both Sulla and Pompey, who was accused of various crimes including adultery, fraud, ominous astrological readings (concerning the outlook for the imperial house), and poisoning. Tacitus, who points out that she was disreputable and guilty, records that "the trial was interrupted by games. While they took place, Aemilia Lepida, together with other distinguished ladies, entered the theater and with weeping and lamentation called upon her ancestors, including that same Pompey whose monuments and statues stood there visible to all. The crowd, moved to pity and weeping, howled savage curses down upon Quirinius [the prosecutor]" (Tac. *Ann.* 3.23). Clearly Lepida understood how to use the theatrical potential of her own tragic circumstance and the suggestive power of the setting; to "work" the audience, she secured a markedly lenient sentence of banishment.

One of the major factors encouraging the use of the theaters and circus for political exchange was the gradual disappearance of such expression from the traditional voting assemblies and the displacement of their function into public entertainments where the populace could directly express its opinion to the emperor. As noted in the previous chapter, Augustus had limited the opportunity of competing politicians to use the games to further individual ambition, as had so often occurred in the late Republic with malignant results. Although nominally allowing the venerable popular assemblies to continue functioning, Augustus ensured that their decisions closely reflected the judgment of the *Princeps.* Tiberius transferred the elections to the Senate at the very beginning of his rule, and the popular assemblies were employed merely to ratify the list of candidates. "The people would thereafter play only a ceremonial role in certain official pageants" (Veyne 1990, 385).

The new arrangement pleased almost everyone. Tiberius was generally able to approve all the candidates, and those he endorsed directly were assured of election. Although regretting the loss of genuine power, the senators were glad they no longer had to endure the trouble and indignity of traditional canvassing — under Augustus it had become illegal to give largess to the electors — and the public raised no serious objection to the loss of its former privilege (Suet. *Aug.* 40; Tac. *Ann.* 1.15). Increasingly the assemblies had become irrelevant as the people took advantage of the opportunity provided by the games to address their grievances directly to the one most effectively able to satisfy them. In effect the games "performed the safety-valve function of the Republic's popular assemblies" (Nippel 1995, 87). Thus the new conditions reinforced and extended an important political function of the games that had first begun to emerge in them during the last years of the Republic. "The theater became the single most important locus of contact between the leaders of the State and their people" (Potter 1996, 144).

In light of their enhanced importance, Tiberius's neglect of the games must have decidedly offended the populace, whose reactions in turn irritated the emperor. He was particularly alarmed by the tendency of the senatorial and equestrian order to display themselves on stage and in the arena. Senators and their sons had been banned from such performance since 38 B.C., and in 22 B.C. the ban was extended to the equestrian order, whose members were entitled by birth to seats in the first fourteen rows of the theater (Dio 48.43.2, 54.2.5). But these measures had little effect — Suetonius notes (*Tib.* 35.2) that to evade the law and appear on stage or in the arena, both senators and knights deliberately got themselves expelled from their orders — and by A.D. 11 they were so disregarded that in a new regulation the prohibition on knights was at least relaxed for particular occasions, if not lifted entirely. Thereafter even Augustus watched their contests (Dio 56.25.7 ff.), and in A.D. 15, Tiberius allowed the precedent, although he would not himself deign to attend. The measure of A.D. 11 did, however, place restrictions on the age of participants: freeborn women had to be twenty or older, and men twenty-five .[4]

Tiberius continued (and even extended) Augustus's policy of reinforcing traditional social structures and class distinctions, in part by defining and maintaining the particular privileges appropriate to each rank. The Augustan marriage laws, for example, had encouraged intermarriage within the upper classes while outlawing members of senatorial families down to great-grandchildren in the male line from marrying freed persons, actors, and their children. The elaborate seating regulations in the theater and amphitheater reflected a similar concern to maintain social cohesion by demonstrating to those who benefited from the increased upward mobility that the winning of greater status did not mean appropriate rules for conduct could be relaxed. "What had to be made clear to the established aristocracy and to those who were moving up into and within it was that its values were unchanged and that it was worth entering" (Levick 1983, 115).

Although not mentioned by ancient historians, a senatorial decree of A.D. 19 inscribed on a bronze tablet found at Larinum in northern Apulia recorded further measures by Tiberius against public performances by members of the upper orders.[5] It reintroduced the ban on performance by knights, condemning those who "had become professional gladiators or had appeared on stage," and reiterated the age restrictions that had been imposed in A.D. 11. The decree made it unlawful for any descendant of a senator down to great-grandchildren to appear on stage or in the arena; for knights the restriction applied down to their grandchildren and also forbade the appearance by anyone whose brother was a knight. The decree emphasized that restrictions upon such relatives was intended to address the possibility that its reimposition of the ban on knights (relaxed in A.D. 11) might again induce them deliberately to have themselves expelled from their order so that they might perform in public. Their curiously persistent desire to do so may indicate that some in the upper orders found the recently imposed restrictions on traditional political rivalry and competition — which for generations had been a defining feature of the Roman character — so intolerable that they turned to other outlets through which to express and satisfy the impulse. "Competition did not cease, but . . . the possibility of competing with all one's wits and powers against a worthy foe, an equal opponent, was absent, and thus a fundamental condition of *gloria* and *dignitas* was absent" (Barton 1993, 28). In any case, the new measures were apparently successful in bringing an end to public performances by members of both the senatorial and equestrian orders for the rest of Tiberius's reign.

Public dislike of Tiberius was forcefully demonstrated at the end of A.D. 19. In October the vastly admired hero, Germanicus, died at Antioch at age thirty-three. Amid hysteria and the near collapse of public order, it had been rumored that Tiberius himself had a hand in the suspicious death of his adopted son. Germanicus was a handsome, intelligent, charismatic, and occasionally histrionic leader — he even composed comedies in Greek — "with the ability of winning universal respect and affection," whose popular esteem probably in part reflected the contempt widely felt for Tiberius (Suet. *Tib.* 3). Only two and a half years earlier, on May 26, A.D. 17, he had enjoyed a memorable triumph at which there was a great display of spoils and captives as well as scenic reconstructions of the mountains, rivers, and battles that had figured in his German campaign (Tac. *Ann.* 2.41.2–4).

There were now extraordinary displays of public sorrow as Germanicus's thirty-one-year-old widow, Agrippina the Elder, grief-stricken and ill — but evidently understanding the importance of timing — undertook a dangerous winter sea voyage to bring his ashes back to Italy, arriving in late December or early January. Following a grand entrance at Brundisium that was watched by vast crowds of mourners as her oarsmen rowed into the harbor at a funereal pace, she made a spectacular procession on foot all the way back to Rome. She was accompanied by two cohorts of Praetorian Guards and joined by local officials, ordinary citizens and, on the outskirts of the city, consuls as well as senators (Barrett 1996, 30–31; cf. Kokkinos 1992, 37–39). After such a prelude, the resentment and suspicion directed at Tiberius was raised to fever pitch when it was observed that Germanicus's funeral lacked pageantry and that the emperor (evidently disdainful of the frenzied atmosphere) had not taken part in the ceremonies. "What had become of the traditional customs? The image placed upon the bier, the poems of eulogy, the panegyrics?" (Tac. *Ann.* 3.5–6). Resentment seethed for months, and Tiberius eventually issued a statement seeking to assuage such protest, urging the public to "return to your usual occupations — and with the *ludi Megalenses* at hand, to your pleasures" (Tac. *Ann.* 3.5–6). But this message — with its air of condescension — could not atone for his failure to be *seen* to participate in the funeral spectacle.[6]

The resentment felt over the lack of appropriate funereal pomp was reawakened four years later, in A.D. 23, by the impressive funeral of Tiberius's own son, Drusus, at which "Aeneas . . . all the Alban kings, Romulus . . . the Sabine nobles . . . and images of all the others of the Claudian line were exhibited in a long procession" (Tac. *Ann.* 4.9). On this occasion, Tiberius initially won sympathy when he addressed the Senate but lost it when, overplaying his part, he destroyed his credibility by "insincere and ridiculous talk of restoring the Republic and returning the government to the consuls, or anyone else willing to assume the burden."

Drusus's death left the pantomimes without their greatest advocate in the imperial household. That, or the increasingly intolerable behavior of the performers and their partisans, finally encouraged the emperor to take decisive action. "After frequent and ineffective complaints by the praetors, Tiberius denounced the licentiousness of the pantomimes as subversive of public order and private morality. . . . They were banished from Italy" (Tac. *Ann.* 4.14). Dio notes specifically that the performers had "debauched women and stirred up tumults" (57.21.3), and Suetonius adds that the problem arose above all from the violence of partisan support for rival actors. Tiberius exiled the faction leaders *(capita factionum)*, who presumably directed the claques, and the performers themselves, and thereafter adamantly refused public pressure for their return, which did not occur until Caligula recalled them in A.D. 37 (*Tib.* 37.2;

cf. Tac. *Ann.* 1.77; Dio 59.2.5). This action and, for good measure, similar strictures against the beloved Oscan farces, which "had become so degraded and influential" that they ought to be repressed, further solidified popular resentment.

For all this the public took its revenge. Early in his reign his frequent but unhonored promises that he was about to tour the provinces "earned him the nickname of 'Callipedes' after a comic actor famous for his realistic imitation of a long-distance runner, in which he never moved from the same spot" (Suet. *Tib.* 38). Later, the worsening relationship between the emperor and his people led to more bitter criticism. He was even blamed for a terrible accident that occurred in A.D. 27 when a temporary amphitheater collapsed, resulting in a huge loss of life. It had been hastily constructed by unscrupulous speculators a few miles north of Rome in Fidenae after Tiberius (having already expelled the pantomimes) had restricted hunting and gladiatorial spectacles in the city. "The people, deprived of their usual diversions by Tiberius, had flocked to the site, eager for entertainment" (Dio 58.1; Tac. *Ann.* 4.62).

Eventually the emperor was deeply unpopular; in the course of his reign, he became increasingly morbid and paranoid, more repressive of dissent, and, in his last years of self-imposed exile on Capri, cruel and vindictive. This tendency was particularly marked after the conspiracy of Sejanus in A.D. 31, whom a decade earlier Tiberius had termed "the partner of my labors" and even honored with a bronze statue in the theater of Pompey when it was repaired following a fire (Tac. *Ann.* 4.2, 3.72; Dio 57.21).[7] Tiberius remained on Capri from 26 until his death eleven years later.

"Tiberius' departure for Capri was the last straw. The people wanted their leader to be near them, wanted him to grieve with them in the misfortunes and rejoice with them in their joys. To the *plebs urbana* the presence of the emperor in Rome was a matter of importance, since a gift from afar was unwelcome" (Yavetz 1969, 112). The Roman people evidently assuaged their resentment at his contempt for their entertainments and his refusal even to show himself by sharp jokes at his expense and the spread of lurid tales about alleged depravities on his island retreat. The rumor that a woman he had attempted to ravish had subsequently killed herself cursing "that filthy-mouthed old goat" resulted in "a joke slipped into an Atellan farce at the next games, prompting great applause and widely recounted, that 'the old goat was licking the does'" (Suet. *Tib.* 45).[8] A playwright who composed a tragedy that provocatively presented Agamemnon as a tyrant is said to have been accused of slander and publicly executed. Both he and a writer of history who dared to speak well of Brutus and Cassius "were punished and their writings destroyed, although these had won approval several years earlier when they were recited with Augustus himself in the audience" (*Tib.* 61). Unlike Augustus, who evidently understood that an overtly negative response would serve only to ratify the offensive potential of such writings, Tiberius, as Dio notes, "in scrutinizing in detail and accuracy everything that people were accused of saying about him slanderously, reviled himself with all the bad things being said" (57.23.1). When Mamercus Aemilius Scaurus wrote a tragedy on the myth of Atreus, Tiberius took offense at the line (quoted by Scaurus from Euripides' version) advising a character "to bear with the folly of the ruler," claiming that the line was spoken against him and that "he was Atreus because of Atreus' bloodthirstiness." Demonstrating both his knowledge of mythology (and also, it would seem, the correctness of the offending accusation), Tiberius remarked, "I in turn will make of him an Ajax," and forced the playwright to commit suicide (Dio 58.24.3–5).[9]

Tiberius's sensitivity on matters relating to the theater was further demonstrated when the orator Junius Gallio (who adopted Seneca the Younger's elder brother, Lucius Annaeus) made the mistake in A.D. 32 of suggesting that former praetorian guardsmen should be honored with seats in the fourteen rows reserved in the theater for the equestrian order. Tiberius sent a letter to the Senate that was written as if he were there in person sternly reprimanding Gallio. He reminded Gallio that only the emperor gave orders and rewards to the soldiers and, moreover, who was Gallio to improve upon the arrangements laid down by the Divine Augustus? Or was it his intention to gain subversive influence over the soldiers by offering such privileges? Gallio was exiled and later confined to Rome under house arrest (Tac. *Ann.* 6.3). Tiberius may possibly have been reminded that as a young general back in 41 B.C. Octavian (as he was then) had arrested a soldier who dared sit in the equestrian section of the theater, and that the mutinous reaction of his comrades had nearly cost the future emperor his life (Suet. *Aug.* 14; cf. Appian *B.C.* 5.15).

As Tiberius smoldered on Capri, surrounded by sycophants and soothsayers, he was joined at about this time by Caligula, the twenty-year-old son of Germanicus. Following the arrest and subsequent exile (ordered by Tiberius) of his mother, Agrippina the Elder, he had lived with his maternal great-grandmother, Augustus's widow, Livia. When she died in A.D. 29 at age eighty-six, Caligula gave the funeral oration in her honor and then passed into the protection of his paternal grandmother, Antonia the Younger, a daughter of Mark Antony by Octavia. Both women are plausibly thought to have influenced his development and character. Certainly Livia, whom he characterized as a "Ulysses in female attire" (Suet. *Calig.* 23.2), was a master of court intrigue and guile, and Antonia may have instilled in him some dream to emulate the regal splendor and histrionic excess that had raised his renowned great-grandfather to near-mythic status. At the age of two, Caligula accompanied his mother to Germanicus's headquarters on the German front, where his taste for dressing up and parading around in soldier's clothes won affection among the troops and the nickname "Caligula" — "little boots" (Suet. *Calig.* 9; Tac. *Ann.* 69.5). In May of A.D. 17, Caligula, not yet five, rode in the triumphal chariot with Germanicus, who took his son later that year on a great progress through the East. There splendid entertainments and pageantry were provided reminiscent of Antony's glorious procession half a century earlier. Their grand tour included such sites as Byzantium and Troy; at Assos on the northwest coast of Asia Minor, Caligula, barely six, first displayed his considerable oratorical promise by addressing the people (Barrett 1990, 13). According to Josephus, this talent was put to good use later. He records that Caligula became "a first-rate orator, deeply versed in Greek and Latin. He understood how to reply impromptu to speeches which others had painstakingly prepared, and instantly to show himself more persuasive than anyone else" (*Ant. Iud.* 19.2.5).

Little is known of Caligula's life on Capri during the reign of terror unleashed by Tiberius upon his real and imagined enemies, which along with many others engulfed the young man's family: his eldest brother, Nero, had been executed in 31, his mother, Agrippina, had been exiled in 29 and starved herself to death in 33, and his other brother, Drusus, first imprisoned in 31, was killed in 33. Yet, according to Tacitus, all this had no visible effect on Caligula, who instead (and perhaps prudently under the circumstances) disguised whatever feelings he might have harbored "faithfully mimicking Tiberius' daily moods, his manner, and almost his words. This prompted the epigram . . . that 'never was there a better slave or worse master'" (Tac. *Ann.* 6.20). Suetonius echoes this assessment, noting that while on Capri, Caligula displayed an "incredible gift for dissimulation," resisting every attempt to lure him into voicing any murmur of dangerous dissent. He goes on to claim that what Caligula could not completely disguise there was "his natural cruelty and viciousness, eagerly witnessing torture and executions, reveling in nocturnal lust and gluttony, disguised in a wig and long gown, and passionately devoted to the theatrical arts of dancing and singing" (*Calig.* 10–11). A former *Consul,* Lucius Arruntius, was so convinced of his evil character that he took his own life as soon as Tiberius fell sick with his final illness, declaring, "I cannot in my old age become the slave of a new master like him" (Dio 58.27.4). Even Tiberius, who earlier had praised Caligula for his sense of "duty and good character," was said to have lamented later, "I am nursing a serpent for the Roman people, and a fiery Phaethon for the world" (*Calig.* 11).

Nevertheless, Tiberius had appointed Caligula his heir in A.D. 35. When the emperor died two years later, on March 16, 37, at age seventy-eight, Caligula resisted the cries of "Tiberius into the Tiber" from a jubilant public, who also suggested facetiously that the cremation of the theater-hating ruler be staged as a popular entertainment in the amphitheater of Atella, the home of farce (Suet. *Tib.* 75). Instead, on April 3, when Caligula himself delivered the funeral oration, he asked the Senate (who had hailed him as emperor on March 18) to grant the same divine honors to Tiberius that they had to Augustus — a request the senators declined to take up (Dio 59.3.7–8). As a great-grandson of both Augustus and Mark Antony (out of whose now near-mythic struggle the principate had been born), the only surviving son of the beloved Germanicus, and one whose accession had been looked to with longing by the masses to whom Tiberius's rule was a burden, Caligula was rapturously welcomed by the Roman people. His triumphal progress from Misenum to Rome and his entry into the city on March 28 were brilliantly stage-managed, with a great mass of people "greeting him uproariously with altars, sacrifices, torches," and expressions of affection (Suet. *Calig.* 13).

For its part the Senate may have felt that the new twenty-four-year-old emperor (who had played almost no previous role in public affairs) could be manipulated or at least restrained from the malevolent and vengeful behavior that had kept them in a condition of cringing terror during the last years of Tiberius. Whether naively, or in response to his studied show of deference, they at once and in a single session conferred absolute powers on him, the first time a *Princeps* had been thus honored. Caligula's early demonstration of a taste and talent for the dramatic was soon confirmed. In April he made a great show of personally carrying back the ashes of Agrippina (who as the widow of Germanicus and a relentless foe of Tiberius was popularly revered as a martyr) and those of his brother Nero from their places of exile, transporting them on an impressively decorated warship up the Tiber to Rome. They were then conveyed with great display by members of the equestrian order to the Mausoleum "at noon when the streets were at their busiest"; the ceremony was subsequently commemorated by annual games and the display of Agrippina's image in the *pompa circensis*.

The population ecstatically celebrated the accession of their *Princeps exoptatissimus* (most earnestly desired *Princeps*), whom they were quick to embrace as a hero and a redeemer: a true heir to the enlightened Augustan principate after the dreary aberration of Tiberius's grim rule (*Calig.* 13). As the contemporary Philo observed, "Rome, all Italy and the nations of Europe and Asia exulted. . . . Nothing was to be seen throughout the cities but altars, oblations, sacrifices, men in white robes and crowned with garlands . . . goodwill, feasts, public meetings, musical contests, horse races, revels, nightlong frolics with harp and flutes, celebration, freedom, holiday-making and every kind of pleasure. . . . Indeed the golden age pictured by the poets no longer seemed a myth, so great was the prosperity and happiness, the freedom from grief and fear, the joy which pervaded everywhere" (*Leg.* 11–13). In the same spirit, the Senate decreed that the day he had become *Princeps* should be celebrated annually as a second *Parilia,* the holiday already marked by games each April 21 to commemorate the founding of the city, "as though Rome had been born again." (Suet. *Calig.* 16)

Mad, Bad, and Dangerous to Know

A few months after his accession, following a brief period of benevolent rule, Caligula's behavior (if not his character) radically changed. The reasons for this are difficult to discern.[10] The ancient historians Tacitus, Suetonius, and Dio, writing long after the fact, regarded him as mentally unsound, if not in fact mad, although there was some doubt over whether this condition was congenital, had been caused by some illness, or possibly even had resulted from poison. Modern commentators tend to endorse the opinion that his caprice, depravity, and cruelty were proof of madness, and some have attempted to designate this more specifically as schizophrenia. Two ancient writers who knew Caligula personally, Seneca and Philo, provide ambiguous evidence. Seneca (who was deeply hostile) emphasizes his savagery and utter lack of restraint and uses language to describe his character that implies insanity but might also be appropriate to unbridled (but not demented) arrogance and viciousness. Philo clearly thought him a lunatic, but his account (as I discuss later) has to be evaluated in its particular context. Recently the suggestion has been made that the symptoms Caligula displayed strongly indicate "interictal temporal lobe epilepsy," an assertion supported by Suetonius's report that he had a history of epileptic seizures (Benediktson 1989; Suet. *Calig.* 50). In particular, many of the character traits associated with this disease — such as a marked change in personality, aggressiveness, paranoia, a feeling of personal destiny, sexual aberrations (including transvestism), and a heavy-handed sense of humor — read like a case description of the evidence available for Caligula.

Two of the symptoms identified in those suffering from temporal lobe epilepsy are evident in accounts of Caligula's behavior: "a profound deepening of emotional responses" and "increased religiousness" (Benediktson 1989, 371). These traits were combined in a most remarkable fashion with some of the more peculiar expressions of his obsessive theatricality. Of course, an impulse toward self-dramatization must have been exacerbated (and given ample scope for expression) by the circumstances in which the new emperor found himself. Upon his accession he had been readily granted awesome authority by a fawning Senate: "power and authority over all things" and the immediate bestowal of political supremacy that both Augustus and Tiberius had acquired (if at all) gradually over many years (Dio 59.3; Suet. *Calig.* 14). Such absolute power might easily have unhinged even a more mature and stable individual; in the case of Caligula it went to his head. He frequently boasted of his power of life and death over every person (e.g., *Calig.* 29) and, not content with "surpassing every king or tribal chieftain, insisted on being treated as a god" (*Calig.* 22). He was "a youth invested with irresponsible dominion over all. And youth coupled with absolute authority is subject to unrestrainable impulses" (Philo *Leg.* 190). Indeed, "when some called him a demigod and others a god, he fairly lost his head. . . . He was eager to appear to be anything other than a mortal and an emperor." (Dio 59.26.5, 59.26.8).

As Philo records, Caligula eventually put such notions into action when "as if in a theater he assumed different costumes; sometimes a lion skin and club as Heracles, sometimes . . . making himself up as the Dioscuri, or another as Dionysus with ivy, thyrsus and fawn's skin" (*Leg.* 79). He lists additional roles among Caligula's repertoire, including Mercury, Apollo, and Mars (*Leg.* 93 ff.). Dio, writing later, confirms these details (as does Suetonius), adding that he "often took on the role of Juno, Diana or Venus . . . assuming all the attributes belonging to the various gods, so that he might resemble them. Now he would be seen as a woman, holding a wine-bowl and thyrsus . . . at one time appearing clean-shaven, later with a full beard. Sometimes he wielded a trident, and again he brandished a thunderbolt. Now he would impersonate a maiden outfitted for hunting or war, and a little later would play the married woman. Thus by varying the style of his dress and by the use of props and wigs, he achieved accuracy in a great many roles" (59.26.6–8). Philo reports that these appearances were often enhanced by a "trained chorus at his side, singing paeans, calling him Dionysus" (*Leg.* 96), and Suetonius notes that "he often danced at night, and once . . . summoned three senators of consular rank . . . who half dead with fear, were led to a stage where, amid a tremendous racket of flutes and heel-taps, Caligula suddenly leapt out dressed in cloak and ankle-length tunic, performed a song and dance and vanished" (*Calig.* 54; cf. Dio 59.5).

Caligula's reign (which lasted just under four years, and concluded sensationally in a theater) offers a rich, varied, and suggestive array of theatrical material, ranging from the expressions of his own intensely histrionic personality through his extensive espousal of extraordinary spectacles as both patron and participant to the pervasive significance of the games for the political life of the period.

There is ample documentation of his propensity for extravagantly theatrical demeanor and gestures. Apart from the strange case of "the emperor's new clothes," it embraced a number of idiosyncrasies and quirks of personality. For example, he practiced grimacing in the mirror to make himself as fearsome as possible (*Calig.* 50), a talent that he combined with "the natural ugliness of his pale face . . . the wildness of his eyes lurking under the brow of an old hag, the hideousness of his bald head" as an additional device to torture his victims (Seneca *Cons.* 18.1; *De Ira* 3.19.1). Philo quotes him as asserting, "I speak not just with my voice, but quite as much with my eyes in every intimation I make" (*Leg.* 264). He was fond of mimicry and greatly prided himself on his ability as an orator, often composing speeches both for and against the accused and determining a final verdict according to his whim (Suet. *Calig.* 53). He frequently argued cases before members of the Senate or simply harangued them, on one memorable occasion engaging in a feigned dialogue before the astonished senators with the deceased Tiberius (Dio 59.16.3–7). On another his intended victim narrowly saved himself by expressing amazement and extravagant admiration for the rhetorical attack that Caligula had mounted against him. Caligula acquitted him, and when asked later why he had brought the charge in the first place, he replied, "It would not have been right for me to keep such a speech to myself" (Dio 59.19.1–7).

His playfulness — of the sort that a panther might indulge in with its prey — and particularly an inclination toward black humor, are copiously documented. These characteristics are strikingly evident in the eyewitness account of the Jewish historian Philo of his own encounter with Caligula while serving as a member of an embassy that visited the emperor, probably in the spring of 40. To the utter horror and dismay of the Jews, Caligula had decided to place his own image in the "Holy of Holies" of the temple of Jerusalem, to them an act of almost inconceivable sacrilege and desecration. Through the intercession of Caligula's close friend Herod Agrippa I (whom he had recently made king and ruler of portions of Judaea), the emperor agreed to receive Jewish envoys in Rome, allowing them to plead their case before he implemented his decision. Philo begins his account with an extended description of Caligula's character, noting in particular his love of theater and spectacle. He records that he sometimes would become "frantic with excitement at the sight of dancers, sometimes joining in, or greeting an enactment of scandalous scenes with a loud youngster's guffaw" (*Leg.* 42). The same trait was noted by Suetonius, who added that "even at public performances he could not resist singing along with the tragic actor as he delivered his lines, or from openly imitating his gestures, to praise or correct them" (*Calig.* 54). Philo remarks that Caligula was advised by Macro, head of the Praetorian Guard (who had helped smooth his assumption of power), that such behavior was unseemly; a little later Macro himself was executed, a victim to the emperor's "deceptive and cunning character . . . his artificial and dissimulating disposition" (*Leg.* 59).

The Jewish delegation was duly received — in a state of deepest foreboding and terror — by this man who "like an actor wearing in turn many masks, beguiled spectators with the deceptive appearances he assumed" (*Leg.* 111). According to Philo's account (*Legatio ad Gaium,* 349–70), Caligula lived up to his reputation. He received the delegation in his private estate on the Esquiline Hill (inherited from Tiberius), which he was in the process of redecorating. "This was the stage where the tragedy aimed at our entire nation was to be performed with us as the immediate victims." Philo himself summed up what followed as "a kind of farce." And indeed, Caligula clearly enjoyed stage-managing and playing the scene for all it was worth, keenly aware that half of his audience was terrified of him and probably thought him mad. With the delegation literally on its knees before him, he "sneered and snarled, 'so you are the god-haters who refuse to think me a god, a god recognized by all the World, but not acknowledged by you?' " Lifting his arms, he delivered a prayer so scandalous that Philo disdained to repeat it. Caligula flitted from room to room, giving instructions for decoration, picture hanging, and the arrangement of furniture, while the Jewish delegates and Caligula's entourage scurried after him through what was something "between a theater and a prison rather than a court; theater-like in the cackling of their hisses, mockery and unrestrained jeering, prison-like in the blows inflicted on us, the torture and racking of the soul through the blasphemies and menaces launched against us by this mighty tyrant."

Caligula engaged in jokes and verbal whimsy — the humor of which the Jewish delegates failed to appreciate — and at one point suddenly demanded, "Why don't you eat pork?" to peals of laughter from the others present. His attitude by turns was menacing and moderate; momentarily attentive to the emissaries, he might suddenly interrupt or feign utter indifference, all the while thoroughly enjoying himself at their expense. The delegates' carefully scripted defense was "utterly mangled and disjointed" by this Marx brothers scenario. Caligula ended the meeting — without announcing a decision — by observing that the Jewish delegates seemed not so much criminals as benighted lunatics unable to perceive his manifest divinity. Later, after an impassioned plea from Agrippa, the order for the imposition of the statue was rescinded.

The impression of instability, irresponsibility, and a volatile tendency to "show off" evident on this and similar occasions was exhibited more expansively in the great state spectacles that Caligula staged. At the beginning of his reign, to signal his festive nature, he even extended the length of the Saturnalia by a day to five days (Dio 59.6.4; Suet. *Calig.* 17.2). He gave many gladiatorial shows, was avidly partisan, and lavished huge sums of money on gladiators and actors. He undertook to construct a new amphitheater (adjacent to the Saepta) but failed to complete it (*Calig.* 21). For his own chariot races, he had a private circus laid out in his mother's gardens (where the Vatican is today) and competed there at times with the future emperor Vitellius (Dio 59.14.6; Suet. *Vit.* 4).[11] He took intense interest in every aspect of production, at first as a spectator, but eventually (presumably in private) "he came to perform and contend in many events, driving chariots, fighting as a gladiator, giving exhibitions as a pantomime, and acting in tragedy" (Dio 59.2.4–5, 59.5.2–5).

Caligula kept his favorite, the tragic performer Apelles, with him constantly as companion and counselor (Philo *Leg.* 203–6; Dio 59.5.2; cf. Petronius 64.2–5), although this relationship did not shield the most famous actor of his day from punishment when he hesitated to answer a query about who was greater, Jupiter or Caligula. "Caligula had him flogged, commenting on the musical quality of his groans for mercy" (Suet. *Calig.* 33). Apelles survived, and many years later he may even have returned to the stage as an honored veteran actor when Vespasian celebrated the rededication of the theater of Marcellus (Suet. *Vesp.* 19.1; Leppin 1992, 204). Caligula also had an intimate relationship with the pantomime Mnester, with whom he smooched in public view in the theater and for whom he demonstrated further affection by dragging from the auditorium and whipping any spectator who dared to talk during Mnester's performance (Dio 60.22.3–5, Suet. *Calig.* 36, 55). This actor too survived to be a prominent player in the reign of Claudius, until the fall of Messalina cost him his life in 48.

A few months after becoming emperor, at the end of August 37, Caligula celebrated the completion and dedication of the temple of Divus Augustus (begun by Tiberius) with extensive entertainments and spectacles. A grand procession, hymns, banquets, and a variety of dramatic, musical, and sporting activities marked the event, including an increase in the number of racing events from the normal ten to twenty on the first day, and to forty on the second (August 31), which — not coincidentally — fell on Caligula's own twenty-fifth birthday and the last day of his first (two-month) consulship. He viewed these races (together with his sisters and fellow priests of Augustus) from a prominent bank of seats at the front of the Circus. To encourage everyone to attend the theater and to remain until the end of the performances, he formally suspended public lawsuits and private mourning (Dio 59.7.5). When the weather was particularly hot, the entertainments took place in the cooler Diribitorium (adjacent to the Saepta Iulia), which was the largest roofed building in Rome (Steinby 1995, 17–18). The spectacles were rounded off with an exhibition of four hundred bears (duly slain) and a performance of the *lusus Troiae.*

Caligula followed a similar pattern on many other occasions. Indeed, the following year he held celebrations marking the anniversary of the commencement of his first consulship on July 1, his birthday on August 31, and the anniversary of his taking the title *Pater Patriae* on September 21; all this was during a period of official mourning for his sister, Drusilla, who had died in June.[12] He increased the number of combatants in the gladiatorial contests, some of which were staged as battles, probably in the Saepta, which on another occasion he excavated and filled with water for a naumachia. Occasionally nighttime performances took place, for which the whole city was transformed into a festively illuminated stage set (Dio 59.10.5–6; Suet. *Calig.* 18).

The Magnificence of Megalomania

In addition to such frequent and lavish entertainments, Caligula provided several unprecedented spectacles. Suetonius recalled his great pleasure barges "equipped with ten banks of oars, sterns studded with gems, multicolored sails, with ample space for baths, porticoes, and dining rooms, and with a great variety of vines and fruit-trees; reclining on these ships throughout the day he would sail along the Campanian shores amid choral dancing and singing" (*Calig.* 37). Remains of two such vessels (bearing Caligula's name) were found and recovered in Lake Nemi between 1927 and 1931 but destroyed by fire during the Second World War. The largest of these extremely well-built and technologically advanced boats was 78 feet wide and 240 feet long. The oak decks were overlaid with tiles that in turn had a marble and mosaic pavement. Elaborate fluted marble columns were part of a substantial superstructure, and there is evidence of walls variously decorated with paint, mosaic, marble, and terra-cotta. The ceilings were inlaid with copper-plated tiles. The presence of an arrangement of pipes indicate that these floating villas had heated bathing facilities. They are thought to have been used for celebrations associated with the worship of the goddess Diana, whose temple stood on the lakeshore (fig. 22).[13]

Caligula displayed similar extravagance—more than a little tinged with megalomania—in his Baiae Bay–bridge folly during the summer of 39. Both Suetonius and Dio (differing only in minor details) described the project, which is also referred to by such contemporaneous commentators as Seneca and Josephus. A pontoon bridge was constructed that spanned the portion of the bay of Naples from Puteoli to a site at or close to Baiae, a distance (depending on the precise positions of these sites) of between 2¼ and 3¼ miles. A

Fig. 22. Artist's conception of Caligula's pleasure barge. (Drawing by J. Glover)

great number of purpose-built vessels, supplemented by ordinary merchant ships, were linked in two lines between which planks were laid and covered with earth to provide a stable surface. On the first day of the spectacle, Caligula donned what was reputed to be the breastplate of Alexander the Great, a purple silk gown decorated with gold and jewels, and a garland of oak leaves, the *corona civica*. Thus adorned, he mounted a suitably embellished horse, after making sacrifices to various gods, including Neptune and Envy. Then, closely followed by ranks of cavalry and infantry, he charged from one end of the bridge to the other "as if in hot pursuit of an enemy" (Dio 59.17.5). Suetonius recalled having heard from his grandfather that Caligula's curious behavior was intended to prove wrong an assertion made by the soothsayer Thrasyllus to Tiberius: "Caligula has no more chance of ruling than of racing across the bay of Baiae on horseback" (*Calig.* 19.3). Surely so great a miracle-maker was fit to rule!

The main event followed the next day when Caligula staged a fanciful form of mock triumph. Wearing a gold-embroidered tunic and standing in a chariot drawn by two renowned racehorses, he led a long and dazzling train composed of spoils, some Parthian hostages, and a great assemblage of carts bearing his friends and supporters in flowered robes; this was followed by the Praetorian Guards with a mass of the general public in fancy dress bringing up the rear. To crown this pageantry the emperor delivered an address in his own honor (from a platform erected at the midpoint of the bridge) in which he recounted and extolled his many amazing achievements and, in keeping with the triumphal mood, praised his soldiers for their hardships and perils, presumably incurred in erecting the bridge itself. According to Josephus, "That, he said, was the sort of road-building appropriate to a god!" (*Ant. Iud.* 19.6). Implicit in all this was the notion that Caligula had daringly engaged in an act surpassing in hubris the awesome feat of Xerxes (a paradigmatic villain of Hellenic history), who at the beginning of the Persian War had bridged the Hellespont, thus yoking Asia and Europe. Apart from the monumental theatricality of such a gesture, "Caligula may be seen as trying to demonstrate his own power by appealing to a facet of 'tyrannical' behavior with a well-established place in the literary tradition. Rhetoric and 'reality' are inseparable" (Edwards 1994, 87). Augustus had drawn in a more positive manner upon the same tradition (and in particular Aeschylus's *Persians*), when he staged as his great naumachia of 2 B.C. (during the dedication of the temple of Mars Ultor) a reenactment of the battle of Salamis at which Xerxes' forces discovered the consequences of defying limits set by the gods.

Evidently innocent himself of any sense of nemesis, Caligula capped his harangue with a distribution of money and a huge party (staged on the bridge and adjacent ships) that lasted the remainder of the day and through the night. Dio reports that because "the place was crescent-shaped, fires were lit on all sides, as in a theater, so that the darkness was not noticed at all; indeed, it was his desire to make the night day, as he had made the sea land" (59.17.9). The whole affair ended in drunken mayhem, with Caligula pushing his guests bodily into the sea or ramming and overturning their boats. Fortunately, because of exceptionally calm seas, the farce caused little loss of life, a fact that, characteristically, Caligula boasted, proved "even Neptune was afraid of him" (fig. 23).

If Caligula failed to see that his behavior might be tempting fate, others were more prescient — at least in hindsight! Seneca, in remarking upon Caligula's death (eight years after it), claimed that when he "built his bridge of boats and trifled with the resources of the Empire . . . in imitation of a mad and falsely proud king," the Roman people had been reduced almost to starvation with the risk of the "near destruction of the city, famine, and the general revolution that follows it" (*Brev. Vit.* 18.5–6). Dio confirms that in constructing the folly, Caligula exhausted his funds (replenished subsequently from the proceeds of a great tide of lucrative plots, trials, and confiscations) and that the requisition of all available shipping had caused a severe famine throughout Italy, particularly in Rome (59.18.1–3).

Caligula exhibited similar qualities the following year (A.D. 40) in another act of hubristic bridge building. He extended his palace out and down from the Palatine so that the temple of Castor and Pollux in the Forum provided a

Fig. 23. Artist's conception of Caligula's bridge at Baiae. (Drawing by J. Glover)

grand vestibule where the emperor would position himself adjacent to the statues of the twin gods, to be admired and even addressed as "Jupiter Latiaris"
(the archaic god of the Latin league) by visitors (Suet. *Calig.* 22.2; Dio 59.28.5;
Steinby 1995, 106–8). He consecrated priests drawn from the nobility (who
were required to pay him handsomely for the privilege) to his service and
erected a golden statue that was "dressed every day in clothes identical to those
that he happened to be wearing" (Suet. *Calig.* 22.3). Earlier he had attempted
to have that wonder of the world, Pheidias's statue of Zeus at Olympia, trans-
ported to Rome and provided with a new portrait head of Caligula himself,
but the project proved unfeasible (Dio 59.28.3–4; Jos. *Ant. Iud.* 19.9–10).
Styling himself (with Jupiter's own title) as *optimus maximus Caesar,* he then
"announced that Jupiter had persuaded him to share his home; and therefore
connected the Palace with the Capitol by spanning a bridge across the Temple
of Augustus."

   He held daily conversations with Capitoline Jupiter, whispering in the ear of
the statue or putting his ear to its mouth, and had rigged a simulation of
thunder and lightning, thereby enabling him to pose as a celestial master of
ceremonies. According to the account of Seneca (written for readers who may
have been eyewitnesses to the event), Caligula "was angered at heaven when
its thunder interrupted pantomimes whom he was more keen to imitate than
to watch." Apparently when this show was "washed out" by a storm, and "the
thunderbolts — surely they missed their mark — scared off the participants, he
challenged Jove to a fight to the finish" (*De Ira* 1.20.8). Both Dio and Suetonius echo Seneca, asserting that Caligula directly challenged Jupiter (when it

thundered, according to Dio) to determine which of them was the most powerful (Suet. *Calig.* 22.2–4; Dio 59.28.4–6; cf. Jos. *Ant. Iud.* 19.8).

Balsdon suggests that "his disparagement of Jupiter *Capitolinus* . . . probably had as its basis . . . anger that Jupiter was in possession of the Capitol.
Jupiter was chief of the Roman gods, and his temple on the Capitol the center
of the State religion under the early Empire as it had been under the Republic.
Now the three cults which Augustus especially favored, those of Mars *Ultor,*
Apollo . . . and Venus, constituted a new triad in contrast to the old Capitoline
triad, Jupiter, Juno and Minerva. In a sense the Palatine became a religious
rival to the Capitol. . . . Gaius wished to go farther and abolish the supremacy
of Juppiter . . . in the religious cult of the State . . . to make the Capitol, like
every other part of the Roman Empire, bow to the accomplished fact of his
own autocracy" (1934, 170).

On one occasion when Caligula was "uttering oracles from a high platform
in the guise of Jupiter," a Gaul began laughing, and when challenged by Caligula's query "What do I seem to you to be?" answered "a great buffoon"
(Dio 59.26.8–10). The man was not, however, punished by the notoriously
brutal emperor; thus Dio concluded that "apparently persons of Caligula's
rank can bear the frankness of the common herd more easily than that of the
powerful élite."

Although Caligula's behavior was certainly madcap (if not mad), there was
some method to his acting. The type of roles that he assumed and the manner
in which he staged the events he took part in suggest that Caligula chose roles
that an emperor could play without ceasing to be imperial. Professional acting
at Rome was *infamis;* for any citizen (much less a member of the upper orders)
to appear for profit publicly on stage or as a gladiator was to sink to the depths
of social degradation and suffer such formal disabilities as the limitation of
marriage rights and barring from public office. In such legal texts as the *Lex
Iulia municipalis* (45 B.C.) those practicing the *ars ludicra* ("show business")
were listed alongside other professionals "who make a profit from their body,
as a trainer of gladiators, or as a pimp" (cf. Frederickson 1965, 194 ff.).
Actors represented the very negation of such Roman virtues as *gravitas, dignitas,* and *fides* because their profession required them to disguise themselves,
misrepresent the truth through their action, use public speech to lie, and employ their bodies as objects of commerce.

The accounts of Caligula's theatrics indicate that he did not "act" publicly;
for example, the nocturnal song and dance routine performed before the terrified senators took place privately in the palace, and even his ventures as a
charioteer were shielded from the public in his own circus. The Baiae bridge
pageant was staged as a military triumph—a perfectly legitimate imperial

activity even if technically unearned — and in any case Caligula did not explicitly assume any role other than himself in presenting it. As for the many divine guises he assumed, just as it had been established practice to worship the *Genius* of Augustus while he was still alive, so too it could plausibly be asserted that the various divinities that Caligula dressed himself to resemble were already immanent in the persona and office of emperor and its attendant priesthoods. If he claimed already to be *Divus* (and it is not certain that he ever did), he could be severely criticized for jumping the gun in a manner that his successors Claudius and even Nero were wisely careful to avoid.[14] As Tacitus pointed out, "Honors that belong to the gods are not paid to the *Princeps* until he has ceased to be active among men" (Tac. *Ann.* 15.74).

The distinction in Roman religion between the individual and god was not sharply defined because it was possible to recognize (and revere) the divine qualities that an exceptional mortal might possess without overtly worshiping him as a deity. In this sense it had, moreover, become customary in Rome to worship privately the *Genius* of the emperor "without crossing the line completely and acknowledging him as divine, although it is far from certain that the unsophisticated were aware of the distinction" (Barrett 1990, 142). Early in his reign Caligula had even forbidden that images of himself be set up and refused to allow sacrifices to be made to his *Genius* (Dio 59.4.4). Tiberius (Dio 58.8.4) earlier enforced the same ban on sacrifices to himself (as opposed to those offered on his behalf) that Claudius (60.5.4) did later. Although Caligula eventually dropped this policy, it is possible that he still adhered to earlier precedents in allowing only his *Genius* to be worshiped in Rome, although in the East he encouraged and received the divine honors customarily paid to emperors (cf. Price 1980, 29–33). On the other hand, he freely allowed his sycophants to call him by divine names and to honor him "as if a god" (Dio 59.27.2–6).

Perhaps where Caligula most grievously transgressed established practice was in allowing a temple dedicated to the cult of his *Genius* to be built in Rome, with public worship by an official body of priests (*Calig.* 22.3). Although dressing up as various gods and goddesses — which even Augustus had done on one unfortunate occasion (Suet. *Aug.* 70) — could be deemed an offense against propriety and possibly reckless pride, it did not constitute an explicit claim to divine status. Its probable appeal to Caligula (apart from indulging his innate exhibitionism and providing an opportunity to force wealthy Romans to pay huge sums for the privilege of serving as his priests) was that it pushed, extended, and tested the outer limits of acceptable imperial behavior. For one who, according to Suetonius, claimed that "he admired and approved of nothing in his character more than what he termed *adiatrepsia,* which is to say his shameless impudence," it must have been irresistible. And to any who might object, he responded, "Remember, I am allowed to do anything to anybody" (*Calig.* 29).

The ambiguous nature of the emperor's divine status introduced a high degree of tension into Caligula's relationship with his people and (perhaps even more significantly) into his conception of the limits of his authority and his exercise of power. Caligula may — whether encouraged by some illness or not — genuinely have believed himself divine. Or he may simply have enjoyed extending his playfulness (for which there is abundant evidence) into behavior that he felt his position empowered him to explore and exploit. If so, then his case is a particularly telling example of how disguise can often be dangerous and sometimes result in disaster — especially among a people as sensitive to and dependent on visual expression and meaning as the Romans. Under the emperors (as later in fascist or communist dictatorships), potent political messages were signified through imagery and spectacle, which the public were adept at reading. Caligula broadcast highly volatile signals that in the end alienated a significant portion of the masses and outraged the elite.

As noted earlier, he was greatly welcomed at first, and his initial actions brought him widespread popularity, which he consolidated through the distribution of large sums of money on his accession (Suet. *Calig.* 15; Dio 59.2.2, 59.6.4). One of his first acts was to recall the pantomimes whom Tiberius had banished fourteen years earlier (Dio 59.2.5). He increased the frequency of the festivals, including a new provision for Circus games honoring his mother in 37 and the birthday of Drusilla (after her death in 38) in 39. In 40 even Tiberius's birthday was celebrated by two days of horse races (Dio 59. 7.3, 59.13.8–9, 59.24.7). He diversified the gladiatorial contests with such events as boxing and sponsored theatrical presentations in many unusual venues — even holding them at night with the whole city illuminated. He was fond of distributing gifts and food to the spectators by having these flung out (a practice termed *sparsio*) over their heads in the auditorium (*Calig.* 18; cf. Josephus *Ant. Iud.* 19.93). For special presentations, he decorated the Circus in red and green and occasionally introduced animal hunts or the *lusus Troiae* between races. He was so hungry for popularity that on one occasion, when inspecting equipment in the Circus from his Palatine properties overlooking the site, he ordered that impromptu games be held on the spot when asked to do so by a few bystanders (Suet. *Calig.* 18).

Caligula lavished money on the entertainments and the actors, and on the gladiators and charioteers who provided them (fig. 24). He allowed, and even conducted, bidding wars among those wishing to take charge of the games and lifted the legal restriction on the number of gladiators permitted to appear in

Fig. 24. Mosaic depicting a charioteer wearing the colors of his faction. National
Archaeological Museum, Rome. (C. M. Dixon)

the arena at the designated festivals (Dio 59.14.2–4). He took a personal (and
occasionally intimate) interest in the performers' affairs and granted them
numerous privileges (Dio 59.5.2–4, 59.27.1). They in turn catered to his demands and flattered him by sponsoring a festival of their own and giving
performances in his honor, as well as by dedicating statues to him and the
deified Drusilla (Dio 59.24.7–8). Mindful of how important it was to the
people that the emperor enjoy their pastimes, Caligula not only assiduously
attended these events, but also assigned prominent theater seats among the
Vestal Virgins to his sisters Agrippina the Younger, Drusilla, and Livilla and
also allowed them to appear in the imperial box at the Circus (Dio 59.3.4). To
encourage comfort and informality he allowed people to attend the theater
without having to pay elaborate respects to him and even lifted the ban that
Tiberius had imposed on attending the games barefoot. Senators were permitted at the theater to use cushions and to shield themselves from the sun with
hats (Dio 59.7.6–8).[15]

In 38 he attempted to restore to the popular assemblies the voting rights that Tiberius had removed, but whether because, as Dio asserts, they had "lost the habit of freemen" or because Caligula's support and enhancement of the games provided more direct means of expressing popular concerns, his proposal aroused little enthusiasm among the urban plebs, and the following year the elections were again abolished (Dio 59.9.6, 59.20.3). To lift the morale of the masses and strengthen his role as their patron and protector, he readily catered to their resentment of their "betters": members of the wealthy and powerful elite. Apart from various judicial measures censuring such people and private gestures designed to humiliate them, Caligula also used the theater publicly to demean them through mortifying loss of face (Dio 59.28.9–10; Suet. *Calig.* 26; Seneca *Ben.* 2.12.1–2, 2.21.5). At some performances he distributed free tickets in advance, allowing equestrian seats to be usurped by members of orders normally restricted to other sections. After gladiatorial displays he would sometimes coerce wealthy senators and knights to purchase the surviving combatants for exorbitant prices at public auction, at once replenishing his coffers, bankrupting theirs, and entertaining his plebeian supporters. Occasionally he forced members of the upper orders to fight as gladiators themselves (Dio 59.10.1–4).

The Mise-en-Scène of Murder

As Caligula's antics degenerated from the merely madcap to the maniacal and mad, "even his most ardent adherents were unable to tolerate his cruelty for long, particularly when he began to maltreat the common people not less than members of the upper classes" (Yavetz 1969, 116). Suetonius says that in the arena he sometimes removed the *vela* (which sheltered spectators from the sun) during the hottest part of the day and forced a captive audience to swelter while constrained to watch deliberately boring, mediocre, or degrading presentations. When disturbed by spectators assembling at night to obtain circus seats, he had them driven away with cudgels; many died in the panic, including more than twenty knights (*Calig.* 26.4–5). The author of an Atellan farce containing a jibe at the emperor was executed (*Calig.* 27.4). In 38, on a whim, he ordered that several spectators be seized randomly and thrown to the beasts. To prevent their cries from disturbing him, he ordered that their tongues first be cut out (Dio 59.10.3; cf. *Calig.* 27). Such behavior (apart from its incontinent cruelty) was deeply subversive in its violation of the vital distinction between Roman citizens and "others," a distinction that confirmed the boundaries and values necessary for social cohesion and that the staging of executions was in part intended to validate and demonstrate. Caligula was creating a "theater of anarchy." By 39 his relationship with the masses had completely broken down. In place of the curious political balance that, with the demise or displacement of traditional institutions, the games had tenuously achieved between the ruler and his people, expressions of discontent and increasing displays of mass opposition "were clearly evident, with an angry emperor on one side and a hostile populace on the other. . . . The emperor no longer showed any favors even to the mob, but opposed absolutely everything they wished, and consequently the people resisted his desires." Dio continues: "The contest was unequal. . . . Caligula could destroy his opponents, dragging many away even while they were witnessing the games and arresting many more after they left the theaters. The chief causes of his rage were, first that they did not show enthusiasm in attending the spectacles . . . and that they did not always applaud the performers that pleased him, or even favored those he disliked. . . . Once he said, threatening the whole people, 'would that you had but a single neck' " (59.13.3–7).

The spectators even boycotted some of the shows — to criticize them risked execution — exasperated by being forced to remain waiting until Caligula chose to appear and offended by his behavior when he did (*Calig.* 27.3). As Bartsch has pointed out (1994, 10), "Unequal distribution of power between participants in any human interaction invariably introduces an element of acting into the behavior of at least one of the participants . . . making actors out of human beings placed in situations in which they feel themselves watched . . . [and] subject to the evaluation of a superior who must be watched in turn to gauge his reactions." By refusing to play their role any longer in this dangerous and quintessentially public theatrical transaction by "walking out" of the show, the audience delivered a stunning rebuke to the emperor. Moreover, they never forgot or forgave the outrageous insult and threat delivered in turn to the Roman people by one who was supposed to be their patron and protector. The threat about the collective Roman neck became proverbial for its provocative insolence (Dio 59.30.1c; Suet. *Calig.* 30; Seneca, *Brev. Vit.* 18.5; *Ira* 3.19.2). Caligula's attitude, however, remained (quoting the playwright Accius), "Let them hate me so long as they fear me."

During his journey back to Rome in 40 following a bizarrely conducted campaign in Britain (with seashells gathered as "trophies of war"), he issued a proclamation that he was returning only to those who sincerely wanted him back, not to the senators whose failure to vote him sufficient honors had infuriated him (Suet. *Calig.* 49.1–2). Soon after reentering the city, he showered the populace in the theater with gold and silver (allegedly mixed with dangerous chunks of metal), causing such a stampede that many were killed (Dio. 59.25.2–5).[16] He exasperated the people further when, after imposing severe new taxes, he inscribed the relevant decree in such small letters and placed it so high that many failed to read it and thereby made themselves liable to its penalties. A great mass of citizenry, outraged by this cruel hoax, poured into the Circus (mindful of its acquired function as a veritable institution of government and public opinion) to raise a furious protest and to petition that the taxes be rescinded. "But he would not listen, and when they shouted louder he sent men into various sections of the crowd to arrest those shouting, drag them out and execute them on the spot" (Jos. *Ant. Iud.* 19.25–26). Dio confirms that Caligula "had them slain by the soldiers; after that they all kept quiet" (59.28.11).

He had gone too far. Murder in the Circus, where it was the emperor's duty to provide popular entertainment and demonstrate his respect for the masses, was intolerable. Moreover, there seemed no end to his abuse of the admittedly ill-defined precedents for the *Princeps'* behavior. "Nothing distressed the people so much as their expectation that Caligula's cruelty and licentiousness might go to still greater lengths" (Dio 59.24.1). It is important to note that under the principate, imperial autocracy had been accepted and formalized through the bestowal of imperium upon each successive emperor; Caligula provides an early and instructive example of how the condemnation of an emperor (either by the elite or the masses) resulted not because of absolutism, but because of its abuse. "Freedom" remained revered as an ideal not of self-government but rather of the right of freedom of speech and personal freedom under the law, which only a tyrant would violate. As Brunt put it (1983, 66), "The emperors themselves professed devotion to certain moral standards, and it was by their observance of these standards that they were judged . . . [and] condemned when they suppressed freedom, set justice aside in punishing men for mere disrespect or on unproven suspicions of treason, or for the purpose of filling their coffers, violated the code of personal morality and indulged tastes unbecoming to a Roman and a ruler, exuberantly and ostentatiously." Members of the Praetorian Guard, many palace officials, and members of the Senate formed a plot. There was no lack of people who felt threatened, scandalized, or humiliated by Caligula's behavior: even those not directly taking part in the conspiracy gave covert support. Josephus, drawing in part on eyewitnesses, left a vivid account of what followed.

The outrage at the Circus had probably taken place during the *ludi Romani* held in early September of 40. The conspirators evidently felt that in light of that incident and the general political significance the games had acquired — possibly motivated too by the desire that tyrannicide should take place in a suitably theatrical venue — Caligula should be assassinated on such a public occasion. Indeed, conscious that they were reenacting the lofty scene of

44 B.C., they took as their watchword *libertas,* the same word used by Caesar's assassins. Although the leader of the conspiracy, Cassius Chaerea (a tribune commanding one of the cohorts in the emperor's personal militia, the Praetorian Guard), "had at several times been on the point of making an attempt at the games; calculation had held him back" (Jos. *Ant. Iud.* 19.27). Now it was decided to strike at the *ludi Palatini,* the games that Livia had instituted in A.D. 14 to commemorate Augustus and that were held annually for three days, beginning on January 17, their wedding anniversary. These were attended by the Roman nobility and their families, a group smoldering with hostility toward Caligula. A temporary wooden stage was erected on the Palatine, close to the imperial residence. "It would be easy for them to make their attempt as he entered, with so many thousands of people crowded into a narrow space" (*Ant. Iud.* 19.76). Plans to act on the first day of the games were frustrated; Caligula, however, had prolonged them by three more days, according to Dio, because he intended himself "to dance and act a tragedy" (59.26.6). Suetonius adds that "he ordered an all-night festival solely to take advantage of the licentious atmosphere in order to make his stage debut" (*Calig.* 54). Chaerea was determined to act on the final day (probably January 22, 41) of the extended games and arrived at dawn to stage-manage the event.

"There was already a noisy, jostling crowd converging on the Palatine to get their places early for the show. Caligula liked popular enthusiasm at such events and had not therefore reserved any places for senators or knights; the seating was indiscriminate" (Jos. *Ant. Iud.* 19.86). He further encouraged confusion by tipping various treats into the auditorium, then watching the scuffles "as the audience snatched and scrambled for them" (*Ant. Iud.* 19.93). The emperor took his seat in the tribunal to the right of the stage. Apparently at least some in the audience were aware of the drama about to be enacted; one senator even covertly remarking to another in Greek that "today's play is to be a tyrannicide" before being quickly told to keep quiet. In fact, the actual presentations were of the mime *Laureolus,* about the exploits, capture, and execution of a real-life brigand, and a pantomime depicting the myth of Cinyras, who unwittingly fathered Adonis by his own daughter, Myrrha, and then committed suicide (Ovid *Meta.* 10.298 ff.). The title role of this was danced by Mnester (Suet. *Calig.* 57.4, 36.1, 55.1). The vast amount of stage blood consequent to these performances — Suetonius notes that the supporting actors of the mime had been keen "to display their proficiency at dying" — was seen as a potent omen, though not by Caligula, who, unaware of the role marked out for him, was preoccupied with trying to decide whether to remain in the theater or retire for lunch and a bath.

The conspirators were on the verge of attacking him in his seat — aware that it would inevitably result in heavy casualties among those in the audience — when Caligula rose, left the theater, and entering the palace complex progressed down a narrow passage on his way to inspect a troupe of dancing boys who had come from the East to participate in the festivities planned for that night as well as to present pyrrhic dances — mythological ballets — at the theater.[17] There, relatively isolated, and without his usual complement of guards, he was easy prey to the conspirators, who cornered him, struck, and then "stood round him as he lay there, and at a single word hacked at him with their swords, urging each other on and even competing with each other in the deed" (Jos. *Ant. Iud.* 19. 110). Undoubtedly, like Dio in his account many years later, they could not resist observing that "thus he learned by actual experience that he was not a god" (59.30.1). He was twenty-eight years old.

According to Josephus, when, a short while later, the emperor's wife, Milonia Caesonia (with their infant daughter and only child, Drusilla), were discovered cowering by his body, "she bared her throat quite willingly and cried aloud . . . 'Don't wait. Finish the last act of the drama you have written for us.' In this courageous manner she met her death" (19.199–200). Drusilla was also slain. Josephus's account records that meanwhile, back in the theater, the audience was in a state of shock, with no one quite sure which role it was prudent to assume. "Those to whom the news of his death would be sheer pleasure . . . were too afraid to believe it" and even suspected a trick staged by Caligula to entrap them. On the other hand, a portion of the audience — "women and children, all the slaves, some of the soldiers" — were "reluctant to accept the truth" because they "had been won over by popular delights — games, gladiatorial shows and the enjoyment of free distributions." Members of each faction were afraid to unmask their true state of mind, as rumors raced through the auditorium. Suddenly a mob of German soldiers from the emperor's Praetorian Guard surrounded the theater, blocking the exits. "The audience all expected to die. . . . The theater rang with cries for mercy as the audience begged on their knees." The soldiers raged through the palace, searching for the conspirators, and butchered the first person they met, Asprenas, a senator whose toga had been accidentally — but, it appeared, incriminatingly — stained with blood during the animal sacrifice preceding the performance. His head and those of others murdered by Caligula's enraged bodyguards were placed as grisly props on the altar in the theater, evoking the most potent pity and fear in the spectators, who, "remembering the men's high rank and pitying their fate, were equally terrorized themselves by the imminent danger." Only through one final act of make-believe did they escape, when an auctioneer (whose powerful voice made him equal to the role he now assumed), though "hating Caligula as much as anyone . . . feigning an attitude of the deepest possible grief . . . proceeded to the theater, where he formally announced the death of Gaius." Gradually the Germans were persuaded to put away their weapons, an act that "undoubtedly saved the lives of the people packed in the theater," who eventually were allowed to leave the scene of the crime.

When (a possibly reluctant) Claudius was forcibly installed as emperor by the Praetorian Guard—frustrating the senators who had fondly hoped to restore the Republic and even exterminate remaining members of the imperial family—he found himself in an exceedingly delicate situation, the ambiguous nature of which was immediately highlighted by his treatment of Caligula's assassin, Chaerea. Senators who supported the assassination were confronted and intimidated by the praetorian cohorts who realized that the very survival of the corps was threatened if its special relationship to the *Princeps* should come to an end, a relationship that Claudius had confirmed by the promise of fifteen to twenty thousand sesterces each for the loyalty of its members. Yet Claudius also had to secure, if not the loyalty, at least the acquiescence of the Senate. In the end he decided that "the deed had been a glorious one, but the man who did it was guilty of disloyalty" and must be executed "as a deterrent for the future" (Jos. *Ant Iud.* 19. 268). For their part, the Roman people (or that portion who hated Caligula), after first dragging down his images and statues (Dio 59.30.1a), took the opportunity of the festival of the Parentalia (held in February and at which the dead were appeased) "to burn portions also in honor of Chaerea, appealing to his ghost to be gracious to them and not angry at their ingratitude" (*Ant. Iud.* 19.272; cf. Barrett 1996, 80).

Claudius: Imperial Improvisations

Having thus narrowly survived only to find himself thrust onto the political stage after a life spent obscurely in the wings, Claudius took up his part with caution. Certainly his attitude toward the games indicates that he consciously attempted to benefit from the examples of his predecessors. He avoided Tiberius's mistake of remaining aloof from and denigrating the great public spectacles, yet he was careful to avoid Caligula's fatal error of making a grotesque and deadly spectacle of himself. Nevertheless, it was exceedingly difficult to strike the right balance in the volatile atmosphere of the games, in which increasingly both emperor and people were on "show," the latter quite able to voice its disapproval of a ruler judged a failure in his role.

Claudius did resemble Tiberius in his tendency to dissimulate, a trait that probably had been a necessary condition for survival. Decades earlier, Augustus had expressed astonishment to Livia at how his great nephew "who is so obscure in his conversation can speak with such clarity and good sense when he declaims" (*Claud.* 4.7). Nevertheless, because of his physical condition (he may have suffered from cerebral palsy), Claudius's public appearances had been severely restricted.[18] When at age fourteen he assumed the *toga virilis,* normally staged as a joyous public ceremony, the event took place furtively at night. That same year (A.D. 6), at the games given by Germanicus and Claudius to honor their dead father, Drusus (son of Livia by her first marriage), he had appeared tightly wrapped in a cloak to conceal his condition, and at games given in A.D. 8 by Augustus in the names of Germanicus and Claudius himself, he may not have been allowed to appear at all (Dio 55.27.3, 55.33.4). Four years later at the annual games celebrating the anniversary of the dedication of the temple of Mars Ultor, Augustus still worried that allowing the twenty-year-old to take a conspicuous part in the ceremonies would "invite ridicule both for him and us before a public which is prone to scoff at and deride such things." He consented to let Claudius preside at the priestly banquet so long as he took care "not to do anything to make himself obvious or ridiculous" but would not allow him to be placed on prominent view at the Circus in the *pulvinaria* (*Claud.* 4.2–3). When seated or standing still, Claudius managed to appear dignified, but this was often compromised by "unseemly laughter, and when angry, a tendency to drool. . . . He stammered and had a persistent tick" (Suet. *Claud.* 30). Some thought him a fool, although Claudius later "asserted that his simple-mindedness had been deliberately feigned under Caligula, because otherwise he would not have escaped alive" (Suet. *Claud.* 38; cf. 9). In fact, he was intelligent and learned, having written in Greek extensive histories of the Etruscans and Carthaginians as well as a lengthy work on the reign of Augustus.[19]

It was now evident that the imperial system was based on a dynastic principle, something that its founder, the great illusionist Augustus, had gone to great lengths, if not to avoid, at least to disguise, because to have created a hereditary succession and "established an overt autocracy would have been to fly in the face of five centuries of history and discard much that was of immense psychological significance and solid practical value" (Stockton 1988, 128). Claudius, however, had no obvious qualification for his office beyond that of blood, and it was therefore important for him to demonstrate that Caligula had died not because the system was flawed but because Caligula himself was evil. He had to display a clear distinction between his own behavior and that of his predecessor. Although under Caligula it had become clear that the Augustan constitutional settlement was over and that emperors were not *principes* but autocrats, it was politic to camouflage the fact. Shortly after his accession, Claudius attempted to appeal to the upper orders by providing an amnesty to senators, offering consulships to conservative republican partisans and even restoring to a descendant of Pompey the surname Magnus (which Caligula had forbidden him to use) and allowing him to marry Claudius's eldest daughter, Antonia (Dio 60.3.2–7, 60.4, 60.5.9).[20] Claudius knew he needed to adjust the image of the emperor in the eyes of the broader public as well. Early in his principate, Claudius acted prudently to restore popular confidence — one of his first acts was to repeal the taxes that had contributed to Caligula's downfall — and restricted the awarding of titles to himself, forbidding anyone to worship or sacrifice to him and curtailing excessive formal acclamations from the crowd at the spectacles. In the spirit of Augustus, who in 22 B.C. had acted to limit the provision of gladiatorial displays (Dio 54.2.4), in A.D. 41 Claudius "ordered the praetors not to give the customary gladiatorial exhibitions and commanded that if anyone else gave them, anywhere else, it should not be recorded that they were given for the emperor's preservation" (Dio 60.5.6).

Restrictions were imposed on abuse of the custom of *instauratio* whereby any minor failure in the ritual attending the games was used as an excuse "by those who benefited from the performance" to repeat them in full (Dio 60.6.4). By way of curbing the unseemly display in which, under Caligula, certain members of the upper orders had indulged, he now forced them to return to the stage "not because he took any pleasure in their performance, but to expose and reprove their conduct in the past." Dio notes that this measure proved successful; thereafter such indecorous behavior was not repeated during his reign (50.7.1). Inspired perhaps by Augustus's imposition of regulations determining seating in the theaters and arenas, Claudius reserved a section of seats for senators at the Circus, while allowing them the option of sitting wherever they wished. In February 41, when Messalina gave birth to Britannicus, the son of the forty-nine-year-old emperor, Claudius refrained from using the occasion for conspicuous celebration and from awarding the title of Augustus to the boy or Augusta to his wife, Messalina, aged fifteen.

Gradually, however, such moderation gave way, if not to the manic indulgence displayed by Caligula, to what was probably a deliberate attempt to use the spectacles in the manner of Augustus — in whose household Claudius had been raised: giving visible expression to imperial power and policies. Claudius possibly hoped as well to attract to himself the public esteem and popularity that his brother Germanicus had enjoyed. Although unlike both Germanicus and Augustus, "Claudius lacked that personal charm without which no ruler could become popular with the common people" (Yavetz 1969, 120), he used the games as best he could. Shortly after his accession he established annual circus games in honor of his parents. In January of A.D. 42 (exactly a year after he became emperor) he marked the anniversary of Livia's marriage to Augustus by declaring her a goddess and honoring her with a state cult. Circus games were given at which elephants drew a carriage bearing her image — the same honor that had been accorded Augustus (Dio 60.5.2; Suet. *Claud.* 11). These games conveniently took place on the anniversary of Caligula's assassination, a fact that it would have been both unnecessary — who could forget it? — and tasteless to have stressed.

In contrast to Tiberius, Claudius strove to exhibit the common touch so crucial to the people's perception and appreciation of an emperor's attitude toward their amusements. Occasionally he would hold short, impromptu games (not scheduled as annual holidays), which he staged in the Saepta and termed *sportula* (roughly, "potluck") "because before giving them . . . he proclaimed that he invited the people 'as if to a make-shift meal, hastily prepared' " (Suet. *Claud.* 21.5). The term was also that used for the fee that a client received from his patron in exchange for service; used in the context of entertainments it therefore implied reciprocity between the emperor and his people (cf. Veyne 1990, 395). On such occasions he tried to convey an impression of easygoing informality, referred to the audience as *domini* ("masters"), communicated written messages to the spectators by having placards carried among them, and, like a modern master of ceremonies, made impromptu jokes, gestured with his fingers, and counted out loud with the crowd the amount of the contestants' prize money as it was awarded to them. Later emperors followed Claudius's practice, seeking to show that they were not contemptuous of the people's pastimes and were pleased to assume a deferential familiarity. "By their freedom of speech, or *libertas,* the public tried to prove to itself that the emperor was a familiar, complaisant and loving master" (Veyne 1990, 403). Eventually, however, Claudius's enthusiasm was deemed to have become excessive, particularly, as Dio notes, because "he was constantly giving gladiatorial contests in which he took such pleasure that he even aroused criticism on this score. . . . Once he had become accustomed to feast his fill on blood and carnage, he had recourse more readily to other kinds of murder" (60.13.1, 60.14.1). Suetonius claims that he demanded that all gladiators who fell accidentally should have their throats cut and that on some occasions he would order combats between those responsible for various scenic devices and machinery that had not functioned properly during the games (*Claud.* 34.).

By expedient use of the gladiatorial contests and wild beasts, he rid himself of the slaves and freedmen who under Tiberius and Caligula had acted as informers or falsely accused their masters or associates. Indeed, the bloodshed was so great that he was said to have moved a statue of Augustus to prevent it witnessing such carnage, an act that brought ridicule upon himself, because Augustus's own pleasure in viewing these public slaughters was well known

(Dio 60.13.3–4). In 43 following the campaign in Britain (invaded on the pretext of the expulsion of two British kings allied to Rome), Claudius accepted the title Britannicus for himself and his son and allowed the Senate to mark the occasion with annual games, while bestowing on Messalina the right (once granted to Livia) to sit with the Vestal Virgins at the theater. The following year, after spending a mere sixteen days in Britain, he celebrated a triumph at which he closely followed the precedent of Julius Caesar (even to the extent of climbing the steps to the Capitol on his knees) and freely bestowed the *ornamenta triumphalia* upon many who had taken part in the campaign, "a thing he was accustomed to do most lavishly on the slightest excuse" (Dio 60.23.2).[21]

For his British victories and those won by his legates, he eventually took twenty-seven formal imperial salutations, six more than Augustus had garnered during a reign three times as long. His British triumph was embellished with a festival celebrated with simultaneous performances in the theaters of Pompey and of Marcellus, and the Circus races were enhanced to include interludes for animal displays, athletic contests, and pyrrhic dances. A second festival was sponsored (with special consent of the Senate) by the members of the theatrical professions. In honoring Claudius, they also conspicuously demonstrated the status that their own profession increasingly enjoyed under imperial patronage (Dio 60.23.4–6). Indeed, in A.D. 43 Claudius formally confirmed, and five years later extended, various rights and immunities that had earlier been granted by Augustus to the international synod of performers, the "Artists of Dionysus" (Millar 1977, 460–61; Csapo and Slater 1994, 254–55).

In the meantime one notable member of the profession, the pantomime Mnester, former consort of Caligula, was becoming a source of embarrassment. Messalina was so enamored with him that to show gratitude for his sexual services she erected bronze statues of the actor, fittingly fashioned (it was said) from metal attained by melting down Caligula's coinage. Her demands upon Mnester, however, vexed the spectators by limiting his opportunities to perform for them, who "were as greatly pleased by his skill, as the empress was by his good looks" (Dio 60.22.3, 60.28.3–5). When the theater audience persistently badgered Claudius to confirm just why Mnester failed to appear, Claudius, feigning ignorance and making various excuses, would insist that he was most definitely *not* in the palace.[22]

On another occasion, the public responded to an actor's line about the insufferable arrogance of underlings by gesturing to one of the emperor's own freedmen, Polybius, known and resented for such behavior. Polybius aptly responded by quoting another line by the same poet — Menander — "who once were goatherds now wield regal power," without incurring any reprimand from Claudius (Dio 60.29.3). The audience's reaction had thereby created "an allusion to a powerful court figure, rendering the line a criticism expressed in the public realm . . . without risk" (Bartsch 1994, 76), while Polybius's haughty riposte only validated the criticism. Such exchanges could not fail to diminish imperial dignity and stature; Claudius sought to restore it in part through more generous provision of entertainments curtailed earlier in his reign.

He completed the restoration of Pompey's theater first begun by Tiberius and continued by Caligula — inscribing his own name and that of Tiberius together with that of Pompey — and rededicated it with games (*Calig.* 21.1; *Claud.* 21.1; Dio 60.6.8). He opened these with a stunning theatrical gesture of his own when, after donning triumphal dress and sacrificing at the temple of Venus towering over the rear of the auditorium, he descended slowly through all the tiers of seats to take his place on a raised dais in the orchestra, while the many thousands of spectators stood in silent anticipation of the signal for the festival's formal commencement. He gave games in the circus that Caligula had constructed in the Vatican area, enhanced the Circus Maximus with marble starting gates and gilded turning posts, and often interspersed the chariot races with animal hunts. On one occasion the games presented a panther hunt by the Praetorian cavalry led by their tribunes and prefect, and on another Thessalian horsemen pursued bulls before leaping upon them and wrestling them to the ground by their horns. In the Campus Martius, as a sort of historical pageant, he staged a mock battle (presiding in military garb) in which a town was besieged and sacked and the surrender of British kings reenacted (Suet. *Claud.* 21.1–3).

Such striving for novelty was complemented by a growing impulse toward excess. In 47 he ordered that the quaestors designate should provide annual gladiatorial displays at their expense, which in Tacitus's opinion had the malign effect of making what had once been an honorable (if very junior) elected office virtually for sale to the highest bidder (Tac. *Ann.* 11.22.). In April of the same year, to mark the eight hundredth anniversary of Rome's founding (and Claudius's fourth consulship), *ludi Saeculares* were held, modeled on those given by Augustus sixty-four years earlier. Suetonius notes that there were still some alive who remembered the earlier celebrations, and consequently the heralds' ancient formula summoning them to attend a "festival of a type which has never before been seen, nor shall again" was greeted with amusement (*Claud.* 21.2). The three-day festival included the full panoply of presentations in the Circus and theaters as well as a performance of the *lusus Troiae* in which both Claudius's young son Britannicus and Nero (probably born December 15, A.D. 37), three years Britannicus's elder, appeared.[23] Prophetically,

Nero received the greater applause for what was considered an exceptionally good performance (Suet. *Nero* 7; Tac. *Ann.* 11.12). As son of Claudius's niece Agrippina the Younger, he was the only surviving male descendant of his grandfather Germanicus (dead over a quarter of a century but still revered), while on his father's side his status as great-grandson of Mark Antony and Octavia, Augustus's sister, lent further luster. The mood of the masses — which later would pressure Claudius to marry Agrippina the Younger (Tac. *Ann.* 12.2) — is not difficult to understand. "Germanicus . . . had stirred the imagination of the common people. . . . After the reign of the embittered Tiberius and . . . the inhuman Caligula, Claudius pleased the masses but inspired them with no enthusiasm. It was therefore to the last scion of the house of Germanicus that the people henceforth pinned their hopes" (Yavetz 1969, 121).

Although the sentiment and support from the audience for Nero may have been welcomed insofar as it bolstered the regime, Claudius viewed other demonstrations occurring at this time less serenely. Various high-ranking women, as well as the former Consul and playwright Publius Pomponius Secundus, were insulted by an unruly audience in the theater; Claudius issued edicts demanding better behavior, though he soon had to deal with far more indecorous affairs in his own household. Messalina, alarmed perhaps that Nero showed signs of eventually eclipsing the prospects of her son and not content with managing innumerable lovers, in 48, while Claudius was temporarily in Ostia, formally attempted to take a second husband, the Consul designate Gaius Silius. According to Tacitus, who like Suetonius was concerned that his readers would find the story incredible, "the idea of being called his wife appealed to her because of its sheer outrageousness — a sensualist's ultimate satisfaction" (Tac. *Ann.* 11.27–26; cf. Suet. *Claud.* 26.2, 29.3).[24] As plots and intrigue in the palace multiplied, many feared the worst should Claudius be replaced by his vengeful and rapacious wife, who stood to gain ultimate power through an emperor of her own making. "It was shameful enough when a pantomime performer violated the emperor's bedroom," but now not just his honor but his very life was in grave danger.

While a member of his staff hastened to Ostia to warn Claudius, Messalina was staging an extraordinary costume ball in her gardens in Rome. "She was performing a make-believe bacchanalia . . . surrounded by women capering in skins like sacrificing or frenzied maenads. She herself, hair streaming, waved a thyrsus, while Silius in ivy-wreath and theatrical boots stood beside her rolling his head and accompanied by a scandalous chorus" (Tac. *Ann.* 11.31). When word came that Claudius knew all and was hastening back to Rome in fury, those participating quickly assumed far more serious — but equally false — roles in an attempt to disguise their treachery. Messalina, Silius, and their accomplices were executed, along with the versatile Mnester, for good measure, despite an impassioned final performance in which he pleaded for his life, reminding Claudius that he had himself ordered the actor to perform whatever Messalina might command of him (Tac. *Ann.* 11.36; cf. Dio 60.22.5). Although nearly persuaded by Mnester, Claudius felt — or feigned — indifference to the fate of his wife. When news of her death was brought to him, "he called for more wine, and went on with his party as usual. In the following days he gave no hint of hatred, satisfaction, anger, distress, or any other human feeling — even when he saw the accusers exulting, and his children mourning" (Tac. *Ann.* 11.38). His earlier "survival training" as an actor evidently continued to serve him well.

The emperor's niece, Agrippina the Younger, had nursed ambitions for both herself and her son, Nero. She now served the former by marrying Claudius early in A.D. 49, following a senatorial degree allowing marriage between uncle and niece — a vestigial gesture to the notion that an emperor was not above the law. She advanced the latter by securing the betrothal of the emperor's ten-year-old daughter, Octavia, to her son, whom Claudius adopted on February 25, 50.[25] The following year the eminence and ambition of Claudius's thirty-four-year-old wife were spectacularly demonstrated at a military show staged to display the captured British chieftain Caratacus, to which the eager and curious Roman public "were summoned as though for a fine spectacle." The climax of the ceremony occurred when Caratacus, "released from his chains, offered to Agrippina, conspicuously seated on a separate dais, the same homage given the Emperor. That a woman should sit before Roman standards was an unprecedented innovation." Tacitus's account is confirmed by Dio, who notes that such a sight was one of the most remarkable novelties of the time (Tac. *Ann.* 12.37; Dio 60.33.7; Barrett 1996, 123–24; Levick 1990, 72).

More followed. At about the same time Agrippina was given the title of Augusta, the first wife of a living emperor to be thus honored (Tac. *Ann.* 12.26.1; Dio 60.33.2a). "Perhaps more than anything else, it conveyed the notion of empress . . . as someone who could lay equal claim to the majesty that the office of emperor conveyed" (Barrett 1996, 108). She was also granted the privilege of using a special covered carriage, the *carpentum,* normally reserved for priests (Tac. *Ann.* 12.42.3–4; Dio 60.33.2). In 51, Nero, aged thirteen, was allowed to assume adult garb (the *toga virilis*) a year early, and the Senate proposed that he hold the consulship as soon as he turned nineteen, applying a precedent of remission of statutory years employed for Marcellus, Augustus's nephew. In the meantime, as Consul-designate games were held in his name where, in stark contrast to Britannicus, who wore child's clothing, Nero, honored by the Senate as *Princeps Iuventutis* (the same title once awarded to

Augustus's grandsons Gaius and Lucius), donned triumphal dress and all the trappings of command (cf. *R.G.* 14). The message conveyed through such historical parallels, pomp, and imagery was clear and was underscored that summer when Nero held court as city prefect during Claudius's absence to celebrate (as Consul) the *Feriae Latinae* on the Alban Mount. He was also given an opportunity to demonstrate his rhetorical skill by thanking Claudius in the Senate for the honors bestowed upon him (Suet. *Nero* 7.2; cf. Barrett 1996, 134–35, 286).

In 52 Claudius staged a naumachia of unprecedented scale and grandeur. It was presented by a cast of nineteen thousand sailors and soldiers on the Fucine Lake in central Italy before a multitude positioned on stands. Claudius had undertaken to drain this lake (a task that Caesar had contemplated but never executed) and employed thirty thousand men over eleven years to do so (Suet. *Div. Iul.* 44; *Claud.* 20; Pliny *N.H.* 36.124; Dio 60.11.5). Just prior to the draining, he staged a spectacle on it. The combatants, made up for the most part of condemned men, were fashioned to represent "Rhodians" and "Sicilians," each side commanding fifty ships, including twelve triremes apiece. Because these in turn were surrounded by rafts manned by soldiers charged with preventing the actors from escaping, the participants' famous salute, "Hail Caesar! We who are about to die salute you," introduced another element of verisimilitude into the proceedings (Dio 60.33.3–4; cf. Leon 1939).

"The coast, the slopes, and the hill-tops were thronged like a theater with those come from neighboring towns and Rome itself to see the show or pay respect to the Emperor. Claudius presided in a splendid military cloak, with Agrippina in a mantle of gold cloth" (Tac. *Ann.* 12.56; cf. Pliny *N.H.* 33.63). Suetonius adds that the signal to mark the start of the battle "was given on a bugle by a silver Triton which rose by mechanical means out of the middle of the lake" (*Claud* 21.6). In addition to Claudius and Agrippina, Nero was there as well, arrayed in military garb. Following the show, the sluices were opened but produced only a dispiriting trickle of water. The channel was quickly made deeper, after which a second show was staged, this time with an infantry battle presented by gladiators fighting on pontoons. This, however, was spoiled when a section of the walls erected as part of the drainage system collapsed, causing general dismay and mayhem and almost drowning Claudius and the imperial retinue who were banqueting nearby.

It was Claudius's grandest and last recorded spectacle, although the next year (A.D. 53) Nero, at his mother's prompting, used the opportunity presented by the emperor's illness to promise circus races should he recover. "Agrippina was leaving no stone unturned to make Nero popular and cause him to be seen as the only successor to the imperial power. Therefore she selected the horse races to which the Romans were especially devoted" (Dio 60.33.9). Claudius did recover, the races were conducted with great magnificence, and, in the same period, Nero married Octavia as a further boost to Agrippina's ambitions.

To ensure that power ultimately passed to Nero, however, rather than to Claudius's natural son, Britannicus, it was essential to remove all doubt by removing Claudius. This Agrippina accomplished (the consensus of ancient historians and their contemporaneous sources) by feeding him poisoned mushrooms on October 12, 54, either when he presided at a priestly banquet on the Capitol to celebrate the Augustalia or a few hours later in the palace.[26] The accusation may be true (see Grimm-Samuel 1991; Barrett 1996, 139–42) or propaganda circulated by Nero's opponents. In any case, intrigue and dissimulation followed. Claudius's illness, but not his death, was announced. Agrippina, "with broken-hearted demeanor, clutched Britannicus as though to draw comfort from him," then confined him and his sisters to house arrest while issuing "frequent encouraging announcements about the emperor's health" (Tac. *Ann.* 12.68). Suetonius adds that "the farce was kept up by summoning a troop of actors under pretense that Claudius had asked to be entertained" (*Claud.* 45) . When all the preparations were complete, early on the afternoon of October 13, a proclamation announced his death, asserting that he had died while happily watching the performance of the comedians (Seneca *Apocol.* 2–4).

Nero (two months short of seventeen) was hailed as emperor on the palace steps. He was conducted first to the source if not the seat of power — the camp of the Praetorian Guards — to exchange promises of mutual support, and then went immediately to an obsequious Senate. There the accession was ratified, and (following the precedent of Caligula) appropriate honors of tribunicia *potestas*, proconsular imperium, and the sweeping right to do whatever he deemed to be in the interest of the state were bestowed. "Agrippina and Nero pretended to grieve for the man whom they had killed" (Dio 60.35.2). At the funeral on October 18 (which exactly followed the established scenario set by Augustus), Nero gave the oration. He had as his speechwriter Seneca, the most celebrated playwright of his age. The senators vainly struggled to keep straight faces (Tac. *Ann.* 13.3). Claudius's will (possibly naming Britannicus as an equal heir with Nero) was suppressed (Levick 1996, 145–46). Nero, indulging in "mimicries of sorrow," proposed that Claudius be declared a god, and Agrippina kept up the charade by "imitating the grandeur of her great-grandmother Livia" (Tac. *Ann.* 13.4, 12.69).[27] She was also made a priestess of the new cult of Divus Claudius, her murdered husband, which Nero estab-lished when he addressed the Senate, probably on October 25 (Tac. *Ann.* 13.2; Levick 1996, 147–50). Only later is he reported to have let the mask of devoted stepson slip by remarking that "mushrooms are the food of the gods, since Claudius by means of them has become divine" (Dio 60.35.4).

Nero

No Business but Show Business

These were the deeds, these the arts of our high-born Prince whose delight was to prostitute himself by vile singing upon an alien stage.
— Juvenal, 8.224–25

Even now everybody wishes he were still alive. And the great majority do believe that he is. — Dio Chrysostom, *Oration* 21.10.

Nero, although later reviled and ridiculed by Roman historians drawn exclusively from a class deeply hostile to his memory — Pliny the Elder characterized him as the "destroyer of the human race" and the "poison of the World" (*N.H.* 7.45, 22.92) — soon became, and arguably remained until the end of his reign, the idol of the Roman populace, who, flattered, fed, and feted, were delighted to serve (in Pliny the Younger's words) as the "spectator and applauder of a stage-playing Emperor" (*Paneg.* 46.4). After quickly securing the support of the soldiers and consequently the Senate, he skillfully built on the popular affection and hope directed toward him as the last of Germanicus's line and son of the great-granddaughter of Augustus. The teenaged "ruler of the world" soon established a genuine rapport with the people, whose support and displays of affection encouraged him to indulge in and develop the demagogic arts. His psychology and education undoubtedly assisted him in what was both a political and personal mission; even Tacitus conceded that along with artistic gifts and a "lively mind" he "possessed the rudiments of culture," while Suetonius noted his training in other pursuits, including painting and sculpture (Tac. *Ann.* 13.3; Suet. *Nero* 52). He must have been particularly interested in music as well in light of his later activities and the fawning assertion that Seneca (shortly after Nero's accession) put in the mouth of Apollo, who said that Nero was "similar to me in his countenance and similar to me in beauty, and not inferior to me in voice and song" (*Apocol.* 4).

Family Dramas

Nero's artistry, and subsequently his crimes, began at home. Tacitus points out that the emperor became well known for his efforts as a poet and that he often gathered together like-minded artists at dinner to recite works they had composed in advance or, at Nero's suggestion, might extemporize for the occasion. Tacitus considered the emperor's own attempts at poetry inept, derivative, and uninspired, an assertion that Suetonius disputed, claiming to have studied the surviving drafts firsthand and to have found them both vigorous and obviously Nero's original work (Tac. *Ann.* 14.16; *Nero* 52).[1]

Nero's artistic banquets, although later notorious for their excess, were based on firm precedent. Even Augustus, whose dinners Suetonius praised for their modesty, had "exhibited performers, pantomimes, or even ordinary players from the circus, and quite often story-tellers" (*Aug.* 74), and by Nero's day it was common for wealthy households to hire such entertainers or even to keep troupes of them as part of their retinue.[2] Pliny the Younger noted that when dining with his friends, "the dinner is frequently enlivened by comic recitations so that even pleasures may be seasoned with learning" (3.1.9); Plutarch discussed the relative merits of a variety of banquet diversions, ranging from enactments of Platonic dialogues, through mime, pantomime, and poetry recitations accompanied by the lyre, cithara, or pipe, to — most worthy of all — performances of New Comedy, and in particular the works of Menander (*Mor.* 711Aff.).[3] In addition to offering relaxation and entertainment, Roman dinner parties were by tradition interludes during which the customarily rigid rules of status were suspended to encourage a more saturnalian sense of equality and openness (cf. Barton 1993, 108 ff.).

The most famous account of dinner theater is the narrative of Trimalchio's banquet written by Nero's contemporary Petronius. Although clearly satirical in vein and exaggerated in its manic depiction of fashionable indulgence, the basis for its humor undoubtedly lay in actual practice. The whole meal is staged as a variety show, with one sensational effect following another and frequent allusion to such things as mime, pantomime, gladiatorial displays, staged animal hunts, acrobats, musical fanfares, and spectacular scenic effects. Trimalchio of course lacks Nero's artistic tastes, confessing that acrobats and trumpeters are his favorite performers and that "I have bought comedians too, but I prefer them to act Atellane farces, and have ordered my [Greek] singers to perform in Latin" (*Sat.* 53), rather as if a modern patron who employed operatic singers should insist they do country and western. Although "at first Nero was moderate in the dinners he gave, and his revels, drinking and amours . . . later he began to indulge more openly and extravagantly in these pursuits" (Dio 61.4.3). Eventually Nero's feasts bore comparison with Petronius's parody, "lasting from noon till midnight"; on one occasion a host was forced to spend four million sesterces feeding him (Suet. *Nero* 27).

Early in Nero's reign, an extraordinary scene had taken place at one of his artistic soirées, held during the Saturnalia in mid-December of A.D. 54, on the occasion of his seventeenth birthday.[4] Britannicus would have come of age on February 13, 55, following his fourteenth birthday, and (after formally assuming the *toga virilis* in March) his claim to power as Claudius's natural son could then pose a threat to Nero, installed as *Princeps* after Claudius's demise the previous October (Tac. *Ann.* 13.15.1). Nero was further alarmed by the meddlesome behavior of Agrippina, who "became angry and menacing" and even allegedly asserted in his presence that "Britannicus was now grown and was the genuine and deserving heir to succeed to his father's power" (Tac. *Ann.* 13.14). In the course of the Saturnalian celebrations, the unfortunate Britannicus — whose own mother had been executed when he was seven and whose father had recently died — revealed an unsuspected (but foolhardy) ability to upstage Nero himself. During a game in which Nero assigned various tasks for his young companions to perform, "he bade Britannicus to rise, advance to the center and sing a song — expecting thus to mock a boy unaccustomed to sober parties, much less drunken ones. But his victim with equanimity began a song alluding to his own expulsion from his father's house and throne. This aroused a rather too obvious pity, since night and revelry had banished dissimulation" (Tac. *Ann.* 13.15). The spectators, in response, revealed a subversive empathy. "Violating the first tenet of a world lived by the rules of theatricality . . . Britannicus . . . at this appropriately Saturnalian moment . . . enacted his own short-lived power reversal" (Bartsch 1994, 14). Nero redoubled his hatred and determined to have Britannicus poisoned, according to Suetonius, "not less from jealousy of his voice, which was better than his own, than from fear he might win a higher place than himself in popular regard" (*Nero* 33.2).

Shortly thereafter, at a second banquet, those assembled demonstrated that they had regained the ability to dissemble, upon which their lives depended. Concealed poison was administered in a drink to Britannicus, who collapsed. "A commotion arose among those seated around, and the less cautious fled; those, however, with a clearer understanding sat motionless, staring at Nero," who calmly suggested that Britannicus had suffered an epileptic fit, which should give no cause for alarm. "Agrippina's face showed such fear and mental distress, although she tried to conceal them," that she clearly was unaware of the plot. Britannicus's fourteen-year-old sister, Octavia (married the previous year to Nero), although equally surprised, evidently understood the role she was constrained to play in Nero's script, because "despite her youth she had learned to conceal pain, love, and every emotion. Thus after a brief silence, the festivities resumed" (Tac. *Ann.* 13.16). She had clearly taken to heart Seneca's advice that "the restraint of sorrow is necessary, particularly for those whose lot it is to dine at the table of a king. . . . In the company of kings . . . they must laugh at the funerals of their loved ones" (*Ira* 3.15.2–3).[5] Nero thereby ably demonstrated his role as an impresario with "the ability to impose [his] own fictions upon the world," because "the point is not that anyone is deceived by the charade, but that everyone is forced either to participate in it or to watch it silently" (Greenblatt 1980, 13).

This black comedy continued when Britannicus's funeral and interment in the Mausoleum of Augustus took place with unseemly haste in pouring rain, according to the accounts of both Suetonius and Tacitus. The latter noted that Nero sought to excuse this slight and mollify the crowd (which saw the storm as a portent of the gods' anger) by asserting that it was "a tradition in the case of untimely deaths not to oppress the public with eulogies and processions" and that that same public — because the state was now the only object of its emperor's devotion — must support him in the loss of his dear brother (Tac. *Ann.* 13.17). No report was given to the Senate. The scenario may not, however, have gone exactly as Nero scripted it: according to Dio, the corpse had been made up with gypsum to disguise the ghastly evidence of poison, but the lashing rain washed this away as the body was carried through the Forum, publicly revealing the crime. Another source adds the theatrical detail that the body "became livid all over and his eyes were wide open, calling upon the rulers for vengeance" (Dio 61.7.4; Johan. Ant. fr. 90 M. 92–93).

Following this domestic interlude, Nero took up an extraordinary public persona with renewed fervor and determination, one that would secure for him not just contemporaneous popularity but lasting fame as the most flamboyantly theatrical of all Rome's emperors. One of his first acts displayed a trait that characterized much of his subsequent policy: the ability to win favor with the broad mass of the city populace by sharing and promoting their enthusiasms while simultaneously delighting them by denigrating the power and status of the aristocracy. He increased the number of prizes and consequently the number of races in the Circus, which of course resulted in more expenses for the responsible magistrates. He championed the charioteers, encouraging them to inflate their demands for pay and "to treat both the praetors and the consuls with great insolence." When the praetors and consuls reacted by refusing to employ the charioteers (the praetor Fabricius Veiento threatened to run dogs instead), Nero himself graciously stepped in to supply the prizes and ensure that the races took place (Dio 61.6.2–3; Suet. *Nero* 22.2; cf. Rawson 1991b, 402).

He may have encouraged similarly subversive behavior in the theaters, where again the professional personnel ignored the stricture of the praetors and consuls and were "both disorderly themselves and led others to act likewise." Nero (often observing the chaos incognito) was accused by Dio of indulging in and indeed instigating such behavior when late in 55 he removed the military cohort customarily stationed in the theaters "to allow those who wished to create disturbance the fullest scope" (Dio 61.8.2–3). Tacitus by contrast suggests that the measure was taken to prevent the troops from being corrupted "by the licence of the theater" and to "test if the plebs would maintain orderly behavior when its custodians were removed" (Tac. *Ann.* 13.24). But he notes that the following year trouble returned to the performances, with Nero watching covertly or even openly, offering prizes to those engaging in such brawls and encouraging battles between rival claques. The situation eventually grew so serious, "with the population divided against itself and still graver disturbances feared," that the soldiers were again stationed in the theaters and the rival pantomimes once more expelled from Italy (Tac. *Ann.* 13.25).[6] In addition to provoking disorder in the established venues, Nero, according to the three primary ancient historians of his reign, began around 56 to indulge in a peculiar sort of street theater as well; disguised in various costumes and wigs, he would wander through the streets and alleys of the city, engaging in acts of wanton violence, robbery, lewdness, and, when accompanied by his followers, gang warfare (Suet. *Nero* 26; Dio 61.9.1–5; Tac. *Ann.* 13.25). In the same period he undertook more subtle subversion and pleased the urban plebs by allowing, if not compelling, members of the upper orders to compromise their irksome *gravitas* and *dignitas* by displaying themselves in public animal hunts or fighting as gladiators, a practice that his predecessors had occasionally allowed but that had been suppressed by Claudius.[7]

In 57 Nero banned provincial magistrates and procurators from giving displays of gladiators or animals as well as theatrical shows of any kind (Tac. *Ann.* 13.31). Concentrating such popular pastimes in Rome and as a precursor of later extravaganzas, in the same year he inaugurated in the Campus Martius a large wooden amphitheater, which was probably erected on the site chosen earlier by Caligula for his abortive arena "adjoining the *Saepta*" (Suet. *Calig.* 21; cf. Tac. *Ann.* 13.31.1). Nero's structure was built from remarkably massive beams and supported by stone foundations faced with marble (Pliny *N.H.* 16.200). Its podium (the flat terrace closest to the arena) had a balustrade encrusted with jewels and decorated with golden netting stretched between marble posts (or elephants' tusks) beneath which a smooth-surfaced revolving cylinder inlaid with ivory provided protection from any overambitious animals (Calp. Siculus. *Ecl.* 7.47–55; Townsend 1980, 171). At its dedication the arena was first flooded to display various aquatic creatures and a mock naval engagement depicting the battle of Salamis between Persians and Athenians; after the water was drained off, it accommodated a series of armed combats and animal hunts (*Nero* 12; Dio 61.9.5). The audience sat sheltered from the sun by sky blue awnings *(vela)* decorated with stars that spanned the semicircular structure (Pliny *N.H.* 19.24).

Probably at the same occasion and venue, an artificial forest was fashioned to ascend out of a hypogeum sunk deep beneath the surface of the arena. According to Calpurnius Siculus (who has an elderly Roman assert that "all the shows we saw in former years now seem shabby to us"), the ground yawned open to reveal a glittering grove filled with exotic beasts (*Ecl.* 7.69–72). This rose mechanically into view while fountains sprayed the spectators with saffron "rain" in the manner referred to by Seneca, who describes (in different contexts) "a means for spraying saffron to a tremendous height from hidden pipes" as well as "a jet of water surging up from the center of the arena to shoot all the way to the top of the amphitheater" (*Epis. Mor.* 95.15; *Nat. Quaest.* 2.9.2). The success of this particular scenic formula was such that a century later Apuleius would describe a strikingly similar presentation in a fictionalized account that undoubtedly reflected contemporaneous staging practice (*Met.* 10.30, 10.34).[8] At what was probably part of the same entertainment (Suetonius mentions it in this context), an aerial display ended in disaster when the performer enacting the flight of Icarus "fell at his very first attempt close to the imperial couch, splattering the emperor with blood" (*Nero* 12.2). Again Seneca verifies both such flying devices *(pegmata)* and the sort of machinery used to fashion the magic forest, cataloguing them as belonging to the "arts of entertainment which give amusement to the eye and ear." He continues: "Amongst these you may count the engineers [*machinatores*] who contrive a structure that soars up by itself, or wooden panels that rise silent aloft, and many other unexpected devices such as objects fit together which come apart, or things separate which automatically join together, or objects which stand erect, then slowly collapse. The eyes of the ignorant are astonished by such things" (*Epis. Mor.* 88.22).

The following year (A.D. 58) provided two graphic demonstrations of the continuing power of the theater as a medium not just for spectacular diversions but for the mass communication of popular sentiment as well. The first of these involved persistent complaints and public demonstrations (indulging in the license customarily allowed at the games) against the methods of the collectors responsible for assessing and exacting indirect taxes in Italy and the provinces. Nero's first impulse was to make a magnificent public relations gesture by abolishing all such taxes and thereby present the crowd with the "noblest gift to the human race. His impulse, however, after much preliminary praise of his magnanimity, was checked by his older advisers," who warned that it risked the destruction of the empire (Tac. *Ann.* 13.50). Instead, various reforms were instituted. Later that year, the second demonstration of the political potential of events at the theater involved two leaders of the Frisians, Verritus and Malorix, who had attempted to lead their people to new settlements in lands reserved for Roman troops. When ordered to desist, they went to Rome to lodge a direct appeal, and while waiting for an audience with the emperor

> they visited the usual places shown to barbarians including the theater of Pompey, where they could observe the huge crowd. There to pass the time (they were too ignorant to take in the show) they inquired about the seating in the auditorium, the distinctions between the orders; who were the knights; and where were the senators located. Seeing seated among the senators men in foreign clothes, they asked who these were, and on being told they were delegates thus honored for their courage and friendship with Rome, they exclaimed that no race on earth was braver or more loyal than the Germans, and went down and sat among the senators. The spectators approved of this noble and impulsive primitive pride. Nero made them both Roman citizens.
> [Tac. *Ann.* 13.54]

This anecdote highlights several salient features of the imperial theater: the symbolic depiction of Roman social organization; the sense of national qualities on display; the opportunity for significant gestures to be broadcast in public, provoking a response that, because it conveys the opinion of the congregation, takes on authority and legitimacy; and, of course, the capacity of a skillful and opportunistic ruler to direct the feeling inherent in the situation to his own advantage. Nero was particularly adept at this and acutely aware of the importance of being seen by his public. Suetonius records that he placed himself prominently at the theater, sitting at the top of the *proscaenium* directly over the stage (*Nero* 12), while Calpurnius Siculus states that even a humble rural theatergoer perched at the very back of the amphitheater could thrill at the sight of the emperor's face from afar; one such audience member recounted: "The splendor of the scene struck me from every side. I stood transfixed and admired it all with mouth agape" (*Ecl.* 7.79–82, 7.26 ff.).

To ensure the continuation of such promising public initiatives and the favor they won, Nero turned his attention to the problem of Agrippina, whose behavior and ambition seemed (or was construed by others to seem) increasingly subversive of her son's interests (e.g., Tac. *Ann.* 13.18–21; Dio 61.11–12; cf. Seneca *Octavia* 156, 159). "She was now arguably the most powerful person in Rome" (Barrett 1996, 150). From the beginning of his reign, she had indicated her desire to be viewed as a virtual empress and demonstrated this wish only a few months after his accession. During a public ceremony at which an Armenian embassy was received, Nero was giving audience on a raised tribunal when, to the astonishment of all present, Agrippina entered with the clear intention of joining him there, perhaps recalling (and expecting to surpass) the Caratacus incident when she had occupied a separate dais adjacent to that of Claudius. With a deft sense of stage management, Seneca quickly advised Nero to descend and greet his mother to avoid what to the Romans would have been the gross public scandal of visibly sharing his supreme power with a woman (Tac. *Ann.* 13.5.3; Dio 61.3.3–4; cf. Barrett 1996, 164–65). Somewhat later, steps were taken to diminish her power by moving her out of the imperial residence on the Palatine; this limited the grandeur and size of her customary morning assembly of clients — an important symbolic ritual visibly validating a public figure's prestige and status (Tac. *Ann.* 13.18).

In A.D. 55 Agrippina was the target of an intrigue encouraged by Nero's aunt Domitia. For this she employed her freedman, Paris, the most prominent pantomime of the day, who was sent to Nero (with whom he customarily engaged in late-night debaucheries) to accuse Agrippina of seditious conspiracy. Agrippina, however, managed to defend herself against the charges — which she characterized as "a comedy staged by Domitia with the help of her actor Paris" — and to exact revenge on several of her accusers, although "Paris himself played too important a part in the emperor's vices to be punished" (Tac. *Ann.* 13.21–22). For a while, she was able to restore and exercise her former power, enjoying a volatile reconciliation with her son "based on fear rather than goodwill and affection." The next year, there were even games dedicated to her at Naples (Barrett 1996, 179–80).

In March 59, however, Nero resolved, as in the case of Britannicus, to dispose of his menacing mother in an appropriately theatrical manner. According to Suetonius, he attempted to poison her but failed when she anticipated his attempts and conditioned herself with antidotes (*Nero* 34.2). Tacitus points out, moreover, that to restage the dinner-table demise of Britannicus risked exposure (Tac. *Ann.* 14.3). Nero therefore contrived to cause the ceiling of her bedroom to collapse upon her while she slept, but the plot was exposed. He was next urged to dispatch her by shipwreck, Dio recounts that his advisers "had seen in the theater a ship that automatically fell apart to release beasts contained inside," a copy of which they constructed (61.12.2–3). Both Suetonius and Tacitus report the tale of the collapsible boat (which evidently resembled the type of stage device mentioned by Nero's close adviser, Seneca), and the elaborate dissimulation employed by Nero to lure her to the trap. It was sprung shortly after the celebration of the Quinquatria festival sacred to Minerva (March 19–23) following a banquet given in Agrippina's honor by Nero in his villa at Baiae, on the bay of Naples. After she departed to sail to her own nearby villa, the boat duly broke apart. Agrippina, however, escaped, although another woman who foolishly called out from the water that *she* was Agrippina was beaten to death with oars by conspirators following the stage directions (if not the plot) of their script.

After swimming to fishing boats that took her safely to shore, and upon reaching her villa, Agrippina desperately attempted to save the situation by denying the scenario that Nero had contrived: she pretended to think the event an accident and sent a messenger to tell her son of her fortunate escape. The emperor then "himself set the stage [*parat scaenam*] for a charge of treason" (Tac. *Ann.* 14.7) by theatrically throwing a sword at the feet of Agrippina's messenger before summoning guards and "accusing him of being hired to kill the emperor" on her orders (Suet. *Nero* 34.3). He then directed that his mother be killed so that it would appear she had committed suicide when her plot was foiled. Thus each protagonist in a grim family drama sought to impose a script upon the other. Even when the assassins sent by Nero arrived, Agrippina vainly kept up the charade to virtually the final moment. Believing her last hope lay in giving a convincing performance showing that she did not suspect her son, she said, "If you have come to visit me you may report that I am safe; but if you are assassins, I will not believe it of my son: he has not ordered matricide" (Tac. *Ann.* 14.8). He had, and she died, "pointing to her womb and crying 'strike here, here, for this bore Nero'" (Dio 61.13.5; cf. Tac. *Ann.* 14.8). She was forty-three years old.[9]

The murder took place at the end of March 59, and Nero delayed his return to Rome until June 23. Dio suggests that the people of Rome, while forced publicly to play the role of rejoicing for his safety, privately condemned him, turning to the theater to characterize his deeds; "in many places one could read the inscription 'Orestes, Nero, Alcmeon, all matricides.'" Tacitus is more cynical about the public response amid the festivals held to mark Nero's deliverance from Agrippina's "plots," describing it as the emperor's "triumph over the servility of the people" (Tac. *Ann.* 14.13). Annual games were added to the festival of Minerva immediately after which the conspiracy against Nero had come to light.[10] The ancient historians all suggest, however, that at first Nero himself was terrified by the enormity of his deed, haunted with fear of supernatural retribution; there was no lack of portents to fuel his anxiety, the most public of which occurred when "the elephants which drew the chariot of Augustus [in the *pompa circensis*], upon entering the Circus proceeded as far as the senator's section, stopped there, and refused to go farther" past the imperial box (Dio 61.16.4). Even the location of the crime oppressed Nero because, unlike the inhabitants of the social and political world, "landscapes cannot dissemble" (Tac. *Ann.* 14.10).

With no overt signs of effective opposition, Nero eventually may have begun to believe in his own theatrical poses as well as the roles he imposed on others, because he never heard "a word of truth from anyone, and saw none who condemned his actions. . . . He thought perhaps there was nothing wrong in them . . . believing that anything he had the power to do was right, and that words inspired by fear or flattery were utterly sincere" (Dio 61.11.1). Tacitus asserts that Nero declared, following his mother's murder, "that on that day power was given to him" (Tac. *Ann.* 14.7.6). Plutarch (in a more sympathetic and near-contemporaneous assessment of Nero's career) suggested that in one sense the emperor was himself a victim of the fawning audience that he was, paradoxically, compelled to serve by both the pressures of imperial propaganda and personal psychology. "What constructed a tragic stage for Nero and put upon him masks and buskins? Was it not the praise of the flatterers?" (*De Adul. et Amic.* 56F).

The Pursuit of Popularity

At celebrations upon his return to Rome, Nero sought to counter any criticism by appearing in a great procession staged as a triumph (even sacrificing at the temple of Mars Ultor in the tradition of returning triumphators), with spectators seated along the route (Tac. *Ann.* 14.13). Through such spectacle, he clearly sought to "associate the State's deliverance from Agrippina with a triumphant victory over its enemies" (Barrett 1996, 193). A little later he simultaneously staged magnificent shows in six theaters, which (with a blunt sense of irony) he dedicated to Agrippina. The extravagance of these games was augmented by lavish gifts that Nero dispersed to the crowds, probably employing the *linea,* a sort of sling suspended over the auditorium, to throw out inscribed balls entitling those who caught them to such treats as horses, slaves, gold, silver, and fine cloths (Dio 61.18.1–2; cf. *Nero* 11.2). Once again, the masses were enchanted (and traditionalists appalled) by the spectacle of men and women of the equestrian and senatorial orders appearing as musicians, charioteers, and gladiators. Some now even danced as pantomimes or acted in stage plays. For those who venerated conservative values it was a deeply unsettling and lamentable sight to watch as the descendants of the great republican families, "whose temples and trophies were everywhere visible, engaged in activities which once they would not even have deigned to watch others performing," while visitors from abroad observed the antics of those whose ancestors had been their conquerors (Dio 61.17.4).

Such graphic displays of a tendency toward leveling support evidence from other sources that Nero followed a deliberate policy of eroding the pomp, privilege, and power traditionally reserved for the upper orders. For example, the proportion of consulships held by men from the old republican nobility declined from around 50 percent at the time of Augustus to only 15 percent during Nero's reign, while there was a marked increase in the advancement of parvenus.[11] Increasingly, effective power lay not in formal office but in the imperial court, often staffed by trustworthy slaves and freedmen whose newly acquired prestige reversed the traditional strata of Roman society. There was a "dissonance between status and power which was much resented by aristocrats, and probably by many free born Romans" (Hopkins and Burton 1983, 184). To secure advancement, aristocratic Romans had to curry favor with their social inferiors. Tacitus had observed that "even Tiberius who was no friend of public liberty . . . as he left the Senate used to exclaim in Greek: 'what men are these, so ready to be slaves!' " (Tac. *Ann.* 3.65.8). As Epictetus, writing shortly after Nero's reign, observed, "For the sake of these great and glorious offices and honors, you kiss the hands of other men's slaves, so as to be the slave of ex-slaves. And then you strut around solemnly once you have become praetor or consul" (*Dis.* 4.1.148 ff.).

Immediately after his accession in 54, Nero (assuming an "Augustan" pose) had promised to correct abuses of the previous reign and complained that the Senate under Claudius had been too limited in the exercise of its powers and had neglected to perform its traditional duties (Tac. *Ann.* 13.4; cf. Barrett 1996, 161). Nevertheless, and despite his willingness to leave much of the business of government in their hands, Nero did little to increase senators' prestige and eventually much, in the eyes of conservatives, to compromise it. Under the emperors, senators had lost their contact with the popular electorate and thus the opportunity to acquire an effective personal power base and its status. Moreover, after the demise of popular voting, although most quaestors, tribunes, aediles, and praetors were (in theory) elected by the Senate, from the reign of Nero onward, consuls were formally appointed by the emperor, and their access to popular favor, military glory, and provincial profits was greatly reduced. Senators no longer appointed commanders of legions or provincial governors, thus becoming further divorced from the effective exercise of political power. Again, Epictetus called attention to their plight: "A man becomes a slave when he enters the Senate; there he serves the finest and sleekest slavery. . . . You can see him cringing, flattering, not for the sake of a meal, but for a governorship, or a consulship. He is a slave on a grand scale, a slave in a magistrate's toga, a slave to ambition. That is why in the Senate, he cannot say what he thinks, even though his opinion shouts at him from within" (*Dis.* 4.1.40, 4.1.139 ff.). In contrast to his treatment of senators, to whom he offered little more than "a world turned upside down," Nero had a great desire to please the general populace. He was motivated in part by the counsel of Seneca, who stressed throughout an essay of advice and praise written early in Nero's reign *(De Clementia)* that the only security even for a ruler so universally admired and greatly gifted as Nero lay not in a political elite but in the steadfast love of his subjects.

According to Suetonius, "He was above all crazed by a desire for popularity, and jealous of all who in any way excited the emotions of the mob" (*Nero* 53). Now, with Agrippina out of the way, "he plunged into all the excesses which a certain regard for his mother had up to now retarded if not entirely controlled" (Tac. *Ann.* 14.13) and, foremost among these, he displayed his own talent to amuse. His grandfather Lucius Domitius had been an avid promoter of hunts and unusually cruel combats in the arena — for which Augustus had first reprimanded and then legally constrained him (*Nero* 4) — as well as a renowned charioteer in his youth. Nero had long aspired to follow his precedent, noting that racing was a "sport of kings that had been practiced by ancient leaders, honored by poets, and sacred to worship of the gods" (Tac. *Ann.* 14.14). He thus appealed in part to an essentially Greek tradition whereby chariot racing was an important element of the great sacred and venerable *agones:* the Olympian, Pythian, Nemean, and Isthmian festivals.

Although in earlier times aristocratic Romans had followed the Greek practice of having great men enter and sometimes drive their own teams, the custom lapsed during the early Republic, and for centuries chariot racing — although not suffering the ignominy and legal penalties *(infamia)* of stage performance — had nevertheless been considered an unworthy profession for reputable citizens; most drivers were slaves (cf. Rawson 1991b, 406–7). As Veyne points out, "hunting was polite, but fencing and charioteering were not. More precisely, the Emperor had to decide whether making a spectacle of oneself was proper (as the Greeks thought) or degrading (as the Romans thought)" (1990, 386; cf. Tac. *Ann.* 14.20; Nepos *Att., Prol.* 5). Nero now drove a four-horse chariot in a private circus in the Vatican area (first used by Caligula), which he enclosed so that "he could race his horses without the spectacle being public," thereby preserving the form of established strictures. He soon violated their spirit, however, when an audience was encouraged to attend, and it praised him rapturously, "as is the manner of the mob, eager for entertainment, and delighted when the emperor shares its taste" (Tac. *Ann.* 14.14).

In effect, Nero skillfully exploited the deep cultural ambiguity that attempts to reconcile Roman and Greek customs had created in imperial society. In the Hellenistic world, it had long been an admirable and highly esteemed practice for members of the upper orders both to develop artistic skills and to compete in a variety of athletic and artistic contests. Although this attitude had gradually permeated some sections of the Roman upper classes — Nero's own grandfather, as consul and praetor, had staged farces in which Roman knights and matrons appeared (Suet. *Nero* 4) — official tradition was relentlessly hostile to such behavior (particularly any type of public performance), considering it foreign and indecorous. Cornelius Nepos, writing in the time of Augustus, pointed out that a Roman reader of history would feel that it denigrated great men to record who taught them music or to praise them for dancing and playing instruments and that although the Greeks thought it admirable to win contests or appear on stage, "making a spectacle of oneself to the people [*populo esse spectaculo*]" for Romans these activities are "classed as infamous [*infamia*], disgraceful [*humilia*] or beyond all bounds of honor" (*Vitae* pref. 5). Those adhering to traditional values found the increasing tendency toward such performances by fellow citizens repugnant and, if compelled to participate themselves, deeply demeaning. Nero would certainly have recalled that his uncle Caligula had been assassinated when rumors were rife that he intended to appear on stage for the first time. On the other hand, some less conservative aristocrats were undoubtedly willing performers. In any case, as Nero increased the degree and openness of his own presentations and provided "command" performances from sometimes reluctant aristocrats, he undoubtedly won gratifying favor and vital support from the urban masses.

Nero's activity therefore represented not just an indulgence of personal inclination but also a degree of political calculation. Unlike his immediate predecessors, he was content to limit his direct involvement in the day-to-day affairs of government. Indeed, early in his reign he had asserted his hope of avoiding the unpopularity that the overzealous meddling and murdering by Caligula and Claudius had occasioned, promising the Senate that it would again be allowed to exercise many of its traditional prerogatives without interference.

For his part, he pledged that "he would govern according to the model of Augustus and he never missed an opportunity to show generosity, mercifulness or affability" (Suet. *Nero* 10). Calpurnius Siculus saw in this the "rebirth of a Golden Age" of peace, clemency, and the rule of law. "No longer will the fettered Senate in funeral procession weary the executioner, no longer will the miserable Senate house be empty and the prison full" (*Ecl.* 1.42, 1.59 ff.; cf. Seneca *De Clem.* 1.9–12; *Apocol.* 1). Even Tacitus conceded that at least at first "Nero kept his promise: many affairs were freely administered by the Senate" (Tac. *Ann.* 13.5; cf. Barrett 1996, 162–63).[12]

Nero learned further from the examples of the previous emperors that the handling of the games could lead either to deep disillusion and unpopularity (the fate of the dour and unfestive Tiberius) or conversely to the sort of adulation enjoyed by Caligula at the beginning of his principate. As Seneca had advised him, it was important above all to establish a relationship of identification, trust, and affection between the emperor and the Roman people upon which the prosperity and safety of each depended. Rulers "are held more dear even than those bound to us by private ties. . . . Caesar and the State have for so long been merged that they cannot be separated without the destruction of both" (*De Clem.* 1.4.3). Locked in this narcissistic embrace, for his part Nero could enjoy that vision of wise governance that Seneca described as "the supreme pleasure of viewing your own image" (1.1.1), while citizens could see "hovering before their eyes, the happiest vision of a government" of freedom and prosperity (1.1.8). In Nero's case, to further this relationship, and in the absence of firm or prescriptive precedents, there was in a literal sense "everything to play for." It was not yet clear within the still developing imperial ideology what the appropriate restraints either upon the political or personal behavior of the *Princeps* should be, because these had not been constitutionally determined. "Where the boundaries were, nobody knew, nor the limits of what might be said by a senator or done by an emperor" (Levick 1990, 97).

An Actor Prepares

The success of his charioteering display quickly led to further ventures through which it is possible to discern Nero deliberately extending the boundaries of acceptable behavior. As a direct consequence (according to Tacitus), in A.D. 59 he staged a series of games, the Iuvenalia, within the park adjacent to the artificial lake constructed sixty years earlier by Augustus for his naumachia (Dio 61.19.1). These were a sort of coming-of-age celebration, marking the first shavings of his beard (which were placed in a pearl-studded golden receptacle in the temple of Jupiter on the Capitol). Traditionally, *ludi Iuve-*

nales were performed by and before young members of the aristocracy for their private amusement (cf. Morel 1969, 208 ff.). Livy notes that earlier the performance of the Atellane farces in particular were reserved for such amateur dramatics (whose presenters performed them without incurring disgrace or suffering various legal penalties), although later these were taken over by professional performers (7.2.12). "The activities of the *iuventus* from before the introduction of scenic games down to Livy's own time are placed firmly in a tradition of native Italian performances and these performances are given a minor role in the total picture of Roman public stage presentations" (Jory 1995, 141). Nero, however, co-opted this convenient custom and used it in part to prepare the ground for his own performances and for a more general espousal of Greek culture by a process of "aesthetic indoctrination" directed at the Roman public.[13] Tacitus records that although "not yet ready to dishonor himself on a public stage," Nero employed the occasion to allow (or persuade) large numbers of upper class participants "to act in Greek or Latin style — even indulging in gestures and songs hardly appropriate for men — prevented by neither rank, age, or official career. . . . Even distinguished women played indecent roles, and places for assignation, drinking, and every incentive to vice" were freely provided. "Promiscuity and degradation thrived. Roman morals had long been impure, but never was there so favorable an environment for debauchery as among this filthy crowd" (Tac. *Ann.* 14.15).

Dio provides further details of attractions, including (in addition to dramatic performances, music, pantomimes, and choral presentations, enacted by people of both sexes and all ages) "everyone displaying to best advantage whatever talent they possessed, and all the most distinguished people . . . and everyone taking instruction for the purpose" (Dio 61.19.2). Writing in this period, Seneca (possibly with the Iuvenalia in mind, and notwithstanding his office as Nero's adviser) laments the fondness of well-born Romans for developing such pursuits as an example of the depravation of morals through soft living. "The house of [the pantomimes] Pylades and Bathyllus continues through its successors. For their arts there are many teachers and students. Throughout the whole City the private stage resounds; it is trod upon by both men and women; wives and husbands compete over which displays a more sensuous thigh. In the end, when a brow has grown smooth from wearing a mask, it dons a gladiator's helmet!" (*Nat. Quaes.* 7.32.3).

Traditionally, young aristocrats performed wearing masks, but unlike professional actors they did not have to remove these masks at the end of the performance (Festus 238L). This, along with the essentially private nature of the performances, preserved at least formally the participants' anonymity and ensured the avoidance of *infamia*. Nevertheless, Nero induced his retinue to remove their masks, "pretending that this was demanded by the spectators, and exhibited the performers to a crowd whose magistrates they had been but a short while before" (Dio 61.19.2–4). This gesture, although it probably had no legal consequences, would nevertheless have been viewed by traditionalists as shameful exhibitionism and a calculated flouting of established practice. In the absence of the political rivalry of open elections that had flourished in the republican period and persisted to a limited degree under the early principate, it is likely that such personal display had become fashionable in some circles because the traditional opportunities for conspicuously extravagant individualism through competitive public patronage were no longer available. The new conditions of the imperial era engendered a sense of disorientation and insecurity. On a psychological level, recourse to previously taboo performance may have represented an attempt to seek compensation in the form of new honors and modes of achievement.

Both Tacitus and Dio note that the climax of these private games was the stage appearance—presumably in a theater constructed on the imperial grounds (cf. Pliny *N.H.* 37.19)—of the emperor as a *citharoedus,* accompanying himself as he sang from the poems *Attis* and *The Bacchantes,* which were possibly his own compositions. He thus fulfilled a long-standing "ambition to sing to the cithara like a professional," having earlier pointed out that "such song was sacred to Apollo" and adding, perhaps with a degree of self-consciousness, that this "great and prescient god was represented attired as a singer in Greek cities and Roman temples" (Tac. *Ann.* 14.14). Even Nero's choice of instrument was provocative. Whereas in Greek tradition the lyre had long been regarded as a preeminently aristocratic instrument that educated citizens might learn to play, the cithara (with its larger sound box and louder volume) was an instrument favored by professional (particularly solo) musicians (cf. Comotti 1989, 59–64). Suetonius confirms that Nero "had longed to appear on the stage, and from time to time would confide this to close friends citing the Greek proverb 'unheard melodies are wasted.' . . . Having gained some knowledge of music in the course of his education, as soon as he became emperor he sent for Terpnus, the greatest master of the cithara at the time, and after many days of hearing him sing after dinner until late at night little by little he began to practice himself" (*Nero* 20.1).[14] The emperor was dedicated to his studies, following a strict regimen that entailed a limited diet, exercises, regular purging, and working out with weights, all intended to strengthen and refine his voice, which according to Suetonius was "weak and husky" (*Nero* 22). Pliny the Elder provides details of the diet, noting that onions and garlic in particular were believed to impart brilliance to the voice. Taken with Suetonius's assertion that Nero suffered from body odor (*Nero* 51), this practice presumably did not sweeten the prospect of dining in the emperor's presence, which, as Britannicus's fate demonstrated, must in any case be undertaken with caution (*N.H.* 19.108, 20.47, 49, 53–54). While developing his singing voice, Nero was also instructed in dance by his intimate, the pantomime actor Paris,[15] and practiced as an instrumentalist, eventually mastering, in addition to the cithara, the tibia, bagpipe, and water organ (*Nero* 54).[16] Recognizing the importance of such arts to the young emperor (if not his actual achievement within them), Seneca flattered his former pupil shortly after his accession by describing him as the equal of Apollo, the singer and cithara player (*Apocol.* 4).

Having done all he could physically and mentally to prepare himself for successful performance, Nero turned his attention to the audience. In addition to a cohort of militia and their commanding officers brought in for the occasion, a claque of some five thousand youthful supporters — the *Augustiani* — swelled the crowd. These had been recruited from sycophantic and ambitious members of the equestrian order and (according to Dio) from the military. He was so impressed by the rhythmic style of chanting and applause practiced in Alexandria that he imported some of its inhabitants to teach their acclamations to his own recruits. These "would lead the applause, and all the rest, however loath, were obliged to shout with them" (Dio 61.20.4). Tacitus adds that "day and night they thundered applause, showering divine epithets on Nero's beauty and voice," for which they received the honors and pomp normally associated with respectable endeavors (Tac. *Ann.* 14.15). Suetonius notes that eventually the claque (whose leaders were paid four hundred thousand sesterces each) was divided into three sections according to the type of rhythmic sounds that each produced and that their regular members were "conspicuous for their bushy hair and fancy dress" (*Nero* 20.3).

The existence of theatrical claques in Rome was not a new phenomenon; although Ovid claims that in early times "there was no art of hand clapping" (*Ars. Amat.* 1.113), it had certainly developed by the late Republic. The earliest direct reference to claques is found in Cicero's speech for Sestius (of 56 B.C.) in which he even used the expression *theatrum populusque Romanus* to distinguish the genuine expression of popular opinion from that which was organized or "purchased by the frivolity of some people . . . [and] easy to see how and by whom it is started" (*Pro Sest.* 54). Elsewhere he noted that he never paid much attention to such demonstrations unless they arose from all sections and levels of the theater (*Phil.* 1.37). In the early principate the claques had become sufficiently well established (and disruptive) to ensure that their leaders were banished by Tiberius in A.D. 23 along with the actors themselves. Nero dramatically strengthened the claque's significance, in part to ensure that the crowd would be encouraged (or coerced) to overlook any inadequacies in his performance, because, according to Dio, "he had only a weak and indistinct voice, and moved the whole audience to laughter and tears simultaneously." In addition to the huge cohort of partisan supporters, he received further moral support from his adviser Seneca and from Burrus, prefect of the Praetorian Guard, who Tacitus asserts "praised as he grieved" (Tac. *Ann.* 14.15). Both "would wave their arms and togas at every utterance of his and lead others to do the same" (Dio 61.20.2–3). To ensure that his performance was favorably remembered, Nero hosted a great public banquet on boats within the large lake *(stagnum)* prepared by Augustus for his naumachia in 2 B.C. before sailing away at midnight down a canal linking it to the Tiber (Dio 61.20.5).

Nero followed these initial *divertissements* with the establishment in Rome in 60 of a new type of festival to be held every four years, modeled on Greek practice and called the *Neronia*. It comprised three areas of activity — athletic contests, chariot racing, and musical competitions including singing, poetry, and recitation. Nero's innovation was directly inspired by such venerable Greek periodic festivals — the sacred *agones* — as the Olympic and Pythian games. Victory in these festivals was rewarded not by money prize but by a crown, together with various honors and privileges and international recognition for the "Sacred Victors" within the Hellenistic world. By the imperial period the original sacred contests within Greece itself had been extended to cities throughout the east with indigenous local contests being upgraded to international status to constitute an extensive circuit in which leading artists would compete. Although such *agonistai* had since the early second century B.C. occasionally taken part in exhibitions in Rome or appeared in the normal *ludi scaenici* there, no *agon* as such had ever been permanently established in the city. Augustus had instituted the Actia at Actium to commemorate his victory over Antony there, and this later equaled the major Greek *agones* in importance (Dio 51.1.2). He had, moreover, inaugurated a festival *(ludi Actiaci)* in Rome itself in 28 B.C. to be held every four years to mark the same victory. According to Dio (53.1.5) in addition to gladiatorial displays by slaves in a wooden stadium (set up in the Campus Martius), Augustus had encouraged highborn citizens to participate in events in the Circus. The involvement of citizens strongly suggests that these celebrations deliberately emulated the sacred contests of Greece. But they did not, apparently, continue after Augustus's death.

Also under Augustus, an *agon* at Naples, the *Italika Romaia Sebasta Isolympia* had been established in A.D. 2 and became permanent (taking place thereafter every four years), limited at first to athletic and equestrian events but later including musical and dramatic competitions. The *Sebastoi* were conceived as "an indeterminate number of members of the imperial house, past and present" (Price 1980, 34), and the festival was therefore linked to the imperial cult. Augustus had himself attended it just prior to his death in A.D. 14 (Dio 59.29.2). Afterward (if not indeed during his lifetime), according to surviving detailed regulations, it included a procession by competitors and officials to his shrine and sacrifice to his divinity (Geer 1935). As emperor, Claudius had arranged and attended the posthumous presentation there of a play by Germanicus that was awarded the crown by the judges (Suet. *Claud.* 11.2; Dio 60.6.1).

The high status and honors enjoyed in the Hellenistic world by *agonistai* (who were usually freeborn citizens) were in stark contrast to the social disgrace and *infamia* traditionally incurred by public actors and musicians (generally slaves or freedmen) in Rome. Roman athletes, however, did not normally incur such penalties, and it appears that at least by the beginning of the principate this dispensation was extended to those who performed as contestants in Greek-style competitions, indicating, as Leppin notes (1992, 141), that "prominent Romans despite their contempt for performers were undoubtedly in a position to react pragmatically to prevailing Grecian conditions."[17] Thus it seems likely that members of the upper orders in Roman society could take part in sacred *agones* so long as they did so *virtutis gratia:* for the honor of the thing. Nevertheless, the disinclination of the emperors prior to Nero to establish an *agon* in Rome itself may suggest a degree of ambivalence and probably a reluctance to avoid appearing less than a *vir vere Romanus* through overenthusiastic espousal of Greek culture. Although when in Naples Claudius had done as the Grecians did, "adopting the Greek manner in all respects, wearing a cloak and high boots, for example at the musical exhibitions" (Dio 60.6.2), he apparently did so not in the role of emperor but "as an ordinary citizen." Nero felt no such restraint.

Nero was fascinated with Greek culture, and his admiration for its achievements was widely shared among more sophisticated members of upper-class Roman society, some of whom, through their voluntary participation as performers in the "private" entertainments staged early in his reign, had demonstrated a willingness to test the limits of conservative tradition and tolerance. Seneca put it down to a love of luxury, which meant that "vice continues to make progress. . . . We continually stifle whatever remains of our morality" (*Nat. Quaes.* 7.31.1–2). Later, as the process continued and accelerated, Tacitus complained that "nowadays our children are handed over at their birth to some silly little Greek maid. . . . They grow up in an atmosphere of sloth and pettiness, in which they gradually lose all sense of decency and all respect both for themselves and for others" (*Dial. de Orator.* 29).[18] Nero, however, displayed abundant admiration for "this race so dear to our wealthy men . . . this nation of play-actors" (Juvenal 3.58, 100). The establishment of a Greek agon in his own name must have been immensely attractive, calculated to celebrate Hellenistic culture (and vex conservative elements at Rome), provide a massive platform for the presentation of his favorite artistic entertainments, and of course lend splendor and an air of divinity to his own person. It was irresistible.

Our scant knowledge of the content of the Neronia derives from the historians who chronicled Nero's reign; for its probable format we can assess what we know about the sacred *agones* of the Greek East, which served as its model.[19] An extensive inscription from A.D. 124 detailing the establishment and procedure of an agon at Oenoanda in northern Lycia during the reign of Hadrian (and through his authorization and foundation) broadly suggests the form of the Neronia a half century earlier. It was organized and managed by a presiding officer, the *agonothetes,* an office that would probably have been held in Rome by Nero himself, wearing the customary golden crown and purple robe. The prizes for the various categories of contest were in the form not of money but of honor symbolized by the presentation of crowns, which at the Neronia would have been a wreath of oak leaves. These were determined by a panel of judges, which consisted of ex-consuls chosen by lot (Suet. *Nero* 12.30). The contests may have taken place over a period of several weeks and, if they conformed to those at Oenoanda, consisted of competitions among trumpeters, heralds, poets, orators, aulos players accompanied by a chorus *(chorauloi),* comic and tragic actors, and *citharoedi,* as well as a variety of gymnastic and equestrian events, including chariot racing. There may also have been an award for those providing the stage machinery and scenery. This was also the pattern of competitive events at the *agon* instituted by Domitian a quarter of a century after the Neronia, called the Capitolia (Jones 1992, 103–4).

Prior to the contests there would have been an elaborate series of sacrifices and a spectacular procession prominently featuring images of the emperors and gods, with perhaps particular emphasis given to Apollo, who was closely associated with the *agones* and with Nero himself. Separate processions and rituals probably took place subsequently at each of the competition venues, with special altars set up and decorated to mark the events. These would later be stored with the intention of rededicating and using them at subsequent celebrations of the festival, which was held every four years. The competitions would be entered by members of the various guilds *(synodoi)* of performing artists *(technitai)* and athletes *(xystici).*[20] In A.D. 43 these had their status and privileges (granted earlier by Augustus) confirmed by Claudius in a formal letter addressed to the "Performers, Sacred Victors, and Crown-Winners of the Whole World Devoted to Dionysus," and five years later the emperor had undertaken to preserve and increase these rights (Millar 1977, 459–61). In accord with long-standing Hellenistic custom, local citizens could also take part. Nero followed Greek practice too by allowing the Vestal Virgins to attend the athletic contests, specifically citing as his justification the precedent of "the Olympian games where the priestesses of Ceres were allowed the same privilege" (Suet. *Nero* 12). This departed markedly from accepted Roman practice, which notably had been strictly enforced by Augustus himself. Although allowing the Vestals a reserved section at the gladiatorial shows (other women were relegated by him to the upper tier), he banned them from athletic contests, in which most of the participants wore little or no clothing (*Aug.* 44).

Tacitus's account of the Neronia (which began in on October 13, 60, the anniversary of Nero's accession) suggests that it did indeed provoke a heated debate and reassessment of the appropriate role for such entertainments in Roman society (Tac. *Ann.* 14.20–21). Traditionalists insisted that the practice of generations should not be overturned because to do so threatened morality and risked an influx of "imported licentiousness" and "foreign tastes . . . at the instigation of the emperor and Senate," who not only had lifted the legal liabilities that by custom were a consequence of public performance but even had compelled "Romans to pollute themselves on the stage under the pretext of delivering an oration or poem." Others, however, pointed out that even in olden days Romans had amused themselves with spectacles and entertainments of various sorts, many of them imported, and yet for centuries no highborn Roman had ever "sunk to the level of performing in the professional theater." Moreover, to have the costs of the entertainments paid for by the state would ensure that magistrates did not risk bankruptcy and corruption in trying to cater to popular demands. In any case, it was argued that the display of rhetorical and poetical skill could encourage and inspire such admirable talents, which were "reputable arts and legitimate pleasures." Tacitus, whose view of Nero was otherwise entirely hostile, concluded his account by conceding that "it must be admitted that the spectacles took place without notable scandal or outbreak of even minor partisan disturbances." He attributed this to the fact that although Nero had allowed the pantomimes banished by Claudius to return, they were prohibited from taking part in these sacred contests, which limited their popular appeal. Even the regrettable vogue for donning Greek clothing (indulged in by many of the spectators) proved mercifully short-lived.

According to Suetonius, Nero (who did not himself perform) was offered the prize for Latin oratory and poetry "for which all the most eminent men had competed, but which was given to him by unanimous consent" (*Nero* 12).

He descended from his seat of honor in the tribunal to the senatorial section in the orchestra to accept the prize. Tacitus confirms the honorific awarding of the prize for oratory to Nero but fails to mention that for poetry (Tac. *Ann.* 14.21), although Dio (without mentioning these at all) asserts that Nero was also given the crown as *citharoedus* "without a contest, since everyone else was barred on the assumption that they were unworthy to be victors. . . . All the crowns awarded for the cithara in all the contests were sent to him as the only artist deserving of victory" (61.21.1–2). This suggests that despite the ostensibly "private" nature of the emperor's previous performances, they were in fact well known. Suetonius records that Nero dedicated the prize at the feet of a statue of Augustus, while Dio adds that the emperor, decked out in the dress of the guild of the cithara players, was immediately enrolled as victor in his newly built gymnasium.

As part of the preparation for the festival, Nero had constructed and dedicated a grand and sumptuous bathing and gymnasium complex in the Campus Martius close to the Pantheon. This building — probably the first such harmoniously combined establishment in Rome — embodied in architectural terms the same impulse toward Hellenistic practice displayed in the Neronia itself. Earlier Vitruvius had described baths and *palaestrae* as separate entities, noting that the latter were not "customary in Italy" (5.11); Nero's complex integrated provision for both bathing and athletic activities, and its dedication was marked by a further Greek-inspired innovation, the distribution of oil to the knights and senators (Suet. *Nero* 12.3; Tac. *Ann.* 14.47). In this gesture, Nero "set himself to counter the Roman prejudice against Greek athletics, a contempt based on the belief that such exercising in the nude encouraged homosexuality and generally undermined the qualities essential in good soldiers. . . . In Nero's day professional gymnastic displays were no longer novel, but the introduction of the habits of the gymnasium into the private life of the upper orders was actively opposed not only by philosophers but by traditionalists" (Griffin 1985, 44). Indeed, Tacitus cited as one of the objections raised against the Neronia the worry that young citizens "would strip naked, put on gloves, and practice this type of conflict instead of the bearing of arms" (Tac. *Ann.* 14.22).[21]

Nero was particularly vulnerable to such criticism. His own soldierly qualities (which had never been demonstrated) were asserted with the construction in 62 of an elaborately decorated triumphal arch in the center of the Capitoline Hill, to mark the Eastern victories of his general Corbulo for which Nero himself had been hailed and celebrated as *imperator*. Tacitus suggests that this too owed something to the theater: "Appearances were emphasized, while truth had to be ignored" (Tac. *Ann.* 13.41, 15.18). Not only were triumphs reserved for the emperor alone, but, indeed, a general who was too ostentatiously victorious risked retribution from an envious *Princeps*. Corbulo had himself experienced this fifteen years earlier in the reign of Claudius, during an overly successful Germanic campaign that he was forced to curtail, remarking, "Happy the Roman generals before my time!" (Tac. *Ann.* 11.20). After further successes in the East, culminating in the pacification of Tiridates of Armenia (which provided Nero with a pretext for a splendid celebration), in 66 he was compelled to commit suicide (Dio 63.17.5).

Meanwhile, in A.D. 63, following the birth of a daughter, Claudia, by Nero's second wife, Poppaea Sabina, a new *agon* in the child's honor was decreed, to take place every four years at Antium (the site of her birth and of Nero's), which was to be modeled on the Actia of Augustus. The infant died after less than four months, however, so the festival was canceled, and she was instead commemorated by having her image placed among the divinities represented in the *pulvinar* during the annual games (Tac. *Ann.* 15.23). In the same year — possibly as a gesture intended to reinforce his popularity with the equestrian order — Nero granted its members permanent reserved seating in the Circus Maximus (Tac. *Ann.* 15.32; Suet. *Nero* 11.1), thus extending to them a privilege given senators twenty-two years earlier by Claudius (Dio 60.7.3; Suet. *Claud.* 21.3). To create additional spectator space, Nero at this time filled in the deep ten-foot-wide ditch *(euripus)* created by Caesar in 46 B.C. that had encircled the inside perimeter of the Circus to provide a protective barrier between audience and performers (Pliny *N.H.* 8.21; Steinby 1995, 239). Perhaps because animal displays increasingly took place in purpose-built amphitheaters, such security was no longer deemed essential.

The Player King

Not content to wait for the next Neronia, and dissatisfied with his role as theatrical impresario, with being awarded prizes for performances he had not actually given, and with what he regarded as his "too modest" exhibitions at the Iuvenalia, Nero was "impelled by a desire that grew stronger each day, to appear regularly on the public stage" (Tac. *Ann.* 15.33). Because "he did not yet dare to undertake this at Rome, he chose Naples as a Greek city" for his public stage debut. Tacitus notes the emperor's intention, after a successful reception at Naples, to tour Greece and only then, "his reputation enhanced, to seek the plaudits of his countrymen." This suggestion accords with the impression conveyed by Nero's earlier activity that, recognizing the lamentable tendency of many in the upper stratum of Roman society to view performance as scurrilous, he in effect followed a policy of escalation, through which he gradually tested and extended the limits of tolerance. The final silencing of his critics and the triumph of this policy and of his art would come when his performance in Rome could be "backed by the approbation of Greece, the consummate and acknowledged judge of quality in these matters, where he could be sure of a favorable reception" (Bolton 1948, 86). In May 64 Nero sang publicly for the first time, in the theater in Naples before an enormous crowd drawn by rumors of the performance from both the city itself and neighboring communities. Both Tacitus and Suetonius record that, ominously, the event was marked by an earthquake (according to Suetonius, *during* Nero's performance), which damaged the theater, though fortunately not until the audience had dispersed. Nevertheless, he gave a series of subsequent recitals there, occasionally resting his voice but evidently so stagestruck (despite the omen of the earthquake) that he was unable to stay away from the place. He even dined publicly in the orchestra, promising the spectators in Greek that "as soon as he had freshened his voice he would belt out something nice and loud" (Suet. *Nero* 20.2). He also composed a poem marking the occasion and offering thanks that there was no loss of life in the earthquake, during which, in his words, "you would have thought it had thundered underground" (Suet. *Vit. Luc.*).[22]

This clearly marked a turning point in Nero's artistic career because thereafter he seems to have felt little scruple about publicly performing. Although the exact chronology of events is unclear,[23] it appears that having first intended to set out for Greece immediately to compete in the various *agones* there, he changed his mind "for reasons that are uncertain" (Tac. *Ann.* 15.36) and instead returned to Rome in June, where — as Suetonius asserts, "considering it of the utmost importance to appear at Rome as well" — he decided to hold the second Neronia at once (*Nero* 21). It is likely that despite holding it "before the appointed time" (as a four-yearly event it was presumably due in October), after only a day or so — just long enough for him to compete in and win the competition amongst the *citharoedi* — he curtailed the rest of the contests. These facts, together with further details provided by Suetonius, suggest something of Nero's psychology and the degree to which this affected his "stage-management" of the contests. Having finally overcome in Naples the irksome inhibition imposed upon him by tradition and what he must have viewed as contemptible "philistine prejudice" in some circles against public performance, he now was anxious to benefit from this advance and indulge both his own desire and that of the public by giving presentations in Rome itself. For this it was not necessary to mount the full panoply of competitions appropriate to the Neronia; a token performance by himself was sufficient precedent for future ventures.

Even so, he still exhibited a becoming reticence of the sort often witnessed in artists who, though longing to perform, desire the additional gratification of being urged to it by their partisans. Suetonius describes how "when there was a general demand for his 'divine voice,' he replied that should any wish to hear him, he would favor them in the gardens; but when the guard of soldiers on duty added their entreaties to those of the mob, he happily agreed to appear at once" (*Nero* 21). Suetonius adds that he therefore immediately put his name forward among the contestants in the cithara contest, addressed the audience briefly, and, using an ex-consul as his master of ceremonies, announced he would sing *Niobe,* a performance that duly lasted the rest of the afternoon. Then "he postponed both the prize-giving and the rest of the festival to the next year in order to allow himself freer scope for further singing."

A potent example of how the theatrical dynamic extended beyond the auditorium itself to color and condition imperial behavior was displayed in the great public banquet hosted (probably shortly after Nero's Roman debut, in the early summer of 64) by Tigellinus, commander of the Praetorian Guard. Following the postponement of his intended tour of Greece, Nero prepared instead to journey to Egypt and issued proclamations to that effect. He again changed his mind, however, claiming that having "seen from the dejected looks of his countrymen . . . that the shortest absence was painful for a people used to drawing comfort in adversity from the sight of their emperor. . . . He must yield to their desire that he stay" (Tac. *Ann.* 15.36). Tacitus adds wryly that "this and similar expressions were much to the liking of the mob, with its passion for amusements." To confirm the impression that Rome and its people were first in the heart of the twenty-six-year-old "Father of His Country," Nero began to hold a number of great public banquets and "to treat the entire city as his palace" (Tac. *Ann.* 15.37). Rather as Versailles became under a later absolute monarch, Louis XIV (who like Nero was pleased to associate himself with the sun), Rome now was an extension of the emperor's no-longer-private domain, duly imbued with his aura of theatricality and excess and obsessed with him and his affairs. Tacitus describes Tigellinus's banquet as typical of such prodigality.

It was staged in the middle of a pool constructed around 20 B.C. by Agrippa, probably in connection with his baths in the Campus Martius in an area lying northeast of the theater of Pompey and south of the Pantheon (Richardson 1992, 367). Both Tacitus and Dio provide extensive details of the arrangement and content of the entertainment. In the center of the pool a great raft was constructed and floated on casks, then towed into place by barges fashioned from gold and ivory and rowed by a crew of obliging young "joy-boys" *(exoleti)* chosen for their "lascivious talents." Nero and his immediate guests dined, resting on cushions and purple rugs. Encircling the pool was an extensive wooded park, which Nero had stocked with exotic birds and animals, while at the water's edge structures were built to serve as brothels and pleasure pavilions. "First came obscene gestures and dances; then as darkness drew on, the whole of the neighboring grove and all the buildings round about began to echo with song and blaze with lights" (Tac. *Ann.* 15.37). Both historians note that women of high and low birth, virgins, married women, courtesans, young and old were all freely available, as "every man had the privilege of enjoying whomever he wished as the women were not allowed to refuse anyone. Consequently the mob both drank and debauched riotously" (Dio 62.15.5). Predictably the whole thing ended in a general orgy, uproar and violence engulfing participants and spectators alike.

According to Tacitus, a few days later Nero, already "defiled by every natural and unnatural lust," conceived a "crowning abomination for his vicious existence" by staging a wedding. In it he took the role of the bride, and with witnesses present to savor this spectacular refinement, was subsequently enjoyed by his "husband," the freedman Pythagoras. According to Suetonius, "he imitated the cries and shrieks of a virgin being deflowered" (*Nero* 29).

Shortly after these events, on July 19, 64, fire broke out in Rome. It began among the wooden shops flanking the Circus Maximus along the base of the Palatine Hill, and apparently the wind passing through the open expanse of the Circus then fanned its initial progress. The fire lasted nine days, during which three of the fourteen regions into which the city had been divided by Augustus were destroyed and seven more damaged. Eventually it engulfed not only vast areas in which the population lived but also many of the most ancient monuments and temples of the city. In addition to the Circus, the amphitheater of Statilius Taurus (built in 29 B.C. under Augustus) was destroyed, as was Nero's still incomplete palace, the Domus Transitoria, which ran from the Palatine through the valley where the Colosseum now stands, toward the gardens of Maecenas on the Esquiline Hill (Steinby 1995, 199–202). This fact, together with the skepticism of Tacitus (*Ann.* 15.38), throws some doubt on the consensus of Suetonius (*Nero* 38), Dio (62.16.1), Pliny (*N.H.* 17.5), and the author of the nearly contemporaneous tragedy *Octavia* (831–33) that Nero himself had instigated the catastrophe either out of desire for the glory of rebuilding Rome or, more madly, to experience the thrill of witnessing the sort of spectacle seen by Priam at the destruction of Troy. The emperor, it is true, had displayed an early fascination with and sympathy for the plight of Troy, having in A.D. 53 defended the modern Trojans' interests by recounting the derivation of Rome from Troy, and the Julian family from

Fig. 25. "The Christian Martyrs' Last Prayer." Jean-Leon Gérôme, 1883. The artist depicts Christians sacrificed to the lions and used as human torches. (The Walters Art Gallery, Baltimore)

Aeneas, and thereby winning their town immunity from taxation (Tac. *Ann.* 12.58.1; cf. Suet. *Nero* 7.2). Tacitus concedes that rumors of Nero's complicity flourished at the time of the fire, and had proponents even in his own day, but allows the possibility of an accident. He does, however, record that Nero was said to have mounted his private stage to recite verses on the fall of Troy (presumably from his own composition, the *Troica*), while elsewhere he quotes the charge by one of the Pisonian conspirators, the tribune Subrius Flavus, that Nero was an arsonist (Tac. *Ann.* 15.67).

Aware of such rumors, Nero sought convenient scapegoats in the Christians, who were subjected to appropriately theatrical means of punishment. He executed "vast numbers of them" either "disguised with wild beasts' skins and torn to death by dogs, or fastened on crosses and burnt by night as human torches" (Tac. *Ann.* 15.44; cf. fig. 25). Immolation *(crematio)* was customary for arsonists (Dig. [Callistr.] 48.19.28.12). One version of this (the *tunica molesta*) required that the clothes of the condemned (which to add mockery were often made of gold and purple cloth) be covered in pitch and set alight (cf. Juv. 8.235; Martial 10.25.5, 4.86.8; Seneca *Epis. Mor.* 14.5). In this case, however, it aroused pity and compassion from the spectators, because it was felt the condemned were "sacrificed not for the welfare of the State, but to the ferocity of a single man." Nero himself attended these illuminations — which were held in the gardens of his private Vatican circus — dressed as a charioteer and demonstrating the common touch by mingling and exchanging pleasantries with the crowd.

Whether guilty or not of the fire, Nero unquestionably seized the opportunity it provided to fashion in the rebuilding of Rome "the greatest show on earth," with himself as star attraction. Despite the condemnation that this building program attracted from ancient historians who saw in it another expression of Nero's degeneracy and viciousness, modern commentators concede that "it represented an outstanding and innovative phase in the history of Roman art and architecture" (Elsner 1994, 119). In addition to the restoration and embellishment of the buildings that had been destroyed or damaged, the central area of the city was to be reconceived and made aesthetically more pleasing through the provision of parks, groves, and fountains, with a complex of imperial buildings scattered among them. In this Nero was extending an imperial precedent that viewed architecture as a particularly effective visual and three-dimensional medium for self-presentation that could be used by the ruler both to dramatize himself and to distinguish his rule and role from those of his predecessors. It is impossible to determine Nero's plans in detail because they were left incomplete at the time of his death and were abandoned by his successors, together of course with his reported intention of naming the newborn city after himself: Neropolis (Tac. *Ann.* 15.40.2; Suet. *Nero* 55). What is certain, however, is that vast areas of the new city were set aside for the construction of Nero's own megalomaniacal fantasy palace: the Domus Aurea.

The extravagance, decor, technical ingenuity, and architectural innovations of Nero's palace complex are too extensive to detail here.[24] What deserves particular emphasis, however, are its innate theatricality and its function within the larger mise-en-scène of the urban landscape. According to MacDonald (1982, 42), "Nero . . . wanted not only to belong to the world of art but also to surround himself with a visible proclamation of what he considered to be his power and his majesty. . . . In the *Domus Aurea* a theater of architecture and color was created for him. . . . His architect made brilliant use of the morphology and sensory impact of vaulted space, creating a unique dwelling for a despot of cosmic pretensions." The main house had a revolving dining room and other chambers outfitted with provision for showering guests with flowers or (as in the theatre) sprinkling them with perfume. With several hundred rooms, extensive colonnades, mosaic vaulting, splendidly coffered ceilings (some fashioned from ivory panels), and probably a private theater or odeum, it featured a magnificent *nymphaeum*: a "folly" for displaying cascading fountains amid statuary and architecture presented in the form of a stage facade. Elsewhere, "fountains . . . with many jets and streams, artificial grottoes, water

Fig. 26. An engraving of a painting, now lost, from the Domus Aurea in the form of a *scaenae frons*. (From N. Ponce, *Description des Bains de Titus* [1786], pl. 25)

stairs, and rigoles (stepped troughs producing continuous movement) added dimensions of motion and sound" (MacDonald 1982, 178). The baths of the palace were supplied with both seawater and sulfur waters.

The walls of the rooms were noted for sumptuous decorations executed by the painter Famulus (or Fabullus), who, according to Pliny, worked for only a few hours a day on his "florid" paintings, carrying out his labors with gravity (he was kept in virtual "imprisonment for his artistry") and wearing a toga even when mounted on scaffolding (*N.H.* 35.120). The surviving frescoes (or ones known from earlier engravings) prominently feature, among other motifs, the type of fantastical depiction of highly ornate *scaenarum frontes* characteristic of the so-called fourth Pompeian style of decoration, dating from Nero's reign, possibly originating with Famulus himself (fig. 26).[25] Such paintings, in representing the architecture of theatrical facades, themselves a mixture of both real and trompe l'oeil elements, draw the viewer into a pictorial fantasy. "Like the portrayals of Nero onstage and off, these paintings merged the theatrical with the 'real' and disabled both as a frame for viewing" (Bartsch 1994, 227). Moreover, in fashioning a dreamworld of architectural perspectives receding into the distance, glimpsed through the doors and windows of a *scaenae frons,* such paintings (executed in a particularly refined form in Nero's palace) have "scarcely any parallel except in the art of the spectacle: the theater and present-day cinema. The spectator has before him, beyond the plane of the stage set or screen, a world at once imaginary and real" (Picard 1968, 74).

These "scenographic" decorations, in which the wall is opened up illusionistically — with figures depicted in it as if set in a real environment — provided a harmonious enhancement of the effect that Nero's palace complex sought to instill in those experiencing it: wonder, admiration, and a degree of pleasurable disorientation. In a similar fashion "this effect of ambiguity and suggestion of incommensurability was completed by the continuity of the vault surfaces. They never came to any kind of linear or angled change of direction . . . so there was no reference point or structural angle from which the senses could derive an impression of load or structural membering" (MacDonald 1982, 177).

In addition to incorporating much of the existing imperial residential complex that had developed on the Palatine, the Domus Aurea stretched out over some two hundred acres (twice the size of Vatican City), crossing the Velian hill overlooking the Forum on the east, then sweeping northward; its main section was located on the Oppian hill forming the southwestern portion of the Esquiline, where it connected to the gardens of Maecenas, already renowned for their works of art and luxuriousness. This palatial complex sat amid extensive parkland, fields, vineyards, meadows, and woods, the latter incorporating a zoo filled with wild and domestic animals. A large lake — possibly forty feet deep — was created (where the Colosseum now stands), which was playfully fashioned to look like a sea surrounded by buildings in imitation of cities (*Nero* 31.1; Steinby 1995, 51–55). Immediately to the south of this, Nero converted the northern (as well as the eastern) side of the great platform and substructures supporting the temple of Divus Claudius (begun by Agrippina but not yet completed) into a series of ornamental fountains and cascades channeled into the lake (Barrett 1996, 148–50; Steinby 1993, 277–78; Richardson 1992, 88), providing a huge scenic backdrop. The symbolism was potent: Nero had abandoned the shrine of his recently deified stepfather and now converted its foundations into a piece of impressive scenery gracing his own godly domain. Tacitus notes that the marvels of the palace were not so much its "gold and gems . . . as its fields and lakes, and the sense of solitude conveyed by the settings of woods and open vistas" created by engineers "who had the ingenuity and courage to test the power of art against the strictures of nature, and to squander the wealth of an emperor" (Tac. *Ann.* 15.42). Nero was intent on rearranging both nature — cutting through the Velian hill and trimming the Oppian — and existing buildings, as he manipulated art and nature to create a vast and dazzling theatrical set.

His attempt to bring *rus in urbem* (the country into the city) and his linking of symbolic and sacred spaces in Rome that had forever been set apart were

seen as an outrageous transgression of "boundaries approved by Roman custom and upheld by moral rhetoric" (Elsner 1994, 122). It seemed as if Nero
had deliberately set out to provide the ultimate example of what his tutor,
Seneca, had characterized only a few years earlier as the soul-destroying vice
of unbridled luxury. "It desires to rest on ivory, to be arrayed in purple, to be
roofed with gold, to rearrange land, to confine the waters of the sea, to hurl
artificial rivers headlong, and to suspend gardens in the air" (*Ira* 1.21.1). Later
(perhaps even as the Domus Aurea was being built) he exclaimed, "Happy the
age before there were architects and builders!" or "houses as big as cities"
(*Epis. Mor.* 90.9, 43).

The entrance to the palace was approached from the Via Sacra in the Forum
along a magnificent triple colonnade eventually leading steeply upward into a
great vestibule decorated in gold and precious gems (Steinby 1995, 50–51,
55–56). Before this, crowning the summit of the Velian hill, the *Colossus,* a
120-foot-high nude statue of Nero himself (possibly with a radiant halo evoking the sun god, Sol), dominated the landscape (Suet. *Nero* 31; Pliny *N.H.*
34.45). Nero had summoned the Greek sculptor Zenodorus and offered him
the commission after learning of a huge statue of Mercury that the artist had
constructed over a period of ten years at Augustodunum (Autun) in Gaul. The
emperor had desired to have his giant image executed in gold and silver, but
Zenodorus preferred to cast it in bronze. Excavation reveals that the base
required to support such a giant measured some fifty-five by forty-five feet
(Steinby 1993, 295–98). Although nudity was no longer unusual in Roman
portrait statues, this Greek-inspired influence had been viewed with deep dis-
quiet by Romans of the late Republic, whose heroes — including military figures — were conventionally represented clad in the toga. By contrast, however, "in the Hellenistic world such statues celebrated the ruler's superhuman
strength and power. The pose and nudity are borrowed from statues of gods
and heroes, to whom the subject is thus implicitly likened, [and] must be
understood in relation to the ruler cults that were established in . . . the East on
the model of divine cults" (Zanker 1988, 5).

The message that Nero conveyed through the scenic emblem of his statue
overlooking the Forum and guarding his stately Xanadu was far removed
from the sobriety, experience, modesty, and virtue embodied in traditional
Roman statues. Its suggestion of an awesome divine presence towering over an
enormous vestibule that was itself a "great Neronian version of the patron's
meeting place with his clients" (Elsner 1994, 121) urged the citizen-spectators
to think of themselves as participants in a fantastic version of the traditional
relationship between dependents and patrons. According to Pliny (*N.H.*
35.51), Nero also created "the ultimate lunacy in painting" in the form of a

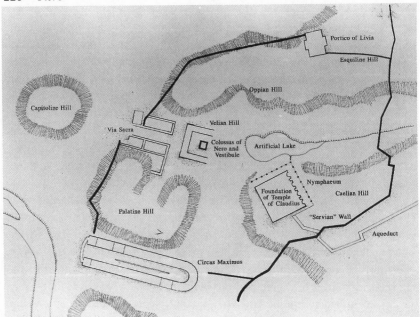

Fig. 27. Diagram showing the approximate area encompassed by the Domus Aurea. (Drawing by J. Glover)

second 120-foot-high image of himself depicted on a great canvas flat. "A thing unknown up to that time," it was erected in the Horti Maiani, which adjoined the Gardens of Maecenas, possibly on the same imperial estate where Caligula had received and terrified Philo and his fellow Jewish ambassadors twenty-five years earlier and where his ghost was reputed to have haunted the gardens after his burial (Philo *Leg.* 358 ff.; Suet. *Calig.* 59). Nero's image, situated near the summit of the Esquiline, approximately three thousand feet away from the *Colossus.* on its hill beyond the valley and lake below, would have served as a secondary iconic figure that, together with its twin, "guarded" and set off as a sort of "magic kingdom" the main body of the Domus Aurea lying between them. Pliny records that it was later struck by lightning and burned, "together with the best part of the gardens."

Tacitus observed that Nero had earlier treated all of Rome as if it were his palace, but now it seemed to the city's inhabitants that "one palace occupied the whole of Rome" (Martial *De Spect.* 2.4). Just as his residence—where he declared that "at last he could begin to live like a human being" (Suet. *Nero* 31.2)—was conceived as a theatrical "pleasure dome," so Nero increasingly began to employ the city itself as a stage set at the service of its actor-manager emperor (fig. 27). His expansionist impulse was another stark violation of traditional Roman decorum, epitomized by Horace's condemnation of one who "tears down the borders marking your plot, and in your greed transgress the boundaries of your tenants," warning that "no palace more surely awaits the wealthy lord than ravenous Hades' destined realm" (*Ode* 2.18.23–31). In thus rapaciously extending his *private* space, Nero went far beyond the practice of earlier emperors who had defined their principate primarily through the provision of prestigious *public* buildings. According to Suetonius, the spectator-inhabitants began to fear that they would be literally overwhelmed by the show. An epigram was circulated claiming that "Rome has become a house; move to Veii, citizens, if that house has not already occupied it too." Nero viewed this whimsical call for "flight to the suburbs" indulgently, it seems, together with other more critical allusions. Even the actor Datus, who in an Atellan farce pointedly illustrated his line " 'farewell father; farewell mother' with gestures of drinking and swimming, obviously referring to the death of Claudius and Agrippina," was punished with mere banishment (*Nero* 39.2–3; cf. Dio 61.16.2–3).

In A.D. 65, in the midst of his immensely expensive and controversial building program, Nero sent ships to North Africa in search of a welcome windfall: buried treasure. There, on the basis of a wild tale related to Nero by a madman who had bribed his way into the imperial presence, workmen frantically dug and searched for the site of a cave where centuries earlier Dido, queen of Carthage, had reportedly hidden a vast treasure trove of gold. "On the strength of this vain hope, Nero's extravagance grew and existing wealth was squandered as if new means were assured for financing further profligacy for years to come" (Tac. *Ann.* 16.3).[26] Much of the fantasy-fed Roman populace was immensely intrigued by the venture and enthusiastic about its anticipated benefits. Nero (possibly seeking to exploit this popular feeling) chose this moment to stage the second Neronia, which had likely been postponed following a brief "preview" early in the summer of 64. Not surprisingly, the orators charged with creating a suitable theme for these shows were inspired by the treasure hunt, developing the theme "with great eloquence and no less sycophancy, confident of Nero's gullibility." They merged it into the time-tested Golden Age motif, praising Nero's rule as one when "the earth gives forth a new form of fertility, and the gods bestow unsought wealth" (Tac. *Ann.* 16.2).

Command Performances

The gold was never found, but the show went on, nevertheless. At the first Neronia, Nero had been awarded prizes without actually performing. Suetonius (as cited earlier) records that although Nero had performed as *citharoedus* at the earlier installment of the second Neronia, he had then immediately postponed the rest of the contests, without taking his prize. Now the Senate tried to avert the scandal of further actual performance by offering him in advance both the crown for singing as well as (in the name of the first Neronia) granting him a prize for the more respectable skill of eloquence to veil the stigma implied by the "show business" connotation of the award for song. Nero refused outright to indulge their sense of propriety, insisting that he had no need for either the power or favor of the Senate: "He was meeting his rivals on equal terms, and relying on the conscience of the judges to award him the prize deserved" (Tac. *Ann.* 16.4). According to Pliny, Nero's previous, less public performances had all taken place at venues other than the great theater of Pompey (*N.H.* 37.19). Now, for the first time, he stood upon its vast stage and recited a poem. According to Dio, he selected a portion of one of his own compositions, the *Troica* (62.29.1). Presumably it would have been tactless to have recited any parts relating the burning of Troy so soon after the disastrous fire at Rome, particularly in light of rumors that Nero had sung of Troy's destruction during the conflagration.

In any case, the crowd soon clamored for him to "display all his accomplishments," demanding that he next perform, singing, as a *citharoedus*. Tacitus records that he once more obligingly took the stage; Suetonius adds: "Nero wished to compete amongst the citharoedi, but did not dare to do so, despite the general demand for him, and he left the theater. Vitellius [the future emperor who was presiding at the contests] called him back, alleging he came as an envoy from the insistent audience, thus allowing Nero to yield to their entreaties" (*Vit.* 4). Vitellius evidently had a gift for ingratiating himself with emperors, having won Caligula's friendship because of his chariot racing, Claudius's company "through his passion for dice," and now Nero's affection for his timely sycophancy. Nero in effect now played two roles: that of humble competitor as well as the character evoked by his arias. The former he performed impeccably, following all the prescribed conventions, which evidently sought to preserve a dignified and hieratic attitude, dictating that the performer remain standing, that he not carry or use any cloth (except his robe) to deal with perspiration, and that he not visibly clear his throat or nose. Tacitus concludes by recording that "finally, on bended knee, with a hand extended in humble supplication to that mob, Nero feigned anxiety awaiting the verdict of the judges" (Tac. *Ann.* 16.4).

It is difficult to determine the nature, much less the quality, of his presentations because the evidence suggests a wide divergence of opinion concerning what were to a significant degree political rather than artistic events. The urban plebs, according to Tacitus, at least pretended to be hugely entertained, while those members of the audience whose business had brought them to the city from remoter parts of Italy (where old-fashioned values were adhered to) "were neither able to endure the spectacle, nor competent to their degrading task" of rapturously cheering and applauding the performing *Princeps*. They failed to keep time with the acclamations and the studious rhythmic clapping of the trained supporters and had to be exhorted or disciplined by the "soldiers stationed in the aisles to ensure that not a moment was wasted in temporary disharmony or interruption" (Tac. *Ann.* 16.5).

His performances were, obviously, a particularly potent form of political theater, and so too was the reaction to them. The spectators' response differed not only according to the extent of their experience with theatrical performance but also inevitably along political lines, depending on the degree to which factions supported or opposed Nero. Tacitus states that some members of the equestrian order were crushed as they struggled to reach the exits (attempting presumably to "vote with their feet" as they rose from their reserved seats in the first fourteen rows) and were engulfed by the crowd surging downward, possibly seeking a closer view of the extraordinary spectacle. He asserts too that it was dangerous not just to attempt to leave but indeed to be *seen* to do so, "since there were a great many spies both openly present and more concealed, noting the names and faces, the enthusiasm or disapproval of the crowd" (Tac. *Ann.* 16.5). Unimportant spectators might be punished on the spot, while those of greater standing were noted and could anticipate deferred retribution. Thus, the spectators were themselves unwittingly taking part in the performance: they were being watched. The total architectural enclosure afforded by the structural unity of the Roman theater (reinforced by its awesome scenic embellishment) was thus joined to a form of rigid psychological containment to create a totalitarian artwork: the ultimate "environmental theater."

It is in part because of this situation that the nature of any genuine reception of Nero's performance is difficult to determine or assess. As Bartsch points out (1994, 11), "In those contexts in which there exists a well-defined, self-conscious audience (as with Nero's stage performances — or modern metatheater), it entails a reversal of the normal one-way direction of the spectators' gaze, so that they know themselves watched by the object of their view and respond accordingly even as the categories of spectacle and spectator lose all stability." Under such circumstances, Bartsch continues, the reception of the performance is largely determined according to the agenda of the more powerful "performer/spectator," because "the dominant member is felt to have a stake in controlling the appearance, and so the public meaning, of the interaction." In such an unequal balance of power, those who already have grounds to envy the power or resent the activity of the dominant performer are likely to find the situation particularly offensive and disturbing, and this is precisely the impression conveyed by Tacitus and the other historians upon whom our knowledge of Nero's performances depends. Under the circumstances, however, such accounts cannot be uncritically relied upon because they arise from a historical tradition whose origins lie in that section of the audience — the senators — most immediately compromised by the conditions in which the performances took place. Indeed, the particular resentment felt by the senatorial class with regard to the *position* (in the literal sense) in which they found themselves in the theater may well have colored their perception and accounts not just of Nero's behavior in the theater but of his reign in general.

Because of the prominent location of their seats in the focal point of the orchestra, senators were visible and vulnerable not just to scrutiny by Nero himself on the stage immediately above them, or to his spies, but also to the great mass of the audience. What had traditionally been a prestigious place of honor on account of its high visibility now became a veritable "hot seat," and indeed the only specific citations of failure to applaud name senators.[27] Consequently "the mass acquiescence that the sources pointedly attribute to the efficacy of an audience surveillance (which these writers may have borne the brunt of) could simply conceal the fact that the great mass of the common people enjoyed and encouraged the imperial performances" (Bartsch 1994, 30).

Senators certainly had excellent grounds for being wary and self-conscious. Shortly before the Neronia, a conspiracy against the emperor's life had been uncovered. It was led by Gaius Calpurnius Piso, who was a Hellenist and, like Nero himself, sang and played the cithara, although probably only in private. Tacitus relates only that Piso had sung costumed as a tragedian, which may indicate that the plot was perhaps not primarily a reaction against Nero's histrionic excesses per se. They were, however, clearly an issue, because in the course of the conspiracy some suggested that Piso should be disposed of in turn, for "as far as disgrace went, what difference did it make if a *citharoedus* was removed, and replaced by a *tragoedus?*" (Tac. *Ann.* 15.65). Moreover, one of those making this suggestion (the praetorian tribune Subrius Flavus) subsequently confessed that primary among his reasons for hating the emperor was indeed his behavior as an actor (Tac. *Ann.* 15.67). The plan had apparently been to murder Nero in the Circus Maximus while the *Cerealia* — games that traditionally had strongly plebeian associations — were being held (April 12–19, 65), because "the emperor went regularly to the Circus entertainments and could be approached with comparative ease in the gaiety of the spectacles" (Tac. *Ann.* 15.53).

In choosing this murder plan, the conspirators sought to script a bit of "political theater" themselves, as well as to "stage a revival" of the tyrannicide-drama that characterized the deaths of Caesar and Caligula. "It is as though the conspirators intended that spectators should not after all be deprived of a *ludus scaenicus* on the final day: namely, the reenactment of the murder of Julius Caesar, which itself had been staged in a place with theatrical connections" (Woodman 1993, 107). It also, of course, would have fittingly followed the pattern of theatrical murders staged by Nero himself.[28] Following the discovery of the plot, fifty-one people were charged, including nineteen senators and seven equestrians. Nineteen alleged conspirators were executed and another thirteen were banished. Those sentenced to death included Seneca (who had served as Nero's most prominent adviser and assisted as "cheerleader" at the Iuvenalia performances) and the poet Lucan (who had himself been awarded the prize for poetry at the first Neronia). Following this bloodbath, Tacitus records that the Senate voted that sacrifices and thanks be offered to Sol, whose ancient temple was located in the Circus Maximus where the assassination was to have taken place. The Cerealia were celebrated with additional horse races, and the month of April was renamed Neroneus (cf. Suet. *Nero* 55). As a suitably histrionic gesture, Nero inscribed the dagger that had been intended for him to "Jupiter the Avenger," consecrating it on the Capitol. He modestly turned down the suggestion that a temple be dedicated at once to Divus Nero out of concern that it might be tempting providence: divinity was bestowed by Roman citizens upon an emperor only "once he has ceased to live and move among men" (Tac. *Ann.* 15.74). As the survivors now gathered under the watchful eye of the emperor and his spies for the second Neronia, such things must have preoccupied their imagination and starkly colored their perception of the "show."

On the Art of the Theater

Before further assessing the probable impact of such imperial performances, it is useful to consider the genres of theatrical expression practiced in Nero's era. Leaving aside mime, comedy, and comic pantomime, serious theater consisted of the tragic pantomime *(tragoedia saltata)*, concert recitals of tragic material *(tragoedia cantata)*, closely related presentations by *citharoedia*, and possibly enactments of complete works in the form of traditional tragedy. Although Nero was sometimes called *histrio* — a term commonly applied in Latin of the imperial period to pantomimists — the word could also mean simply "actor" or even "performer," and it is unlikely that Nero ever actually participated in pantomimes. Suetonius, however, asserts that at the end of his reign Nero revealed an ambition to dance the *Turnus,* a tragic pantomime presumably based on Vergil's text (*Nero* 54). The suggestion that Nero did indeed intend to extend his repertoire is strengthened by Suetonius's report that Nero executed the pantomime performer Paris "as a dangerous rival," although Dio claims he was condemned because "the emperor had wished to learn dancing from him, but lacked the talent" (63.18.1). Such assertions may of course have been only malicious rumor, and it is important to note that in the various catalogues of Nero's aesthetic "offenses" recorded by the ancient historians, none mentions pantomimic dancing. In particular, the scornful allusion made by Dio Chrysostom, a contemporary of the emperor who probably was in Rome during his reign, to the extensive skills *(technai)* that Nero sought to master does not include pantomime. "A certain king of our time was ambitious to be clever in this sort of knowledge, believing he knew a great deal . . . such as acting as herald, singing to the cithara, reciting tragedies, wrestling, and participating in the *pancration*. Moreover he is said to have painted, sculpted, and played the pipe: was he not then a clever man?" (*Dis.* 71.5–9).

It is difficult to distinguish between the content of *tragoedia cantata* and the *citharoedia* beyond the important fact that the latter term could be extended to include a variety of songs not directly derived from tragic material. The *citharoedus* accompanied himself on his instrument while singing tragic arias, odes, hymns, or other types of songs. His tragic pieces may have resembled or even been the same as those sung by the chorus (or soloist) that normally accompanied the performance of the mute pantomime as he used his movements, gestures, and masks to depict a variety of characters and situations. The *citharoedus* generally wore a "neutral" costume consisting of a loose, flowing ungirted robe (often with a long cloak) and slippers or half boots and performed without a mask or props. The *tragoedus,* who both sang and acted his role, wore an appropriate mask whose elongated forehead *(onkos)* and gaping mouth gave it a decidedly unnatural aspect. He also had a full-length tunic, belted at the waist, that was usually ornate in its embroidery, colors, and decorations. The most characteristic element of tragic costume was a high platform shoe, which, together with the mask and padding of the torso, turned the actor into an overgrown simulacrum of a man, tending perhaps to stumble rather than to strut upon the stage. Indeed, Lucian, in his mid-second-century A.D. essay on pantomime, characterizes the appearance of the tragic actor as "a dreadful hideous sight! A man out of all proportion, perched on high clogs, mask stretching far over his head with a great gaping mouth fit to swallow the audience. Not to mention all that padding for chest and stomach so as not to betray a slender figure. And inside, the man himself, howling away, rocking back and forth as he chants out his lines and—how awful can you get— making a song out of his disasters" (*De Salt.* 27).

The tragic performer might present his role solo, accompanied by a chorus, or in the company of other actors with whom he engaged in spoken dialogue. These options would depend on (and in turn determine) the degree of "performance values" desired, ranging from simple concert recitations (which in their most austere form would be read rather than sung) to full-scale productions with a cast of characters and a chorus. These choices would be reflected in the venue selected: lecture hall, private house, or theater. There is textual evidence for this entire spectrum of presentations during Nero's era. The first recorded purpose-built public indoor theater in Rome, which probably held five to seven thousand spectators and was ideally suited to small-scale production as well as music and recitations, was the odeum erected in the Campus Martius during the reign of Domitian (A.D. 81–96). Such structures, however, had long been evident elsewhere in Italy; the earliest, built in Pompeii, appeared early in the first century B.C. It is likely that Nero himself established an odeum — by remodeling an existing basilica — found in Cosa a hundred miles north of Rome where a small-scale artistic center had flourished during his reign (Izenour 1992, 114–18).

Tacitus composed a dialogue evoking a conversation with his friend Curiatius Maternus,[29] who (perhaps at such a venue) had given a spirited recital of his historical play *Cato* — a *praetexta* — that had offended certain powerful figures. Nevertheless, the poet (who is also credited with both a tragedy, *Medea,* and an earlier historical drama, *Domitius,* prior to his *Cato*) announces his intention in the near future to compose and recite a further work: his tragedy *Thyestes.* Maternus points out that some years back it was through the recitations of his drama that he had first gained fame, when a play he had written about Nero (presumably presented shortly after his fall) successfully broke the power of a particularly disreputable Neronian courtier, Vatinius.[30] Apart from the obvious political risk of reciting potentially subversive works, Tacitus refers in passing to the fact that the poet must "rent a house and prepare an auditorium, hire seating and distribute programs" (*Dial. de Orator.* 9).

Evidence that tragic performances in Rome in this period could extend beyond mere recitation is found (apart from accounts of Nero's activity) in such writers as Pliny the Younger, who states that he revises his own compositions by reciting them before a select audience, which he contrasts with tragic performances that require "not a lecture hall, but a stage and actors," while lyric poetry needs a chorus and lyre (*Epis.* 7.17). Seneca (in addition to writing tragedies himself) notes that "we are attracted to the theater to satisfy the pleasures of the ear, whether by a speech, or by a song, or by a play" (*Epis. Mor.* 108.6); elsewhere he refers to the skill of "actors in the theater who imitate the emotions, express fear and nervousness, depict sorrow, and portray bashfulness by hanging their heads, lowering their voices, and fixing their

eyes on the ground" (*Epis. Mor.* 11.7). Although the extent of public performance elsewhere in the Empire is difficult to assess,[31] the various inscriptions
relating to the *agones* document not only that staging did continue to take
place but also that at least some new works were still being composed for
performance. For example, a decree from this period relating to the Athenian
festival of the Great *Panathenaea* notes that a particular individual "was *cho-
regos* and . . . directed a brand new tragedy" (Csapo and Slater 1995, 206). At
the end of the first century A.D., Plutarch records that a friend (who is known
from other evidence to have been a tragic author himself) had recently been a
victorious director of a tragic chorus *(chorodidaskalos)* at the most venerable
of all dramatic festivals, the Athenian Dionysia, and this too may have been
new work (*Mor.* 628A). Writing in the same period, Quintilian frequently
refers to performances, noting for example that he has "often seen actors both
in tragedy and comedy leave the theater still drowned in tears after finishing
acting some moving role" (*Inst. Orat.* 6.2.35).

Although the late-second-century account by Apuleius of a lavish myth-
based ballet production cited earlier demonstrates that elaborate stagings of
some types of subject matter were mounted and presumably popular, it is
likely that full-scale performance of tragedy was relatively infrequent and
new tragic writing intended for the stage rare. About a century earlier, Dio
Chrysostom notes that although comedies are still presented intact, only the
"stronger portions" of tragedy remain: the sensational arias and emotional set
pieces, but not the linking passages or lyric choruses (*Orat.* 19.4–5). This
trend was probably already evident by the reign of Nero. Although there is
ample evidence for the presentation of tragedies at the agones, the competitive
element at these would have itself tended to require short pieces, possibly
fashioned by condensing full-length originals. An inscription of A.D. 127 cata-
loging the Caesarea of Corinth mentions contests between performers of both
tragedies and comedies, as well as between authors of newly composed comedies, implying that there were no new tragedies available for entry (see C. P.
Jones 1993, 46).

Seneca, in a suggestive passage, speaks with contempt of the tragic actor
"who sweeps grandly across the stage and says with head thrown back, 'lo, I
rule Argos: my kingdom I have from Pelops . . . ' He is a slave; he gets his five
measures of grain and five denarii. And look at the actor who with such pride
and abandon and confidence in his power swellingly proclaims, 'And if you
hold not your peace, Menelaus, this right hand will fell you.' He gets his daily
wage and sleeps under a patch coat" (*Epis. Mor.* 80.7–8).[32] And yet, this was
the profession — so scorned in Roman society — that Nero, ruler of the world,
now embraced. According to Suetonius, following the second Neronia, Nero

embarked on numerous public appearances. "He put on the mask and sang tragedies representing gods and heroes, and even goddesses and heroines, with the masks made to resemble himself or the women he happened to fancy" (*Nero* 21). In addition (presumably) to reciting lengthy passages or even complete tragedies, he also presented such sensational excerpts as *Orestes the Matricide, The Blinding of Oedipus,* or *The Madness of Hercules.* He was even alleged to have considered lowering himself to appear among professional actors at ordinary games given by the public officials, when one of the responsible praetors sought — like a modern opera producer — to add splendor to his games with the performance of an emperor, purchased for a fee of a million sesterces (*Nero* 21). Tacitus details his performances only in the less disreputable guise of a *citharoedus* — the portions of his history that would have covered the full flowering of Nero's acting career are lost — but he does record (verbatim) that one of those who conspired against Nero in 65, when questioned before Nero himself about his motives, replied, "I began to hate you when you turned into the murderer of your mother and wife — a chariot-driver, an actor *(histrio),* an arsonist" (Tac. *Ann.* 15.67; cf. Dio 62.24.2). The evidence of other sources is conclusive. Nero performed as a tragic actor, probably first in Rome in 65–66 and then later (from which most references are drawn) during his extraordinary histrionic odyssey in Greece in A.D. 66–67.

Strange Interlude

The effect on public opinion of Nero's debut upon the public stage was profound. Apart from the politically based resentments and fears of many in the senatorial class — who resented the emperor's popularity and felt that his excessive desire for acclamation revealed a tyrannical conception of his authority — a substantial segment of the upper orders would have opposed it on moral grounds alone. Actors performing professionally for pay had of course been subject to *infamia* and various legal restrictions for many years (*Dig.* [Ulpian] 3.2.2.5; cf. Ducos 1990). But the feeling and expression of public disapproval among traditionalists was not limited to formal sanctions. Rather, the repugnance felt for actors arose from the perception that historically their craft was an essentially foreign art, practiced by people of little social consequence whose whole business involved trafficking in a *levitas* inappropriate for serious-minded citizens. Cicero pointed out that traditionally Romans had viewed "the art of entertaining and the act of appearing on stage in general as a disgrace" (*De Rep.* 4.10). Even to display too great an interest or ability in learning to dance might be considered morally suspect by Romans, in marked contrast to its esteem among the Greeks, who valued dance as an important element of aristocratic education (cf. Macrobius *Sat.* 3.14.4–15). Actors, moreover, presented themselves in public but used the highly revered art of rhetoric to feign personalities other than themselves while appealing for support not on moral, political, or intellectual grounds but purely for their capacity to entertain by, in a most literal sense, offering (or if professionals, selling) their bodies as virtual slaves (Cic. *De Off.* 1.150). Indeed, by contrast, would-be orators were specifically warned to avoid any hint of overtly theatrical gestures or language in pursuing their craft.[33]

Undoubtedly in part because of their positions outside respectable society, actors had also developed an almost proverbial reputation for behaving badly, associated with prostitution, duplicity, informing, and, of course, a great deal of public disorder.[34] As ever in the prevalent Roman vision of a relentlessly decaying moral order, there was felt to be an imminent danger that vices, once taken root, would spread to infect all of society. As Juvenal later put it, "With an emperor as *citharoedus,* is it strange a noble should act as a mime? What else remains except the school for gladiators?" (8.198–99). Although more sophisticated members of the aristocracy had a good deal of respect for the performing arts and were quite willing to grant a particular "dispensation" for those performing in the sacred *agones,* many more — conditioned to resent Nero and his works — viewed his public performances as an unmitigated and unforgivable scandal.

It was not merely that Nero through his performances tactlessly demonstrated his power to abolish the normative rules governing society, causing his political opponents to wish to deny and curtail that power. It was rather that such behavior engendered a giddy sense that reality and illusion had merged, that the ordinary categories and signs by which a deeply conservative society made sense of itself had collapsed into a black-comedy world of topsy-turvydom.

"We unmask the actor playing the emperor and find the same face underneath. . . . The theater, where appearances ought to be deceptive, was the only place the emperor really was the emperor, while, everywhere else, appearances had become quite unreliable, as the emperor roamed about his own city in disguise" (Edwards 1994, 93). Writing at the time, Seneca the Younger used the metaphor of a distorting mirror to describe the moral confusion of a society transfixed by "illusion and the insubstantial imitations of real objects," unable to distinguish the fantastic from the real (*Nat. Quaes.* 1.16–17).

Of course the principate itself was based on a fragile and even absurd state of affairs whereby on the one hand the emperor sought to act as sovereign by absolute right, even though his power notionally was conferred on him by the Senate "which was too powerful to behave like a mere council without responsibility and yet was not powerful enough to be able sometimes to impose its sovereign will" (Veyne 1990, 411). The Senate and *Princeps* tolerated each other at the cost of hypocrisy and a consequent ambiguity and irreality that permeated the system. At the same time, within the broader mass of the urban population, the reaction to an acting emperor was relatively straightforward and strongly positive. Even Tacitus, who elsewhere consistently expresses the view of his own outraged senatorial class, concedes in a melancholy passage that "the urban plebs, accustomed to encourage the behavior of even an ordinary actor, thundered their approval in rhythmic and measured cadences. You might have thought them to be rejoicing, and perhaps they were rejoicing, oblivious to the national shame" (Tac. *Ann.* 16.4). During the half century since the death of Augustus, the image and role of the *Princeps* had evolved from that of "first citizen" guiding government primarily by virtue of superior *dignitas* and *auctoritas* to that of virtual demigod, reigning by divine right. Both Augustus and Claudius had been deemed gods after their demise, and Caligula, living, had assiduously embellished himself with divine trappings. The ideology of the principate had increasingly created through every aesthetic means a cult of flattery, adulation, and reverence with little to distinguish it—particularly in the popular mind—from outright worship of the emperor as a living god (cf. Price 1980).

As this melding of aesthetics and politics progressed, the boundaries between art and life, between emperor and god, and ultimately between reality and illusion became ever more permeable. Commentators then and later were struck by the uncanny similarity, for example, between what Nero did onstage and off and, in particular, between his real-life crimes and those his fictional roles enacted in the theater. Those dramatis personae for which he was specifically noted—-Alcmeon, Orestes, Oedipus, Thyestes, and Hercules—were characters who had themselves engaged in such alleged Neronian acts as matricide, incest, usurpation of the throne, and murder of close relatives (cf. Dio 63.22.6). As Bartsch notes (1994, 47), "Nero, who was already seen as reproducing his life on the stage, did so at an inescapably visual level as well and almost *inflicted* the equation of his persona with his tragic roles upon the audiences at these plays." Both Suetonius and Dio record the intriguing fact that when playing these mythic parts, Nero frequently wore a mask depicting his own features (Suet. *Nero* 21; Dio 63.9.5).

What was a spectator meant to see, or think? In one important sense, of course, the audience was not intended to think at all. The whole purpose of such political pageantry was not ultimately to persuade, nor even to work as propaganda, because by and large its audience now was not expected to make a choice or required to express any opinion. Rather, the object of such artistry was to employ all the available means of expression to appeal through the perceptive senses directly to the emotion of the spectators and thereby to create in them a feeling of exaltation, celebration, and awe, in effect "for the sole pleasure of being acclaimed and reigning absolutely in their hearts" (Veyne 1990, 378). It was intended first to demonstrate the glory and triumph of power itself and then, through ritual and ceremony, to organize it as public drama. The emperor was himself the "star" of his shows, which began by involving the audience in extending ritual homage to him with the different sections of the crowd rhythmically chanting and singing their acclamations.[35] The choice of later tyrants (such as Hitler or Mussolini in this century) to adapt such imperial, "fascist" imagery — military display, the scenic use of crowds, vast processions, visually emotive graphics, and costumes coordinated with stirring music and mass choreography — to the service of the cult of the leader and his sacred mission was calculated and frequently quite successful. As Walter Benjamin observed, fascism was based in part on the "aestheticization of politics and the politicization of aesthetics," for which it drew extensively upon ancient example (Taylor 1990, 11). The "rhythmic and measured cadences" of the organized acclamations in the imperial Roman theater echoed distantly in the slogans and "Sieg Heils" of fascist rallies.[36]

Nero could wear a mask of himself because in a most literal sense he was playing himself, fulfilling for the crowd its expectation of what its godlike leader should be — imbued with all the potency that myth, patriotism, and religion could provide — as he simultaneously thrilled and flattered it with the overwhelming joy of being in his very presence and, at the same time, the object of his affection and benevolence. His histrionic activity was a further extension and concession to the syndrome whereby "every gesture represented a new act in imperial self-definition" that invited comparison with his predecessors and determined therefore that "the fulfillment of the imperial office was beset by a permanent anxiety of influence" (Elsner 1994, 113). Other emperors had provided the Roman people with gifts and entertainments and impressed it with the spectacle of their presence; Nero gave *himself* to the people by seeking to please them with his talents while petitioning their approval of his artistic service.

The magnitude of this service was enhanced and made more precious coming as it did from one who claimed, correctly, "I have the power to destroy kingdoms and to create them" (Dio 63.5.3). Nero's desire to exhibit this power, and his taste for adulation, grandeur, and extravagant display (unfettered by clear constitutional restraints) drew him relentlessly toward an absolutist view of his "office." Although not actually calling himself by the unacceptable title of "king," the traditional Hellenistic concept of "the absolute monarch, splendid in wealth, dress and abode, adored by his subjects to whom he was both a source of awe and a fountain of benefits" (Griffin 1985, 219) exercised a powerful pull on his imagination. At the same time, the venerable patriotic and religious connotations of the theater in Roman cultural life allowed him to broadcast this vision of his own role as *Princeps* while simultaneously entering into a powerful, mutually supportive relationship with his audience, the Roman people, whom Cicero had once characterized as "princes [*principes*] of all the world and every people" (*Phil* 3.14) and "master of kings, conqueror and *imperator* of all the world" (*De Dom.* 90). In marked contrast to all emperors since Augustus, Nero used the potent title *imperator* not just according to established tradition as an exceptional salutation bestowed under specific circumstances but (after several travesties including an award following the defeat of the Pisonian conspiracy) by eventually adopting it as a permanent *praenomen,* a prefix to his own name comparable in usage — and increasingly in its meaning — to that of "king" (cf. Griffin 1985, 231–33).

Nero's role, therefore, was literally that of "he who plays the king": an embodiment of national identity, by means of the iconography of his theatrical appearance and actions, he reflected upon the audience their own flattering image. At the same time, an influential segment of that audience — the old senatorial elite — would have been appalled not just by the notion of a play-acting *Princeps* but also by what they must view as a highly inappropriate role: an absolute ruler grotesquely trampling upon the last vestiges of the republican constitution. The drama being played out in the theater therefore (both on stage and in the audience) was in a direct sense "The Final Decline and Fall of the Roman Republic," whose plot, however well known to the participants, was nevertheless now brashly broadcast in a manner certain to offend many in its audience by overwhelming much of the carefully crafted ambiguity and deceptive stagecraft of the early principate.

In addition to their impact upon the audience, such performances may also have transfigured Nero himself. The consciousness and ostentatious celebration of absolute power — as many other historical examples affirm — can exercise an almost unbearable psychological strain, as the individual's innate physical and sensual limitations are confronted and challenged by a notional power that by contrast is virtually limitless, commensurate only with what an unbridled and overwrought imagination can conceive and encompass. Theater as the "art of the impossible" provides an escape of sorts from the intolerable burden that finitude and mortality places on those to whom everything is otherwise allowed, but it can also lead to destructive delusion and even to madness.

"That Nero escaped more and more into a world of fantasy from the time of the second *Neronia* is a conclusion difficult to resist, even allowing for malicious distortion in our sources" (Griffin 1985, 164). Soon after the contests, his second wife, Poppaea, died while pregnant, allegedly having been kicked by Nero in a fit of anger caused, according to Suetonius, by her having scolded him for returning late from the chariot races (Tac. *Ann.* 16.6; Suet. *Nero* 35.2). Whether from real or feigned grief, he held an elaborate funeral, her body embalmed like an Oriental queen before being placed in the Mausoleum of Augustus. Nero himself delivered the funeral oration and had her declared a goddess. Thereafter when he performed female roles in tragedies, he often wore a mask representing her face "so that, though dead, she might take part in the spectacle" (Dio 63.9.5). Nero also chose a eunuch, Sporus, as consort because his looks reminded the emperor of her (Dio 62.28.2–3) and, if Suetonius and Dio are to be believed, later "married him with all the usual ceremonies . . . and thereafter treated him as his wife . . . decked out in the finery of an empress and riding in a litter . . . fondly kissing him from time to time" (*Nero* 28.1–2; cf. Dio 63.13.1–2). Suetonius follows this report with an account of even more bizarre behavior with another favorite, Doryphorus. The emperor chose him to serve as his "husband" and also sometimes used him in a peculiar sexual scenario "in which, covered with the skin of some wild animal, Nero was let loose from a cage and attacked the private parts of men and women tied to stakes until, having satisfied his lust, he was 'finished off' by his freedman" (*Nero* 29; cf. Dio 63.13.2–3).

Apart from these private *divertissements,* shortly after Poppaea's death Nero instituted another reign of terror, ordering that various real or imagined enemies be prosecuted for treason. As they were duly eliminated, "he boasted that no prince had ever known what power he really had, and began frequently to give unambiguous hints that he would not even spare those of the Senate who survived, but one day would wipe out their entire order" (*Nero* 36.2). Foremost among those accused was Thrasea Paetus, a distinguished conservative senator and former consul of impeccable integrity. In Nero's eyes his offenses ranged from his lack of enthusiasm at the Iuvenalia back in 59, through his avoidance of taking the customary annual vows ratifying the acts of previous emperors and those for Nero's own welfare, to his absence from Poppaea's funeral and consecration (Tac. *Ann.* 16.21–22). Augmenting such irksome "passive resistance" and apart perhaps from irritating Nero with an unfestive sobriety that gave him "the appearance of a school-master" (*Nero* 37.2), Thrasea infuriated the emperor because, far from being ignorant or dismissive of the fine arts, he was actually something of a connoisseur; it was Nero's art that he disdained. "He would never listen to Nero's singing or cithara-playing, nor sacrifice to his Divine Voice like all the rest, nor give public exhibitions, even though it was known that at Patavium [modern Padua], his home, he had himself once acted in a tragedy performed by custom at a festival" (Dio 62.26.3–4; cf. Tac. *Ann.* 16.21.1). His performance then had probably been part of some ritualistic observance rather than mere public entertainment. Now he demonstrated that he also knew how to die in an appropriately tragic mode, exclaiming as he opened his arteries, "to thee Jupiter, Patron of Freedom, I pour this libation of blood."

At the time of Thrasea's trial in May 66, there was a further highly public display of Nero's growing megalomania. An extraordinary celebration was held to mark the state visit of Tiridates, king of Armenia, who as part of a peace settlement three years earlier had ceremoniously laid down his crown before a chair and statue of Nero on the understanding that he would resume it only from the emperor's own hand in Rome (Tac. *Ann.* 15.29). Nero had used this purely diplomatic "victory" as an excuse to hold a triumph (Dio 62.23.4; cf. Griffin 1985, 231). Now, after a journey of nine months (during which the Roman treasury had footed the daily cost of some eight hundred thousand sesterces), Tiridates' exotic and impressive entourage — including some three thousand Parthian cavalry — was conducted to Nero's residence at Naples. There he knelt, paying obeisance to the emperor and calling him master. Nero responded by escorting him to Puteoli — where in the previous year the amphitheater had been refurbished and enlarged — for a magnificent gladiatorial display staged upon sand imported from the Nile, with the entire ensemble of combatants — males, females, adults, and children — composed of Ethiopians. Tiridates joined in the fun by shooting at wild beasts from his elevated seat, bagging (according to Dio's skeptical report) two bulls with a single arrow (Dio 63.3.1).

The grand retinue then progressed to Rome, where Tacitus notes that "the entire population streamed out to welcome the Emperor and stare at the King" (Tac. *Ann.* 16.24). Dio adds details of what was clearly intended — as indeed Suetonius specifically termed it — to be a magnificent spectacle of state. "The entire city was decorated with torches and garlands, huge crowds everywhere, and the Forum particularly full. Its center was occupied by civilians, arranged according to rank, clad in white and carrying laurel branches; everywhere else were soldiers, lined up in shining armor, weapons and standards flashing like lightning. The very roof-tiles and all the surrounding buildings were entirely hidden from view by spectators who had clambered onto the roofs. Everything had been thus arranged during the night; and at daybreak Nero, wearing the triumphal garb and accompanied by the Senate and the Praetorian Guards, entered the Forum" (63.4.1–3; cf. Suet. *Nero* 13.). Nero took his seat in a curule chair on the *rostra,* which was decked out with banners and standards. As Tiridates and his entourage approached, they were stunned by the glittering array and momentarily halted in their tracks by a great approving roar from the audience. Then he approached, ascending along a sloping ramp set up for the occasion and flanked by heavily armed troops. After prostrating himself and kissing the earth in the elaborate Oriental gesture of worshipful obeisance (known as *proskynesis*)[37] and addressing Nero as "my god to worship as I do Mithras," Tiridates servilely praised Nero and delivered his sons and nephews as hostages while his words were translated and proclaimed to the rapt spectators. Nero first directed him to sit at his feet, then extending his hand raised him up, kissed him, replaced his turban with a royal diadem, and formally declared him King of Armenia while a great shout went up from the spectators. Everyone adjourned to the theater of Pompey.

Special games had been decreed, and the stage and the entire interior of the theater of Pompey were gilded to mark the occasion (Dio 63.6.1–2; cf. Pliny *N.H.* 33.54). There, before the assembly, Tiridates once again formally performed the role of suppliant, while the crowd gazed down from beneath the great purple *vela* spanning the theater " in the center of which was an embroidered figure of Nero driving a chariot, with golden stars gleaming all about him" (Dio 63.6.2). The unsubtle but highly emotive imagery — golden theater, subservient king, and Apollonian emperor — was calculated to make an indelible impression on all who witnessed it, as clearly it did; afterward the occasion was popularly referred to as the "golden day." As a crowning touch, Nero held a sumptuous banquet, performed on the cithara and later drove a chariot dressed and helmeted in all the appropriate gear of his favored circus faction, the Greens. To conclude this extravagant "total work of art" and synthesis of politics, pageantry, patriotism, and religion, Nero placed a triumphal wreath in the Capitol and closed the doors of the temple of Janus, formally signifying that the entire empire was now at peace. Tiridates was honored with an equestrian statue in Rome (Steinby 1995, 232) and sent home with costly gifts — worth one hundred million sesterces according to Suetonius, twice that much in Dio's account — and permission to rebuild his capital city of Artaxata (burned by the Romans in A.D. 58), which he renamed Neronia.

The entire event ranged far beyond the bounds of mere propaganda to become a suggestive ritual of vivid symbolism, fashioning through every medium a masterful expression of Nero's own self-image and mythmaking and then making a "gift" of this to entertain his clients and dependents, the Roman people. Pliny refers to a more private motive as well. Tiridates was accompanied by a number of his holy men, the Magi, and Nero sought to be initiated into certain of their rites, hoping thereby to control the gods by magic. Failing to acquire the necessary powers, he abandoned his efforts (*N.H.* 30.15, 17).

Although the realm of the supernatural may have exceeded even his expansive grasp, in the artistic sphere there were still glittering prizes to win and other worlds left to conquer.

"The Only Victor of the Grand Tour, the Only One from the Beginning of Time"

Prompted by the honor and flattery extended by the emissaries of the *agones* in Greece, who customarily conveyed to him the crowns for the citharoedic contests, and after declaring in response to their enthusiastic endorsement of his talents that "the Greeks alone are worthy of my genius; they know how to listen to music" (Suet. *Nero* 22.3), Nero commenced his previously delayed trip to Greece. He departed probably in September 66, returning around January 68 — sixteen months later — an absence from Rome that exceeded any emperor's since Tiberius's extended (and greatly resented) sojourn on Capri. To enable him to compete in all the major *agones,* these four-yearly events were rescheduled (and in several cases repeated) to create a probable grand-touring sequence during which Nero first appeared at the Actian and then at the Pythian, Isthmian, Nemean, and Olympian festivals before returning to perform a second time at the first three contests. The traditional content of some of the festivals was altered, with tragic acting introduced to the *Isthmia* of Corinth and a musical contest interpolated into the *Olympia.*

Despite the later lamentations of Dio, Suetonius, Juvenal, and others over such behavior, and the scorn expressed for what they characterized and castigated as the grossly sycophantic and undeserved honors heaped upon a dangerous and deranged buffoon, both Nero's intentions and the achievements of his Grecian circuit deserve more respectful analysis. They should not be dismissed as mere demagoguery and dementia. Leaving aside for the moment the question of the actual quality of Nero's performances (and therefore the "validity" of his artistic successes), the tour was valuable as a calculated act of diplomacy. The sacred agones had long been a vitally important element of Greek civic life, and indeed both their number and their role grew significantly during the imperial period, providing a vital focus for national identity, the communication and sharing of experience, and through the celebration of a common culture supplying a significant "safety valve" to curb resentment of and resistance to Roman rule. By endorsing such occasions, Nero encouraged at a popular level the type of growing homogeneity of culture, including the integration of the arts, already widely evident in aristocratic circles. The activities of the festivals represented a major common cultural denominator, unifying the people of the empire by stressing shared values. Such assimilation, both cultural and political (including the granting of Roman citizenship), was a favored imperial practice, which had been memorably endorsed two decades earlier by Claudius (Tac. *Ann.* 11.24; Dio 60.17.4–5; Levick 1990, 163–65). Moreover, it had long been an acknowledged imperial policy (and one that would be aggressively promulgated by subsequent emperors) to "encourage games in the East as a means of spreading largess and fostering local support. . . . Nero's activity could be viewed simply as an extension — admittedly a major extension — of Roman interest and participation in these festivities" (Alcock 1994, 100; cf. Roueché 1993, 2–11).

However sullen dissident opinion back in Rome (both Nero's enemies and the general populace were restless during his absence), the response of the Greeks to Nero's undertaking was overwhelmingly positive, and at the close of his tour he solidified such support by a gesture of stunning if grandiloquent diplomacy. Having ordered that as many inhabitants as possible be present in the marketplace at Corinth during the Isthmian festival there on November 28, A.D. 67, he publicly proclaimed the liberation of the entire province of Achaia, granting it a degree of governmental autonomy and freedom from Roman taxation. His actual words (preserved on an inscription) give something of the flavor of the occasion.[38] "Unexpected is the gift, men of Greece, which I present you — though perhaps nothing can be thought unexpected from munificence like mine — and so vast you could not hope to ask for it. . . . Not through pity, but through goodwill, I make you this benefaction, thanking the gods . . . that they have granted me the opportunity of so great a benevolence. Other Emperors have freed cities; Nero alone a whole province!" Apart from exhibiting the ingrained Roman trait of competitive "one-upmanship," and the particular "anxiety of influence" that emperors habitually displayed in light of the achievements of their predecessors, Nero, ever the showman, went a step further. He staged it as a reenactment of the memorable event 263 years earlier when, at the same venue and occasion (in what had since taken on the sheen of myth) the Roman general Flaminius had similarly decreed Greece's freedom. Significantly, although Flaminius had his edict proclaimed by a herald, Nero delivered his "in person from a tribunal set up in the market-place amidst the multitude" (Plutarch *Flam.* 12.8). After all, one of the contests in which he regularly competed was that for heralds, and throughout his tour he had announced his own invariable formula for victory: "Nero Caesar wins this contest and crowns the Roman people and the inhabited World which is his own" (Suet. *Nero* 24; Dio 63.14.4).

Dio noted this, only to add contemptuously: "Thus, though possessing a World . . . he nevertheless continued on as a *citharoedus*, herald, and tragic actor!" Nero's participation, however, and the precise words used to acknowledge his victories (apart from cleverly co-opting the entire Roman people as victorious performers) demonstrated in the most graphic way possible a policy of assimilation and integration as well as an enthusiastic espousal of a culture toward which Romans had long demonstrated either outright hostility or a divisive and no doubt resented — as far as the Greeks were concerned — ambivalence. The vilification that his Greek venture suffered from Romans is in part itself an expression of the continuation of a deeply rooted Hellenophobic tradition. That it was also condemned by some Greek writers with strong Roman connections and sympathies, such as Dio, Philostratus, and Plutarch — although the latter two praised his liberation of Archaia — reflects in part the extent to which the official *damnatio memoriae* later decreed upon him conditioned, colored, and calls into question the objectivity of their assessments.

Even hostile historians made certain concessions in their accounts to such things as Nero's scrupulous observance of the rules (Suet. *Nero* 24), his elaborate anxiety about his performances (Dio 63.9.2), and his humility toward the judges (*Nero* 23.2–3), from whom he asked no favor except that "being men of wisdom and experience, they should ignore anything that was fortuitous." Two mishaps are recorded. In the first of these, while portraying a king, Nero dropped his scepter and was terrified he might be disqualified from the competition, which nevertheless continued "amid the delight and acclamations of the public" (*Nero* 24.1). Then, as a charioteer at Olympia, he fell from the chariot (drawn by an unusual ten-horse team) and, although reinstalled, failed to complete the course. Both Suetonius and Dio claim that he was nevertheless awarded the prize — the only overt example of apparent favoritism recorded (*Nero* 24.2; Dio 63.14.1).

When preparing or relaxing "off-stage" as well as in his performances, he behaved in speech and gesture exactly as ordinary actors; moreover, adopting the common touch, he treated them as if "they were exactly the same status as himself" (*Nero* 23.2). When not performing he could be seen "training, practicing various songs . . . [or] walking about with one or two attendants, looking askance at his rivals, and often uttering taunts to them." When acting he fully engaged with such roles as Oedipus, Thyestes, Canace, Heracles, Alcmeon, and Orestes, "begging in the role of a runaway slave, led about as a blind man, giving birth, acting a madman, or an outcast." The only concession to his status was that when he was bound, gold chains were used since "it was thought improper for a Roman Emperor to be bound in iron shackles" (Dio 63.9.2–6).

Nero employed a former consul, Cluvius Rufus, to announce his appearances. He had earlier performed the same service at the Neronia and would later compose a history, now lost, centered on Nero's reign (Tac. *Ann.* 13.20,

14.2). The emperor was accompanied too by an enormous entourage of soldiers, courtiers, and senators, as well as, of course, a claque of Augustiani. Both Suetonius and Dio echo Tacitus's earlier allegation of audience surveillance at the Neronia, stating that on the Grecian tour during the sometimes extremely long performances, the spectators (particularly the senators) "were constantly subjected to the closest scrutiny in their entrances, exits, attitudes, gestures and shouts" (Dio 63.15.2), and that as a result some secretly climbed out of the theater, or even feigned death to be taken away for burial (*Nero* 23.2; Dio 63.15.3). But balancing this depiction of the ultimate "captive audience," the accounts nevertheless concede that Nero (while observing the presumably well-defined rules), was welcomed, approved, and applauded by huge crowds. Suetonius acknowledges that the judges did not promise victory, and that Nero was extremely deferential and uncertain himself about the outcome of his efforts. There is no suggestion of the expectation or delivery of bribes in advance to the judges (although Suetonius claims Nero did bribe his better rivals and that at the end of his tour the judges were given Roman citizenship and a sum of money) nor did any other participants make any charges of improper conduct (tantamount to sacrilege) in the contests.

To maintain that it was all a farce and a travesty requires that the respected judges were uniformly dishonest, cowardly, and intimidated; that while following the strictly defined rules, Nero still won despite poor performances; and that huge crowds of experienced and sophisticated spectators (up to forty thousand in the stadium at Olympia) were content or coerced to give their vociferous approbation, even though Nero was known to be remarkably indulgent toward personal jests and lampooning and patient even when faced with popular criticism and abuse (*Nero* 39.1–3). Whatever their quality, Nero's efforts appear to have engendered a genuine and lasting affection among the Greeks.

Helius, his freedman minion left behind to keep order in Rome, warned Nero that conspiracy was at hand (fomented in part by the executions and confiscations carried out by Helius himself), news of which prompted Nero's return to Italy at the end of 67 or early in 68. Following the custom of Agonistic victors, he entered Naples in a chariot through a breach made in the wall to mark the occasion (Dio 63.20.1–2). This was a long-established honor in the Greek world, whereby "in acknowledgement of the glory that a city obtained when their citizen was victorious, they would reward him . . . with the right to drive into the city in a triumphant return" (Roueché 1993, 3). Nero, having explicitly competed and won "for the Roman People," simply extended the concept to include the whole of Italy. Following his reception in Naples, he made his progress through Antium and Alba Longa to Rome. There he cleverly (if rashly) joined Greek with Roman precedent by staging his entry in the style of a traditional Roman military triumph. For his "actor's triumph" he employed the triumphal chariot first used a century earlier by Augustus. He wore the traditional purple robe and a cloak with golden stars. In place of the usual triumphal props, however, Nero donned the Olympic olive crown, holding in his hand the Pythian laurel; behind him in the place of the traditional admonishing slave stood a famous *citharoedus*, Diodorus (cf. Leppin 1992, 231). His car was preceded not by captive warriors but by attendants carrying his winnings of 1,808 wreaths and crowns, together with banners listing the places of his victories, whom he had defeated, and the titles of his songs or roles (Suet. *Nero* 25.1; cf. Dio 63.20.2–6). To complete the travesty, in his wake, instead of victorious soldiers, there followed an army of his claques, the Augustiani, shouting, "Hail Olympian Victor! Hail Pythian Victor! Augustus! Hail Nero, our Hercules! Hail Nero our Apollo! The only Victor of the Grand Tour, the only one from the beginning of time! Augustus! Augustus! O, Divine Voice! Blessed are they that hear thee."

Along the route, which wound through the Circus and Forum, "sacrifices were made, the streets were sprinkled with perfume, birds, ribbons and sweets were showered upon him" (*Nero* 25.2), and the city was bedecked with garlands and ablaze with lights. The mocking parody of Roman military tradition continued as Nero made his way not to the temple of Jupiter on the Capitoline, but rather to that of Apollo, patron of the arts, built by Augustus on the adjacent Palatine (cf. Morford 1985). He then announced a series of races in the Circus, where he deposited his crowns beneath the Egyptian obelisk of Rameses II that Augustus had brought from Heliopolis in 10 B.C. and dedicated to Sol, a god with whom Nero had developed a special relationship (Pliny *N.H.* 36.70–75). Finally, he gave a command performance as a charioteer to conclude an extraordinary spectacle calculated in every detail not only to cast the aura of a triumphant military hero upon the *scaenicus imperator* (Pliny *Paneg.* 46.4) but also to bestow on him the greatest of all accolades: the "New Augustus." Throughout there had been persistent reminders of Augustus—the reiterated incantation of his name, the use of the chariot first employed (in 29 B.C.) at the celebration of his great Eastern victories, the dedication of trophies at the temple of Apollo that he had constructed adjacent to his home, and the ceremony at the obelisk—developing a theme sounded two years previously, when, like Augustus a century earlier, Nero closed the doors of Janus's temple.

"Qualis Artifex Pereo!"

A Roman emperor's survival depended on the support of the military—including, crucially, the nine resident praetorian cohorts, which might be supplemented by the three urban cohorts (Tac. *Ann.* 4.5.3) — reinforced if possible by some understanding with the Senate sufficient to secure if not its members' active support then at least their passive acquiescence. Popularity with the masses could exercise useful pressure and was valuable in lending an emperor desirabie prestige, dignity, and "presence" but was rarely itself politically decisive. "Rome was not a city where people were likely to mount the barricades, and after the creation of the Praetorian Guard, their swords were the only ones that counted politically" (Veyne 1990, 385; cf. Tac. *Ann.* 14.61). Long before his Greek tour, Nero had alienated much of the Senate and punished a portion of it; during the tour he persecuted (and executed) many more despite their increasingly frantic attempts to please or appease him (Dio 63.15.1, 63.18.2–3). He had also severely undermined the support of the military — many of whose generals were themselves drawn from the senatorial order — by the summary execution of the great general Corbulo (whom he had summoned treacherously to attend him in Greece); by employing soldiers (in a manner their ethos found demeaning) as attendants, audience, and "fans" at his performances; and, most outrageously, by what they must have viewed as the utter degradation of sacred military tradition by his "actor's triumph."

Even before the Pisonian plot in 65, the praetorian tribune Subrius Flavus was said "to have conceived an impulse to attack Nero while he was performing on the stage" (Tac. *Ann.* 15.50). Following the betrayal of the plot itself, Piso had been urged as a last desperate measure to get to the headquarters of the Praetorian Guard or, failing that, even to mount the *rostra* to test and if possible rally the support of the troops and people. After all, "what likelihood was there that this play-actor [*scaenicus*] . . . would answer force with force?" Piso did not, however, attempt this and was forced a little later to kill himself "when a body of soldiers arrived, recruits . . . deliberately chosen by Nero, since veterans were distrusted" (Tac. *Ann.* 15.59). In the course of the purge that followed the plot, in addition to Flavus, a centurion was executed and four praetorian tribunes dismissed. Two other tribunes were spared for cooperating but later killed themselves (Tac. *Ann.* 15.60–61, 15.71). The plot was a disturbing and dangerous show of disloyalty, particularly because, as the case of Claudius's accession had clearly demonstrated, the Guard could make, and undoubtedly also break, emperors. Nero afterward attempted to secure his position through a gift of two thousand sesterces and a free corn allowance to each of the praetorians (Tac. *Ann.* 15.72).

Now, however, following further follies in the course of and at the conclusion of his Greek venture, opinion in the ranks turned decisively against the emperor. In March 68, a Gaul of senatorial status, Gaius Julius Vindex, serving as a Gallic legate, probably in the province of Lugdunensis (Lyon), urged mutiny (Plutarch *Galba* 4.2). Acknowledging that other rulers had committed murder, robbery, and scandals, he pointed out that Nero had surpassed them all in outrageous behavior and vices.

> What words can describe them? I have seen him — believe me — I have seen that man . . . in the orchestra of the theater . . . sometimes holding the cithara and dressed in loose tunic and buskins, and again wearing the high-platform shoes and a mask. I have often heard him sing, play the herald, and act in tragedies. . . . I have seen him imitating all the situations of mythology by his own speech, by what was said to him, by what he did, and had done to him. Will anyone style such a person Caesar and Emperor and Augustus? Never! They were sacred titles. . . . This fellow should be called Thyestes, Oedipus, Alcmeon or Orestes since these are the characters he acts on stage, and the titles he has assumed in place of the others. Therefore rise now finally against him; save yourselves and the Romans; liberate the entire World! (Dio 63.22.4–6)

Nero was first informed of the uprising while viewing a gymnastic contest at Naples; his only response was to leap from his seat and take part in the competition. He then sent a letter to the Senate excusing his failure to attend them because of a sore throat, "implying that he would like, even in the crisis, to sing to them" (Dio 63.26.1). Suetonius adds that he fully reacted to the threat only when one of the insulting edicts issued by Vindex included the "taunt that he was a terrible *citharoedus*," which Nero then used to argue that all the other criticisms leveled at him were equally unfounded because "he was being taunted with being unskilled in an art to which he had devoted much attention and had perfected himself. . . . Did anyone know of any artist who was his superior?" (*Nero* 41.1). Even after finally returning to Rome, Nero was more concerned with displaying to his advisers a newly invented variety of water organ that he could use to produce louder and more musical tones ("which with Vindex's permission he would soon demonstrate for everyone in the theater") than in discussing the crisis with them (*Nero* 41.2; Dio 63.26.4).

The emergency deepened when the governor of Spain, Galba, led a revolt of his armies after intercepting a dispatch from Nero to the procurator in Spain ordering his death. He was soon joined by the governor of Lusitania, Otho. Even then, Nero busied himself with writing ribald verses about the leaders of the growing rebellion and, on one occasion, after entering the theater incognito, sent a note to a rival actor chiding him for taking advantage of the emperor's preoccupation to in effect "steal the limelight." At the end of April 68, he assumed the consulship as a gesture toward taking military command, but his efforts to mount a campaign were less than decisive; "his first care was to obtain wagons to carry his theatrical props," and he announced that upon reaching Gaul he would stand "unarmed in front of the soldiers and do nothing but weep" as a means of subduing his enemies. Then having won them over through the force of his art, they would all rejoice and sing victory songs "which he really ought to be composing right now!" (*Nero* 43.2). Dio adds that he consoled himself with the fantasy that even if defeated and removed as emperor, he could always support himself in the East as a professional *citharoedus* (63.27.2a).

Nero's cherished and carefully nurtured popularity with the masses was at low ebb because of a disruption of the grain supply then causing food shortages, which moreover promised to grow far worse following a further defection by the legion in Africa where much of the supply originated (Plutarch *Galba* 6). Meanwhile, it was rumored that ships were still arriving laden with special sand for use in the arena! Offensive and subversive graffiti began to appear (*Nero* 55). In the light of a rapidly deteriorating situation, Nero at first considered dressing in black and making a direct impassioned address to the people from the *rostra* but, fearing he might be killed before reaching the Forum, decided to flee. He was unable to persuade the leaders of the Praetorian Guard — possibly including his former fellow debauchee, Tigellinus — to support or accompany him (Jos. *Bel. Iud.* 4.9.2.). This failure proved fatal. Seeing its chance, at this crucial juncture the Senate roused itself, declared Nero a public enemy, and withdrew his personal unit of praetorians, whose reluctance to forsake their loyalty oath and declare for Galba was overcome with a bribe of thirty thousand sesterces each (Dio 63.27.2b; *Nero* 48.2, 49.2; Tac. *Hist.* 1.5). As Plutarch wryly noted, "This quickly brought Nero to his grave, and soon after Galba too; they murdered the first in expectation of the promised gift, and a little later, the second because they did not get it from him" (Plutarch *Galba* 2.2.).

Accompanied by four freedmen including his "spouse," Sporus, Nero set out hoping to reach the port at Ostia from which to escape. The dramatic irony of his fall from prominence and power was explicitly described in the Roman historians' later accounts of his last hours on June 9, 68, and must have tortured his own desperate imagination as well. It was said that in playing out "his tragic part" he thought constantly of a verse from his last performance as Oedipus; "Wife, Father, Mother drive me to my death" (*Nero* 46.3; cf. Dio 63.28.5). Dio observed that "such was the drama that Fate now prepared for him: that he should no longer play the parts of other matricides and beggars, but only now at last, himself." Thus, at the end, the actor and his role truly and indissolubly merged for the final curtain. Just as his pursuers arrived, he managed (with help from friends) to stab himself, uttering the subsequently famous last lamenting line, "Qualis artifex pereo!" — "What an artist dies in me!" (*Nero* 49.1; Dio 63.29.2). He was thirty years old.

Fig. 28. Watercolor depicting the theater of Taormina in the imperial period. Viollet le Duc, 1839. Centre de recherche sur les monuments historiques, Paris. (Fototeca Unione at the American Academy in Rome)

His final request had been that his body not be mutilated. This was re-spected, and his remains were buried at great expense in the Domitian family tomb on the Pincian hill overlooking the Campus Martius. For a long time thereafter mourners decorated the tomb with flowers (*Nero* 57.1). Tacitus simultaneously concedes and disparages the fact that a large portion of the urban population regretted Nero's fall. "The dregs of the city, haunting the Circus and the theater, and the scum of the slave population or those who . . . had depended on Nero's degrading charity, were sorrowful and eager for ru-mors" (*Hist.* 1.4). His memory long continued to be widely cherished among portions of the Roman people and particularly in the Greek East, both for his role in securing a Parthian settlement and above all for his liberation of Achaia. For this gift, Plutarch — who despised Nero's rule but viewed him as a tortured soul — claimed "some good thing is owed him by the gods," thought-fully suggesting that he deserved to be reincarnated as a frog singing in the marshes and lakes (*Mor.* 567F). In fact, as a gesture that Nero himself would have preferred and viewed as particularly appropriate, he enjoyed the flattery of imitation: for decades afterward a number of "false Neros" appeared, claiming to be the lost emperor and attracting wide popular support from those who "longed for revolution and hated the existing state of things" (Tac. *Hist.* 2.8.1; cf. Suet. *Nero* 57.2; Dio 66.19.3b). Over a thousand years later, in 1099, Pope Paschal II built a small chapel to exorcise Nero's malevolent ghost and attendant demons at what was thought to be the site of his tomb, which, rural at the time, later came to mark Rome's monumental northern entrance: the church of Santa Maria at Piazza del Popolo (Richardson 1992, 355).

Thus the last Roman ruler drawn from the "descendants of Aeneas and of Augustus" (Dio 63.29.3) — the last emperor of the Julio-Claudian dynasty — lingeringly left the stage. Meanwhile, the spectacle entertainments that his princely predecessors had conceived and established, and that he had come to personify, continued in Rome and throughout its empire for a further five centuries (fig. 28).

Notes

Chapter 1: The Setup

1. Early examples of such games are those given by Scipio Africanus in 205 and 200, by Fulvius Nobilior in 186, by Lucius Scipio in the same year, and by Lucius Anicius in 167. Subsequent examples are numerous.

2. A similar situation arose in the case of "votive" games. If the Senate approved, a sum could be set aside from the booty carried in a triumph in order to honor a vow made by the general prior to achieving victory. Livy notes that M. Acilius Glabrio, who had triumphed in 190, was a formidable candidate for the censorship the following year, primarily because he had given lavish public benefactions "by which he had attracted a large part of the population to himself" (Livy 37.57.10–11). As early as 182 the Senate attempted to limit the gathering of resources for *ludi,* but the measures proved ineffective (Livy 40.44.8–12). Gruen (1992, 188 ff.) provides a useful analysis revising the standard opinion about the extent to which the provision of entertainment may actually have influenced political advancement. He believes there is little evidence to support this belief prior to the first century B.C..

3. For an analysis of the situation in this period, see Millar (1986).

4. For a discussion of this aspect, see Brunt (1988, 127 ff.), as well as Yakobson (1992, 33, 48).

5. Tragedy — at least that intended for staging — apparently died out soon after Accius, whose latest known play, *Tereus,* dates from 104. Early in the next century Julius Caesar Strabo, a prominent aristocratic politician and orator, wrote several tragedies that evidently were staged (Val. Max. 5.3.3., 3.7.11; Cicero *Brut.* 48.177; *De Orat.* 3.8.30;

Marius Victorinus in Keil [1855, 6.8], who suggests that Strabo's *Tecmessa* was staged). There are occasional references to comic playwrights in the first century B.C. Horace, for example, mentions Fundanius, who "alone of living poets can charm us with the chatter of comedies, where the sly courtesan and Davus trick old Chremes" (*Sat.* 1.10.40–42).

6. Cicero undertook as stylistic exercises the translation of passages from Greek tragedy, and his younger brother Quintus Tullius Cicero was an avid admirer of Sophocles, several of whose works he translated or in some cases adapted. (See *Tusc. Disp.*, *De Fin.*, 5.1.3; *Ad. Quint. Frat.* 2.15.3, 3.1.13, 3.6.7, 3.9.6). As a young man, Julius Caesar composed an *Oedipus* (Suet. *Div. Iul.*, 56.).

7. Wiseman (1985a, 33–34) argues for the continued composition of the praetextae; while Gratwick (1982, 127–28) cites Cicero's assertion in defending the poet Archias in 62 B.C. that the poet's highest task was to celebrate the deeds of famous persons and points out that Accius was still writing praetextae at least as late as the 130s. Literary versions, which may have been staged or recited, were composed still later. See Chap. 5, n. 29, for the case of Curiatius Maternus as a composer of praetextae in the imperial period.

8. Cicero *Pro Rosc. Com.* 20, a speech given about 76 B.C. See Garton (1972), chap. 7, "How Roscius Acted Ballio," for an intriguing discussion based in part upon Cicero's evidence.

9. As Rawson (1991d, 469) pointed out, "Most of our scanty information about the playwrights and actors of the republican period comes from the Roman grammatical tradition, and especially the Varronian tradition." Varro (116–27 B.C.) had collected a great deal of information describing and classifying Roman dramatic and theatrical practice. These alas, are lost and can be assessed only through fragments and the probable reflection of his works in other writers. But according to Rawson (1985, 272 ff.), they included a "*De Poematis*, supposedly theoretical, and the *De Poetis*, biographical and chronological . . . a *De Scaenicis Originibus*, the *De Comoediis Plautinis*, five books *Quaestionum Plautinarum*, . . . *De Personis*, about masks, the *De Actis Scaenicis*, [and] *De Actionibus Scaenicis*."

10. As Wiseman (1985a, 34) notes, "Our sources tell us about the scholars and the literary men . . . but for every Roman aristocrat who appreciated *their* talents, there must have been ten who could find work for actors." Gruen (1992) provides an excellent and persuasive account and analysis of the assimilation and adaptation of Greek culture by the ruling elites of the middle and later Republic.

11. Sallust *B.J.*, 85.39; Plutarch *Marius* 2. The occasion was Marius's triumph of 101 B.C. Gruen (1992, 269) argues that Marius's abrupt departure from the exhibition of Greek plays that he had arranged for his triumph did not indicate disdain but rather that he had "financed and produced the show for the edification of the public, attended its opening, and then withdrew," thereby demonstrating "that his nation controlled the cultural products of Greece and could employ them for the advantage of its own citizens."

12. For the revival of Satyr-plays in the period, see Szilágyi (1981), Sifakis (1967, 124), and Wiseman (1988, 1–13). For a recent analysis of the continuation of Greek drama in the imperial period, see C. P. Jones (1993, 39–52).

13. For an interesting discussion of this subject see Goldberg (1993). He writes (63): "Plautus had made comedy too absurd and Terence had made it too alien to be taken

seriously at Rome. . . . Within a century of his death Roman literature had achieved greatness, but ancient comedy as a creative genre was gone for good." Hunter (1985) provides an extensive account of New Comedy, including an analysis of variations in treatment between Greek and Roman playwrights.

14. In 55 B.C. in a rare display of tolerance, Cato left the theater during a mime so that his unfestive presence would not detract from the spectators' enjoyment of the customary naked conclusion. The anecdote is recounted by Valerius Maximus (2.10.8) and cited by Seneca (*Epis.* 97.7) and Martial (1. Praef.) An excellent recent discussion of the mime is provided by Fantham (1989). See too Beacham (1992, 129–39).

15. According to Strabo (5.3.6), however, Oscan plays were still given in Rome at a particular festival in his time (the period of Augustus), and Cicero refers to "Oscan plays" at Pompey's games of 55 B.C. (*Ad Fam.* 7.1.3).

16. Wiseman (1985a) devotes a section entitled "The Poet and His Audience" to the subject (124–29), and notes that it was sufficiently important for Varro in documenting cultural life of the Republic to devote three volumes to the subject and the practice of recitation: *De Lectionibus.*

17. For comments on the art of acting, see inter alia Cicero *Paradoxa* 25–26; *De Orat.*, 1.128, 1.159, 2.193, 3.196, 3.2.14, cf. 3.98; *Or.* 173; *Acad.*, 2.20, 2.86. Horace, however, did not apparently share such sentiments about the spectators' discernment and taste; cf. *Ars Poetica* 263–67.

18. Plautus *Poenulus* 1011–12: "Didn't you hear? He says he wants to provide the aediles with some African mice for the procession at the games." The use of elephants in 275 and 251 are recorded, respectively, in Seneca *De Brev. Vitae* 13.3, Eutropius, 2.2.14, and Varro *Ling. Lat.* 7.389.39; and in Seneca *De Brev. Vitae* 14.2 and Florus 1.18.26.

19. He also provided more lasting monuments to his glory in the form of buildings and porticoes erected near the Circus Flaminius, including a temple honoring Hercules and the muses. See Richardson (1992, 83, 187), Wiseman (1974a, 5–7), and Steinby (1993, 269–72).

20. According to Plutarch (*Sulla* 5), when Sulla first put himself forward for the praetorship, without having stood for the lower office of aedile, he attributed his defeat "to the populace, who knowing his intimacy with King Bocchus, and for that reason expecting, that if he was made aedile before his praetorship, he would then show them magnificent hunting-shows and combats between Libyan wild beasts, chose other praetors, on purpose to force him into the aedileship." But Sulla was nevertheless elected praetor the following year, according to Plutarch by bribery and perhaps by the promise of the games that duly followed.

21. Pliny *N.H.*, 8.64, 8.96, and 8.65 ff. Scaurus also erected an extraordinary theater for the occasion, discussed below. Hopkins (1983, 11) points out that "by contrast, after Roman times, no hippopotamus was seen in Europe until one was brought by steamship to London in 1850; it took a detachment of Egyptian soldiers to capture it, and a five-month journey to bring it from the White Nile as far as Cairo."

22. Wiedemann (1992, 2 ff.) discusses this aspect of the munera and asserts (7) that "there is no conclusive evidence that in the late Republic munera were ever given by magistrates in their public capacity. . . . The idea of publicly provided gladiatorial shows in the late Republic has to be dismissed." This view is supported by Edmondson (1996,

79). Welch (1994, 61–2), however, disputes it, citing as evidence a charter dating from 44 B.C. from Urso in Spain that "calls for gladiatorial games to be dedicated to the Roman State gods, and specified that the State was to contribute to their cost" and also referring (footnote 10) to the Quinquatria festival of Mars and Minerva (March 19–23) at which gladiatorial combats evidently took place. Golvin (1988, 18) asserts that from 105 B.C. republican magistrates *were* required to provide munera.

23. Wiedemann (1992, 30–34) notes that the argument presented by Georges Ville (1981) for a Campanian origin is persuasive, and the same is suggested by Boethius (1978, 170–71) and Golvin and Landes (1990, 39 ff). This, however, is disputed by Welch, who while suggesting that the *munera* may have originated in Rome itself concedes that "there was a debate even in ancient times about where gladiatorial games originated; the Romans themselves did not have the answer." (1994, 59).

24. The figures given by Augustus (*Res Gestae* 22) suggest that on average some 1,250 gladiators fought in each of his shows.

25. Cicero defended Murena against the charge that the provision of games during his campaign for the consulship in 63 came under the law forbidding *largitio* (bribery). Cicero insisted that Murena's practice constituted legitimate *beneficium* without disputing the facts, or that such provision had helped ensure Murena's popularity both then and earlier when he held the praetorship in 65.

26. This figure was for the funeral of Paullus, at which Terence's *Hecyra* had failed to win a hearing. It is a perennial difficulty in Roman scholarship to convey some accurate idea of the relative value of sums of money. To qualify for the title of "knight" *(eques)* a man must show a capital worth at least 400,000 sesterces. To be eligible for election to a local council, 100,000 was required. The price of a slave varied from 800 to 2,500 sesterces, and the holder of a higher public office such as a procurator drew an annual salary, depending on rank, of sixty, one hundred, or two hundred thousand sesterces. Other literary evidence suggests that an annual income of between 20,000 and 25,000 sesterces was necessary to live in comfort in Rome. See White (1978, 88–89). Thus, the cost of a stylish funeral would have supported approximately thirty people for a year.

27. For a full discussion of the role of electoral bribery in the late Republic, see the important article by Yakobson (1992), particularly his analysis of the Murena affair, 35–37.

28. Also, in 63, Gaius Marcellus was expelled from Capua for attempting to gain the support of gladiators for a rebellion.

29. Wiedemann (1992, 5). The numbers come from Servius *Ad Aeneid* 6.862 and Appian *B. C.* 1.105 ff.

30. For a discussion of such masks, see H. Drerup (1980).

31. The competitive presuppositions of the speech are stressed by Wiseman (1985b, 3 ff).

32. The accounts are given by Appian *B.C.* 1.106 and Plutarch *Sulla* 38.3.

33. The differing theories are comprehensively described and analyzed in Versnel (1970) and include suggestions that the triumphator represents a king or a god (Dionysus, Mars, or Jupiter) and that the ceremony is related to a New Year ritual, or to an entry rite, by which the god and his blessings were formally brought into a community. Recently Coleman (1996a) has called attention to the marked similarity between Roman

and Hellenistic practice, using the example of the Grand Procession of Ptolemy Philadelphus in 275 B.C.

34. A triumph was originally granted only to consuls, praetors, and dictators but was later extended to pro-magistrates and in the second half of the first century B.C. to legates (Senate envoys) who had commanded separately and led an army to victory in their native province. The individual had to achieve victory over a foreign enemy, and to slay at least five thousand of them, while he was in possession of imperium (essentially the formal right to command an army) and acting under his own *auspicia* (divination that he was formally entitled to conduct).

35. Versnel (1970, 83) suggests that the cry originally was an Etruscan invocation for the god Jupiter to appear in the shape of the triumphator/king, but he believes that in the republican period this earlier meaning had been forgotten and an epiphany was no longer acknowledged.

36. It is not certain whether the pompa preceded all of the *ludi circenses;* in addition to the *ludi Romani,* however, it is attested for the *ludi Megalenses,* votive games, and probably was part of the Cerealia. For a detailed analysis of the pompa, see Piganiol (1923, 15–31) and the article by F. Bömer, "*Pompa,*" in Paulys Real-Encyclopädie der classischen Altertumswissenschaft, Vol. 21, Stuttgart, 1934, cols. 1878–1994.

37. For this particular occasion we have striking evidence of the type of difficulties that such foreign innovations could encounter in the boisterous and sometimes xenophobic Roman audience. The proceedings came close to general mayhem when the Romans were confronted by unfamiliar Greek fare that they either misunderstood or regarded with contemptuous mockery. Possibly the performance was too refined for the festive mood of a triumph, or, because it took place in the Circus, the audience expected something more robust. In any case, they were dissatisfied and turned the performance by the hapless Greeks into a confused burlesque and near riot. Gruen (1992, 215–18) suggests that Anicius himself deliberately caused the affair. "By turning it into a fiasco and inviting a Roman audience to egg on the entertainers in activities that discredited their talents, he braced the spectators' sense of the own cultural superiority" (218). Other interpretations are found in Garton (1972, 65), Crowther (1983, 270), and Gilula (1989, 106–7).

38. For an account and analysis of the development of stage architecture at Rome, see Beacham (1980) and (1992) Chapter 3 as well as Rumpf (1950), Frézouls (1982), Neppi (1961), and Lauter (1976).

39. Mitens (1988) records examples in both Sicily and Magna Graecia of the front rows (*prohedria*) of the auditoria being distinguished by either larger seats or arm rests. See too Rawson (1991c, 536). The three front rows of the theater at Pietrabondante dating from the late second century may have been intended for the local senate. In Greece itself there had been special seating as early as Aristophanes (cf. *Birds* 794). For senatorial seats in the orchestra, see Garton (1972, 53) and Rawson (1991c, 537–39). For an analyses of the provision of senatorial seating in 194, see Gruen (1992, 202–5).

40. The procession is recorded by Dionysius of Halicarnassus (*Ant. Rom.* 2.71) and Tertullian (*De Spect.* 10.1–2). For the chair either of the god or of a mortal being honored by the games, see Dio 44.6.3, 53.30.6, 58.4.4, 72.31.2, 73.17.4, 75.4.1, and Lucretius *De Re. Nat.* 4.78–80. Hanson (1959, 13 ff.) details the relation between theater sites and

temples and discusses the sellisternium (82 ff). Lucretius also refers to "the stage freshly sprinkled with Cilician saffron, and the nearby altar exhaling its Panchaean scents" (*De Re. Nat.* 2.416–417). Propertius too mentions the use of saffron (4.1.15–16), as does Ovid (*Ars. Amat.* 1.103–6). For the presence and location of the altar, see Hanson (1959, 87–89).

41. In 186 expenditure was limited for the games of M. Fulvius Nobilior, which he had vowed to Jupiter on his Aetolian campaign, and a similar curb was in force for the votive games of Q. Fulvius Flaccus in 179 who had sought to lavish on the games money which had been raised in Spain. In 182 excessive collection from Roman subjects to finance the games given by Tiberius Sempronius Gracchus as aedile were so burdensome that the Senate passed a decree preventing such impositions. Livy 39.5.6–12, 39.22.1–3, 40.44.8–12.

42. Garton (1972, 55–56) discusses the stage and Demetrius.

43. For a survey of practice outside Rome, see Rawson (1991d) and Lauter (1976), as well as the extended treatment by Mitens (1988).

44. Such a device is known to have been used earlier at Pompeii and possibly at Capua as well, and it eventually became customary in the permanent Roman theaters, circuses, and amphitheaters. Vitruvius, writing about 25 B.C., indicates that it was widely used in temporary structures as well (10. Praef.). Its use at Pompeii is illustrated in a wall painting showing its operation in the amphitheater, and corbels survive in the large theater in which masts were placed to hold the awning taut. Rainer Graefe (1979) has prepared a massive two-volume study of the subject, describing its operation in great and persuasive detail in vol. 1, 147–69. He points out (10) that Greek inscriptions sometimes use the Latin word *vela* to refer to the awning, suggesting that the Greeks first encountered it through the Romans. Graefe's attempt to construct a working version of *vela* is the subject of a television documentary, *Secrets of Lost Empires: The Colosseum* (NOVA/ WGBH Boston Science Unit Production, 1996). Lucretius noted (*De Re. Nat.* 4.74–84) how the awning created a multicolored effect as the light played through it. "Awnings often do this, as they ripple and flap across beams, stretched over huge theaters in red, yellow and purple. For all below — the audience on the tiers, the stage's show, the [Senate] fathers, the Mother of the gods — are dyed and made to ripple in the awnings' colors" (trans. Wiseman [1974b, 15–16]). See too Goldman (1982), which includes a bibliography. For Capua, see Rawson (1991d, 476).

45. Plutarch *Cicero* 13.2–4; Macrobius *Sat.* 3.14.12; Pliny *N.H.* 7.117; Cicero *Ad Att.* 2.1.3. Cicero had to come to the theater from the nearby temple of Apollo where the Senate was meeting, and assembled the theater audience in the adjacent emple of Bellona. As Parker (1997) shrewdly observes, Cicero could not demean himself by speaking to the crowd from within the theater and, moreover, had to first change the psychological situation by transforming the audience into a public assembly *(contio)*. "The orators ruled in the *contio;* they made the rules; they spoke. The people ruled in the theater. In the theater they made the rules; they were in charge of who spoke and what it meant." See the detailed discussion in Rawson (1991c, 530–36). See too Crawford (1993, 213–18), who discusses the fragment of Cicero's speech and the circumstances.

46. Polybius 6.56, trans. Scullard (1981, 33).

47. Pliny (*N. H.* 36.6) notes that the largest of the theater's stone columns, some thirty-

eight feet in length, were set up in Scaurus's atrium and were so heavy that he had to provide a guarantee against damaging the sewers when they were dragged to his home on the Palatine. Scaurus's house was famous for the lavishness of its decoration, which Pliny condemned. It has recently been the subject of excavations, which reconstructed the dimensions of its atrium based on the length of the columns mentioned by Pliny. See Coarelli (1989). According to Asconius (*In Scaur.* 27C), these onyx columns were later removed on Augustus's orders and installed in the permanent theater of Marcellus.

48. Many of the major "players" in late republican politics lived close to one another. Scaurus, Claudius Pulcher, Cicero, Clodius, and Catulus were all neighbors, and their rivalry was reflected in their homes — inside and out — which were frequently decorated with spoils recalling the achievements of both present and previous owners. See Patterson (1992, 200–204).

49. The *Lex Appuleia*, passed by Saturninus around 100 B.C., defined *maiestas minuta* (according to Cicero *De Inventione* 2.53) as detracting "in any way from the dignity [*dignitas*] or the stature [*amplitudo*] or the power [*potestas*] of the people [*populus*], or of those to whom the people have given power." For other measures incorporating the concept see Yavetz (1983, 79–85).

50. For the underground passages, see Carettoni (1956–58). Cicero mentions them in describing how Appius Claudius used them to slip unseen into the stands to avoid the booing of the crowd (*Pro. Sest.* 124–126). Pliny mentions Caesar's awnings (*N.H.* 19.23), as does Dio (43.24.2). The gladiatorial displays given by Tiberius honoring his father around 25 B.C. (Suet. *Tib.* 7.2) are the last explicitly identified as taking place in the Forum. For a discussion of how the combats were staged there, see Coarelli (1985, 143, 222–30) and Giuliani and Verduchi (1987, 52–66.) J. C. Golvin suggests that the shape of the purpose-built permanent amphitheaters (Statilius Taurus built the first in Rome in 30 B.C.) may have been influenced by the oblong shape of the Forum (1988, 20, 56 ff.). The term *amphitheatrum* was not used to designate the venue until the time of Augustus. Cf. Vitruvius (1.7.1), Strabo (14.1.3), and Augustus's own *Res Gestae* (22).

51. Patterson (1992, 190–94) provides an excellent survey of recent analysis and argument concerning the architecture and use of the Forum in the republican era.

52. See too Millar (1986, 1–2). For a full discussion of Roman funeral orations and their interpretation, see Kierdorf (1980). For an account of Roman funeral practices in general, see Toynbee (1971).

53. This assumes that its traditional identification with the temple situated on an east-west alignment along the north side of the Forum is correct. But recent work has suggested this building might have been the Basilica Fulvia, of 179 B.C., and that the Basilica Aemilia is represented by remains of a structure on a north-south axis running from the Temple of Castor and Pollux, beneath the later-built temple of Divus Iulius. See M. Gaggiotti (1985) and E. M. Steinby (1987).

54. The information has been analyzed by L. Pietilä-Castren (1987, 154–58).

55. Translation from Scullard (1981, 216–17).

56. See Rawson (1991c, 515 ff.).

57. Cf. Cicero *Planc.* 45; *Mur.* 70. For a detailed discussion of the situation, see A. Wallace-Hadrill (1989, 71 ff.) and J. Linderski (1985).

Chapter 2: Playing for Power

1. For analysis and discussion of Rome's population in the late Republic, see Brunt (1971, 382–83), Hopkins (1978, 96–98), and Rickman (1980, 175–79).

2. Wiseman (1985, 4 ff.) gives examples of the competitive emphasis on superlatives that characterized the Roman sense of personal worth and achievement. He points out how, even at moments of supreme danger, Cicero's letters reveal that he looked in evident sincerity not to expediency but to Homeric ideals of honor and duty; he even considered how history would view his conduct a thousand years hence.

3. The date cannot be determined with certainty. Livy (*Epit.* 89) puts it in 81, but Greenhalgh (1981, 235) thinks it was in March of either 80 or 79.

4. For a discussion of the problems of "blockage" in a political career, see Wiseman (1971, 143–69).

5. Pompey may have been intentionally drawing upon the practice and imagery of Hellenistic monarchs. Similar "floats" were employed in their grand processions. See Coleman (1996, especially 52–54), who describes the procession mounted by Ptolemy Philadelphus at Alexandria in 275 B.C.

6. The other measures passed on January 4 decreed that the grain dole be free, that restrictions be placed on the use of the *auspices* to delay legislation (benefitting Caesar, whose legislative program had been the target of such attempts at delay), and that the censors not stigmatize a person unless a trial had taken place (Dio. 38.14.1–3). The measure concerning the *auspices* was returning a favor to Caesar, who had assisted Clodius in the adoption procedure (noted below) that gave him access to the tribuneship.

7. An account and analysis of Clodius's activity is provided in Lintott (1967); a brief description is given by Nippel (1995, 70–78). The Compitalia are described in Scullard (1981, 58–60), and the controversy surrounding them in Salerno (1984).

8. Clodius first attempted to be declared a plebeian not by adoption but by plebiscite in January of 60, but the attempt was blocked in the Senate (Cicero *Ad Att.* 1.18.4; 1.19.5; 2.1.4–5.; *Har. Resp.* 45). He succeeded in being adopted in 59 under a law passed by Caesar (Cicero *De Dom.* 41; *Har. Resp.* 45; *Ad Att.* 2.12.1; 8.13.5.).

9. This suggestion is put forward by Frézouls (1983, 199 ff.).

10. The following account of these events is taken from Cicero's speech, *Pro Sestio*, 50 ff.

11. Wiseman (1974b) in his contribution "Clodius at the Theater" (159–69), discusses the incident and suggests that (as Cicero's report clearly indicates) two "theaters" were involved: one was the stepped terrace of the Great Mother's temple on the Palatine, where an enactment of the Goddess's myth took place, and the other a temporary theater erected for the festival at the bottom of the cliff below the temple.

12. It was enacted the following year under the *Lex Licinia* proposed by Crassus, who shared the consulship with Pompey.

13. On the other hand, the Greek experience suggests that the theater could also help to preserve peace. In Athens, under Pericles, a special fund, the *theorikron,* had been established to subsidize the attendance of poorer citizens at the theatrical festivals. A century later, around 350 B.C., a law was passed stipulating that all surplus revenue was to be incorporated into this fund, as opposed to the *stratiotikon,* a fund to support military

operations. "This law gave the poorer citizens a financial interest in preserving peace; for should Athens undertake a major war, the surplus would have to go not to the Theoric Fund but to the military fund" (Hammond 1991, 532). Indeed, a person who suggested during peacetime that the *theorikron* be used for military purposes could be punished by death. In defending, it the prominent politician, Demades, pointed out in an epigram that the Theoric Fund was as vital to the democracy as glue to a book, and in 331 as chief commissioner of the Fund he vetoed Demosthenes' proposal that Athens join Sparta against Macedon, arguing that "war would mean the people sacrificing all Theoric Monies" (Hammond 1991, 619). Any such suggestion of giving primacy to the provision of theater over war would have been viewed with contempt by prominent Romans.

14. For details of Pompey's financial affairs, see Shatzman (1975, 389–93).

15. In Book 10 of the lost *Antitquitates Rerum Divinarum,* which was devoted to *ludi scaenici.*

16. References to the animals at Pompey's games are found in Seneca *De Brev. Vit.* 13.6; Pliny *N.H.* 8.20–21, 8.53, 8.64, 8.70, 8.71; Dio 39.38.2–4; Cicero *Ad Fam.* 7.1.3. A full account is given in Jennison (1937, 51–55). For the use of elephants in games, processions, and religion in Rome, see too Scullard (1974, 250–59). Pompey also used the occasion to bring the most famous tragic actor of the day, Aesopus, before the public once more. But, alas, according to Cicero, he had lost his once-fine voice and was a great disappointment (*Ad Fam.* 7.1.2). More successful was the appearance of the retired dancer Galeria Copiola, who had made her debut in 82 B.C. and was presented as a living legend in A.D. 9, at the age of 105! (Pliny *N.H.* 7.158).

17. See Capoferra Cencetti (1979) for an analysis based on the groundplans of existing structures built on the site of the theater that preserve its dimensions. An account of the excavation of the Porticus of Pompey is reported by Gianfrotta et. al. (1968–69). For a discussion of the nature of the theater's *scaenae frons,* see Sear (1993).

18. See Hanson (1959). As Rawson points out (1991d, 472), "theater-like structures also form part of the grandiose rebuilding now dated to the late second century at the sanctuary of Fortuna at Praeneste, and that of the early first at the temple of Hercules Victor at Tibur." The story of using the temple to validate the theater is told by Tertullian *De Spect.* 10, and the inscription placed on the completion of the temple in 52 during Pompey's third consulate is described by Aulus Gellius 10.1.7. Pliny gives the year of dedication as 55 (*N.H.* 8.20–21). Tacitus (*Ann.* 14.2) mentions the alleged censure of Pompey for building a permanent theater. It is possible that when first constructed, the theater of Pompey had only a temporary and removable scaenae frons built (as was the custom) of wood (see Crema [1959, 95] and Boethius [1978, 206], but against this theory, Sear [1993]). If so, then the assertion that the seats in the cavea had the appearance of a great staircase to the temple is more plausible, because this is indeed how it would have appeared to those outside the theater gazing toward it, if no scaena obstructed their view. That the theater (and specifically its scaena in A.D. 80) is reported several times to have been damaged by fire lends weight to the theory that during its early history the theater had a scaena at least partly constructed of wood, later replaced by stone. It was restored by Augustus in 32 B.C. but burned in A.D. 21 and, following its restoration by Caligula and rededication by Claudius, yet again in A.D. 80. (Tac. *Ann.* 3.72; Suet. *Calig.* 21; *Claud.* 21.1; Dio 60.6.8, 66.24.2).

19. Seneca too refers to the invention of "a process for spraying saffron perfumes to a tremendous height from hidden pipes" (*Epis.* 90.15), while surviving "advertisements" (*CIL.* 4.1203, 4.9983a) for the theater and amphitheater at Pompeii announced those special occasions when similar novelties were provided for the provincial spectators (Graefe 1979, 1:6–8).

20. The theater was probably not brought within the formal city boundaries until the *pomerium* was extended by Claudius (Richardson 1992, 294–5). By then, the matter of retaining imperium was no longer an issue. The Emperor's *imperium maius* extended throughout Italy and could also be exercised from within the city of Rome.

21. It was therefore called the Domus Rostrata. After Pompey's death, Mark Antony acquired it (Dio 48.38; Florus 2.18.4), and still later it became an imperial property, was occupied briefly by Tiberius before his accession (Suet. *Tib.* 15), and later served as the palace of the Gordians (S.H.A. *Gord.* 2,3,6,17). This house, which had earlier belonged to Pompey's father and was near the temple of Tellus, was where Pompey had sought refuge in 58 B.C. when he feared assassination. In Steinby (1995, 159–60), however, it is argued that the Domus Rostrata should instead be identified with the house Pompey constructed as part of his theater complex.

22. Ovid *Ars Amat.* 3.387; Propertius 2.32.11–20, 4.8.75; Martial 11.47.3. Pliny (*N.H.* 35. 114,126,132) describes some of the famous paintings included in the porticus. Martial mentions it as a place for pleasant strolls and relaxation (11.1.11, 11.47.3). Gleason (1990 and 1994), gives an intriguing account and interpretation of recent work on the site.

23. In the same year, 53 B.C., Marcus Favonius gave games as aedile. Plutarch records that Favonius's friend Cato the Younger attended and, instead of the magnificent awards and presents that were usually made, offered the actors and audience very basic gifts, "doing this in derision of the great expenses that others incurred, and, to teach the crowd that in amusements men ought to seek amusement only . . . not great preparations and costly magnificence for things of little importance" (Plutarch *Cato Minor* 46.2–5). Ironically, the public was so fascinated by the spectacle of the famously austere Cato enjoying himself in the theater that they "deserted the games of Curio who at the same time was giving very magnificent entertainments in another theater."

24. For a detailed presentation and discussion of the events leading to Caesar's break with Pompey, and the outbreak of civil war, see Gruen (1974, 451–97).

25. Although not dedicated until September of 46 (or completed until the time of Augustus), Caesar had for some years been amassing money for his forum, the site of which alone, according to Pliny, cost him a hundred million sesterces (*N.H.* 36.103). It is described in Steinby (1995, 299–306).

26. Cf. Gruen (1974, 358–65) and Brunt (1971, 100–12). Plutarch makes the same assertion about the provision of entertainments, owing to "the great calamity which the civil wars had wrought, and the large portion of the Roman population which they had consumed" (*Caes.* 55.6).

27. Theodor Mommsen, *History of Rome*, vol. 4, 581.

28. In reporting afterwards to his colleague Q. Cornificius, Cicero noted, "I have grown so thick a skin that at our friend Caesar's show . . . I heard Laberius' and Publilius' verses with perfect composure" (*Ad Fam.* 12.18.2). Jory suggests that in fact Caesar may

have been doing Laberius a favor: "The real reason for his acting was probably that Laberius was in such financial straits that he was in danger of being excluded from the fourteen rows reserved for the *equites*. The decision may have already been taken and it is possible that Caesar offered Laberius a way out of the impasse" (1995, 144; see too Lebek 1996, 45–48).

29. The evidence is comprehensively assembled and analyzed in Weinstock's extensive study (1971).

30. According to Dio (37.21.4), Pompey exercised this privilege only once.

31. In 49 B.C., having hastened back to Rome from Spain and planning to push on to confront Pompey in Greece, Caesar delayed for eleven days, one of which he spent in holding the Feriae Latinae, possibly because of the significance he placed in his Alban ancestry.

32. Rawson (1991a, 185–86) suggests that popular opinion of kings was influenced not just by accounts from Roman history but by literature and above all by the theater, where tragic playwrights had long put kings — frequently unhappy or villainous ones — on the stage. The truth about Caesar's own views and motives in regard to the question of the bestowal both of kingship or of divine status are ultimately unknowable. This has not, of course, curtailed an immense amount of scholarly speculation. Yavetz (1983) provides in his first chapter an excellent summary of the various arguments and their proponents.

33. Nicolaus of Damascus 130.81, 92, 94, 98; Appian *B.C.* 2.118; Dio 44.16.1–2. Velleius Paterculus notes that the conspirators were "escorted by a band of gladiators belonging to Decimus Brutus," the *Consul* designate (2.58.2). Some of the gladiators were intended to assist the conspirators and according to Nicolaus, were placed within the *porticus* complex "between the theater and the *curia*." For the history of the statue and the question of the authenticity of one now located in the Palazzo Spada, see Sapelli (1990, 180–85).

34. Dio's extended but probably less accurate account of the funeral is found at 44.35–51.

Chapter 3: The State Craft and Stagecraft of Augustus

1. A few days later Cicero reported to Atticus (who had helped to finance the games as a favor to Brutus and Cassius) that in fact Brutus had thought that a performance of the *Brutus* had taken place (*Ad Att.* 16.5.1). The incident is discussed in Vanderbroeck (1987, 80–81). Galinsky succinctly summarizes the events in the weeks following the assassination (1996, 42 ff.).

2. The manipulation of these games and the composition of the audience are analyzed by Alföldi (1976, 55 ff., 96–98) and in Veyne (1990, 403).

3. For a discussion of Antony's attitude toward attempts to promote deification, see Taylor (1931, 80 ff.).

4. For expressions of popular feeling on Caesar's deification, see Yavetz (1969), chap. 4, "The People and the Worship of Caesar."

5. Octavian's soldiers (four hundred centurions) entered the Senate and demanded the consulship. According to Suetonius, the centurion Cornelius, leading the deputation, showed the senators the hilt of his sword and said, "This will make him Consul, if you do

not." (*Aug.* 26). Dio reports that Cicero's response, "If that is the way you ask, he will surely get his consulate," sealed Cicero's doom (46.43.4–5). For good measure the Senate also decreed that an equestrian statue be erected in Octavian's honor in the Forum. With the exceptions of Sulla, Pompey, and Caesar, no Roman had been thus honored for three hundred years (Vell. Paterculus 2.61.3).

6. Asinius Pollio magnificently rebuilt the Atrium Libertatis to provide Rome's first public library, which included an extensive collection of sculpture; Gaius Sosius (as noted below) rebuilt the temple of Apollo; Domitius Ahenobarbus refurbished the shrine to Neptune; Domitius Calvinus restored the Regia; L. Marcius Philippus repaired a temple to Hercules; and Aemilius Lepidus Paullus completed extensive restoration work during his consulship (34 B.C.) on the venerable Basilica Aemilia, which had been begun by his father. The amphitheater of Statilius Taurus may have been semiprivate in nature, maintained by his family and therefore not favored for use in the great state occasions, such as the funeral of Agrippa in 7 B.C. or the dedication of the temple of Mars in 2, when the Saepta Iulia was employed (cf. Steinby 1993, 36).

7. Dio 47.18.4, 51.22.2, 51.19.1–2; Augustus *R.G.* 19; 21. This *rostra* did not replace that built by Caesar himself (the Rostra Caesaris) when he displaced the old republican *rostra* with the construction of the Curia Iulia. The Rostra Caesaris was later enlarged by Octavian and remained the principal *rostra* of the imperial period (Richardson 192, 334–37). That attached to Caesar's (Rostra Iulia) temple was later used principally for funerals of the imperial family. The arch of 29 B.C. (*Arcus Octaviani*) is believed to have been built next to the temple, but no trace of it has been recovered. In 19 B.C. a second arch (Arcus Augusti) was erected along the southwest side of the temple to celebrate the return of the standards of Crassus, captured by the Parthians. This was a lofty triple arch, which has been hypothetically reconstructed from fragments. It was elaborately decorated and crowned by a *quadriga,* with statues of barbarians surrendering the standards mounted on the flanking gables. See Richardson (1992, 23) and Steinby (1993, 80–81). For the development of the Augustan arch, see Kähler (1963, 61–66).

8. For a discussion of Apollonian imagery in the principate, see Zanker (1988, 49–53, 62 ff, 84–89) and Galinsky (1996, 188–89, 215–19, 277–99).

9. They are recorded by Dio as having been first decreed in 30 B.C. (51.19.2), later taking place in 20 (54.8.5), 13 (54.26.2), 11 (54.34.1), becoming annual in 8 (55.6.6), and held for the last time during Augustus's life, in A.D. 13 (56.29.2).

10. For the bestowal of the title, see Macrobius *Sat.* 1.12.35.; Augustus *R.G.* 34; Livy *Per.* 134; Suetonius *Aug.* 7; Ovid *Fasti* 1.608 ff; and Dio 53.16.6–8. It is discussed in Taylor (1931, 159–60), and Galinsky (1996, 315–17) analyzes the suggestive etymology of the word. The vitally important concept of Augustus's *auctoritas* is extensively described by Galinsky, 11–41.

11. In the festivals and building works of 29–28 alone he spent perhaps eighty million sesterces. With the additional sums paid to 250,000 citizens and 120,000 veterans, together with funds used to purchase land for his soldiers and thereby avoid the resentment and danger of confiscations, he spent around one billion sesterces. See Eder (1990, 102). Shatzman (1975, 357–71), gives a full account of Augustus's finances.

12. According to Dio, from 18 B.C. on Augustus "allowed the praetors who so desired to spend on the public festivals three times the amount granted them from the treasury"

(54.17.4). He further reports that later, in A.D. 7, under financial pressure, Augustus "ordered that the money which was regularly paid from the treasury to the praetors who gave gladiatorial combats should no longer be expended" (55.31.4). It was probably also in 22 that Augustus stipulated that an annual gladiatorial display be provided by two praetors, chosen by lot. For the negative effects of competitive *munera* in the last years of the republic, see Ville (1981, 57–88).

13. The office carried the *ius auxilii,* the important right for the holder to be protected and to provide protection to the plebs, and the *ius cum plebe agendi,* the right to intervene on behalf of plebeian interests. For an analysis of the significance of Augustus assuming these powers, see Cuff (1973).

14. The letter, which is particularly important for the information it conveys about the Roman theater, is comprehensively treated in Brink (1982). On the reference to Augustus's *numen,* see Galinsky (1996, 316–18). Horace had expressed similar feeling in *Odes* 4.5.33–36. "Thee with many a prayer, thee with pure wine poured from bowls, he worships; and mingles thy majesty (*numen*) with his household gods, like Greece mindful of Castor and great Hercules."

15. The evidence relating to the concept of the *saecula* is concisely presented and discussed in Weinstock (1971, 191–97, 310). For the concept of the golden age and its relationship to the Augustan principate, see Zanker (1988, 167–92) and Galinsky (1996, 90–121).

16. The 1890 inscription (*CIL* 6.32323) and related material are in translated in Chisholm and Ferguson (1981, 150–55), from which the following citations from the oracle and inscription are taken. The more recent discoveries are detailed in Moretti (1984).

17. The coins are discussed by Kellum (1990, 289–90), Zanker (1988, 168), and Galinsky (1996, 105–6).

18. The legislation was so greatly resented that Augustus was unable to enforce it, eventually having to withdraw or amend much of it. Even so, many years later, when a protest was mounted in the theater against certain tax advantages linked to these laws, Augustus "had the children of his adopted grandson Germanicus brought in, held one in his arms and had the others sit in their father's lap, and by his expression and gesture demonstrated that the protestors should take the young man as their model" (Suet. *Aug.* 34). See too n. 24, below.

19. In the same vein, Horace elsewhere relates how the wealthy politician and patron L. Licinius Lucullus was asked to lend a hundred cloaks for use in a stage production. At first doubting he had so many, he later reported he found five thousand. "Take some or all," he said (*Epis.* 1.6.40–41).

20. Asinius Pollio to Cicero, *Ad Fam.* 10.32.3. Cf. Leppin (1992, 244).

21. The best account and analysis of the *Lex Iulia* is that by Elizabeth Rawson (1991c), to which my discussion is indebted. See too Edmondson (1996).

22. Herodian, writing in the late second century (1.9.3), and Arnobius, at the end of the third (*Adv. Nat.* 4.35), provide piecemeal evidence that at least some aspects of the regulations were still in force. Inscriptions in the Colosseum indicate that senators still enjoyed reserved seating in the late fifth century.

23. The famous passage from the prologue to Plautus's *Poenulus* certainly establishes

their presence from earlier times. In Cicero's account of Clodius's disruption of the Megalesia in 56 B.C., discussed in Chapter 2 of this volume, he implies that the presence of slaves (at least at that festival) was unusual, if not unprecedented. Possibly he exaggerates, or uses the term "slaves" as a general term of abuse for Clodius's followers, who were assuming inappropriate privileges on that occasion.

24. Under the *Lex Papia Poppaea* of A.D. 9, special prominent seats were allotted to those who had fathered three children; this right could also be conferred as a particular honor even upon childless men. See Martial 3.95.5–10, 2.91.6, 2.92, and Edmondson (1996, 103).

25. Martial too describes circumstances in which it was impossible to find a seat in the fourteen rows (5.8, 5.14). On one occasion when a freedman of Maecenas named Sarmentus (who had subsequently attained equestrian status) took his seat, the crowed chanted its disapproval (Scholium on Juvenal *Sat.* 5.3). Horace recorded his hostility toward an ex-slave similarly entitled to such a seat (*Epod.* 4.15–16; cf. Juvenal *Sat.* 3.153 ff.).

26. Caesar had been granted the use of the *sella curulis* everywhere except the theater, where he sat with the tribunes on their *subsellium*. In his absence he was to be honored by the provision of a golden throne with his wreath upon it — an essentially divine honor — and it was this that Octavian attempted to display in the theater following Caesar's assassination. The problems concerning the use of the *sella* in the theater are discussed in detail by Weinstock (1957, 146–54) and Edmondson (1996, 92–93).

27. See Bejor (1979).

28. For acclamations see Klauser (1950), Veyne (1990, 399–401), Cameron (1976, chap. 9), Roueché (1984), and Potter (1996, 132–42).

29. For a concise survey of the topic, see Zanker (1988, 192–215). The Forum itself is analyzed in Anderson (1984, 88–97), Luce (1990, 123–38), and Steinby (1995, 289–95). See too Galinsky's discussion (1996, 141–224) in particular his analysis of the *Ara Pacis* 141–55.

30. See Bosworth (1972) for an analysis of his career and relationship to Augustus.

31. Titus Labienus, an orator and historian who wrote about the period of the triumvirate, was less discreet. He gave public readings at which he passed quickly over the more controversial passages, with the remark that they should be read after his death. Instead, a Senate decree in A.D. 6 ordered his books collected and publicly burned (Seneca the Elder *Contr.* 10 *Praef.* 4–8).

32. *Codd. Parisinus Latinus* 7530 and *Montecassinus* 1086, fol. 64, the latter written in the ninth century. See Heubner (1979).

33. Galinsky, however, cautions against assuming a dogmatic aesthetic orthodoxy dictated by Augustus (whom he believes was humane and tolerant on such matters) and illustrates his argument with an analysis of wall painting, including works from Augustus's own house. "What is Augustan . . . about Augustan painting is, as in the case of Augustan literature, its impulse to variety, its multiplicity of subjects . . . and their associations, its creativity, innovation and experimentation, its eclecticism of styles and themes, and its ongoing development" (1996, 194).

34. For a discussion of the continuing staging possibilities for tragedy in the imperial era, see Kelly (1979) and Jones (1993).

35. Elsewhere Horace provides an account of an impromptu pantomimic performance given by one Sarmentus, a rural jester who danced the cyclops (in a farcical contest) before Maecenas, Vergil, Varius, Tucca, and Horace (*Sat.* 1.5.63). McKeown (1979, 80) says of this that "the incident may or may not be historically true. The important point is that neither Horace nor his friends, including Maecenas, can have objected to having their enjoyment of this type of entertainment advertised and immortalized."

36. H. A. Kelly (1979, 21–24) discusses the relation between pantomime and traditional tragedy. Jory (1996) provides a useful analysis of the surviving visual evidence for the costume and masks of pantomimes and notes that "while there is considerable variation of dress among the full-length pantomime monuments, as would be expected given the 'tragic' roles portrayed, a long tunic reaching to the ankles features on almost all of them" (19). Galinsky compares pantomime to the works of Ovid, particularly his *Metamorphoses*. "The emphasis on singles scenes . . . the narrator's bravura performance, his sophistication, the constant shifts and changes, and the graphic, visual appeal of many scenes all have their counterpart in the pantomime . . . [which] required on the actor's part, a good knowledge of mythology and a superior education. . . . The tragic pantomime became the rage and its stars, the darlings of the higher classes. This is precisely the public for which Ovid wrote" (1996, 265).

37. Not the founder of comic pantomime, but a later dancer of the same name, famous during the reign of Domitian.

38. For opposition (particularly from the Senate) to the moral legislation, see the literature cited in Kienast (1982, 139, 234), Syme (1939, 444), and Raaflaub and Samons (1990, 433–35).

39. These figures indicate that on average Augustus displayed 1,250 gladiators and 135 wild animals per show. This demonstrates a dramatic increase in scale from that of the republican era.

40. From the earliest assessments by ancient Roman historians to the present, the interpretations of Augustus and his policies have widely differed in their analysis and conclusions. In the introductory section of his *Annals* (1–10), Tacitus presents two quite different summary viewpoints for comparison. Other commentators more nearly contemporary with Augustus, e.g., Velleius Paterculus (2.89), Pliny (*N.H.* 7.147–50), Seneca the Younger (*De Clementia* 1.9.1–1.11.2), and Philo (*Legatio ad Gaium* 143–51), also differ greatly in their evaluation. For a recent collection of articles assessing Augustus's legacy (reflecting quite diverse points of view), see K. A. Raaflaub and M. Toher (1990).

41. Galinsky (1996, 312–31) discusses the "Road to Divinity" in some detail.

42. See the discussion and conclusion by Nugent (1990) concerning Ovid's "error" and exile.

43. See Syme (1978, 19–20).

44. Technically speaking, it was not within the boundaries of the actual Campus, although the distinction was probably not important. It was also outside the *pomerium,* and thus formally outside the city. See Steinby (1993, 220–24; Richardson 1992, 294). For an analysis of the meaning of the Mausoleum, see Kraft (1967), Zanker (1988, 72–73), and Galinsky (1996, 352).

45. See Rawson (1991c, 535). Zanker (1988, 215–23) details the honors bestowed upon the two princes.

Chapter 4: Playing for Keeps

1. For a discussion of the climate of opinion and political unease during this period, see Newbold (1974).

2. On this occasion he granted the requests of some knights that they be allowed to fight as gladiators in Drusus's games, but unlike Augustus, who had attended a similar exhibition in A.D. 11, Tiberius refused to watch the contests, and when one of the equestrian contestants was killed, he forbade the man's opponent to continue (Dio 57.14.3).

3. This is the earliest record of what became the standard practice of maintaining a cohort of soldiers permanently in the Circus, arena, and theaters, the only occasions when troops were regularly present in the city to keep order. See Rich 1991, 194; Nippel 1995, 93–94.

4. For a full discussion and analysis of upper-class participation in the games during the early imperial period and the relevant legislation, see Levick (1983).

5. These measures were the subject of Levick's comprehensive article (1983).

6. Other visible honors were lavished upon Germanicus's memory by order of the Senate, including inscribed arches, innumerable statues, a chair placed in the theater in his honor among the priests of Augustus, the naming of a section of the equestrian rows in the theater after him, the presence of his ivory statue in the pompa circensis, and the display of his image each July 15 at the head of the traditional procession (transvectio equitum) of knights through the city (Tac. Ann. 2.83). This was a venerable ceremony, revived after long disuse by Augustus (Suet. Aug. 38); according to Dionysus of Halicarnassus (6.13.4), it included five thousand knights, who, dressed in purple robes with scarlet stripes and crowned with olive branches, were presented in a magnificent parade as if they were returning from battle. Recent evidence reveals a Senate decree of A.D. 20 commending the equestrian order for attempting through their acclamations at the theater to calm a protest by the plebs and praising those plebs who in turn "agreed with the sentiments of the equestrian order" and through their acclamations "demonstrated piety toward our *princeps* and the memory of his son" during a period of what was evidently considerable popular unrest (Edmondson 1996, 102, n. 148; Potter 1996, 140–41).

7. The theater burned in A.D. 21. Tiberius began the restoration but did not complete it (Suet. *Tib.* 47); it was eventually accomplished under Caligula (Suet. *Calig.* 21). Velleius Paterculus lavished praise on Tiberius for this modest act. "With what magnificent control of feeling did he restore the works of Pompey . . . for a feeling of kinship leads him to protect every famous monument" (2.130.1). By contrast, the honoring of Sejanus with the statue was denounced at the time by the historian Cremutius Cordus as a disgrace to Pompey's memory (Seneca *Marc.* 22.4).

8. The line punned on the word goat, *capra,* and the island Capreae. Augustus too had once suffered insult by the spectators' inclination to perceive a pun. An actor on stage referring to another said, "See how this dandy's [*cinaedus*] finger beats the drum." The audience chose the line's alternative meaning, "See how this dandy's finger sways the world," a reference to Augustus, and loudly applauded (Suet. *Aug.* 68).

9. Tacitus notes that the historian who praised Brutus and Cassius was Cremutius Cordus, who was prosecuted in A.D. 25 (*Ann.* 4.34.1). He also cites the case of Scaurus in A.D. 35 (*Ann.* 6.29.3).

10. A full review of the evidence for Caligula's mental and physical state is provided by Barrett (1990, 213 ff.).

11. The Circus (later used by Nero as well) was not finished until the end of Caligula's reign. The seventy-five-foot-high obelisk erected to crown the central barrier in his circus was brought from Heliopolis, in Egypt. The inscription dedicates the obelisk to Augustus and Tiberius. It was moved in 1586 to its present location in front of St. Peter's basilica.

12. On September 23 she was declared a goddess, the first Roman woman to be thus consecrated.

13. For a fuller description of these remarkable vessels, see Ucelli (1940) and an English summary in MacKendrick (1960, 178–82). Suetonius's assertion that there were ten banks of oars seems technically impossible, recent research having indicated that triremes were the most that could be achieved using separate tiers of oarsmen. Perhaps Caligula's barges employed oars that were each operated by ten oarsmen. In April 1996 a group of Italian archaeologists and experts on naval engineering announced plans to reconstruct the two vessels based on surviving prewar photographs and designs (*Times Higher Education Supplement,* April 26, 1996, 12).

14. For a full discussion of the vexed question of Caligula's divine honors, see Barrett (1990, 140–53). Price (1980) analyzes the ambiguous nature of the "divinity" of emperors and the nature of their cult and notes "the falsity of the picture sometimes presented of the emperor as an unquestioned god in the East" (42).

15. This implies that the shade provided by the vela did not actually extend over the auditorium as far as the orchestral area where the senators were seated, a suggestion consistent with the most likely arrangement of the apparatus used to rig and position this system of awnings.

16. The precise date and this sequence of events are disputed. Caligula may have been in Britain early in the year. He apparently did not stage his grand entry into Rome until the end of August. Barrett (1989, 135 ff.) provides a detailed analysis of the episodes.

17. According to Suetonius (*Calig.* 58.1), Caligula stopped to observe their rehearsals and, but for the fact that their leader was ill, would have arranged a command performance at once. Originally the *pyrricha* are thought to have been the frenetic dance of the Cretan *curetes* or *corybantes,* but by the first century A.D. they had evidently been tamed (cf. Suet. *Nero* 22.2; Apuleius *Meta.* 10.29–34) and sometimes involved animals as part of the performance (Pliny *N.H.* 8.5; Babrius 80).

18. See Levick (1990, 13 ff., 200 n. 8).

19. Dio also asserts that Claudius "feigned a stupidity greater than was really the case, since from childhood he had been prey to illness and great terror" (60.2.5). Despite a certain talent for oratory (so long as he followed a prepared text), his first public recitation had been less than successful; as Suetonius records, "At the very start of his performance a hugely fat man caused several benches to collapse, amidst general merriment. Even after silence was restored, Claudius could not help recalling the sight and breaking into peals of laughter" (*Claud.* 41). For his qualities of speech and intellect, see Levick (1990, 200–201, nn. 11, 18–20).

20. In 47, however, Pompey was put to death, reputedly after being caught in the act with a male lover, although the penalty may have been imposed at the urging of Mes-

salina, who possibly saw him as a political rival to her son, Britannicus (Suet. *Claud.* 27.2, 29.1–2; cf. Levick 1990, 58, 61; Barrett 1996, 88, 274).

21. He was harshly criticized subsequently for such practices. Half a century later, Pliny, in a lengthy tirade, denounced the awarding of *ornamenta praetoria* to Claudius's freedman M. Antonius Pallas (*Epis.* 8.6; cf. Tac. *Ann.* 12.53).

22. On one occasion Mnester delighted the spectators when they demanded that he perform a popular "turn" for them by "sticking his head out from behind the stage and saying 'sorry, I can't comply, I'm in bed with Orestes!' " (Dio 60. 28.5). Poppaea Sabina, reputedly Messalina's rival for Mnester, was terrorized into committing suicide (Tac. *Ann.* 11.1.1, 11.3.1).

23. For the uncertainty over the dates, see Barrett (1996, 234).

24. Other references to the affair are found in Pliny *N.H.* 29.8; Josephus *Ant. Iud.* 20.149; Dio 60.31.1–5; Juv. 6.116–32, 10.329–45; Seneca *Octavia* 257–72; and *Apocol.* 11.1, 13.4. It is discussed by Barrett (1996, 90–94).

25. Tac. *Ann.* 12.3.2; Dio 60.31.8; Suet. *Nero* 7.1 (cf. Barrett 1996, 234). It was first necessary to arrange for the accusation and execution of Junius Silanus, to whom Octavia was already betrothed. This Agrippina managed to do, persuading Claudius of the treachery of this reputable man, whom earlier the emperor had honored by promoting him at an early age to the praetorship and, at his games, shouting for favors as if Claudius himself were merely head of one of the petition-presenting factions (Dio 60.31.7). For the legal ban on marriage between an uncle and niece, see Barrett (1996, 100–101). In contriving to have it lifted, Agrippina and Claudius flattered the Senate by suggesting that giving its assent would establish a precedent enhancing its powers and arranged for popular demonstrations to take place in the Forum calling for the marriage.

26. Tac. *Ann.* 12.66–67; Dio 60.34.1–4; Pliny *N.H.* 2.92; Seneca *Octavia* 21, 44–45, 102, 164; Josephus *Ant. Iud* 20.148, 20.151; Juvenal 5.147–48, 6.620–24; Aurelius Victor *Caes.* 4.12–13.

27. Tacitus notes that later, during Senate deliberations, Agrippina literally positioned herself "behind the scenes," "shut off by a curtain thick enough to conceal her from view but not to prevent her from hearing." Not everything was to her liking. As one of his first acts, Nero had repealed the requirement imposed by Claudius upon the quaestors that they sponsor gladiatorial games, a relatively minor revision that, however, Agrippina unsuccessfully opposed "as a subversion of the acts of Claudius" (Tac. *Ann.* 13.5; cf. Barrett 1996, 164). Pliny later claimed that Nero deified Claudius only to ridicule him (*Paneg.* 11.1). But clearly it was attractive to Nero to style himself (in the manner of Augustus) as *Divi Filius,* and he used the title frequently (see Barrett 1996, 148, 166, 291; Levick 1996, 148).

Chapter 5: Nero

1. The passage from Suetonius suggests that he had seen Tacitus's account and sought to rebut it. There is general agreement among scholars that Tacitus, Suetonius, and Dio all used a common source or sources in their accounts of Nero's life but that Suetonius did not directly rely upon Tacitus, nor Dio upon his two predecessors. Tacitus was writing perhaps half a century after Nero's death, and Suetonius somewhat after Tacitus. Dio

wrote a century after them. The common source may have been Pliny the Elder, Cluvius Rufus, or Fabius Rusticus supplemented by other subsequently lost accounts such as those of General Corbulo and the autobiography of Agrippina the Younger. Martial also mentions poems by Nero (8.70), and Suetonius elsewhere notes a collection of songs for the cithara that probably included both words and music, selections of which were played for the public after Nero's death (*Vit.* 11).

2. Juvenal observed (6.365 ff.) that a resident dancer tended to corrupt the whole household: "If your wife is musical, none of those who sells their voices to the praetor will hold out against her charms." He goes on to suggest that such women become so love-struck they constantly have to pray to Janus for aid. "One woman consults you about a comedian, another wishes to commend to you a tragic actor."

3. It is interesting to note that Plutarch rejects the performance of tragedy at such banquets because it required elaborate enactment of events, and the performance of pantomime because it demanded many masks or characters. For a general survey of such "dinner theater," see C. P. Jones (1991) and D'Arms (1984). Goddard (1994) provides a useful analysis of Nero's table manners.

4. It was probably for this same Saturnalia that Seneca, Nero's former tutor and now his adviser, composed as an entertainment for the court the *Divi Claudii apocolocyntosis* (literally, *The Pumpkinification of the Divine Claudius*), in which he satirized Claudius, presenting him as a buffoon and a murderer, but praised Nero and celebrated the return of the rule of law. Dio says (60.34.2–4) that Seneca wrote such a work, which is as-sumed to be the extant parody now known by that name, although — while attributed to Seneca — it is given a different title in the manuscripts. See Barrett (1996, 202, 303), Griffin (1985, 96–97), and the extended treatment in Horstkotte (1985).

5. Suetonius, Tacitus, and Dio all suggest that Britannicus was murdered by Nero. Suetonius adds the detail that Britannicus's close friend, Titus (the future emperor), who was dining beside him, also drank some of the poison and became seriously ill. "Titus did not forget this, and later set up a golden statue of his friend in the Palace, and dedicated a second equestrian ivory statue, which to this day is carried in the *pompa circensis*" (*Titus* 2). Josephus, who knew Titus personally and would have recorded the version of events adhered to at the time he wrote his account around A.D. 90, also insists on Nero's guilt, while asserting that few at the time suspected an unnatural death (*Ant. Iud.* 20.153). See too Barrett (1996, 170–72).

6. Thereafter, one cohort (probably numbering about 500) from either the Praetorian or Urban Guard was regularly stationed in the theater and Circus. It eventually became the responsibility of the city prefect *(praefectus urbi)* — an office introduced by Augustus in A.D. 13 (Tac. *Ann.* 6.10.3) — to ensure order and control riotous spectators. See too Barrett (1996, 173), who suggests that the earlier removal of the praetorians from the theater was part of a package redefining the guards' duties, one purpose of which was to deprive Agrippina of her personal use of a praetorian detachment and thereby isolating her from men whose loyalty she might otherwise have been able to count on.

7. Caesar had set the precedent by compelling a member of a praetorian family, Furius Leptinus, as well as a former senator, Quintus Calpenus, to fight in the arena (Suet. *Div. Iul.* 39), and even Augustus had allowed members of the equestrian order to appear as gladiators in A.D. 11, when the earlier ban of 22 B.C. had proven difficult to enforce (Dio

56. 25.7). But Tiberius had reimposed and strengthened the restrictions in A.D. 19, which were then relaxed again by Caligula.

8. Apuleius writes, "There was a hill of wood . . . fashioned as a lofty structure, planted with foliage and live trees, from the highest peak of which a flowing stream ran from an artificial fountain. A few goats grazed upon the grass. . . . Then from the summit of the hill through a concealed pipe, there burst on high saffron mixed with wine. . . . And now with the entire theater sweetly scented, an opening in the ground swallowed up the wooden hill." The evidence of Calpurnius Siculus depends on the much debated assumption that he lived at the time of Nero. Coleman (1990, 52) accepts a Neronian dating but then subsequently rejects it (1993, 57). For an assessment of the arguments, see Champlin (1978), Townsend (1980), and Mayer (1980).

9. Assuming that the traditional date of her birth is correct: November 6, A.D. 15. For the issue of the precise date, see Barrett (1996, appen. 1). Barrett also gives an excellent account of Agrippina's murder, as well as an analysis of the various versions and supporting evidence (181–95 and appendix 10). The prefect of the fleet at Misenum (and former tutor to Nero), Anicetus, carried out the murder and was later employed again by Nero in A.D. 62 to help him dispatch his first wife, Octavia. Nero ordered him falsely to confess adultery with Octavia (implying that she had hoped to use his military force to overthrow the emperor), for which Anicetus was first heavily rewarded with money then lightly punished with banishment to Sardinia, where he lived well and died a natural death (Tac. *Ann.* 14.62).

10. Bartsch (1994, 22) suggests that "Tacitus's Nero thus emerges as a man whose power is characterized by his ability to decide what truth in the public realm will be; in a very real sense, his audience is compelled to follow a script over which the Emperor has total control." She cautions against accepting Tacitus's characterization uncritically as the whole truth.

11. See Levick (1990, 95). A useful discussion of the decline of senatorial power and prestige is provided by Hopkins and Burton (1983).

12. For example, in A.D. 58, the Senate heard a request from Syracuse asking permission to increase the number of pairs of gladiators allowed at the games there. In the debate, Thrasea Paetus (who a decade later would fall victim to Nero's "reign of terror") opposed the request and, when challenged to justify his intervention in so trivial an issue, explained that "he was paying members the compliment of making it clear that they would not dissemble their interest in great affairs when they could give attention to even the slightest" (Tac. *Ann.* 13.49). Similarly, following a violent riot in A.D. 59 in the amphitheater of Pompeii between the inhabitants of that city and neighboring Nuceria, Nero referred the matter to the Senate, which banned Pompeii from holding further gladiatorial displays for ten years.

13. For a discussion of these issues, see Griffin (1984, 41–49). For the Iuvenalia, see Bradley (1978a, 82), Gatti (1976, 105), and Warmington (1977, 64–65).

14. Later, on his Grecian tour, Nero competed with and—naturally—defeated his former instructor (Dio 63.8.4). Later still, as a old man, Terpnus was presented to mark the celebrations at the rededication of the theater of Marcellus by the emperor Vespasian, who paid him two hundred thousand sesterces for his appearance (Suet. *Vesp.* 19.1). The

same honor, incidentally, was paid to another of Nero's former competitors, the citharoedus Diodorus (Dio. 63.8.4, 63.20.3).

15. Although as noted above Paris had survived his involvement in the abortive plot against Agrippina in A.D. 55, in 67 he fell from grace and was executed by Nero, in whose overwrought imagination he was said to have loomed as an artistic rival (Suet. *Nero* 54). Paris was recalled a century later by Lucian as a man "who was no fool, and excelled if ever a man did, in remembrance of legends and beauty of movement." He recounted an anecdote in which Paris was challenged by Demetrius the Cynic (who had a low opinion of pantomime) to perform without benefit of musical or choral accompaniment. This Paris did, dancing a complex sequence from Homer's *Odyssey,* depicting the tale in which Aphrodite and Aries are entrapped by Hephaestus in a net while making love and then humiliatingly displayed to all the other gods. He enacted the entire story with all its characters so vividly that Demetrius was utterly enthralled and at the end exclaimed in a great shout, "I *hear* the story that you are acting, man, I do not just see it; you seem to me to be talking with your very hands!" (*De Salt.* 63).

16. For a discussion of Nero's artistic qualities, see Frazer (1966), Morford (1985), and Gyles (1962). A general account of Roman musical instruments and practice is provided by Comotti (1989), chaps. 3 and 4.

17. For an excellent discussion of the vexed question of performers' legal status at Rome, see Leppin (1992, 71–83).

18. Although Roman and Greek culture suffused one another, they were far from identical. As Wallace-Hadrill points out (1989, 164), "Culture does not respond to the food-blender: you cannot throw in chunks of Greek and Roman, press a button, and come out at the end with a homogeneous suspension of bland pap." An excellent description of what occurred is given by Gordon Williams (1978, chap. 3, "The Dominance of Greek Culture," 102–52).

19. Understanding of the nature and significance of the *agones* is chiefly due to the extensive work and publications of Louis Robert. An excellent summary of this work is provided in Robert (1984). Other related discussions are in Spawforth (1989), Herz (1990), Roueché (1993, 1–60), and Leppin (1992, 169–76). For an extensive treatment of the Oenoanda festival, see Wörrle (1988). It is also discussed by Mitchell (1990) and Gebhard (1996, 123–25).

20. For a discussion of these guilds, see Pleket (1973), Leppin (1992, 91–107), and Roueché (1993, 50–60). For organizations in Rome, see Jory (1970).

21. It is interesting to note that Seneca himself condemned a number of practices that Nero not only encouraged but avidly pursued: "I do not deign to admit painting into the list of the liberal arts, any more than sculpture . . . and other aids to luxury. I also ban from the liberal arts wrestling and all knowledge that is contrived of oil and mud . . . for do we really believe that the training they give is 'liberal' for the young men of Rome, who used to be taught by our ancestors to stand straight and hurl a spear . . . ? Neither the new system nor the old teaches or encourages virtue. For what good does it do us . . . to beat many opponents in wrestling or boxing only to find ourselves defeated by anger?" (*Epis. Mor.* 88.18–19).

22. This scrap of poetry attributed to Nero is preserved by Suetonius in his life of the

poet Lucan, who, having earlier been awarded the poetry prize at the first Neronia for a eulogy of Nero, later turned hostile after the emperor snubbed one of his poetry recitals. He expressed this in various ways: "Once in a public latrine, when he relieved his bowels with a remarkably loud fart, he shouted out this half line of Nero's, while those who were there for the same purpose fled in terror." Apparently no place was safe from the imperial spies! Lucan was later executed for taking part in the Pisonian conspiracy.

23. For an analysis of the complicated chronology of events relating to the *Neronia,* see Bolton (1948).

24. The primary accounts are Suetonius *Nero* 31 and Tacitus *Annales* 42. In addition to the book by Boethius (1960), a full summary is provided by Steinby (1995, 49–64),.; Richardson (1992, 119–21), Hemsoll (1990), Griffin (1985, 133–42), and Grant (1970, chap. 10), with illustrations in Nash (1968, vol. 1, 339–48).

25. I analyze in some detail the relationship between Roman wall painting and the theater in Beacham (1992, 68–81, 169–78, and 227–28, nn. 45–46). In addition to the bibliography cited there, see the articles by Cerutti and Richardson (1989), Moormann (1983), and Leach (1982), as well as the various discussions in Ling (1991, including 30–31, 77–78, 143, 159–62), and, more generally, his treatment of the fourth style in chap. 5. For the depiction of *scaenarum frontes* in the *Domus Aurea,* see Vallet et al. (1993, vol. 1, 260 ff.).

26. Elsewhere, Tacitus records that Nero had squandered (possibly in the last years alone of his reign) some two hundred million sesterces in "largess" (*Hist.* 20.2). Plutarch notes enormous sums given to actors and athletes (*Galb.* 16), while Suetonius gives further details of his notorious extravagance (*Nero* 30).

27. Of course, the ruling order had always found itself in effect trapped between two groups: the social outcasts performing on stage and the common crowd in the auditorium behind them. But under traditional political conditions this was tolerable. Nero rendered it volatile, offensive, and dangerous. In Dio's account of Nero's Iuvenalia he notes that Thrasea Paetus failed to applaud "since he would never help Nero in these matters" (61.20.4.). Tacitus reports that the future emperor Vespasian was reprimanded for dozing off during the Neronia (Tac. *Ann.* 16.5); Dio and Suetonius give a similar account but place the event during Nero's Grecian tour (Dio 61.11.2; *Vesp.* 4.4). But the punishment was not harsh; after a brief removal of imperial favor, in A.D. 67 he was appointed as special commander to suppress the Jewish rebellion.

28. It is noteworthy that Tacitus himself uses a good deal of theatrical language as well as a strong suggestion of a dramatic plot in his extended description of the conspiracy. Woodman (1993) provides an excellent analysis of this, pointing out among much else how Seneca's own suicide is described as a role-playing performance, in effect "The Execution of Socrates." Of course, it is difficult to determine whether the theatricality is Tacitus's creation or an accurate depiction of the extent to which the theatrical metaphor dominated public behavior in the Neronian era. The account by both Tacitus (15.70) and Suetonius *(Lucan)* of the poet Lucan's similarly histrionic suicide and the account by Tacitus of Petronius's death (16.19) suggest something of a fashion in such leave-taking.

29. The identity of Curiatius Maternus as a composer of *praetextae* (or whether indeed he may have been a fictionalized character conceived by Tacitus) is a much debated issue.

For an extensive analysis both of this and of the *Dialogue* itself, see Bartsch (1994, 98–126, and notes on 248 and 260). See too Kragelund (1987) and Sullivan (1985, 47, 155).

30. Vatinius was a cobbler who later served as a sort of court buffoon, acquiring wealth and influence in the process to become one of the most contemptible of Nero's favorites. The emperor attended a gladiatorial spectacle given by Vatinius at Beneventum, shortly after his stage debut (and accompanying earthquake) at Naples in A.D. 64. Elsewhere Tacitus characterizes him as among "the foulest creatures of the court . . . endowed with a misshapen body and a scurrile wit. . . . by slandering every decent person he acquired a power which made him in influence, wealth, and capacity for harm, notable even amongst villains" (Tac. *Ann.* 15.34). Tacitus's text concerning Maternus and Vatinius is difficult to understand and much discussed. The interpretation I favor is that Maternus refers to a play, *Nero*, presumably presented sometime during the brief rule of Galba (between June 68 and January 69), when it is likely Vatinius was executed, according to Tacitus in *Hist.* 1.37.5. This brief period of relative liberty and freedom of speech would also have been an opportune time for the composition (and presentation?) of the *Octavia*. For a discussion of the textual problems, see Kragelund (1987).

31. See Kelly (1979) and C. P. Jones (1993).

32. Cf. Lucian *Icaromenippus* 29, "If you take away their tragedians' masks and their gold embroidered robes, nothing is left but a funny little man hired for a competition for seven drachmas." On the other hand, successful actors could earn a great deal of money. The greatest actor of Cicero's day, Quintus Roscius Gallus, commanded a daily honorarium of four thousand sesterces (Macrobius *Sat.* 3.14.13) and according to Cicero was "a rich man" who in a decade could be expected to have earned (had he wished) six million sesterces (*Pro Rosc. Com.* 22–23). His contemporary the actor Aesopus left a legacy of twenty million sesterces, all earned through acting (*Sat.* 3.14.14).

33. Cf. Cicero *De Orat.* 1.128, 3.214, 3.220; *De Off.* 1.129–30; Quint. *Inst.* 1.8.3, 1.11.1–3, 1.11.12, 6.3.29, 6.3.47; for a full discussion of the relationship between actors and orators, see Graf (1991).

34. In the mid-second century A.D., Aulus Gellius records a question posed by Aristotle many centuries earlier: "Why are the artists of Dionysus for the most part worthless fellows?" noting that the question continues, "Is it because . . . much of their time is spent in intemperance and sometimes in poverty too?" (20.4).

35. For the nature and later history of such acclamations, see Peterson (1926), Alföldi (1934, 79 ff.), Klauser (1950), Cameron (1976, chap. 9), the article by Roueché (1984), and Potter (1996, 132–42). For the argument against pageantry as mere propaganda, see Veyne (1990, 378 ff.).

36. As Cross observes, "The sheer pageantry of his [Hitler's] campaign was sufficient to get people worked up; to attend a Hitler meeting was an almost religious experience" (1973, 169). He then quotes the following antiphon: "Versicle: 'Who is responsible for our misery?' Response: 'The System.' Versicle: 'Who is behind the system?' Response: 'The Jews.' Versicle: 'What is Adolf Hitler to us?' Response: 'A Faith.' Versicle: 'What else?' Response: 'A last Hope.' Versicle: 'What else?' Response 'Our LEADER!' Versicle: 'Germany!' Response: 'Awake!' Versicle: 'Germany!' Response: 'Awake!' "

37. The gesture had traditionally been viewed in Rome as a repugnant example of

unseemly oriental servility. For a discussion of this Eastern expression of worship, see Taylor (1975), esp. 256 ff. See also Alföldi (1934, 72 ff.) for its later employment as an element in the imperial cult.

38. The bronze inscription found at Karditsa, northwest of Athens but unquestionably set up throughout Greece, is recorded in Dittenberger (1915–24), no. 814. Ancient references to the event include Plutarch (*Flam.* 12.8), Suetonius (*Nero* 24), Pausanias (7.17.3), and Pliny (*N.H.* 4.6.22). Suetonius says that the ceremony took place in the stadium at Corinth, but the assertion by Plutarch (who was probably present there as a young boy with his tutor) that it was held in the marketplace is more likely (*Mor.* 385B).

Bibliography

Abbot, F. "The Theater as a Factor in Roman Politics under the Republic." *Transactions of the American Philological Association* 38 (1907): 49–56.

Ades, D., et al., eds. *Art and Power: Europe under the Dictators, 1930–1945.* London, 1995.

Alcock, S. E. "Nero at Play? The Emperor's Grecian Odyssey." In J. Elsner and J. Masters, eds., *Reflections of Nero.* Pp. 98–111.

Alföldi, A. "Die Ausgestaltung des monarchischen Zeremoniells." *Mitteilungen des Deutschen Archäologischen Instituts* 49 (1934): 118.

———. "Die Geburt der kaiserlichen Bildsymbolik." *Museum Helveticum* 10 (1953): 103–24.

———. *Die monarchische Repräsentation im römischen Kaiserreiche.* Darmstadt, 1970.

———. *Oktavians Aufstieg zur Macht.* Bonn, 1976.

Alföldy, G. *The Social History of Rome.* Rev. ed. Trans. D. Braund and F. Pollock. London, 1978.

———. *Römische Sozialgeschichte.* Rev. ed. Wiesbaden, 1984.

———. "Eine Bauinschrift aus dem Colosseum." *Zeitschrift für Papyrologie und Epigraphik* 109 (1995): 195–226.

Anderson, J. C. *The Historical Topography of the Imperial Fora.* Brussels, 1984.

Anderson, J. K. *Hunting in the Ancient World.* Berkeley, 1985.

Anderson, W. S., ed. *Essays on Roman Satire.* Princeton, 1982.

André, J. M. "Die Zuschauerschaft als sozialpolitischer Mikrocosmos zur Zeit des Hochprinzipats." In J. Blänsdorf, ed., *Theater und Gesellschaft im Imperium Romanum.* Tübingen, 1990. Pp. 165–73.

Andreae, B. *The Art of Rome.* Trans. R. E. Wolf. London, 1978.

Andreae, M. T. "Tiermegalographien in pompejanischen Gärten: Die sogenannten Paradeisos Darstellungen." *Rivista di Studi pompeiani* 4 (1990): 74–124.

Arendt, H. *On Violence.* New York, 1970.

Arnold, I. R. "Agonistic Festivals in Italy and Sicily." *American Journal of Archaeology* 64 (1960): 245–51.

Artaud, A. *The Theater and Its Double.* Trans. M. C. Richards. New York, 1958.

Auerbach, E. *Mimesis: The Representation of Reality in Western Literature.* Princeton, 1953.

Auguet, R. *Cruelty and Civilization: The Roman Games.* London, 1972.

Aymard, J. *Essai sur les chasses romaines.* Paris, 1951.

Balsdon, J. P. V. D. *The Emperor Gaius.* Oxford, 1934.

———. *Life and Leisure in Ancient Rome.* London, 1969.

Barrett, A. A. *Caligula: The Corruption of Power.* New Haven, 1990.

———. *Agrippina: Sister of Caligula, Wife of Claudius, Mother of Nero.* London, 1996.

Barton, C. *The Sorrows of the Ancient Romans: The Gladiator and the Monster.* Princeton, 1993.

Barton, T. "The *Inventio* of Nero: Suetonius." In J. Elsner and J. Masters, eds., *Reflections of Nero.* Chapel Hill, N.C., 1994. 48–63.

Bartsch, S. *Actors in the Audience: Theatricality and Doublespeak from Nero to Hadrian.* Cambridge, Mass., 1994.

Beacham, R. "The Development of the Roman Stage: A Missing Link Restored." *Theatre Research International* 5, no. 1 (1980): 37–45.

———. *The Roman Theatre and Its Audience.* Cambridge, Mass., 1992.

Beard, M., and M. Crawford. *Rome in the Late Republic.* Ithaca, N.Y., 1985.

Beare, W. *The Roman Stage.* London, 1950.

Bejor, G. "L'edificio teatrale nell' Urbanizzazione Augustea." *Athenaeum* 57 (1979): 126–38.

Bell, J. M., and D. Mullin. "The Problem with Pollux." *Theatre Notebook* 40, no. 1 (1986): 9–22.

Benediktson, D. T. "Caligula's Madness: Madness or Interictal Temporal Lobe Epilepsy?" *Classical World* 82, no. 5 (May–June 1989): 370–75.

Bergmann, B. "Painted Perspectives of a Villa Visit: Landscape as Status and Metaphor." In E. K. Gazda, ed., *Roman Art in the Private Sphere.* Ann Arbor, 1991. Pp. 49–70.

Bieber, M. *The History of the Greek and Roman Theater.* Princeton, 1961.

Billows, R. "The Religious Procession of the *Ara Pacis Augustae*: Augustus' *Supplicatio* in 13 B.C.." *Journal of Roman Archaeology* 6 (1993): 80–92.

Bishop, J. D. *Seneca's Daggered Stylus: Political Code in the Tragedies.* Königstein, 1985.

Blänsdorf, J. "Voraussetzungen und Entstehung der römischen Komödie." In E. Lefèvre, ed., *Das römische Drama.* Darmstadt, 1978.

———, ed. *Theater und Gesellschaft im Imperium Romanum.* Tübingen, 1990.

Blanckenhagen, P. H. von. *Flavische Architektur und ihre Dekoration.* Berlin, 1940.

Boethius, A. "On the Ancestral Masks of the Romans." *Acta Archaeologica* 13 (1942): 226–35.

———. *The Golden House of Nero.* Ann Arbor, 1960.

———. *Etruscan and Early Roman Architecture.* Harmondsworth, 1978.

Bollinger, T. *Theatralis Licentia: Die Publikumsdemonstrationen an den öffentlichen Spielen der früheren Kaiserzeit und ihre Bedeutung im politischen Leben.* Winterthur, 1969.

Bolton, J. D. P. "Was the *Neronia* a Freak Festival?" *Classical Quarterly* 42 (1948): 82–90.

Bömer, F. "Pompa." In K. Wissowa et al., eds., *Paulys Real-Encyclopädie der classischen Altertumswissenschaft.* Vol 21. Berlin, 1931. Pp. 1878–1994.

Bomgardner, D. L. "Amphitheatres on the Fringe." *Journal of Roman Archaeology* 4 (1991): 282–94.

———. "A New Era for Amphitheatre Studies." *Journal of Roman Archaeology* 6 (1993): 375–90.

Bonelli, G. "Autenticità o retorica nella tragedia di Seneca." *Latomus* 39 (1980): 612–38.

Bosworth, A. B. "Asinius Pollio and Augustus." *Historia* 21 (1972): 441–73.

Bradley, K. R. "The Chronology of Nero's Visit to Greece A.D. 66/7." *Latomus* 37 (1978b): 61–72.

———. *Suetonius' Life of Nero: An Historical Commentary.* Brussels, 1978a.

———. "The Significance of the *Spectacula* in Suetonius' *Caesares.*" *Rivista Storica dell' Antichità* 11 (1981): 129–37.

Brantlinger, R. *Bread and Circuses: Theories of Mass Culture as Social Decay.* Ithaca, N.Y., 1983.

Brink, C. O. *Horace on Poetry,* vol. 3: *The Letters to Augustus and Florus.* Cambridge, Mass., 1982.

Brothers, A. J. "Buildings for Entertainment." In I. M. Barton, ed., *Roman Public Buildings.* Exeter, 1989. 97–125.

Brown, S. "Death as Decoration: Scenes from the Arena on Roman Domestic Mosaics." In A. Richlin, ed., *Pornography and Representation in Greece and Rome.* New York, 1992. 180–211.

———. "Explaining the Arena: Did the Romans 'Need' Gladiators?" *Journal of Roman Archaeology* 8 (1995): 376–84.

Brunt, P. A. *Italian Manpower: 225 B.C.–A.D. 14.* Oxford, 1971.

———. "Princeps and Equites." *Journal of Roman Studies* 73 (1983): 42–75.

———. *The Fall of the Roman Republic.* Oxford, 1988.

Cameron, A. *Circus Factions: Blues and Greens at Rome and Byzantium.* Oxford, 1976.

———. "Bread and Circuses: The Roman Emperor and his People." Inaugural lecture, King's College. London, 1973.

Capoferro Cencetti, A. M. "Variazioni nel tempo dell'identita funzionale di un monumento: Il theatro di Pompeo." *Rivista di Archeologia* 3 (1979): 72–82.

Carcopino, J. *Daily Life in Ancient Rome.* Trans. E. O. Lorimer. London, 1941.

Carettoni, G. "Le gallerie ipogee del foro romano e i ludi gladiatori forensi." *Bollettino della commissione archeologica comunale in Roma* 76 (1956–58): 23–44.

———. "Due nuovi Ambienti dipinti sul Palatino." *Bollettino d'Arte* 46 (1961): 189–99.

Carlson, M. *Places of Performance: The Semiotics of Theatre Architecture.* Ithaca, N.Y., 1989.

Cavallaro, M. A. *Spese e Spettacoli: Aspetti economici-strutturali degli spettacoli nella Roma giulio-claudia.* Bonn, 1984.

Cerutti, S., and L. Richardson. "Vitruvius on Stage Architecture and Some Recently Discovered *Scaenae Frons* Decorations." *Journal of the Society of Architectural Historians* 48, no. 2 (1989): 172–79.

Champlin, E. "The Life and Times of Calpurnius Siculus." *Journal of Roman Studies* 68 (1978): 95–110.

Charles-Picard, G. *Augustus and Nero.* Trans. L. Ortzen. New York, 1968.

Chisholm, K., and J. Ferguson. *Rome: The Augustan Age.* Oxford, 1981.

Cianfrotta, P. A., O. Mazzucato, and M. Polia. "Scavo nell'area del Teatro Argentina, 1968–69." *Bolletino della commissione archeologia communale di Roma* 81 (1968–69): 25–36.

Cizek, E. "Suéton et le théâtre." In *Association Budé, Actes IXᵉ Congrès.* Paris, 1975. 480–85.

Clark, G. W. "Seneca the Younger under Caligula." *Latomus* 24 (1965): 62–69.

Clavel-Lévêque, M. *L'Empire en jeux.* Paris, 1984.

——. "L'espace des jeux dans le monde romain." In *Aufstieg und Niedergang der römischen Welt* 2.16.3 (Berlin, 1986): 2405–563.

Coarelli, F. "Il complesso Pompeiano del Campo Marzio e la sua decorazione scultorea." *Rendiconti della pontificia accademia romana di archeologia* 44 (1972): 99–122.

——. *L'Area sacra di Largo Argentina.* Rome, 1981.

——. *Foro romano II: periodo repubblicano e augusteo.* Rome, 1985.

——. *Il Foro boario dalle origini alla fine della repubblica.* Rome, 1988.

——. "La casa dell'aristocrazia romana secondo Vitruvio." In H. Geertman and J. H. De Jong, eds., *Munus non Ingratum.* Rome, 1989. 178–87.

Coleman, K. M. "Fatal Charades: Roman Executions Staged as Mythological Enactments." *Journal of Roman Studies* 80 (1990): 44–73.

——. "Launching into History: Aquatic Displays in the Early Empire." *Journal of Roman Studies* 83 (1993): 48–74.

——. "'The Contagion of the Throng': Absorbing Violence in the Roman World." Inaugural lecture, Trinity College. Dublin, 1996a.

——. "Ptolemy Philadelphus and the Roman Amphitheater." In W. J. Slater, ed., *Roman Theater and Society.* Ann Arbor, 1996b. 49–68.

Comotti, G. *Music in Greek and Roman Culture.* Trans. V. Munson. Baltimore, 1989.

Conforto, M. L., and A. M. Reggiani, eds. *Anfiteatro Flavio: Immagine, testimonianze, spettacoli.* Rome, 1988.

Corbett, P. *The Scurra.* Edinburgh, 1986.

Costa, C. D. N. "The *Dialogus.*" In T. A. Dorey, ed., *Tacitus.* London, 1969. 19–33.

Cousin, J. "Quintilien et le théâtre." In *Association Budé, Actes IXᵉ Congrès.* Paris, 1975. 459–67.

Cozzo, G. *L'ingegneria romana.* Rome, 1928.

Crawford, J. M. M. *Tullius Cicero: The Fragmentary Speeches.* Atlanta, 1993.

Crema, L. *L'architettura romana.* Turin, 1959.

Cross, C. *Adolf Hitler.* London, 1973.

Crowther, N. B. "The *Collegium Poetarum* at Rome: Fact and Conjecture." *Latomus* 32 (1973): 575–80.

——. "Greek Games in Republican Rome." *L'Antiquité Classique* 52 (1983): 268–73.

Csapo, E., and W. Slater. *The Context of Ancient Drama*. Ann Arbor, 1995.

Cuff, P. J. "The Settlement of 23 B.C. : A Note." *Rivista di Filologia* 101 (1973): 466–77.

D'Arms, J. "Control, Companionship and *Clientela*: Some Social Functions of the Roman Communal Meal." *Echos du monde classique* 28 (1984): 327–48.

De Finis, L., ed. *Scena e spettaculo nell'antichità*. Trent, 1989.

Dickison, S. "Claudius: *Saturnalicius Princeps*." *Latomus* 36 (1977): 634–47.

Dittenberger, W. *Sylloge Inscriptionum Graecarum*. 3d ed. Leipzig, 1915–24.

Domerque, C., E. Landes, and J. Pailler, eds. *Spectacula-I. Gladiateurs et Amphithéâtres*. Lattes, France, 1990.

Dorey, T. A., and D. R. Dudley, eds. *Roman Drama*. New York, 1965.

Duckworth, G. E. *The Nature of Roman Comedy: A Study in Popular Entertainment*. Princeton, 1952.

Ducos, M. "La condition des acteurs à Rome." In J. Blänsdorf, ed., *Theater und Gesellschaft im Imperium Romanum*. Tübingen, 1990. 19–33.

Dupont, F. *L'acteur-roi ou le théâtre dans la Rome antique*. Paris, 1985.

Edler, W. "Augustus and the Power of Tradition." In K. A. Raaflaub and M. Toher, eds., *Between Republic and Empire*. Berkeley, 1990. 71–122.

Edmondson, J. C. "Dynamic Arenas: Gladiatorial Presentations in the City of Rome and the Construction of Roman Society during the Early Empire." In W. J. Slater, ed., *Roman Theater and Society*. Ann Arbor, 1996. 69–112.

Edwards, C. "Beware of Imitations: Theatre and the Subversion of Imperial Identity." In J. Elsner and J. Masters, eds., *Reflections of Nero* Chapel Hill, 1994. 83–97.

Ehrenberg, V., and A. H. M. Jones, eds. *Documents Illustrating the Reigns of Augustus and Tiberius*. Oxford, 1949.

Ellis, S. P. "Power, Architecture, and Decor." In E. K. Gazda, ed., *Roman Art in the Private Sphere*. Ann Arbor, 1991. 117–34.

Elsner, J. "Cult and Sculpture: Sacrifice in the *Ara Pacis Augustae*." *Journal of Roman Studies* 81 (1991): 50–61.

Elsner, J., and J. Masters, eds. *Reflections of Nero: Culture, History, and Representation*. Chapel Hill, N.C., 1994.

Engemann, J. "Architekturdarstellungen des frühen zweiten Stils." In *Mitteilungen des Deutschen Archäologischen Instituts, römische abteilung, zwölftes Ergänzungsheft*. Heidelberg, 1967.

Epstein, D. *Personal Enmity in Roman Politics, 218–43 B.C.* London, 1989.

Fantham, R. E. "Mime: The Missing Link in Roman Literary History." *Classical World* 82, no. 3 (1989): 153–63.

Fidenzoni, P. *Il teatro di Marcello*. Rome, 1970.

Flambard, J. M. "Clodius, les collèges, la plèbe et les esclaves." *Mémoires des Ecoles Françaises de Rome* 89 (1977): 115–56.

———. "Collegia Compitalicia: Phénomène associatif, cadres territoriaux et cadres civiques dans le monde romain à l'époque républicaine." *Ktema* 6 (1981): 143–66.

Foucault, M. *Madness and Civilization*. Trans. R. Howard. New York, 1973.

———. *Discipline and Punish: The Birth of the Prison*. Trans. A. Sheridan. New York, 1979.

Fowler, B. *The Hellenistic Aesthetic*. Madison, Wisc., 1989.

Fowler, W. *The Roman Festivals of the Period of the Republic*. London, 1932.

Franciscis, A. de. *Pompeian Wallpaintings in the Roman Villa of Oplontis*. Reckling-hausen, 1975.

Frank, T. "The Status of Actors at Rome." *Classical Philology* 26 (1931): 11–20.

Franklin, J. L. "Pantomimists at Pompeii: Actius Anicetus and his Troupe." *American Journal of Philology* 108 (1987): 95–107.

Frassinetti, P. *Fabula Atellana: Saggio sul teatro popolare latino*. Pavia, 1953.

Frazer, R. M. "Nero the Artist-Criminal." *Classical Journal* 62 (1966): 17–20.

Frederiksen, M. F. "The Republican Municipal Laws: Errors and Drafts." *Journal of Roman Studies* 55 (1965): 183–98.

———. "Caesar, Cicero and the Problem of Debt." *Journal of Roman Studies* 56 (1966): 128–41.

Frézouls, E. "Aspects de l'histoire architecturale du théâtre romain." In *Aufstieg und Niedergang der römischen Welt*. 2.12.1. Berlin, 1982. 343–441.

———. "La construction du *theatrum lapideum* et son contexte politique." In *Théâtre et spectacles dans l'antiquité*. Leiden, 1983. 193–214.

Friedländer, L. *Darstellungen aus der Sittengeschichte Roms in der Zeit von Augustus bis zum Ausgang der Antonine*. 4 vols. 10th ed. Leipzig, 1921–23.

Fuchs, M. *Untersuchungen zur Ausstattung römischer Theater in Italien und den West-provinzen des Imperium Romanum*. Mainz, 1987.

Gaggiotti, M. "Atrium Regium-Basilica (Aemilia)." *Analecta Romana Instituti Danici* 14 (1985): 53–80.

Galinsky, K. *Augustan Culture*. Princeton, 1996.

Galsterer, H. "Spiele und 'Spiele': Die Organisation der *ludi Iuvenales* in der Kaiserzeit." *Athenaeum* 59 (1981): 410–38.

———. "A Man, a Book, and a Method: Sir Ronald Syme's *Roman Revolution* after Fifty Years." In K. A. Raaflaub and M. Toher, eds., *Between Republic and Empire*. Berkeley, 1990.

Garland, R. *The Eye of the Beholder: Deformity and Disability in the Graeco-Roman World*. London, 1995.

Garnsey, P. D. A. *Social Status and Legal Privilege in the Roman Empire*. Oxford, 1970.

Garton, C. *Personal Aspects of the Roman Theatre*. Toronto, 1972.

———. "A Revised Register of Augustan Actors." *Aufstieg und Niedergang der römischen Welt* 2.30.1. Berlin, 1982. 580–609.

Gatti, C. "Studi Neroniani II: Gli Augustiani." *Centro ricerche e documentazione sull'antichità* 8 (1976–77): 103–21.

Gazda, E. K., ed. *Roman Art in the Private Sphere*. Ann Arbor, 1991.

Gebhard, E. R. "The Theater and the City." In W. J. Slater, ed., *Roman Theater and Society*. Ann Arbor, 1996. 113–28.

Geer, R. M. "The Greek Games at Naples." *Transactions of the American Philological Association* 66 (1935): 208–21.

Gentili, B. *Theatrical Performances in the Ancient World: Hellenistic and Early Roman Theater*. Amsterdam, 1979.

Gianfrotta, P. A, O. Mazzucato, and M. Polia. "Scavo nell'area del Teatro Argentina,

1968–69." *Bolletino della Commissione Archeologia Communale di Roma* 81 (1968–69): 25–36.

Gilula, D. "Greek Drama in Rome: Some Aspects of Cultural Transposition." In H. Scolnicov and P. Holland, eds., *The Play Out of Context*. Cambridge, U.K., 1989.

Giuliani, C. F., and P. Verduchi. *L'area centrale del foro romano*. Florence, 1987.

Gleason, K. L. "The Garden Portico of Pompey the Great." *Expedition* 32, no. 2 (1990): 4–13.

———. "*Porticus Pompeiana*: A New Perspective on the First Public Park of Ancient Rome." *Journal of Garden History* 14, no. 1 (1994): 13–27.

Goddard, J. "The Tyrant at Table." In J. Elsner and J. Masters, eds., *Reflections of Nero: Culture, History, and Representation* Chapel Hill, 1994. 67–82.

Gold, B. K., and E. W. Leach, eds. *Literary and Artistic Patronage in Augustan Rome*. Austin, 1982.

Goldberg, S. "Terence and the Death of Comedy." In C. Davidson, R. Johnson, and J. Stroupe, eds., *Drama and the Classical Heritage*. New York, 1993. 52–64.

Goldman, N. "Reconstructing the Roman Colosseum Awning." *Archeology* 35, no. 2 (1982): 57–65.

Göllmann, C. "Zur Beurteilung der öffentlichen Spiele Roms bei Tacitus, Plinius d. j., Martial und Juvenal." Ph.D. diss. University of Münster, 1942.

Golvin, J. C. *L'amphithéâtre romain: Essai sur la théorisation de sa forme et de ses fonctions*. 2 vols. Paris, 1988.

Golvin, J. C., and C. Landes. *Amphithéâtres et gladiateurs*. Paris, 1990.

Graefe, R. *Vela Erunt, die Zeldächer der römischen Theater und ähnlicher Anlagen*. 2 vols. Mainz, 1979.

Graf, F. "Gestures and Conventions: The Gestures of Roman Actors and Orators." In J. Bremmer and H. Roodenburge, eds., *A Cultural History of Gesture from Antiquity to the Present Day*. Oxford, 1991. 36–58.

Grant, F. C. *Ancient Roman Religion*. New York, 1957.

Grant, M. *Gladiators*. New York, 1967.

———. *Nero*. London, 1970.

Gratwick, A. S. "Drama." In E. J. Kenny, ed., *Cambridge History of Classical Literature* 2 Cambridge, U.K., 1982. 77–137.

Greenblatt, S. *Renaissance Self-Fashioning*. Chicago, 1980.

Greenhalgh, P. *Pompey: The Roman Alexander*. London, 1980.

———. *Pompey: The Republican Prince*. London, 1981.

Griffin, M. T. *Nero: The End of a Dynasty*. New Haven, 1985.

Griffith, J. G. "Juvenal and Stage-struck Patricians." *Mnemosyne* 15 (1962): 256–61.

Grimal, P. "Le théâtre à Rome." In *Association Budé, Actes IXe Congrès*. Paris, 1975. 249–305.

Grimm-Samuel, V. "On the Mushroom that Deified the Emperor Claudius." *Classical Quarterly* 41 (1991): 178–82.

Gros, P. "La fonction symbolique des édifices théâtraux dans le paysage urbain de la Rome augustéene." In *L'Urbs: Espace urbain et histoire*. Rome, 1987. 324–25.

Gruen, E. *Cultural and National Identity in Republican Rome*. Ithaca, N.Y., 1992.

———. *The Last Generation of the Roman Republic*. Berkeley, 1974.

——. "P. Clodius: Instrument or Independent Agent?" *Phoenix* 20 (1966): 120–30.

Gyles, M. F. "Nero: *Qualis Artifex.*" *Classical Journal* 57 (1962): 193–200.

Habel, E. "Ludi Publici." In K. Wissowa et al., *Paulys Real-Encyclopädie der classischen Altertumswissenschaft.* Berlin, 1931. Vol. 15: 608–30.

Hammond, N. G. L. *A History of Greece to 322 B.C.* Oxford, 1991.

Hannestad, N. *Roman Art and Imperial Policy.* Aarhus, 1988.

Hanson, J. A. *Roman Theater-Temples.* Princeton, 1959.

Harmon, D. P. "The Religious Significance of Games in the Roman Age." In W. J. Raschke, ed., *The Archaeology of the Olympics: The Olympics and Other Festivals in Antiquity.* Madison, Wisc., 1988. 236–55.

Harris, M. V. *Ancient Literacy.* Cambridge, Mass., 1989.

Hemsoll, D. "The Architecture of Nero's Golden House." In M. Henig, ed., *Architecture and Architectural Sculpture in the Roman Empire* Oxford, 1990. Vol. 29: 10–38.

Henderson, M. I. "The Establishment of the *Equester Ordo.*" *Journal of Roman Studies* 53 (1963): 61–72.

Henry, D., and E. Henry. *The Mask of Power: Seneca's Tragedies and Imperial Rome.* Chicago, 1985.

Herrmann, M. *Die Entstehung der berufsmässigen Schauspielkunst im Altertum und in der Neuzeit.* Berlin, 1962.

Herz, P. "Die musische Agonistik und der Kunstbetrieb der Kaiserzeit." In J. Blänsdorf, ed., *Theater und Gesellschaft im Imperium Romanum.* Tübingen, 1990. 175–95.

Heubner, H. "Zum 'Thyestes' des L. Varius Rufus." *Rheinisches Museum für Philologie* 122 (1979): 358–65.

Highet, G. *Juvenal the Satirist.* London, 1954.

Holliday, P. J. "Time, History and Ritual on the *Ara Pacis Augustae.*" *Art Bulletin* 72, no. 4 (1990): 542–57.

Hölscher, T. "Denkmäler der Schlacht von Actium. Propaganda und Resonanz." *Klio: Beiträge zu alten Geschichte* 67, no. 1 (1985): 81–102.

Hönle, A. *Amphitheater und Circus: Kampf, Blut und Gefahr zu Ehren der Götter, zum Nutzen des Staates.* Freiburg im Breisgau, 1981.

Hopkins, K. *Conquerors and Slaves.* Cambridge, U.K., 1978.

——. *Death and Renewal.* Cambridge, U.K., 1983.

Hopkins, K., and G. Burton. "Ambition and Withdrawal: The Senatorial Aristocracy Under the Emperors." In K. Hopkins, ed., *Death and Renewal.* Cambridge, U.K., 1983. 120–23.

Horsfall, N. "The *Collegium Poetarum.*" *Bulletin of the Institute of Classical Studies* 23 (1976): 79–95.

Horstkotte, H. "Die politische Zielsetzung von Senecas *Apocolocyntosis.*" *Athenaeum* 63 (1985): 337–58.

Hülsemann, M. *Theater, Kult und bürgerlicher Widerstand im antiken Rom.* Frankfurt, 1987.

Humphrey, J. H. *Roman Circuses: Arenas for Chariot Racing.* Berkeley, 1986.

Izenour, G. C. *Roofed Theaters of Classical Antiquity.* New Haven, 1992.

Jennison, G. *Animals for Show and Pleasure in Ancient Rome.* Manchester, 1937.

Jones, B. W. *The Emperor Domitian.* London, 1992.

Jones, C. P. "Dinner Theatre." In W. J. Slater, ed. *Dining in a Classical Context*. Ann Arbor, 1991. 185–98.

———. "Greek Drama in the Roman Empire." In R. Scodel, ed., *Theater and Society in the Classical World*. Ann Arbor, 1993. 39–52.

Jory, E. J. "Dominus Gregis?" *Classical Philology* 61 (1966): 102–5.

———. "Associations of Actors in Rome." *Hermes* 98 (1970): 223–53

———. "The Literary Evidence for the Beginnings of Imperial Pantomime," *Bulletin of the Institute of Classical Studies* 28 (1981): 147–61.

———. "The Early Pantomime Riots." In A. Moffatt, ed., *Maistor: Classical Byzantine and Renaissance Studies for Robert Browning*. Canberra, 1984. 57–66.

———. "Continuity and Change in the Roman Theatre." In J. Betts, J. Hooker, and J. Green, eds., *Studies in Honour of T. B. L. Webster*. Bristol, 1986a. 143–52.

———. "Gladiators in the Theatre." *Classical Quarterly* 36 (1986b): 537–39.

———. "Publilius Syrus and the Element of Competition in the Theatre of the Republic." In N. Horsfall, ed., *Vir Bonus Discendi Peritus: Bulletin of the Institute of Classical Studies*. Suppl. 51 (London, 1988): 73–81.

———. "*Ars Ludicra* and the *Ludus Talarius*." In *Stage Directions: Essays in Honour of E. W. Handley*. London, 1995. 139–52.

———. "The Drama of the Dance: Prolegomena to an Iconography of Imperial Pantomime." In W. J. Slater, ed., *Roman Theater and Society*. Ann Arbor, 1996. 1–28.

Jolivet, V. "Les jardins de Pompée: Nouvelles hypothèses." *Mélanges de l'Ecole Française de Rome* 95 (1983): 115–38.

Josephus, Flavius. *Death of an Emperor*. Trans. T. P. Wiseman. Exeter, 1991.

Kähler, H. *The Art of Rome and Her Empire*. New York, 1963.

Keil, H. *Grammatici Latini*. Leipzig, 1855–1923.

Kellum, B. A. "The City Adorned: Programmatic Display at the *Aedes Concordiae Augustae*." In K. A. Raaflaub and M. Toher, eds., *Between Republic and Empire*. Berkeley, 1990. 276–307.

Kelly, H. A. "Tragedy and the Performance of Tragedy in Late Roman Antiquity." *Traditio* 35 (1979): 21–44.

Kennedy, D. "The Spectator and the Spectacle." Inaugural lecture, Trinity College. Dublin, 1996.

Kienast, D. *Augustus: Prinzeps und Monarch*. Darmstadt, 1982.

Kierdorf, W. *Laudatio Funebris: Interpretationen und Untersuchungen zur Entwicklung der römischen Leichenrede*. Meisenheim am Glan, 1980.

Killeen, J. F. "What Was the *Linea Dives* (Martial 8. 78. 7)?" *American Journal of Philology* 80 (1959): 185–88.

Kindermann, H. *Das Theaterpublikum der Antike*. Salzburg, 1979.

Klauser, T. "Akklamation." *Reallexikon für Antike und Christentum*. Stuttgart, 1950. 213–33.

Knoche, U. *Roman Satire*. Trans. E. S. Ramage. Bloomington, Ind., 1975.

Kohansky, M. *The Disreputable Profession: The Actor in Society*. Westport, Conn., 1984.

Kokkinos, N. *Antonia Augusta: Portrait of a Great Roman Lady*. Routledge, 1992.

Kokolakis, M. "Lucian and the Tragic Performances in His Time." *Platon* 12 (1960): 67–109.

Kolendo, J. "La répartition des places aux spectacles et la stratification sociale dans l'Empire romain." *Ktema* 6 (1981): 301–15.

Kondoleon, C. "Signs of Privilege and Pleasure: Roman Domestic Mosaics." In E. K. Gazda, ed., *Roman Art in the Private Sphere*. Ann Arbor, 1991. 105–15.

Konstan, D. *Roman Comedy*. Ithaca, N.Y., 1983.

Kraft, K. "Der Sinn des Mausoleums des Augustus." *Historia* 16 (1967): 189–206.

Kragelund, P. "Vatinius, Nero and Curiatius Maternus." *Classical Quarterly* 37 (1987): 197–202.

Krautheimer, R. *Rome: Profile of a City, 312–1308*. Princeton, 1980.

Kubiak, A. "Trail and Terror: *Medea* Prima Facie." In C. Davidson, R. Johnson, and J. Stroupe, eds., *Drama and the Classical Heritage: Comparative and Critical Essays*. New York, 1993. 1–28.

Künzl, E. *Der römische Triumph*. Munich, 1988.

Laidlaw, W. A. "Cicero and the Stage." *Hermathena* 94 (1960): 56–66.

Lana, I. "I ludi Capitolini di Domiziano." *Rivista di Filologia e di Istruzione Classica* 29 (1951): 145–60.

Landes, C., ed. *Le théâtre antique et ses spectacles*. Lattes, France, 1992.

Langenfeld, H. "Die Politik des Augustus und die griechische Agonistik." In E. Lefèvre, ed., *Monumentum Chiloniense: Studien zur augusteischen Zeit*. Amsterdam, 1975. 228–59.

Lanciani, R. *Forma Urbis Romae*. Ed. and repr. by F. Coarelli. Rome, 1990.

Lauter, H. "Die hellenistische Theater der Samniten und Latiner in ihrer Beziehung zur Theaterarchitektur der Griechen." In P. Zanker, ed. *Hellenismus in Mittelitalien*. Göttingen, 1976. Pp. 413–25.

Leach, E. W. "Patrons, Painters, and Patterns: The Anonymity of Romano-Campanian Painting and the Transition from the Second to the Third Style." In B. Gold, ed., *Literary and Artistic Patronage in Ancient Rome*. Austin, 1982. 135–73.

Lebek, W. D. "Moneymaking on the Roman Stage." In W. J. Slater, ed., *Roman Theater and Society*. Ann Arbor, 1996. 29–48.

———. "Standeswürde und Berufsverbot unter Tiberius: Das *Senatus Consultum* der *Tabula Larinas*." *Zeitschrift für Papyrologie und Epigraphik* 81 (1990): 37–96.

Lefèvre, E., ed. *Das römische Drama*. Darmstadt, 1978.

Lenaghan, J. O. *A Commentary on Cicero's Oration "De Haruspicum Responso."* The Hague, 1969.

Leppin, H. *Histrionen: Untersuchungen zur sozialen Stellung von Bühnenkünstlern im Westen des römischen Reiches zur Zeit der Republik und des Principats*. Bonn, 1992.

Levick, B. "The *Senatus Consultum* from Larinum." *Journal of Roman Studies* 73 (1983): 97–115.

———. *Claudius*. London, 1990.

Linderski, J. "Buying the Vote: Electoral Corruption in the Late Republic." *Ancient World* 11 (1985): 87–94.

Lindsay, H. "A Fertile Marriage: Agrippina and the Chronology of Her Children by Germanicus." *Latomus* 54 (1995): 1–17.

Ling, R. *Roman Painting*. Cambridge, Eng., 1991.

Lintott, A. "P. Clodius Pulcher — *Felix Catilina?*" *Greece and Rome* 14 (1967): 157–69.

———. "Cicero and Milo." *Journal of Roman Studies* 64 (1974): 62–78.

———. "Electoral Bribery in the Roman Republic." *Journal of Roman Studies* 80 (1990): 1–16.

Little, A. M. *Roman Perspective Painting and the Ancient Stage*. Kennebunk, Maine, 1971.

———. *Décor, Drama, and Design in Roman Painting*. Kennebunk, Maine, 1977.

Luce, T. J. "Livy, Augustus, and the Forum Augustum." In K. A. Raaflaub and M. Toher, eds., *Between Republic and Empire*. Berkeley, 1990. 123–38.

Lugli, G. "L'origine dei teatri stabili in Roma antica." *Dioniso* 9, nos. 2–3 (1942): 55–64.

Lyttelton, M. *Baroque Architecture in Classical Antiquity*. London, 1974.

MacAloon, J. J. *Rite, Drama, Festival, Spectacle*. Philadelphia, 1984.

MacCormack, S. G. *Art and Ceremony in Late Antiquity*. Berkeley, 1981.

MacDonald, W. L. *The Architecture of the Roman Empire: An Introductory Study*. Rev. ed. New Haven, 1982.

MacKendrick, P. *The Mute Stones Speak*. New York, 1960.

MacMullen, R. *Enemies of the Roman Order: Treason, Unrest, and Alienation in the Empire*. Cambridge, Mass., 1966.

———. *Changes in the Roman Empire: Essays in the Ordinary*. Princeton, 1990.

Malandrino, C. *Oplontis*. Naples, 1977.

Malissard, A. "Tacite et le théâtre ou la mort en scène." In J. Blänsdorf, ed., *Theater und Gesellschaft im Imperium Romanum*. Tübingen, 1990. 213–22.

Manning, C. E. "Acting and Nero's Conception of the Principate." *Greece and Rome* 22 (1975): 164–75.

Marek, H. G. "Die soziale Stellung des Schauspielers im alten Rom." *Altertum* 5 (1959): 101–11.

Mauss, M. *The Gift: Forms and Functions of Exchange in Archaic Societies*. Trans. I. Cunnison. New York, 1967.

Mayer, R. "Calpurnius Siculus: Technique and Date." *Journal of Roman Studies* 70 (1980): 175–76.

McKeown, J. C. "Augustan Elegy and Mime." *Cambridge Philological Society Proceedings* 25 (1979): 71–84.

Meier, C. "C. Caesar *Divi filius* and the Formation of the Alternative in Rome." In K. A. Raaflaub and M. Toher, eds., *Between Republic and Empire*. Berkeley, 1990. 54–70.

Meinel, R. *Das Odeion: Untersuchungen an überdachten antiken Theatergebäuden*. Frankfurt, 1980.

Mellor, R. *Tacitus*. New York, 1993.

Millar, F. G. B. *The Emperor and the Roman World, 31 B.C.–A.D. 337*. London, 1977.

———. "The World of the *Golden Ass*." *Journal of Roman Studies* 71 (1981): 63–75.

———. "Politics, Persuasion and the People Before the Social War." *Journal of Roman Studies* 76 (1986): 1–11.

———. "Ovid and the *Domus Augusta*: Rome Seen from Tomoi." *Journal of Roman Studies* 83 (1993): 1–17.

———. "The Last Century of the Republic: Whose History?" *Journal of Roman Studies* 85 (1995): 236–43.

Millar, F. G. B., and E. Segal, eds. *Caesar Augustus: Seven Aspects*. Oxford, 1983.

Miller, N. P. "Dramatic Speech in the Roman Historians." *Greece and Rome* 22 (1975): 45–57.

Mitchell, S. "Festivals, Games, and Civic Life in Roman Asia Minor." *Journal of Roman Studies* 80 (1990): 183–93.

Mitens, K. *Teatri greci e teatri inspirati all'architettura greca in Sicilia e nell'Italia meridionale c. 350–50 a. C.* Rome, 1988.

Mommsen, T. *The History of Rome.* Trans. W. Dickson. London, 1880.

Moormann, E. M. "Rappresentazioni teatrali su scaenae frontes di quarto stile a Pompeii." *Pompei, Herculaneum, Stabiae* 1 (1983): 73–117.

———. "A Ruin for Nero on the Oppian Hill." *Journal of Roman Archaeology* 8 (1995): 403–4.

Morel, J. P. "La *iuventus* et les origines du théâtre romain." *Revue des Etudes Latines* 47 (1969): 208–52.

Moretti, L. "Sulle didascalie del teatro attico rinvenute a Roma." *Athenaeum* 38 (1960): 263–82.

———. "Frammenti vecchi e nuovi del Commentario dei Ludi Secolari." *Rendiconti della pontificia accademia romana di archeologia* 55–56 (1982–84): 361–79.

Morford, M. P. O. "Nero's Patronage and Participation in Literature and the Arts." *Aufstieg und Niedergang der römischen Welt* 2. 32. 3 (Berlin, 1985): 2003–31.

Morgan, M. G. "Politics, Religion, and the Games in Rome, 200–150 B.C.." *Philologus* 134 (1990): 14–36.

Morques, J. L. "Les Augustians et l'expérience théâtrale néronienne." *Revue des Etudes Latines* 66 (1988): 156–81.

Mullin, D. "The Problem with *Periaktoi*." *Theatre Notebook* 38, no. 2 (1984): 54–60.

Nash, E. *Pictorial Dictionary of Ancient Rome.* 2d ed. Vols. 1 and 2. London, 1968.

Neiiendam, K. *The Art of Acting in Antiquity.* Copenhagen, 1992.

Neppi, M. A. *Gli edifici teatrali greci e romani.* Florenze, 1961.

Newbold, R. F. "Social Tension at Rome in the Early Years of Tiberius' Reign." *Athenaeum* 52 (1974): 110–43.

———. "Cassius Dio and the Games." *L'Antiquité Classique* 44 (1975): 589–604.

———. "The Spectacles as an Issue between Gaius and the Senate." *Proceedings of the African Classical Associations* 13 (1975): 30–35.

———. "The *Vulgus* in Tacitus." *Rheinische Museum für Philologie* 119 (1976): 85–92.

Nibley, H. "Sparsiones." *Classical Journal* 40 (1944–45): 515–43.

Nicolet, C. *The World of the Citizen in Republican Rome.* London, 1980.

Nicoll, A. *Masks, Mimes and Miracles: Studies in the Popular Theatre.* London, 1963.

Nippel, W. *Public Order in Ancient Rome.* Cambridge, U.K., 1995.

North, J. A. "These He Cannot Take." *Journal of Roman Studies* 73 (1983): 169–74.

Nugent, S. G. "*Tristia 2:* Ovid and Augustus." In K. A. Raaflaub and M. Toher, eds., *Between Republic and Empire.* Berkeley, 1990. 239–57.

Ogilvie, R. M. *The Romans and Their Gods.* London, 1969.

Ostrow, S. E. "The *Augustales* in the Augustan Scheme." In K. A. Raaflaub and M. Toher, eds., *Between Republic and Empire.* Berkeley, 1990. 364–79.

Palmer, E. A. "Cults of Hercules, Apollo *Caelispex* and *Fortuna* in and around the Roman Cattle Market." *Journal of Roman Archaeology* 3 (1990): 234–44.

Parker, H. "The Observed of All Observers: Spectacle, Applause, and Cultural Poetics in the Roman Audience." In B. Bergmann and C. Kondolean, eds., *The Art of the Ancient Spectacle*. Forthcoming.

Patterson, J. R. "The City of Rome: From Republic to Empire." *Journal of Roman Studies* 82 (1992): 186–215.

Payne, R. *The Roman Triumph*. London, 1962.

Petersmann, H. "Mündlichkeit und Schriftlichkeit in der Atellane." In G. Vogt-Spira, ed., *Studien zur vorliterarischen Periode im frühen Rom*. Tübingen, 1989. 135–59.

Peterson, E. "Eis Theos: Epigraphische, formgeschichtliche und religionsgeschichtliche Untersuchungen." Göttingen, 1926.

Petrochilos, N. *Roman Attitudes to the Greeks*. Athens, 1974.

Picard, G. *Roman Painting*. Greenwich, Conn., 1968.

Pietilä-Castren, L. *Magnificentia Publica: The Victory Monuments of the Roman Generals in the Era of the Punic Wars*. Helsinki, 1987.

Piganiol, A. *Recherches sur les jeux romains*. Strasbourg, 1923.

Plass, P. *The Game of Death in Ancient Rome: Arena Sport and Political Suicide*. Madison, Wisc., 1995.

Pleket, H. W. "Some Aspects of the Athletic Guilds." *Zeitschrift für Papyrologie und Epigraphik* 10 (1973): 191–227.

———. "Games, Prizes, Athletes, and Ideology: Some Aspects of the History of Sport in the Graeco-Roman World." *Stadion* 1 (1975): 49–89.

Poliakoff, M. B. *Combat Sports in the Ancient World: Competition, Violence and Culture*. New Haven, 1987.

Potter, D. "Martyrdom as Spectacle." In Ruth Scodel, ed. *Theater and Society in the Classical World*. Ann Arbor, 1993. 53–88.

———. Review of *Emperors and Gladiators*, by T. Wiedemann. *Journal of Roman Studies* 84 (1994): 229–31.

———. "Performance, Power, and Justice in the High Empire." In W. J. Slater, ed., *Roman Theatre and Society*. Ann Arbor, 1996. 129–60.

Pratt, N. T. *Seneca's Drama*. Chapel Hill, N.C., 1983.

Préaux, J. G. "*Ars ludicra*: Aux origines du théâtre latin." *L'Antiquité Classique* 32 (1963): 63–73.

Price, S. R. F. "*Between Man and God: Sacrifice in the Roman Imperial Cult.*" *Journal of Roman Studies* 70 (1980): 28–43.

———. *Rituals and Power: The Roman Imperial Cult in Asia Minor*. Cambridge, U.K., 1984.

Quinn, K. "The Poet and his Audience in the Augustan Age." *Aufstieg und Niedergang der römischen Welt* 2.30.1 (Berlin, 1982): 75–180.

Raaflaub, K. A., and L. J. Samons. "Opposition to Augustus." In K. A. Raaflaub and M. Toher, eds., *Between Republic and Empire*. Berkeley, 1990. 417–54.

Rawson, E. *Intellectual Life in the Roman Republic*. Baltimore, 1985.

———. "Caesar's Heritage: Hellenistic Kings and Their Roman Equals." In *Roman Culture and Society*. Oxford, 1991a. 169–88.

———. "Chariot-Racing in the Roman Republic." In *Roman Culture and Society*. Oxford, 1991b. 391–407.

——. "*Discrimina Ordinum:* The Lex Julia Theatralis." In *Roman Culture and Society.* Oxford, 1991c: pp. 508–45.

——. "Theatrical Life in the Republic." In *Roman Culture and Society.* Oxford, 1991d. 468–87.

Rea, R. "Recenti osservazioni sulla struttura del l'anfiteatro flavio." In M. L. Conforto and A. M. Reggiani, eds., *Anfiteatro Flavio: Immagine, testimonianze, spettacoli.* Rome, 1988. 9–22.

Reinhold, M. "Usurpation of Status and Status-Symbols in the Roman Empire." *Historia* 20 (1971): 275–302.

Ribbeck, O. *Die römische Tragoedia im Zeitalter der Republik.* Leipzig, 1875.

Rich, J. W. Review of *Aufruhr und "Polizei" in der römischen Republik,* by W. Nippel. *Journal of Roman Studies* 81 (1991): 193–95.

Richardson, E. "A Note on the Architecture of the *Theatrum Pompei* in Rome." *American Journal of Archaeology* 91 (1987): 113–16.

Richardson, L. *A New Topographical Dictionary of Ancient Rome.* Baltimore, 1992.

Richter, G. M. A. *Perspective in Greek and Roman Art.* London, 1970.

Rickman G. *The Corn Supply of Ancient Rome.* Oxford, 1980.

Rieks, R. "Sebasta und Aktia." *Hermes* 98 (1970): 96–116.

Rives, J. "Human Sacrifice among Pagans and Christians." *Journal of Roman Studies* 85 (1995): 65–85.

Robert, L. "Etudes d'épigraphie grecque." *Revue de Philologie* 4 (1930): 25–60.

——. "Deux concours grecs à Rome." *Comptes Rendus de l'Académie des Inscriptions* (1970): 6–27.

——. "Discours d'ouverture." In *Actes du VIIIᵉ Congrès international d'épigraphie grecque et latine à Athènes, 1982.* Athens, 1984. 35–45.

Robertson, D. S. *Handbook of Greek and Roman Architecture.* 2d ed. Cambridge, U.K., 1954.

Romano, D. *Atellana fabula.* Palermo, 1953.

Rotolo, V. *Il pantomimo: Studi e testi.* Palermo, 1957.

Roueché, C. *Performers and Partisans at Aphrodisias.* London, 1993.

——. "Acclamations in the Later Roman Empire." *Journal of Roman Studies* 74 (1984): 181–99.

Rumpf, A. "Die Entstehung des römischen Theaters." *Mitteilungen des Deutschen Archäologischen Instituts* 3 (1950): 40–50.

Salerno, F. "Collegia adversus rem publicam?" In *Sodalitas: Scritti in onore di A. Guarino.* Naples, 1984. Pp. 615–31.

Saller, R. P. *Personal Patronage under the Early Empire.* Cambridge, U.K., 1982.

Sapelli, M. "Restauro della statua di 'Pompeo.'" *Bollettino di Archeologia* 5–6 (1990): 180–85.

Scamuzzi, U. "Studio sulla *Lex Roscia Theatralis.*" *Rivista di Studi Classici* 27 (1969): 144–56.

Schmidt, P. L. "*Postquam ludus in artem paulatim verterat:* Varro und die Frühgeschichte des römischen Theaters." In G. Vogt-Spira, ed., *Studien zur vorliterarischen Periode im frühen Rom.* Tübingen, 1989. 77–134.

———. "Nero und das Theater." In J. Blänsdorf, ed., *Theater und Gesellschaft im Imperium Romanum.* Tübingen, 1990. 149–63.

Scholler, F. *Darstellungen des Orpheus in der Antike.* Freiburg, 1969.

Scobie, A. "Spectator Security and Comfort at Gladiatorial Games." *Nikephoros* 1 (1988): 191–243.

Scullard, H. H. *The Elephant in the Greek and Roman World.* London, 1974.

———. *Festivals and Ceremonies of the Roman Republic.* London, 1981.

Sear, F. B. *Roman Architecture.* Rev. ed. London, 1989.

———. "The Theatre at Leptis Magna and the Development of Roman Theatre Design." *Journal of Roman Archaeology* 3 (1990): 376–82.

———. "Vitruvius and Roman Theater Design." *American Journal of Archaeology* 94 (1990): 249–58.

———. "The Scaenae Frons of the Theater of Pompey." *American Journal of Archaeology* 97 (1993): 687–701.

Shackleton Bailey, D. R. *Cicero.* London, 1971.

———. *Profile of Horace.* Cambridge, Mass., 1982.

Shatzman, I. *Senatorial Wealth and Roman Politics.* Brussels, 1975.

Sifakis, G. *Studies in the History of Hellenistic Drama.* London, 1967.

Sihler, E. G. "The *Collegium Poetarum* at Rome." *American Journal of Philology* 26 (1905): 1–21.

Slater, W. J. "Actors and Their Status in the Roman Theatre in the West." *Journal of Roman Archaeology* 7 (1994): 364–68.

———. "Pantomime Riots." *Classical Antiquity* 13 (1994): 120–44.

Slater, W. J., ed. *Roman Theater and Society.* Ann Arbor, 1996.

Small, D. B. "Studies in Roman Theater Design." *American Journal of Archaeology* 87 (1983): 55–68.

Spawforth, A. J. S. "Agonistic Festivals in Roman Greece." In A. Cameron and S. Walker, eds., *The Greek Renaissance in the Roman Empire.* London, 1989. Pp. 193–97.

Stambaugh, J. E. *The Ancient Roman City.* Baltimore, 1988.

Steinby, E. M. "Il lato orientale del Foro Romano." *Arctos* 21 (1987): 139–84.

———, ed. *Lexicon Topographicum Urbis Romae.* Vol. 1, Rome, 1993. Vol. 2, Rome, 1995.

Stockton, D. "The Founding of the Empire." In J. Boardman, J. Griffin, and O. Murray, eds., *The Oxford History of the Classical World: The Roman World.* Oxford, 1988. Pp. 121–49.

Styan, J. L. *Modern Drama in Theory and Practice,* vol. 2: *Symbolism, Surrealism and the Absurd.* Cambridge, U.K., 1981.

Sullivan, J. P. *Literature and Politics in the Age of Nero.* London, 1985.

Sutton, D. F. "Cicero on Minor Dramatic Forms." *Symbolae Osloenses* 59 (1984): 29–36.

———. *Seneca on the Stage.* Leiden, 1986.

Syme, R. *The Roman Revolution.* Oxford, 1939.

———. *History in Ovid.* Oxford, 1978.

———. "The Crisis of 2 B.C.." *Roman Papers* 3. Oxford, 1984. 912–36.

Szilágyi, J. G. "Impletae Modis Saturae." *Prospettiva* 24 (1981): 22–23.

Talbert, R. J. *The Senate of Imperial Rome*. Princeton, 1984.

Tatum, W. J. "Cicero's Opposition to the *Lex Clodia de Collegiis.*" *Classical Quarterly* 40 (1990): 187–94.

Taylor, B., and W. Van der Will, eds. *The Nazification of Art: Art, Design, Music, Architecture and Film in the Third Reich*. Winchester, U.K., 1990.

Taylor, L. R. *"The Opportunities for Dramatic Performances in the Time of Plautus and Terence." Transactions of the American Philological Association* 68 (1937): 284–304.

——. *Party Politics in the Age of Caesar*. Berkeley, 1949.

——. *The Divinity of the Roman Emperor*. Reprint. Philadelphia, 1975.

Tengström, E. "Theater und Politik im kaiserzeitlichen Rom." *Eranos* 75 (1977): 43–56.

Thomas, E. "Ovid at the Races." In J. Bibauw, ed., *Hommages à Marcel Renard = Collection Latomus, Revue des Etudes Latines* 101–3 (1969): 710–24.

Thompson, D. L. "The Meetings of the Roman Senate on the Palatine." *American Journal of Archaeology* 85 (1981): 335–39.

Till, R. "Laberius und Caesar." *Historia* 24 (1975): 260–86.

Townsend, G. B. "Calpurnius Siculus and the *Munus Neronis.*" *Journal of Roman Studies* 70 (1980): 166–74.

Toynbee, J. M. C. *Death and Burial in the Roman World*. London, 1971.

——. *Animals in Roman Life and Art*. London, 1975.

Traversari, G. *Gli spettacoli in acqua nel teatro tardo-antico*. Rome, 1960.

Tumolesi, P. S. "*Pyrricharii.*" *La parola del passato* 25 (1970): 328–38.

Ucelli, G. *Le Navi de Nemi*. Rome, 1940.

Ulrich, R. B. *The Roman Orator and the Sacred Stage: The Roman "templum rostratum."* Brussels, 1994.

Vallet, G., et al. *La peinture de Pompéi*. Vols. 1 and 2. Paris, 1993.

Vanderbroeck, P. J. J. *Popular Leadership and Collective Behaviour in the Late Roman Republic*. Amsterdam, 1987.

Versnel, H. S. *Transition and Reversal in Myth and Ritual*. Leiden, 1993.

——. *Triumphus: An Inquiry into the Origin, Development and Meaning of the Roman Triumph*. Leiden, 1970.

Veyne, P. *Bread and Circuses*. Trans. B. Pearce. London, 1990.

Ville, G. *La gladiature en Occident des origines à la mort de Domitien*. Rome, 1981.

Wallace-Hadrill, A. "The Golden Age and Sin in Augustan Ideology." *Past and Present* 95 (1982): 19–36.

——. "Rome's Cultural Revolution." *Journal of Roman Studies* 79 (1989): 157–64.

Wardman, A. *Rome's Debt to Greece*. London, 1976.

Warmington, B. H. *Suetonius, Nero*. Bristol, 1977.

——. *Nero: Reality and Legend*. London, 1969.

Watson, A. *The Law of the Ancient Romans*. Princeton, 1970.

Weaver, P. R. C. *Familia Caesaris: A Social Study of the Emperor's Freedmen and Slaves*. Cambridge, U.K., 1972.

Weber, C. W. *Panem et Circenses: Massenunterhaltung als Politik im antiken Rom*. Düsseldorf, 1983.

Weidenfeld, D. *Der Schauspieler in der Gesellschaft.* Cologne, 1959.

Weinreich, O. *Studien zu Martial: Literarhistorische und Religionsgeschichtliche Unter-suchungen.* Stuttgart, 1928.

Weinstock, S. "The Image and the Chair of Germanicus." *Journal of Roman Studies* 47 (1957): 144–54.

———. *Divus Julius.* London, 1971.

Welch, K. "The Roman Arena in Late-Republican Italy: A New Interpretation." *Journal of Roman Archaeology* 7 (1994): 59–80.

———. "Roman Amphitheatres Revived." *Journal of Roman Archaeology* 4 (1991): 272–81.

Wellesley, K. *The Long Year:* A.D. 69. London, 1975.

White, P. "*Amicitia* and the Profession of Poetry in Early Imperial Rome." *Journal of Roman Studies* 68 (1978): 74–92.

———. "Positions for Poets in Early Imperial Rome." In B. K. Gold, ed., *Literary and Artistic Patronage in Ancient Rome.* Austin, 1982. 50–66.

Whittaker, C. R. "The Revolt of Papyrius Dionysius." *Historia* 13 (1964): 348–69.

Wiedemann, T. *Emperors and Gladiators.* London, 1991.

Wille, G. *Musica Romana: Die Bedeutung der Musik im Leben der Römer.* Amsterdam, 1967.

Williams, G. "Phases in Political Patronage of Literature in Rome." In B. K. Gold, ed., *Literary and Artistic Patronage in Ancient Rome.* Austin, 1982. 3–27.

———. *Change and Decline.* Berkeley, 1978.

Wiseman, T. P. *New Men in the Roman Senate.* London, 1971.

———. "The Circus Flaminius." *Papers of the British School at Rome* 42 (1974a): 3–26.

———. "Clodius at the Theatre." In *Cinna the Poet.* Leicester, 1974b. 159–69.

———. "*Pete nobiles amicos:* Poets and Patrons in Late Republican Rome." In B. K. Gold, ed., *Literary and Artistic Patronage in Ancient Rome.* Austin, 1982. 28–49.

———. *Catullus and His World: A Reappraisal.* New York, 1985a.

———. "*Conspicui postes tectaque digna deo:* The Public Image of Aristocratic and Imperial Houses in the Late Republic and Early Empire." In *L'Urbs: Espace urbain et histoire.* Rome, 1987. 393–413.

———. "Satyrs in Rome? The Background to Horace's *Ars Poetica.*" *Journal of Roman Studies* 78 (1988): 1–13.

———. "The God of the Lupercal." *Journal of Roman Studies* 85 (1995): 1–22.

Wiseman, T.P., ed. *Roman Political Life* 90 B.C.–A.D. 69. Exeter, 1985b.

Wistrand, M. *Entertainment and Violence in Ancient Rome: The Attitudes of Roman Writers of the First Century* A.D.. Götheborg, 1993.

Woodman, A. J. "Amateur Dramatics at the Court of Nero." In T. J. Luce and A. J. Woodman, eds., *Tacitus and the Tacitean Tradition.* Princeton, 1993. 104–28.

Wörrle, M. *Stadt und Fest im kaiserzeitlichen Kleinasien: Studien zu einer agonistischen Stiftung aus Oinoanda.* Munich, 1988.

Wright, F. W. *Cicero and the Theater.* Northampton, Mass., 1931.

Wright, J. *Dancing in Chains: The Stylistic Unity of the Comoedia Palliata.* Rome, 1974.

Wüst, E. "Mimus." In *Paulys Real-Enzyclopädie der classichen Altertumswissenschaft.* Ed. K. Wissowa et al. Berlin, 1932. Vol. 15. 1727–64.

Yakobson, A. *"Petitio et Largitio:* Popular Participation in the Centuriate Assembly of the Late Republic." *Journal of Roman Studies* 82 (1992): 32–52.

Yavetz, Z. *Plebs and Princeps.* Oxford, 1969.

——. *Julius Caesar and His Public Image.* London, 1983.

Zanker, P. *The Power of Images in the Age of Augustus.* Trans. A. Shapiro. Ann Arbor, 1988.

Zanker, P., ed. *Hellenismus in Mittelitalien.* Göttingen, 1976.

Zinserling, G. "Die Programmatik der Kunstpolitik des Augustus." *Klio: Beiträge zu alten Geschichte* 67, no. 1 (1985): 74–80.

Zwierlein, O. *Die Rezitationsdramen Senecas.* Meisenheim am Glan, 1966.

Index